T0326934

GOWANUS

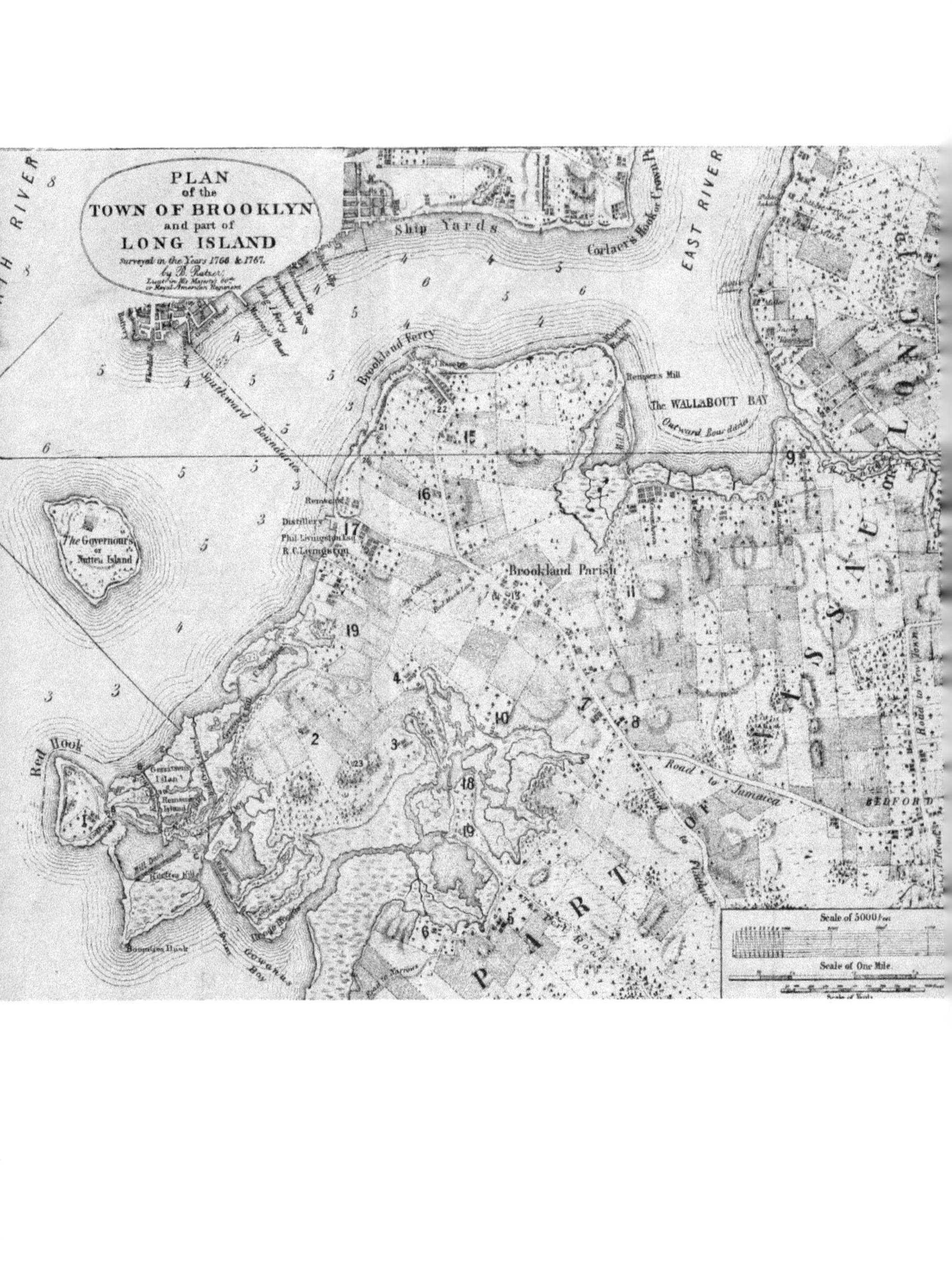

PLAN
of the
TOWN OF BROOKLYN
and part of
LONG ISLAND
Surveyed in the Years 1766 & 1767.
Ship Yards
Corlaers Hook or Crown Pt.
EAST RIVER
Brookland Ferry
The WALLABOUT BAY
Outward Boundaries
Southward Boundaries
The Governour's or Nutten Island
Distillery
Brookland Parish
Red Hook
Road to Jamaica
Road to Flatbush
Road to New Town
BEDFORD
Gowanus Bay
PART OF
LONG ISLAND
Scale of 5000 Feet
Scale of One Mile

GOWANUS

BROOKLYN'S CURIOUS CANAL

JOSEPH ALEXIOU

NEW YORK UNIVERSITY PRESS
New York and London

NEW YORK UNIVERSITY PRESS
New York and London
www.nyupress.org

LIBRARY OF CONGRESS CATALOGING-IN-PUBLICATION DATA
Alexiou, Joseph.
Gowanus : Brooklyn's curious canal / Joseph Alexiou.
pages cm
Includes bibliographical references and index.
ISBN 978-1-4798-9294-5 (hbk. : alk. paper)
ISBN 978-1-4798-0605-8 (pbk. : alk. paper)
1. Brooklyn (New York, N.Y.)—History. 2. Gowanus Canal (New York, N.Y.)—History. 3. Gowanus Canal Region (New York, N.Y.)—Environmental conditions. 4. Waterfronts—New York (State)—New York—History. 5. Industrial districts—New York (State)—New York. 6. Brooklyn (New York, N.Y.)—Social conditions. 7. Brooklyn (New York, N.Y.)—Commerce—History. I. Title. II. Title: Brooklyn's curious canal.
F129.B7A43 2015
974.7'23—dc23
2015013951

New York University Press books are printed on acid-free paper, and their binding materials are chosen for strength and durability. We strive to use environmentally responsible suppliers and materials to the greatest extent possible in publishing our books.

Frontispiece image: A map of Brooklyn based on surveys made in 1766–1767, drawn by British cartographer Bernard Ratzer. Courtesy of the New York Public Library.
Chapter opening art by Lisa Gilman
Book design by Adam B. Bohannon

Manufactured in the United States of America
10 9 8 7 6 5 4 3 2 1
Also available as an ebook

In memory of my grandmother, Esther Braun Sparberg

And what is that you smell?

Oh, that! Well, you see, he shares impartially with his neighbors a piece of public property in the vicinity; it belongs to all of them in common, and it gives to South Brooklyn its own distinctive atmosphere. It is the old Gowanus Canal, and that aroma you speak of is nothing but the huge symphonic stink of it, cunningly compacted of unnumbered separate putrefactions. It is interesting sometimes to try to count them. There is in it not only the noisome stenches of a stagnant sewer, but also the smells of melted glue, burned rubber, and smoldering rags, the odors of a boneyard horse, long dead, the incense of putrefying offal, the fragrance of deceased, decaying cats, old tomatoes, rotten cabbage, and prehistoric eggs.

And how does he stand it?

Well, one gets used to it. One can get used to anything, just as all these people do. They never think of the smell, they never speak of it, they'd probably miss it if they moved away.

—Thomas Wolfe, *You Can't Go Home Again*, 1940

CONTENTS

ACKNOWLEDGMENTS

This book would not have existed without the encouragement, support, and expertise of numerous colleagues, teachers, mentors, and friends. The idea that became a whole book originated under the guidance of seasoned authors Professor Sam Freedman and Assistant Professor Kelly McMasters, who led the narrative nonfiction book seminar at Columbia University's Graduate School of Journalism in 2011. I thank them for their tutelage and detailed edits, questions, and prodding that nurtured a story about the history of Gowanus into sixty-thousand-word book proposal. Furthermore, I extend my heartfelt thanks to Deirdre Mullane, my agent who believed in this project. Her boundless enthusiasm, intelligence, and detailed eye ensured that my dream could become a reality, and I'm grateful for her insight, pep talks, and efforts that extended far beyond her responsibilities. I want to thank Debbie Gershenowitz for bringing me on board with NYU; I want to thank Clara Platter, editor of this tome, for her patience and hard work on toning the manuscript into a readable story; I also recognize the tireless work and guidance of her editorial assistant, Constance Grady. Also, a big thank-you to Dorothea Halliday, Joseph Dahm, Margie Guerra, Betsy Steve, and the numerous and talented staff of NYU Press who were involved in the creation, publishing, and marketing of this book.

There would be no book without the libraries and archives that host the necessary information and hidden historical footnotes, which cannot function without the many librarians and archivists who aided my research. Please forgive me in advance for any unintended omissions, as the noble profession of keeping society's information organized often goes unappreciated: Thank you to the staff of the Brooklyn Museum library, the Brooklyn Public Library—in particular the staff of the Brooklyn Room and the archivists of the *Brooklyn Daily Eagle*. Thank you to the staff of the Pratt Institute library, the Brooklyn College archive, and the library of the Brooklyn Historical Society, including librarians Elizabeth Call and Julie May; archivist Janet Marks at Long Island University and Amy Peck, the Prospect Park historian; the staff of the New York Public Library. And a special thanks to the research experts at the archives of the New York Historical Society, including Tammy Kiter, Joseph Ditta, and Edward O'Reilly. I could not have researched the many historical factoids and eras of this sprawling topic without the expertise of other Gowanus fanatics, including Linda Mariano, Katia Kelly, and Marlene Donnelly—friends, colleagues, and activists who have taught me much more about Brooklyn and the Gowanus than I knew possible (and introduced me to a plethora of inside information, contacts, sources, and other credibility). A special thank-you for each: to Linda for your cheerleading, guidance, and archival knowledge of Gowanus, to Katia for your kindness and tireless effort in maintaining the ongoing Gowanus timeline in your blog, Pardon Me for Asking, and to Marlene for your technical expertise and willingness to share it with us all. Other notable Gowanus obsessives include Celia Cacace, who bequeathed to myself and others a massive archive of South Brooklyn papers (as well as her knowledge, wit, and humor); Glenn Kelly, Margaret Maugenest, Lisa Ackerman, Frampton Tolbert, Sasha Chavchavadze, Leslie Albrecht, Eymund Diegel, Christine Petro, and Hans

Hesselein, all of whom were enthusiastic in sharing their hard-earned knowledge with me. I thank Buddy Scotto and Bill Appell for some of the early interviews in my research, and their time, knowledge, and efforts toward building a better Gowanus. A huge thank-you to Natalie Loney, Christos Tsiamis, and Brian Carr, Environmental Protection Agency employees who have devoted years of their working lives to the Gowanus Superfund designation. Their willingness to speak at length about the science and politics surrounding the Superfund designation of the Gowanus gave me the necessary background to be able to speak about the Gowanus pollution with any kind of authority.

Over the past few years many wonderful people gave their precious time to bestow advice, read chapters and excerpts of this work, and offer the incessant encouragement required to produce a book. I therefore offer my most grateful and heartfelt thanks to the following: my classmates from the 2011 Columbia book seminar, in particular Jaime Joyce, Brian Spitulnik, and Philip Eil; writing mentors Jerry Portwood and Susan Shapiro (and her many students), also Adam Rathe, Mariah Summers, Kevin Coyne, Sean Gannet, Jen Messier, J. Soma, Jamie Courville, and Chris Reynolds. From the start of this process many dear friends offered eyes, ears, uncanny intellect, and support, including Veronica Rutter, Sandra Rothbard, Stephanie Morris, Ed Woodham, Ari Brand, Cait Petre, Joelle Berman, Adam Freelander, Julie Stein, Josh Kesner, Shana Siegel, Annie Orenstein, Aaron Orenstein, Matt Baer, Masha Katz, Ben Pisciotta, Andrew Gordon, Andrew Shield, Conor Yates, Ethan Baldwin, Eva Seligman, Carly Machado, Daniel Lubrano, Sean Billy Kizy, and Steven Valentino. I would never have gotten through this process (or my twenties) without the support and love of Eli Szenes-Strauss, Anne de Turenne, Erica Rosen, and Sara Dalziel.

Finally, the love and support of my family have meant everything to me in this foolish endeavor, and so I offer my most sincere thanks and appreciation to my brother Alex Alexiou, whose level-headed support and encouragement are a continual source of strength, and the same to my sister-in-law Ayşe Asatekin, a brilliant and all-too-modest woman and chemical engineer who answered my many questions about cream of tartar and water pollution. I thank my grandmother, Esther Sparberg, to whom this book is dedicated, for being my lifelong cheerleader and font of unpolluted love; my father, Nicholas Alexiou, for being a source of boundless confidence and guidance while I meander through history and adulthood. And my mother, Alice Alexiou—herself a writer and published author several times over—I thank for her honesty, her earnest encouragement in all of my efforts, her unwavering mentorship and love.

Prologue

The Tale of Sludgie the Whale

On April 15, 2007, a violent nor'easter slammed the New York City metropolitan area, showering its residents with hailstones and heavy rain. First percolating in the Deep South, the storm had expanded eastward as warm Gulf winds and Atlantic cold fronts swirled in combat, blanketing half the country. That Sunday afternoon, the nor'easter hit the East Coast head-on. Winds of nearly a hundred miles an hour raised two-story-high waves that destroyed beaches and damaged riverfronts. Major roads shut down in coastal New Jersey, Connecticut, and New York as hundreds of car accidents were reported. The rainfall in Central Park was the second highest in 138 years of recorded weather history, more than five hundred flights were canceled at local airports, and 18,500 people lost power in the tri-state area.

By Monday morning, the storm had blown itself out to sea. Newspapers, blogs, and wire services reported millions of dollars in damages and at least eighteen people killed across the region. Even the IRS was forced to adapt, granting storm victims an additional two days to file their tax returns. Just hours before, Robert Guskind, a forty-eight-year-old veteran journalist, had posted pictures he had taken of the storm the previous evening on his popular Brooklyn-based blog, the *Gowanus Lounge*. The photos showed the Gowanus Canal, a curious waterway that stretches 1.8 miles from the Upper New York Bay northward into the borough of Brooklyn, overflowing its banks. Water poured across the intersection of Sackett and Second Streets on the eastern border of Carroll Gardens, an old residential neighborhood known mostly for its genteel red brick townhouses. "Also bear in mind," Guskind wrote under the flood pictures, "that during heavy rains like yesterday's, raw sewage flows directly into the canal, so that what you are looking at is (almost literally) crap in the streets."

The *New York Times* covered the deluge with an understated headline, "East Coast Storm Breaks Rainfall Records," and a small feature, perhaps coincidentally, of the Gowanus overflow. The venerable paper also published a photograph of a Brooklyn man, Jorge Aguilar, in the basement of his house at 467 Sackett Street, one block from the canal. In the photo Aguilar is bending over with his pants rolled up as he retrieves a sodden object from gray, ankle-deep water.

The raw sewage Guskind intimated was no accident, per se, but the result of nineteenth-century urban planning. Almost all American cities at the time were built with "combined sewer systems," in which storm water runoff and raw sewage flowed through a single pipe. The term among engineers and city planners for what happened in the Gowanus streets during the storm is "combined sewage overflow," or CSO. In the case of Brooklyn's sewer system, all of the water collected in that area is supposed to flow to one of two catch points nearby, the Owl's Head Wastewater Treatment Plant in Bay Ridge or the Red Hook Wastewater Treatment Plant (which, despite its name, is located in the Brooklyn Navy Yard). However, if the volume of water is too great for the sewer pipes to handle—an all-too-often occurrence, as Brooklyn has grown exponentially since the original sewers were built—sewage flows into the nearest exit channel, usually a body of water like the Gowanus Canal. Today there are eleven outfalls, or sewer exits, emptying into the canal, dumping almost four hundred million gallons of wastewater into the canal every year.

But other headlines that Monday morning competed with the dramatic weather for readers' interest. Some five hundred miles farther south, Seung-Hui Cho, a twenty-three-year-old Korean American student, had gone on a shooting rampage at the Blacksburg campus of Virginia Polytechnic Institute and State University. Cho, a disaffected English major, had killed thirty-two people and wounded twenty-five more before shooting himself, leaving the country reeling in shock. Between the Virginia Tech massacre and the short-lived but powerful storm, it's understandable that many might have failed to notice another small item that followed: in the wake of news of such natural and human violence, on Tuesday morning, April 17, a baby minke whale had been discovered swimming placidly at the mouth of the Gowanus Canal.

John Quadrozzi, the president of the Gowanus Industrial Park (a collection of small businesses surrounding an abandoned grain elevator at the canal's entrance), was the first person to spot the creature. Soon after Quadrozzi contacted the coast guard, a WNBC helicopter captured footage of the whale breaching in the Gowanus Bay, into which the canal empties. When the coast guard arrived to inspect the animal from their boats, it reported never having heard of a whale being spotted in New York's harbor, and then estimated that the heavy waves churned up by the nor'easter had likely separated the young mammal from its mother.

News of the whale quickly spread from WNBC's morning TV coverage to the staff of the *Daily News*, who immediately emailed Guskind, the local Gowanus expert, for verification. He posted the breaking news to his blog, and the story of the whale's arrival soon went viral. By Wednesday morning the *Daily News* had published an article under the headline "A Whale Swims in Brooklyn," referencing Betty Smith's beloved 1943 novel *A Tree Grows in Brooklyn*. The newspaper dubbed the twelve-foot-long, two-ton mammal "Sludgie the Whale," evoking in one stroke both another popular cetacean, Carvel's signature ice cream creation, and the polluted muck of the

Gowanus Canal. The Associated Press, having caught wind of the sighting, ran with the story, and soon Sludgie appeared in newspapers across the nation. During these early days, there were conflicting reports of Sludgie's weight: the *Daily News* first described Sludgie as a "15-ton whale," while the *New York Post* put its heft at "30,000 pounds." A *New York Times* article stated that Sludgie weighed "several tons," while the *Daily News* revised its estimate the following day to 5,000 pounds. In fact, a 30,000-pound whale would have been around the size of garbage truck, while the diminutive Sludgie was more like a motorcycle.

Regardless of her size, within a day of her discovery Sludgie became a media microheroine as New Yorkers flocked to the mouth of the canal, many with children in tow, to grab a glimpse of the unlikely visitor. In a city where a gaggle of actors hobbling down the street dressed as zombies or a flash mob of pantsless subway riders is practically quotidian, Sludgie's sudden appearance was an enthralling reminder of the natural world in a seemingly endless stretch of concrete. That a wild living creature—a cute baby mammal, no less—was swimming in the harbor was reason enough for dozens of locals to grab a pair of binoculars and leave work early. One *New York Times* article, reporting in the shadow of the Virginia Tech tragedy, quoted Sludgie enthusiasts who came out to root for the whale simply because they wanted something to feel good about. After such a violent beginning to the week, the kind of innocent joy associated with spotting a juvenile minke that had survived a massive storm and was flourishing in a stagnant basin of polluted water was practically tangible.

But the joy was short-lived. Pointing out in an interview in the *Daily News* that the nor'easter had drained tons of sewage into the canal, Guskind remarked that Sludgie had appeared at "probably the worst time to wander in there." Arthur Kopelman, president of the Coastal Research and Education Society of Long Island, confirmed the presence of toxins in the canal and deemed it "an incredibly nasty place to be for a whale." According to most reports, the whale had suffered cuts along her head after banging into bulkheads along the Gowanus Bay, and at around four forty-five on Wednesday afternoon, April 17, a witness saw Sludgie thrashing in the water near the mouth of the canal. She then beached herself onto some rocks and, quite suddenly and to the disappointment of many, died just before five o'clock, only a single day into her celebrity.

Guskind reported her death that evening and Thursday morning posted a retrospective: "While we worried about its health . . . the chance that the whale would make it back out to sea or be rescued was enough to counterbalance the concern that it had wandered into water that we knew was especially fouled by this week's Nor'easter. . . . So, yes, we were very depressed when we learned of Sludgie's demise last night, sad that this beautiful creature hadn't survived and a little selfishly upset that the days of Gowanus whale watching had abruptly come to an end."[1] Upon hearing of the tragedy, Mayor Michael Bloomberg remarked from the steps of City Hall, "My thoughts are with the whale."

Sludgie's many fans were understandably saddened by the news. "We just came hoping for good news," said one woman who had arrived at the mouth of the Gowanus with some friends, only to find out that Sludgie was dead. "After Virginia, you come here rooting for the whale. You hope that something good has to happen, because it turns out these are days for tears." Follow-up reports of her necropsy—which revealed that Sludgie was female—failed to find a connection between the whale's death and the quality of the Gowanus waters, although the exact cause was never determined. Sludgie was a baby and very disoriented, and she may have been sick before ever venturing into the Gowanus. Nonetheless, her sudden, startling appearance had focused attention on the murky and mysterious waters of the Gowanus once again.

~ ~ ~ ~ ~

My relationship with the Gowanus Canal began in late 2006, when I moved to the transitioning neighborhood quite by accident. The surrounding area was just at the cusp of its plunge into city-wide "rediscovery," and my having landed in a notoriously seedy, literal backwater afforded me more street cred than any newcomer deserved. I had previously worked as a travel journalist and guide-book researcher, so the countless number of unusual old buildings to discover and odd waterfront corners for exploration became a regular source of satisfaction (and a fantastic metaphor for the self-discovery of a twenty-three-year-old fledgling writer). As I became familiar with the landscape and its crumbling, nineteenth- and early twentieth-century industrial architecture, the innocent intrigue for my adopted corner of Brooklyn became an obsession: What is that odd brick house, that unusual warehouse? Where did this water come from, and why was it here? Who dug this and why, or was it naturally occurring? How polluted is the water really, and how did it get that way? The budding writer in me was full of questions, and thanks to the village-like nature of the community in the Gowanus and Carroll Gardens, there were plenty of people willing to stop with answers.

As it turned out, I was hardly the only person obsessed with the Gowanus Canal. After speaking with many neighbors, other pedestrians, and local store owners and falling into the vortex of reading Brooklyn-based blogs, I found that everybody who "discovers" the Gowanus for the first time always goes back to see it again, and again—even after forty years of living by its shores. With its odd bends and angles, you never see the exact same thing twice, and usually catch a detail missed the first time around. Exploring the neighborhood reveals the dead ends where streets meet the canal water, where unlikely urban plant life grows alongside the rotting wooden docks. Those warehouses, crowned with porcelain signs declaring "Kentile Floors" and "Eagle Clothes," were monuments of long-departed midcentury businesses, but they were hardly abandoned. On the east bank of the canal, the red brick, Romanesque revival building—nicknamed "the bat cave," I later discovered it was the former power station for the Brooklyn Rapid Transit—towering above the low-scale skyline was a haven for squatters and drug addicts, but also a sprawling canvas for graffiti art. Across the street, at the corner of Third Street and Third Avenue, a strange and beautiful concrete house sat in an empty lot, save the crumbling walls doused in more graffiti. Gowanus was a patch of New York that felt untouched, a bit wild—the authentic postindustrial urban experience. I was no artist, but the presence of creative types was palatable in the repurposed former factories and garages, including the saxophone player who practiced at the end of Bond Street by the canal.

Furthermore, because of the unusually pungent pollution, the future of the Gowanus Canal was a matter of great civic importance to a number of people in the community—enough to make it a regular source of new stories in a breadth of subjects: art and culture, environment and health, urban development, politics, and, of course, real estate. The deeper I dug, the more I found—the history of Gowanus indeed extended back to the earliest days of colonization, and beyond.

Gowanus is the name of not only a canal, but a whole region that sprawled out beyond the marshes of this tiny waterway, but the bay and surrounding area on the coast of Brooklyn; to the east arose the hills in today's Prospect Park and Green-Wood Cemetery (the Gowanus "heights"), down to the grassy meadows of today's Sunset Park. Throughout time the name "Gowanus" has invoked diverse meanings and definition, from bountiful farmland to rough-and-tumble industrial thoroughfare. During the past century and a half, it devolved to a befouled, dirty quarter, fit for the poor, working immigrants and the socially maligned. Most recently, the discovery of Gowanus now invokes images of postindustrial decay converted into a creative and popular site of contemporary urban renewal and creativity. Not only because of this relatively recent upgrade in its public relations does the history of Gowanus deserve to be fleshed out—and not only because as a neighborhood with a canal it is unique within New York City. The Gowanus waterway and its environs have been active participants across American history. Through this lens we have a unique vantage point for examining the growth of a great city, like the focal point of a historical microscope. It is one of the earliest sites of settlement in the history of America, one of the oldest places where our recorded history begins. In a way, the Gowanus is a microcosm—a lens through which to view the passage of history, and in particular the growth of Brooklyn and its unique identity in relation to its environs.

From its present polluted state, human documentation of the Gowanus Canal can be traced back more than three centuries. In the 1630s, after the Dutch colony of New Amsterdam was established, officers of the Dutch West India Company purchased huge swaths of land across the western edge of Long Island to develop for agriculture and eventual settlement. Large tracts near the Gowanus Creek, the natural precursor to the Gowanus Canal, were some of the first to get snatched up. The saltwater estuary—a tidal inlet connected to the ocean—was surrounded by mile-wide salt marshes. The region surrounding the marshes was also dotted with hills and meadows, freshwater springs, and abundant wildlife—all of the ingredients attractive to both settlers and speculators. The early Dutch farmers used ponds dug along the creek to power their gristmills and for convenient boat access to Manhattan. The local waters teemed with fish and eels, dinner-plate-size oysters, and dolphins and whales. A curious sea mammal swimming to the mouth of Gowanus Creek would probably not have been an unusual sight to local residents at that time, nor would the estuary have been dangerous to these aquatic visitors.

But progress drove massive change, and the fate of the Gowanus was closely tied to that of Brooklyn itself. After playing a significant role as the site of the Battle of Brooklyn during the Revolutionary War, the former Dutch settlement grew into a city so popular that by the early nineteenth century its population doubled every ten years. As the new country grew rapidly and expanded westward, New York was a nexus of commerce and opportunity. Masses of goods and work-hungry immigrants poured into the expansive bay, and with their proximity to bustling Manhattan, the villages of modern-day Brooklyn transformed and grew as some of the arrivals, smelling opportunity, chose to settle across the East River. Brooklyn's rapid growth would require a serious development of infrastructure.

The idea of turning Gowanus Creek into Gowanus Canal was first proposed in 1848, with the purpose of draining the local salt marshes and establishing a conduit for sewage and storm water. The person who made it possible was an ambitious entrepreneur from Upstate New York named Daniel Richards. His arrival in New York in 1827 led him to the undeveloped tracts of land in the area known as Red Hook, which lay at the outskirts of what would become a thriving industrial metropolis and, for a time, the third largest city in America. Key origins of Brooklyn's explosive growth in the mid-nineteenth century can be found in the urbanization of the boggy marshlands of Red Hook, the personal project of Richards, whose enterprising modernist vision transformed Brooklyn's landscape into one of the first large-scale commercial developments of its waterfront. Richards's drive and creativity triggered the possibility for growth that led to the conception of the Gowanus Canal as we know it today.

The canal, built between 1853 and 1874, would serve as a thriving transport lane for more than fifty years during the height of the industrial era in the heart of the extensive neighborhood development of the large area once referred to as South Brooklyn. This denomination contains the present-day neighborhoods of Cobble Hill, Carroll Gardens, and Park Slope, some of the most sought-after and expensive real estate in all of New York City—much of which owes a great deal to the Gowanus Canal. In addition to providing a conduit for transporting the building materials that engendered these buildings and the commercial goods that filled them, the Gowanus was an energy source for the growing city. As a major site of coal delivery, the canal not only allowed for large shipments of the "black diamonds" but also provided a site for manufactured gas plants—the smoke-belching production centers that furnished heat and light to Brooklyn's growing populace.

Beyond the lost Gowanus history of Daniel Richards is that of Edwin C. Litchfield, a Gilded Age railroad tycoon, also from Upstate New York, who was the archetypical wealthy American social climber. Having amassed a vast fortune in partnership with his brothers, Litchfield bought a square mile of land in today's Park Slope, but in his era it was part of the greater Gowanus area. While Richards may have conceived of the Gowanus Canal as we know today, it was Litchfield who used his money and influence to make it a reality. His goals were utterly American—to make another fortune, but this time through the time-honored tradition of New York real estate. When researching the origins of the Gowanus Canal, I found that Brooklyn's historians had almost forgotten these dedicated and brilliant architects of an urban landscape that rose and fell in its usefulness. The evolution of Brooklyn's lands from agricultural to industrial had a particularly profound effect on the Gowanus waterway and the people who lived and worked in its vicinity. Recalling the successes and mistakes of these historic dreamers of Brooklyn can only inform the current renaissance that Gowanus is experiencing today. These developers responded to the call of speculation in the hopes of achieving a great fortune. But beyond yielding wealth, their ideas morphed the landscape of Brooklyn into never-before-seen shapes, whose results were not always positive, yet echo physically and culturally to the present. Their lives, however distant, recall a previous age of the city, when Brooklyn competed with New York in vitality, business, and culture. Those who struck out into the "wilds" of this other place were at the same time foolish and creative. Their degree of success can be measured in the stories they left behind for us to uncover, more than a century later.

Despite the tireless efforts of figures like Richards and Litchfield to launch a golden age of industry from the Gowanus shores, it was difficult to overlook one of the canal's most distinguishing features: it was an open sewer. In 1858 the city of Brooklyn laid several local sewers that emptied into the new canal, and an influx of raw sewage from Brooklyn households has flowed through the Gowanus nearly every time it has rained since then. In particular, one sewer exit at the end of Bond Street has long been a source of complaint, appearing multiple times in the story of Gowanus, persisting through 150 years of pollution. Thanks to this unfortunate fact of Brooklyn's early city planning, in the late 1870s shoals (or "sandbars") of human waste and industrial byproducts had formed at the exits of four different sewers along the canal. Not only was this a health hazard, it made navigating the waterway especially difficult. Unsurprisingly, a public outcry over the contamination ensued, engendering a neighborhood battle with local government spanning several centuries, and earning the canal the nickname "Lavender Lake."

While some particularly aggressive opponents called for the Gowanus to be filled in with concrete (an opinion that emerges with every generation), almost anybody who used it for commercial purposes agreed that the waterway needed to be regularly dredged. Many complained of the unhealthy stenches and disease-causing miasmas—the nineteenth-century belief, sometimes synonymous with malaria (literally, "bad air") that infectious ailments traveled through the air, which became a reoccurring theme throughout this study. But dredging the waste proved difficult, and not just because the city had to coerce commercial landowners along the canal to fund it. At the one Board of Health meeting in 1877, J. H. Raymond, the sanitary superintendent of the city of Brooklyn, pointed out that "the dredge cannot be used successfully as the filth slides from the shovel back into the water as soon as it is displaced." It seemed at the time that the development of the Gowanus had created as many problems as opportunities.

It also turns out that the contemporary Coast Guard officials had gotten it wrong. Sludgie, the baby minke, was not the first, or even the second, whale recorded to have entered the Gowanus. In a profile published in the *Brooklyn Eagle* on June 22, 1952, a veteran policeman told a reporter that a baby whale had once tried to make a home in the canal sometime during the 1940s, before eventually getting stuck in the flushing tunnel at the canal's northernmost point. Although the officer, Mike Harrigan, didn't specify what had happened to that whale, the profile reported that he "consider[ed] the Gowanus a 'region of the dead,' like the River Styx of mythology." During his twenty-nine years on harbor duty, a beat that included patrolling the canal, Harrigan recalled retrieving "a couple of thousand dead bodies." But before Harrigan, there had been many other bodies over the years. Further back, in 1922—just before Officer Harrigan began his Gowanus beat—a baby sperm whale had appeared in the canal, provoking a bloody battle between man and beast that bears little resemblance to the popular response to Sludgie's rise and fall.

By this era, a large Italian population had settled around the Red Hook and Gowanus neighborhoods, replacing generations of lace-curtain Irish. Their arrival in Brooklyn changed the culture of the area, creating an entirely new street life that was at one time foreign to Brooklyn's population, but now drums up images of the "authentic" urban village. Through this change, the docks and waterfronts of Gowanus also gained notoriety for their association with organized crime—and in the latter years of the twentieth century that of the Mafia. Al Capone grew up near the banks of the Gowanus, and later on it became a center of bootlegging and illegal alcohol production, a main source of mob income. Although the contemporary view of Gowanus is this rough neighborhood of the twentieth century, the true origins of this violent character extend much further back to the industrial era of nineteenth-century Brooklyn. The dangers of too-dense boat traffic or explosions and fires from industrial accidents often caused gruesome deaths; victims of suicides and muggings or the drunks who fell off of the bridges spanning the canal regularly turned up in the murky waters. Yet because it would eventually be the home turf of the Gallo brothers, Albert, Larry, and "Crazy" Joey, members of what would become New York's infamous Colombo crime family, the Gowanus gained a reputation as the dumping ground for their unfortunate victims.

After the stock market crash of 1929 and the Great Depression that followed, the world had changed, and the Gowanus along with it. Army Corps statistics show that during the 1930s commercial activity along the canal steadily declined. Although stepped-up production during World War II eventually revived the economy, the newest commercial sea vessels, with the ability to hold multiple shipping containers, were favored over the smaller barges that once crowded the canal. Cars and trucks became the primary source of transportation of goods on land, as the government oversaw the construction of hundreds of new highways, roads, and bridges. In a final coup de grâce, the Brooklyn-Queens Expressway—a massive highway project advanced by the indomitable Robert Moses in 1950—effectively severed Red Hook and the mouth of the canal from the rest of Brooklyn.

With these developments, entrepreneurs could avoid the cramped spaces and outrageous cost of renting industrial facilities in cities, building their factories and processing plants on cheap, broad tracts of open land. Furthermore, while big metropolises once offered the dense population of potential workers needed to operate these businesses, the automobile made possible the lure of life in suburbia, where the working and middle classes could live in comfortable houses with driveways and backyard patios, instead of tiny apartments, and drove (pun intended) many families out of the city. By 1953, the number of vessels that sailed the Gowanus had shrunk to one-third of those employed in 1924, and the number of businesses numbered less than half. And still the problem of sewage remained. In 1960 a manhole cover was supposedly thrown into the works of the Gowanus flushing tunnel (some residents swear by this story, others consider it apocryphal), causing the whole pumping apparatus to cease functioning altogether. Without an influx of fresh water, the Gowanus's already polluted stream was rendered completely stagnant. That no plans were made now to repair the damage confirmed what everybody already knew, that the canal was simply obsolete, and during the following two decades, the Army Corps stopped recording statistics on the canal's use completely. The breakdown of the flushing tunnel was, effectively, the final, sputtering death of the Gowanus Canal as an industrial waterway.

For the next thirty years, the Gowanus Canal was a stagnant cesspool in a neighborhood that New York City forgot. Local community members, a majority of whom were Italian American, complained of the stench as much as the residents from a hundred years before had, but their voices were unheeded. New York was nearly bankrupt in the 1970s, and many landlords had abandoned their huge and now useless industrial spaces in Manhattan, particularly in the SoHo and TriBeCa neighborhoods. Even though the cheap access to these ample lofts prompted repopulation of those neighborhoods by artists, if downtown Manhattan was the rotten core of a Big Apple, the area known as South Brooklyn—the neighborhoods of Cobble Hill, Boerum Hill, Park Slope, Carroll Gardens, and Red Hook—was little better than a slum. Yet amid the associations of pollution and crime, the possibility for reinvention was built into the DNA of the Gowanus neighborhood, even if its history had been totally forgotten. Through the slow but steady climb of gentrification, South Brooklyn's motivated residents and brownstone settlers recognized the usefulness and beauty in the neighborhood's postindustrial grit. Their sensibilities led the way to the kind of postindustrial urban renewal that defines cities in the twenty-first century. By 2010, the Gowanus Canal had been designated by the EPA as a highly toxic Superfund site, placing it in the company of the approximately thirteen hundred most heavily polluted venues in the country. Yet in that designation lies a seed of Gowanus's renewal.

~ ~ ~ ~ ~

Throughout the biography of this small waterway in the heart of a city are some reoccurring themes. The unique geography of the Gowanus poses an opportunity to urban dwellers, encouraging in its settlers the spark of innovation. From its earliest development until the present day, the waters of Gowanus have been either a problem or a solution, an attraction or a deterrent. This magnetism, for lack of a better term, has inspired generations of creativity and provided a unique identity to the many people who have settled near its waters.

Gowanus is often ignored for long periods until some enterprising person or entity from outside "discovers" the neighborhood during waves of high speculation—and then attempts to introduce sweeping changes. In consequence, throughout its history exists a palatable anxiety about the evolution of this neighborhood. While such anxiety is hardly unique to New York City or the life of all cities, the Gowanus's unique location and character—that of a natural waterway surrounded by a dense urban population—have set it apart from all other areas of the former Dutch colony of New Amsterdam. Through the evolution of Gowanus from the city's earliest years, we can observe centuries of urban dwellers attempting to control their environment.

Because the area was long regarded as a swamp, and then suffered consistent pollution beginning in the modern era, it has a much older association with flooding, poverty, stench, and disease than locals might realize. Only recently has it been considered suitable for dwelling by anybody except the poorest working classes, minorities, and immigrants. Thanks to its historic placement on the frontier between neighborhoods and regions, the Gowanus region has an ancient reputation as a place of the "other" on the fringe of society. While I am almost entering dangerous territory by invoking the following term, over time these exceptional characteristics have given life to unique and "authentic" urban characters—an ever-evolving popular view of a certain kind of Brooklynite. At one point this indicated a person of a certain class who is a bit rough, accented, and usually ethnic, while today's Gowanusian can evoke any number of stereotypes of someone who lives in Brooklyn. While the specifics of this identity have evolved over time, I argue that the unusual environment and buildings that characterize Gowanus have created the ideal setting for the urban sidewalk ballet that persists in celebrating this "authenticity" scholars have discussed since the publication of Jane Jacobs's *Death and Life of Great American Cities*. Because of the ubiquitous nature of this discussion, and the manner in which it has been applied to the development of urban environments the world over, a historical breakdown of the Gowanus to its current state has broad application to all cities in America's postindustrial society.

~ ~ ~ ~ ~

To New York City's approximately eight million residents, a broad, open sky is a luxury, and probably one of the first things one notices while walking around the Gowanus Canal today. Viewed from the Third Street Bridge, magnificent sunsets unfold with nary a skyscraper to interfere (although the skyline is definitively growing). Admittedly, in that same direction (southwest) hulks a giant subway bridge and platform, the Culver Viaduct, which cuts across the Brooklyn horizon like a rickety black zipper. Just under eighty-eight feet tall, it houses the highest subway station in New York City and, according to the MTA, the world. It exists because digging a subway tunnel under the Gowanus Canal was structurally impossible.

Some time around the turn of the twenty-first century, Brooklyn came to be widely acknowledged in the media as the designated stomping ground for New York's young creatives. According to one fading popular image, the borough may be aptly characterized as an extended campus of hip urbanites dressed in skinny jeans and thick-framed glasses, all launching eclectic boutiques and authoring blogs from cafés manned by tattooed baristas. While somewhat fantastic, this representation is shaped around a central truth: by the 1990s, scores of up-and-coming artists and wired media professionals priced out of Manhattan had unleashed a tidal wave of gentrification that spread rapidly across Brooklyn's oldest neighborhoods. The industrial landscape of Gowanus and its low rents had long attracted the city's fearlessly offbeat and creative dwellers who saw beauty in the neighborhood's grit. As in SoHo and the East Village before Brooklyn, the developers arrived on the heels of this creative class, licking their chops and ready to build.

Before the 2008 recession, industrial neighborhoods like Williamsburg and Greenpoint drove these architects and development firms wild with possibility. As they had the chance to restore derelict factories into luxury condos or build shiny residential towers on abandoned lots, any open space was considered a potential goldmine. "Brownstone Brooklyn" neighborhoods like Park Slope, Boerum Hill, Fort Greene, and Carroll Gardens—where rents now rival those in parts of Manhattan—were also the rage for their village-like charm. Until the mid-2000s the popularity of these surrounding brownstone areas overshadowed the less obvious appeal of Gowanus, which had a seedy reputation and, of course, the toxic canal. But at the height of the housing bubble these negatives actually spelled untapped potential: an underdeveloped area that was not too expensive, with copious old industrial buildings in a proximate location. The tight-knit neighborhood, zoned for a mix of residential, commercial, and industrial use, was a Jane Jacobsian utopia ripe for urban renewal.

The *New York Times* has long been publishing stories about the potential of Gowanus property in its real estate pages, but early in this century it amped up the cultural coverage: a 2006 article described a group of artists living in a houseboat docked on the canal. In 2008, *New York* magazine published a short item describing Gowanus—which it termed "Fringeville"—as unmistakably "Brooklyn's newest culture cluster." A week after the EPA had announced the canal's Superfund designation in 2011, *New York* posed the question, "The Gowanus Canal: Toxic wasteland or real-estate hot spot?" and two months later ran a story about the city's decidedly hip "microneighborhoods," cheekily dubbing the Gowanus area "Superfund South." And the notoriety wasn't just local. In 2010, the Jonathan Ames HBO series *Bored to Death*—mostly shot in Carroll Gardens—ran an episode titled "The Gowanus Canal Has Gonorrhea!", while in May 2012, during an episode of *Law and Order SVU* set around the canal, Mariska Hargitay's Detective Olivia Benson exclaims, "Why would anyone go swimming there? It's a Superfund site!"

Once an eyesore of empty shop windows and daytime streetwalkers, Gowanus, as if exerting its newfound Superfund chic, has sprouted a brewery, two popular music venues, a French bakery and restaurant, art galleries, multiple barbecue restaurants, a Whole Foods, a New England–style clam chowder shack, an aikido studio, a tiki-themed shuffleboard court, and a shop dedicated purely to artisanal pies, heralded across the city (to name a few). New ventures pop up practically every month. Light industry and custom craft studios have flourished, and other small businesses have been launched in the many lofts and industrial spaces that dominate the neighborhood. In the beginning of 2014, the neighborhood had reached such an apex of civic and cultural note that it became the platform for that intellectual buffet of the Internet age, a TED conference (technically it was a TEDx, or independently affiliated, day-long lecture series, "TEDxGowanus"; full disclosure—I was a co-curator and speaker).

It appears that the Gowanus, after fifty years of blight, is staging a comeback. But the challenges that have defined the canal throughout its transformation from bucolic stream to functional urban waterway continue to lie ahead. As journalist Robert Guskind wrote in a retrospective following Sludgie's death in 2007, "The fact that we still tolerate rivers of sewage flowing right into the Gowanus during rainstorms—and that the pollution goes right into New York Harbor and eventually into the Atlantic—is as astounding as a whale showing up in the Gowanus Bay. But that is a different issue."[2]

1

Millponds, Oysters, and Early Origins (1636–1774)

While it's difficult to determine exactly when the first European settlers arrived on Long Island—sometime in the early 1630s—according to some of the earliest available Dutch colonial documents one of the first official land purchases was made by two Englishmen named William Adrianse Bennet and Jacques Bentin, who bought a large tract of land in "Gowanus" from an Indian chief known as Sachem Ka in 1636.

In the delightful language of early land deeds, the property was demarcated by rural landmarks such as "a certain tree or stump on the Long Hill," or a "series of white and black oak trees," one "standing by the Indian foot-path, markt with three notches." While the exact date of the purchase was lost when the patent document was later destroyed in a fire, it mentions a dwelling house, and thus, according to Henry Reed Stiles—a physician and highly regarded historian most famous for his nineteenth-century, three-volume work *History of the City of Brooklyn*—suggests that Gowanus was the "first step in the settlement of the City of Brooklyn."[1]

The first European settlers in New Amsterdam arrived from the Netherlands in the early seventeenth century, mostly under the auspices of the Dutch West India Company (hereafter referred to as DWIC) . Many of these early settlers were Walloons, or French-speaking Calvinist Protestants, living in the southern part of modern-day Belgium (often referred to as Huguenots). As Russell Shorto established in his incomparable *Island at the Center of the World*, New Nederland had special appeal due to some outstanding natural features: the massive protected bay and a seemingly limitless supply of fresh water, trees, fauna, and flora that the rumors of the New World had promised. After New Amsterdam was established in 1625, many of new immigrants migrated out in all directions from what is today downtown Manhattan, forded the rivers, and settled around 250 square miles of lush and rugged countryside—in today's New Jersey and Staten Island to the west, Harlem and Bronx to the north, and Long Island to the east.[2]

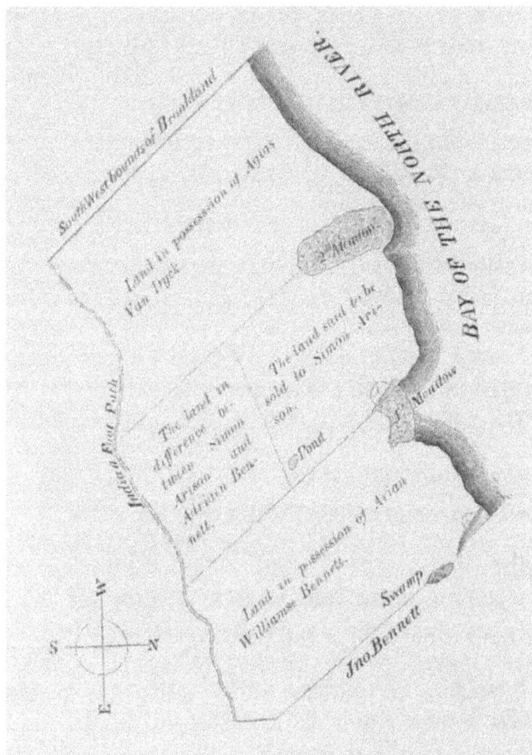

A map of the first land patents of Gowanus, copied from a 1696 survey, printed in the first volume of Henry Stiles's *History of the City of Brooklyn* (Brooklyn, 1867).

Like the spread of dandelion seeds, small farming communities at the tip of Long Island popped up and bloomed in the lush countryside at the western shores of what the natives called Seawanhacky, or "Island of Shells" after *sewant*, the shells used as currency for trade—more popularly known as *wampum* among the New England tribes. Geographically, the modern borough of Brooklyn is a part of Long Island, but in most New York parlance "Long Island" refers to Nassau and Suffolk Counties, the suburban and rural enclaves lying east of the city limits.[3]

More or less at the same time as Bennet and Bentin's Gowanus purchase, records show a grant of several treeless meadows, in the modern-day neighborhoods of Flatbush, Flatlands, and Midwood, purchased from several local natives by DWIC officials on June 16, 1636: "The Director-General and Council of Nieuw Nederland residing at Fort Amsterdam on the Island of Manhattan certify that before them appeared this day, Tenkirauw, Ketaman, Ararykau, Wappettawackensis, owners, who by advice of Penhawis & Cakapeteyno, chiefs in that quarter, have, for certain goods delivered unto them, sold and delivered unto Jacobus Van Curler the middlemost of the three flats to them belonging, called Castateeuw, lying on the island Seawanhacky between the bay of the North River and the East River."[4]

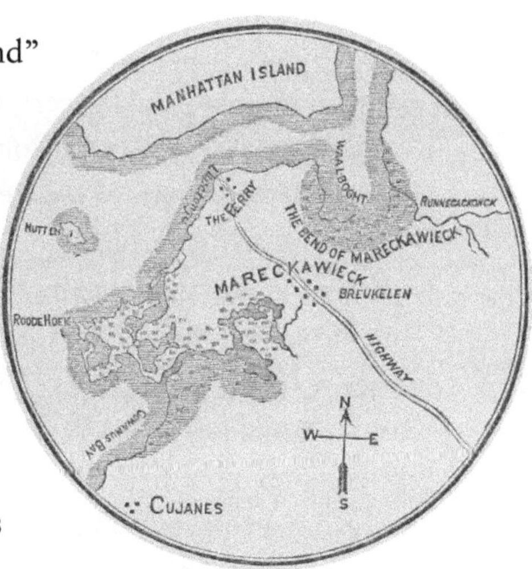

A map of the three Dutch settlements of Brooklyn. Henry R. Stiles, *History of the City of Brooklyn*, vol. 1 (Brooklyn, 1867).

Van Curler, also known as "Van Corlear," was well known in New Amsterdam as an official under the government of Wouter Van Twiller, the director-general. He owned land in Lower Manhattan (where his name graces an area in southeastern Manhattan once known as Corlear's Hook), and on the same day, early Manhattan settlers Andries Hudde and Wolfert Gerritsen purchased flats directly west of Van Corlear's. Director-General Van Twiller himself purchased a massive flat to the east, called Kaskutensuhane, one month later. This massive land grab—the total area of the three plots southeast of the Gowanus amounted to some fifteen thousand acres—was speculative self-interest (an important tradition in New York real estate) since the men neither informed the Amsterdam Council nor asked its permission to buy the property.

On June 16, 1637, exactly one year after the Van Corlear purchase, another settler obtained a patent for a tract of land and freshwater stream called "Rinnegackonck," from two native chiefs Kakpeyno and Pewichaas, undoubtedly the same individuals from the Flatlands purchase. This buyer was Joris Jansen de Rapalie (also spelled Rapalje), a young textile worker and one of the earliest settlers of New Amsterdam. He and his Walloon wife, Catalina Trico, had arrived in the colonies more than a decade previous and were also some of the first landowners in Manhattan. (They were famous throughout New Amsterdam, and their modern-day American descendants number in the millions.) Trico and Rapalie claimed to have produced "the first Christian daughter in New Netherlands," on June 9, 1625, though this distinction has long been in dispute. In any event, Sarah Rapalie married Hans Hansen Bergen—one of the few Norwegian settlers in the colony—who became the patriarch of a prolific Brooklyn family whose scions held land in Gowanus for generations. Many early Walloon settlers (most of whom were political asylum seekers who had been camping out in the Dutch university town of Leiden) had made their homes on the much larger island just east of Manhattan.[5]

Rapalie's settlement, near the modern Brooklyn Navy Yard, was known as 'T Waale Boght (also spelled Wahle-Bocht, Waal-Bogt, and later Wallabout) and was about one mile north of the Gowanus Creek. Stiles dubbed this area, known for its majority Walloon population, to which the word Waale Boght is often attributed, as the second milestone in the establishment of Brooklyn.[6]

(Most of our knowledge of native place-names, such as the Indian settlement known as Werpoes, just west of the head of the Gowanus Creek, or Marechkawieck, the native name of the lands between Werpoes and the Wallabout Bay, derives from such land patents.)[7]

By 1639, Jacques Bentin, who was once New Amsterdam's *schout fiscal*—a Dutch civic position that combined sheriff and attorney general—had sold his Gowanus interest to Bennet for the sum of 360 Dutch guilders.[8] That same year, another of the earliest official Gowanus settlers, Thomas Bescher, obtained a land patent on May 17 for "a plot of 300 paces in breadth," for a certain tobacco plantation "before occupied by John Van Rotterdam, and after wards by him, Thomas Bescher, situate on Long Island, by Gouwanes, in a course towards the south by a certain creek or underwood on which borders the plantation of Willem Adriaensen (Bennet) Cooper; and to the north, Claes Cornelise Smit's; reaching the woods in longitude: for all which Cornelis Lambertsen (Cool) shall pay to said Thomas Bescher 300 Carolus guilders, at 20 stuyvers the guilder."[9]

This patent officially gave Bescher the legal right to own the land as well as sell it, in this case to another settler named Cornelis Lambertsen. The relatively short document reveals several historical gems: Bescher's sale of Gowanus land was the first recorded transfer of property from one colonist to another in early Brooklyn, and he had purchased an already established and previously occupied tobacco plantation. This indicates that by 1639 the land in Gowanus already held significant agricultural value to these earliest settlers and to the DWIC—especially since the latter finally began to regulate the land after a decade of ignoring it. Colonists would not have lived in any of these settlements before the mid-1630s—an unfortified settlement outside of New Amsterdam would be too dangerous in the beginning, with unknown numbers of wild animals and natives controlling the land. The farmers most likely returned home to the safety of Manhattan after a long day's work—New York's first reverse commuters.[10]

Unlike his predecessor, William Kieft, the director-general who replaced Van Twiller in 1638, did not consider Long Island a cheap source of unauthorized patroonships. On August 1 of that year Kieft organized the purchase of a large tract called "Keskaechquerein," which extended from Rapalie's plantation at the 'T Waale Boght up through current-day Greenpoint, and from the East River to the swamps abutting Newtown Creek. It was the first officially recognized purchase of Brooklyn land by the DWIC. For these roughly four thousand acres, Kieft paid the chiefs eight fathoms of duffel cloth, eight fathoms of wampum, twelve kettles, eight adzes, eight axes, several knives and awls, and a few pieces of coral. One month after this purchase, Kieft changed the colony's settlement policy: all of New Netherland was awarded free trade by all its inhabitants and friendly nations, and every immigrant was to be granted "as much land as he and his family can properly cultivate."

Along with this very modern (and very Dutch) policy, Kieft also awarded free passage to the New World to any "respectable" farmers looking to emigrate. This call resonated across Europe and even the English settlements at Virginia and New England. Many farmers, some with considerable means, left to claim their stake to the ample lands in New Amsterdam.[11] Thus, the first settlements in modern-day Brooklyn were established at Gowanus, the 'T Waale Boght, and finally the Ferry, at the foot of present-day Fulton Street in Brooklyn. This last site would prove to be vital to the creation of Brooklyn and to the inhabitants of Gowanus in particular.[12]

Origins and Taxonomy

What is today the teeming borough of Brooklyn once boasted a lush coastline and dramatic topography. During the earth's most recent ice age, nearly twenty thousand years ago, massive glaciers carved these beaches and hills, before slowly melting into the ground. But it was only around fifteen hundred years ago that, as the waters receded into New York Bay, Gowanus Creek emerged. Later, practical nineteenth-century Brooklynites dubbed this meandering "tidal estuary"—a partially enclosed body of saltwater with no current other than the movement of the tides—quite accurately "an arm of the sea." Extending from the watery limb were many streams and offshoots and some freshwater springs, surrounded for nearly a square mile by a lush salt marsh. For good reason and with the same practicality the Gowanus area has often been called a swamp. But modern ecologists would disagree with this nomenclature, since true swamps have trees, while the extensive flooded meadows of Gowanus supported only salt hay and shrubs. These tough grasses are good only for grazing animals or weaving, and grow liberally in the remaining marshes of New York today.[13]

The earliest occupants of the land around Gowanus Creek were Native Americans, particularly the Lenni-Lenape group of Algonquin Indians. Also known as the Delaware, the members of this once-widespread culture spoke a dialect known as Munsee. Different bands used the surrounding area for seasonal fishing and gathering of shellfish, while the outlying lands were sometimes planted with corn. They lived well off of the ample natural resources, as did the European settlers who came along to claim the land and change the course of its destiny. What we know of Indian day-to-day life comes from the earliest accounts of life in New York, when it was a Dutch settlement known as New Amsterdam, part of the colony of New Nederland.[14]

"No Long Island name," wrote the nineteenth-century historian Martha Bockée Flint, "is more puzzling and elusive than Gowanus." The most popular origin story, repeated by historians of the last century to present-day pedestrians, is that the name refers to a Lenape *sachem*, or chief, named Gouwane. According to legend, Sachem Gouwane owned a maize plantation south of the Dutch settlement of Breuckelen, giving a name to the creek, bay, and region.[15] But while the earliest colonial records of that period, mainly deeds and patents for land sales, reveal the names of several prominent natives conveying land to settlers or the newly established government, none of the documents mention a "Gouwane," though Gowanus was already an established area. Nonetheless, this interpretation was canonized in the 1901 reference book *Indian Names of Places in the Borough of Brooklyn*, by William Wallace Tooker, who writes, "The only signification found suggested for [Gowanus] appears in Jones' Indian Bulletin for 1867 as: 'the shallows,' 'flopping down.' . . . From the mark of the possessive case the land probably takes its name from an Indian who lived and planted there, Gouwane's plantation. His name may be translated as 'the sleeper,' or 'he rests,' related to the Delaware *gauwihan* 'sleep,' *gauwin* 'to sleep.'"[16]

William M. Beauchamp, an ethnologist who wrote *Aboriginal Place Names of New York* in 1907, praised Tooker's linguistic expertise and the interpretation of the Gowanus's origins, and also provided translations such as from *gawunsch*, "briery or thorn bush," or *gauwin*, "to sleep," as in Tooker's interpretation. But Beauchamp failed to notice some other names published in his colleague's work that seem rather coincidental: Not far from Lake Erie in Upstate New York lies a village named Gowanda, to which Beauchamp offers the translation of a "contraction of Dyo-go-wand-deh or O-go-wand-da, meaning almost surrounded by hills or cliffs . . . [a term] still used by the Senecas to describe a place below high cliffs or steep hills, especially if the hills form a bend." This accurately describes a preindustrial Gowanus, since the environs were a low-lying, bending creek and marsh surrounded by rolling hills. Even more promising is the name Gowanisque (also spelled Cowanesque), a creek in Painted Post, New York. In his work Beauchamp quoted Major J. W. Powell, an adventurous former director of the Bureau of Ethnology at the Smithsonian Institution, who had stated, "The word Cowanesque seems to be no other than Ka-hwe-nes-ka, the etymology and signification of which is as follows: Co, for Ka, marking grammatical gender and meaning *it*; wan for hwe-n, the stem of the word o-whe-na, an *island*; es, an adjective meaning *long;* que for ke, the locative preposition, meaning *at* or *on*; the whole signifying *at* or *on the long island*. If this is correct the island has now disappeared by changes or drainage."[17] Adding to the intrigue is Lewis H. Morgan, yet another ethnographer and anthropologist, who cited "Gä-wa-nase-geh" as an Oneida word for "a long island" in his *League of the Ho-dé-no-sau-nee, or Iroquois*, first published in 1901.[18]

Although Gowanus is indeed at the western edge of today's aptly named Long Island, scholars are reluctant to draw a connection between the Gowanus and these Iroquois words. Dr. Ives Goddard, senior linguist and Algonquian specialist in the Smithsonian's anthropology department, explains that analysis of such early place-names is "extremely difficult," since the recordings are "too imperfect and the local vocabularies were too poorly known." Even more disheartening, Goddard is certain that an Iroquoian noun could not have ended up as a place-name in Munsee-speaking Brooklyn.[19] Whether or not Chief Gouwane existed, or if Gowanus means "long island," "resting place," or "thorny briars," most can agree that the origins of the unusual word are Native American. The spelling of this elusive name has at least fifteen permutations throughout history—a partial list includes Cujanes, Cowanoes, Gauwanes, Gouanes, and Gouwanes[20]—depending on the era and native tongue of whomever was writing. Regardless of its origins, it is one of the most ancient place-names still in use in the modern-day New York. "Gowanus" is clearly older than "New York" and "New Amsterdam," and certainly much older than the name "Brooklyn."

The earliest European pioneers and their subsequent generations used "Gowanus" in reference to the lands extending outward from the creek and surrounding marshland—once settled by Europeans, the name soon grew to mean the hamlet that formed south of today's Downtown Brooklyn, extending through the neighborhoods of Sunset Park down to Bay Ridge, or the colonial town of New Utrecht. Gowanus was also the name of a village established therein, along the bay between modern-day Twenty-Fourth and Twenty-Eighth Streets. Writes historian Stiles, "It was originally laid out in village lots, and the old stone 'Bennet house' which stood in the middle of Third avenue, near Twenty-seventh street, and was taken down when the avenue was opened, was probably a remnant of the original settlement."[21] The name also refers to the bay that runs along the western coast of Long Island with the present borders lying approximately from Butler

Street down to Hamilton Avenue, and from Bond Street to Fourth Avenue in Brooklyn. And as with all place-names, the definition of what constitutes "Gowanus" may yet again change.

In the early stages of colonial settlement Gowanus stood at a much-trafficked thoroughfare, at both the geographic and economic crossroads of the original five Dutch towns of Long Island (in order of foundation, Breuckelen, Nieuw Amersfoort, Midwout, Nieuw Utrecht, and Boswijck). By the 1640s several farms had been established near this site. Unlike those who worked some of the more landlocked agricultural locales on Long Island, the farmers of Gowanus had several transportation options to bring their foodstuffs to the markets of Manhattan: The first involved trudging through the wooded hills and swamps to the ferry landing, where one could hire a boat or row oneself from the creek across Gowanus Bay—which meant navigating the dangerous shallow waters around Roode Hoek (today's Red Hook). Before the official municipality of Breuckelen was formed, settlers relied on their own skiffs for transport; in 1642, the DWIC approved a public ferry between the two islands.

The official landing point, somewhere in the vicinity of the Fulton Ferry landing in the contemporary neighborhood of DUMBO, Brooklyn, corresponded with the landing at Pecks Slip in Manhattan, a still-extant street and former neighborhood near the South Street Seaport. The Brooklyn side of the landing was in the charge of Cornell Dircksen, a Dutch settler whose house and garden were located just a few steps away. An early New York real magnate, Dircksen also owned the surrounding property at Pecks Slip, which included an inn. The ferry service was the height of seventeenth-century technology: Travelers wishing to cross the river would go to the water's edge, where a conch shell hung from the branch of an old tree. The conch call would summon one of Dircksen's farmhands, who would leave his plough and retrieve a roughly hewn boat hidden under some nearby bushes. He would then row the passengers over for the price of three Dutch stuyvers, paid in pieces of sewant. According to Flint, this business was lucrative, as Dircksen later sold his house, land, and ferriage rights in Breuckelen to a Willem Tomassen for a whopping 2,300 guilders (46,000 stuyvers), much more than the cost of larger tracts of land situated farther south. The system remained roughly the same through the next decade, until the Dutch-backed government instituted fixed rates and a formal ferry license. The cost for transporting a single person to Manhattan was three stuyvers, while Indians had to pay six. A one-horse wagon cost sixteen stuyvers, a two-horse wagon twenty. The ferryman held such a prominent position in the community that he was exempt from any military service.[22]

Although Director-General Kieft was deft in his real estate purchases, in practically every other arena he was considered a terrible governor, mostly due to the bloody war he ignited with the local Lenape tribes, which erupted, like so many conflicts, over problems of cash: New Amsterdam was flooded with all kinds of foreign currency—guilders and florints, stuyvers and sewant—making economic organization difficult. Kieft's expenses included wages for soldiers and officials, and so, he attempted to tax the natives for their continued settlement on the lands they had "sold." Following a failure at tax collection, Kieft retaliated, sending his soldiers to violently attack the same natives with whom many settlers had cultivated beneficial relationships. This response did not bode well with New Amsterdam's colonists, and so Kieft—trying to avoid political unrest—organized a council of the various heads of New Amsterdam families, including wealthy merchants and landowners, to collectively decide how to deal with the Indian "problem."[23]

After some deliberation, that council elected twelve representatives, known as the "Twelve Men," to voice their interests in the matter. One-quarter of this body—Jacques Bentin, Frederick Lubbertsen, and Joris Rapalie—were prominent landowners in or around Gowanus. The Twelve Men advised Kieft to maintain peace with the natives, but in reality the director-general had gathered the group purely to obtain public consent for an even more violent retaliation against the natives. He managed to get their grumbling approval by promising them future representation in a formally elected legislative body, an agreement that, naturally, he later dishonored. Kieft's attacks forced the diverse tribal groups to ally in a previously unheard-of union, and so between 1642 and 1643 a tragic slaughter occurred on both sides. Many of the outlying settlements in Brooklyn were destroyed, including the early structure on Bennet's land in Gowanus. Kieft's foolish policy did eventually subdue the natives, but it left the colony nearly bankrupt. He then attempted to tax the colonists' fur trading and then their beer. Clearly, this line of governance shredded any popular support that remained for the director-general.[24]

In July 1645, a settler named Jan Evertsen Bout determined a particular location on the road from the Ferry to 'T Vlacke Bos—approximately at today's Fulton Street, between Hoyt and Smith Streets—to be the perfect place to establish a new village. It was a very convenient spot, at the center of a triangle drawn between the earliest hamlets on that part of Long Island: Gowanus, the Ferry, and the Waal-bocht. Numerous settlers followed suit, and they called their new settlement "Breuckelen," after a picturesque riverfront town between Amsterdam and Utrecht. The new Breuckelenites quickly applied to the New Amsterdam council for permission to organize a proper town "at their own expense." As one of his last sound decisions, Kieft—soon to be replaced by Peter Stuyvesant as director-general—granted this privilege on December 1, 1646. Jan Teunissen was named the first *schout*, a job he had performed long before being formally designated.[25]

Throughout New Netherland, the DWIC had already been doling out patroonships—a type of Dutch land grant akin to the English manorial system—to its most prominent investors, usually nobles and Amsterdam councilmen. These patroonships were intended to jump-start the colonies, with the grantee, or patroon, responsible for bringing in settlers and heading civil management. After much deliberation, in 1652 Cornelis Van Werckhoven, the *scheffen* or magistrate of the city of Utrecht and a lesser noble, instituted a patroonship on two tracts of Long Island, "one situated to the east of the North River, near its mouth, and joining Gowanus, 'as it was before purchased by the Company,' and stretching in an oblique line through the mountain to Merrakawick (Breukelen)."[26] The second tract, known as "Nyack" or "Najack" after the local Indian tribe, became the foundation for the town of New Utrecht (around today's Bensonhurst), named in honor of Van Werckhoven's native city. Augustine Heermans, the agent for the DWIC in this purchase, paid the Indians six shirts, two pairs of shoes, six pairs of stockings, six chisels, six axes, six knives, two pairs of scissors, and six cans for the first tract; for the second he paid six coats, six kettles, six axes, six chisels, six small looking glasses, twelve knives, and twelve combs.[27]

Despite the favorable deal he had procured, Van Werckhoven never saw his land prosper, as he died two years later during a return visit to Holland. But his contribution to New Nederland was immeasurable: Along with his children, Van Werckhoven had brought along a tutor, a talented young man named Jacques Cortelyou. Already in his late twenties when he arrived in the colony, Cortelyou had been raised in Utrecht by French parents, and spoke both Dutch and his parents' tongue fluently. He was also educated in diverse fields such as Latin, mathematics, philosophy, and land surveying by the time he arrived in the colony, and he was left in charge of Van Werckhoven's estate following his patron's death. Cortelyou soon assumed control from the *scheffen*'s children and, as the de facto founder of the settlement of New Utrecht, became one of the most prominent landed men on Long Island. (Despite his Brooklyn ties, Cortelyou is now most famous for the creation of a celebrated map representing Manhattan in 1660—known as the Castello Plan since the only known copy was discovered at the Villa di Castello near Florence in 1900—one of the earliest and most detailed published maps of the new colony.[28])

In the mid-seventeenth century, Breuckelen was booming. By 1660 there were thirty-one families in the town. Early in that year, Stuyvesant hired Jacques Cortelyou as a surveyor, along with commissioners Albert Cornelissen and Jan Evertsen Bout, "to examine the situation and quality of the land in the neighborhood of the village of Breuckelen, and to report (with a map) how much of it remained undisposed of, how it was cultivated, and how many plantations might be advantageously laid out upon it."[29] But already, the area was dotted with evidence of agricultural prosperity in a truly Dutch character. Putting the local geography to work, the colonists had chosen Gowanus Creek as the site of New Nederland's first tide mill. The oldest Gowanus mill was Brouwer's Mill, or Freeke's Mill, erected sometime before 1661, serviced by a hand-dug millpond. This mill was most likely located in the middle of today's canal path, at the head of the creek where a millpond was clearly documented on maps of the era. While owned by a rich merchant, John C. Freeke, by the late eighteenth century, the mill was first called Brouwer's Mill after its original proprietor, Adam Brouwer, and was also known as the Old Gowanus Mill. The land itself first belonged to Jan Evertse Bout, but it was Bout's tenant, Brouwer, who constructed the mill with business partner Isaac Deforrest. Brouwer eventually acquired Deforrest's share and bought (or traded) the land rights from Bout, who in 1667 bequeathed "the corn and meadows and place whereon the mill is grounded" to the children of Adam Brouwer.[30]

Because the Gowanus is an estuary regulated by tidal flow, the pond was a necessary piece of aquatic engineering to produce a functioning mill. Controlled by a sluice gate, this millpond filled to capacity at high tide; once the tide went out, the gates were opened and a steady flow of water was established, forcing the millstone to turn. African slaves, long employed by the Dutch for agricultural work, likely dug most millponds—the excavation of Cole's millpond has long been attributed to African laborers.[31]

With his successful mill operation, Brouwer was perhaps the first Gowanus entrepreneur and was also the first person to formally suggest digging a canal to aid transportation—he also created the first

Gowanus "canal." At that time, many settlers used their own boats to transport their goods from Long Island to Manhattan, which required a dangerous trip around the shallow waters of Roode Hoek. Brouwer saw the potential usefulness of Gowanus Creek and how one branch in particular (conveniently located next to his mill) could be widened and dredged at the expense of local inhabitants, allowing them to avoid the danger of capsized boats. Brouwer brought his proposal, representing a primordial version of the modern canal, to the governor and Council's attention by a petition dated May 29, 1664, in which he pointed out that "there is situate a kill at the end of Frederick Lubbertsen's land, and between (that and) the Red Hook, which might be made fit to pass through it to the Gouwanes and the Mill, without going west of the Red Hook, where the water is ordinarily shallow, inasmuch as the said kill, which now is blocked up by sand at the end, might be made, without much trouble of digging, fit and navigable for the passage of boats laden with a hundred skepels of grain, full of wood and other articles."[32] Lubbertsen, who owned the great swath of marsh in question bordering Red Hook, offered no objections, and the creek was dredged.

That year that Brouwer sponsored his canal project, 1664, brought other big changes: Peter Stuyvesant surrendered New Nederland to the English and the colony of New York was established. Despite this political upheaval, daily life in the former Dutch colony was hardly interrupted, nor was the flow of colonists to its strategic and desirable location. This same year one of the most prominent early Gowanusians emigrated from the Netherlands to its marshy fields.

The Oysters at Gowanus

In 1664, a Dutch settler named Simon Aertson de Hart arrived in the New World among the wave of prosperous fortune seekers. He eventually settled on the lands owned by Bennet, with the intention of reaping the benefits of the agriculturally rich environment, particularly at Gowanus. We know of de Hart today through his appearances in various colonial records, but mainly thanks to a Dutch missionary named Jasper Danckaerts.

Danckaerts, along with his traveling companion Peter Sluyter, were Labadists, members of a now-defunct Protestant sect that promoted, among others things, early-Christian-style communal living. Their mission was to establish a Labadist colony in the New World, but we can be indebted to Danckaerts mainly for his journalistic efforts. *The Diary of Jasper Danckaerts*, a chronicle of his travels between 1679 and 1680 from New Nederland to Maryland and back north again, until he eventually departed out of Boston, remains an invaluable first-person account of seventeenth-century life in the New World colonies.[33]

The duo first sailed on June 26, 1679, from Texel, an island north of Amsterdam marking the entrance to the North Sea. Their vessel, the *Charles*, was a small fluyt, a Dutch cargo ship, owned by Margriete Flips, a Dutch proprietress and cargo master (the captain in her employ, Thomas Singleton, was English). The Labadists paid seventy-five guilders each for their passage on the small but efficient ship. The initial voyage required several stops before the big jump across the Atlantic from Falmouth, England, in late July. On the eve of their journey, on the advice of their fellow traveler Jan Teunissen, the first *schout* of Breuckelen, the duo stocked up on provisions and dined on oysters. This repast was followed by nearly two months of transatlantic discomfort.[34]

The ship sailed southwesterly across the Atlantic, touching on the South American west coast near Brazil, passing through the Caribbean and northward to New Nederland. Nearly three months after setting out from Amsterdam, on September 23 the *Charles* finally anchored in New York Bay, where Danckaerts was overwhelmed by the activity in the harbor. As soon as they passed through the narrows, around three o'clock in the afternoon, a swarm of private boats hounded the *Charles*, their owners making all kinds of inquiries and assessing the business opportunities to be had from the new arrivals. The wildlife too was plentiful. It was "not possible to describe how this bay swarms with fish," Danckaerts wrote that day, "both large and small, whales, tunnies and porpoises, whole schools of innumerable other fish, which the eagles and other birds of prey swiftly seize in their talons when the fish come up to the surface, and hauling them out of the water, fly with them to the nearest woods or beach, as we saw."[35]

Among the Labadists' fellow voyagers on the *Charles* were some seasoned colonists with many contacts, including Gerrit Evertsen van Duyn, who secured the visitors lodging in his elderly father-in-law's house in Manhattan. Gerrit, a wheelwright and carpenter by trade, was returning to the New World after nearly a decade in his native land. Gerrit's older sister Neeltje had married Jacques Cortelyou, and

Originally drawn by George Hayward, an image of Gowanus Bay from the 1867 manual of the Brooklyn Common Council. On the left is the former home of Simon de Hart, known as the de Hart or Bergen House. George Hayward, *Gowanus Bay, Brooklyn, 1867*. From *Manual of the Common Council of the City Brooklyn for 1867*. Courtesy of the Brooklyn Public Library.

the prominent surveyor had gifted his brother-in-law a land patent, so that Gerrit was a prominent citizen despite his long absence from the colony. The journalists settled in the elder van Duyn's house and spent the next week exploring Manhattan and meeting its inhabitants.

On the afternoon of September 29, Danckaerts and Sluyter ate lunch at Gerrit's father-in-law's and mailed letters they had composed earlier that morning. Then, at two in the afternoon, the men reunited with Gerrit, who would be their guide through the wilds of Brooklyn, as well as Jan Teunissen, who was also traveling to Brooklyn to deliver letters and "transact other business." The little band headed over to the ferry station and paid their fare, three pieces of sewant, as Danckaerts observed that the ferry service, a clever style of rowboat that could be equipped with a sail when the conditions dictated, was surely a profitable business as Long Island was "one of the most populous places in this vicinity." After arriving at the ferry landing on the opposite shore, the group traveled uphill for about a mile, passing farms along the free roads and some forest until they came across "the first village, called Breukelen, which has a small and ugly little church standing in the middle of the road." This apparently unpleasant structure had been completed in 1666. It was the second church built in Kings County and was erected at the northern edge of the neighborhood known today as Boerum Hill.

Our journalist was clearly unimpressed with the village that bestowed the borough of Brooklyn its name, since he wrote less than a paragraph of description before striking "off to the right, in order to go to Gouanes." The group had been traveling eastward from the boat landing, and so this right turn brought the men directly south, where they soon arrived at some plantations where Gerrit knew "almost all of the people." These Gowanus folk (the first of several Danckaerts would encounter) made a big show of their guests and shared "bountifully whatever they had, whether it was milk, cider, fruit or tobacco." It's possible that these farmers and agricultural workers, many of Dutch extraction or allegiance, would have been especially excited to greet kinsman newly arrived from their homeland, offering Danckaerts and Sluyter "first and most of all, miserable rum or brandy which had been brought from Barbados and other islands." Although the people were quite fond of the bad-tasting liquor ("and most of them extravagantly so," Danckaerts noted), strong alcohol was offensive to Labadist sensibilities.

Clearly enchanted by their surroundings, nonetheless, the small party proceeded onward through the plantations, arriving at a place with peach trees so overloaded with fruit that some branches were bent over or broken. It was impossible to walk without stepping on the fallen peaches, while hogs and other farm beasts gobbled up the rotting fruit. According to Danckaerts, the peach orchard was owned by the "oldest European woman in the country." One of her innumerable children, some of whom still lived in the house with her, informed their guests that the matriarch was one hundred years old.

In what is perhaps the earliest caricature of an American frontierswoman, Danckaerts describes the ancient great-grandmother sitting by a fire as she chain-smoked a pipe, blowing plumes of blue smoke around her guests. The elderly woman explained in French that she was from Luyck, or Liège, the economic capital of Wallonia (in today's Belgium) and had lived in the New World for about fifty years, making her quite possibly one of the original Gowanus settlers. The matriarch also claimed to have sired more than seventy children and grandchildren, and knew of a multitude of great-grandchildren as well but couldn't give a hard count for that generation. The hardy settler offered the travelers mugs of fine, freshly brewed cider and some salted and smoked striped bass, already aged a full year but "still perfectly good and in flavor not inferior to smoked salmon."[37]

Taking leave of their generous hostess, the duo, until early evening, walked several miles south to the center of "Gouanes," where they sought out the home of Simon Aertson de Hart, a close friend of Gerrit's. Legal documents show that de Hart was a wealthy man, at least compared to his neighbors, and his manor house, later depicted in numerous lithographs, became a historic property that stood proudly well into the nineteenth century. De Hart and his wife Geertje offered the travelers a warm welcome and invited them to sit before a roaring fire of "clear oak and hickory," which warmed their tired feet. Danckaerts was impressed that they used the expensive fuel with such abandon, but even more so with a pail of Gowanus oysters roasting on the fire, which he called "the best in the country." "They are fully as good as those of England," he wrote, "and better than those we ate at Falmouth. They are large and full, some of them not less than a foot long, and they grow sometimes ten, twelve and sixteen together, and are then like a piece of rock." The discarded oyster shells, explained Danckaerts, were so numerous that they were burned into lime, which was used for fertilizer, and the plentiful oysters were pickled and sold in Barbados and other Caribbean destinations, not to mention more local islands, particularly Manhattan.

After their delicious appetizer—which more than three hundred years later has not lost its popularity in New York, even if the oysters are no longer locally sourced or the size of dinner plates—de Hart served the Labadists a feast of roasted haunch of venison, purchased from Indians for "three guilders and half of *seewant*, that is, fifteen stivers of Dutch money," followed by thick slices of fat, flavorful wild turkey, and wild goose that was "somewhat dry." Danckaerts marveled at the heap of watermelons piled for sale in Manhattan ("a whole hill," he wrote, "as large as pumpkins"), though they were not quite as good as the Caribbean variety he had previously sampled; he blamed the flavor on the fact that the melons were the "last pulling" at season's end. Perhaps unwittingly anticipating the locally sourced food fetish of modern Brooklynites, Danckaerts noted approvingly that everything they ate was "the natural production of the country." Danckaerts was obviously delighted with the Gowanus bounty and the hospitable character of its people, for he would revisit de Hart numerous times throughout his stay in the New Amsterdam area.

On the morning of August 30, Danckaerts and Sluyter awoke to see the de Harts off for their morning boat ride to the Manhattan markets to sell their watermelons. Accompanied by their faithful guide Gerrit, the trio then explored the Gowanus lands farther west and eventually headed south toward the village of New Utrecht. Along the Brooklyn shoreline, amid a series of swampy wetlands, the Labadists happened upon a small island known as Najack, also the name of the Indian population, and their village (known today as Fort Hamilton, at the eastern point of the Verrazano Narrows), where an eighty-year-old woman was fiercely beating a pile of "Turkish beans" with a stick to free the legumes from their pods. Nearby, her approximately two dozen fellow tribesman—about seven or eight families—had settled in several longhouses "15 feet wide and 60 long, dirt floors covered by walls and roof of reeds and chestnut bark and supported by tree limbs."[38] Danckaerts described at length quotidian Najack life: the design of the longhouses and cooking pots, the social arrangement of families and roles within the community, and the how despite being "a poor, miserable people they are, nevertheless, licentious and proud."

He also claimed that Najack Island itself belonged to the esteemed surveyor Jacques Cortelyou, who had developed extensive properties in the colony of New Nederland as well as acted as leader of New Utrecht. Cortelyou had allowed the local Indians to remain on the island, often trading with them and even paying them multiple tributes to the grand confusion of the Labadists (a seasoned settler, Cortelyou clearly understood native land politics enough not to repeat certain past mistakes). "But the worst of it was," Danckaerts lamented, "[Cortelyou] was a good Cartesian, and not a good Christian, regulating himself, and all externals, by reason and justice only; nevertheless, he regulated all things better by these principles than most people in these parts do, who bear the name of Christians or pious persons."[39]

Cortelyou and his wife welcomed the group to New Utrecht with as much hospitality as they could muster, a difficult task since an epidemic of smallpox was raging through the settlement. Still, the Labadists spent several days exploring the southern edges of modern Brooklyn, including a tour of Coney Island. Danckaerts spoke highly of the strong stone houses that were built in New Utrecht, noting they were erected from the ashes of homes burnt in a fire that ravaged the village several years previous. The travelers stayed with Cortelyou and his wife for several days, learning much about the land before returning to Manhattan. In their gratitude the duo left Cortelyou a gift of calamus tincture and sulfur balsam, herbal medicines used for relaxing nerves and treating skin ailments.

After their first instructive visit to Gowanus, the travelers wished to visit Staten Island, with its similar topography and settlements, but they lacked transit. On October 10 they had the luck of a visit from de Hart, now their "old friend," who immediately offered to take the Labadists over in his skiff. That night they accompanied de Hart back to the homestead, where he entertained them with food and drink, no doubt as lavishly as on their first visit,[40] and the following morning de Hart dropped the travelers off on Staten Island, where they explored Indian villages and plantations over the next five days. In anticipation of the approaching cold weather, Danckaerts next set his sights on Maryland and Virginia, which he wished to visit despite the poor opinion that his New Amsterdam contacts held of the southern colonies. Before their departure on November 14, the Labadists visited Cortelyou so that they might copy his folio of Dutch laws. The legal documents were battered and poorly organized, which may explain why little of their translation exists in Danckaerts's account, but in gratitude he lent the secular Cortelyou a copy of Blaise Pascale's *Pensées*, a lengthy defense of the Christian religion.[41]

For the next two months, Sluyter and Danckaerts traveled in the South, where they encountered as many cheap and "Godless" as generous and pious folks. Our faithful journalist describes, with a detectable level of distaste, how farmers in Maryland planted tobacco and little else—few vegetables or fruits and only corn in sizable quantities. He did sample some decent meals, including a supper of fresh

Maryland duck from a local pond, which was followed up by a rather unusual digestive of Maryland or Virginia oysters. "We found them good," Danckaerts wrote in his diary on December 10, "but the Gouanes oysters at New York are better."[42]

When the Labadists returned to New York at the start of 1680, news of their travels preceded them since they arrived to find de Hart waiting with a boatload of wood for their Manhattan stove. Having barely settled down, Danckaerts immediately asked the Gowanusian if they could borrow his boat to travel to Ackquakenon (also spelled Acquackanonk, today's Passaic in southeastern New Jersey), another settlement that had been founded by Jacques Cortelyou. De Hart could not make the trip, but offered his boat, and Gerrit was chosen to lead the journey: he knew his brother-in-law's lands and had knowledge of the local Indian languages. Waiting for warmer weather to begin the journey, the group did not meet again until March 3, at de Hart's land in "Gouanes." While waiting for Gerrit to arrive, the Labadists attempted to buy some oysters from the Indians who had settled on de Hart's beach at the consent of Geertje, his wife, but were interrupted by the arrival of Jacques Cortelyou, who had come to help de Hart deal with a sickly horse. The small party was delayed another night in Gowanus, due to a leak in de Hart's boat, and in the end the simple two-night excursion proved arduous, plagued by the freezing rains of early March and a grumbling, uncalculating guide—whom a frustrated Danckaerts called a "coarse, ignorant man"—whose knowledge of tides was unreliable.[43]

Safely arrived back in Gowanus by the evening of March 6, Danckaerts and Sluyter were startled by the wild cacophony of "shouting and singing in the huts of the Indians." The sight of the natives "lustily drunk, raving, striking, shouting, jumping, fighting each other," in their settlement on the beach near the de Hart House, "foaming at the mouth like raging wild beasts," was shocking for the teetotaling Labadists. Apparently other natives had fled the seventeenth-century mosh pit to hide with their wives and children in the de Hart house, where a drunken hoard tried to break down the door. With some difficulty the two travelers managed to lock out the mob.

Danckaerts laments greatly the disastrous effects of alcohol on the native population, and the apparent godlessness of those Europeans who sold the spirits—so much so that he called upon the wrath and judgment of God, invoking the name of Jesus Christ in anger. The missionary severely admonished de Hart and his wife for providing the natives with the booze. In their defense, the couple claimed that if that hadn't made the sale other colonists certainly would have and then "they would have the trouble and others the profit, but if they must have the trouble, they ought to have the profit." Unmoved by this mercantile claim, Danckaerts recorded that all of the colonists would try to sell the natives as much liquor as they could, "begging their money from them," and even driving them to destitution, compelling the thirsty natives to "leave their blankets, leggings, and coverings of their bodies in pawn, yes, their guns and hatchets, the very instruments by which they obtain their subsistence." Though by the next morning, when the Labadists were leaving de Hart's to head south toward modern-day Fort Hamilton, the natives were already rebuilding the huts they had knocked over,[44] Danckaerts would not be the last to decry the effects of alcoholism among the native communities.

After two more months exploring New Amsterdam, in the spring of 1681 the Labadists' journey concluded. On May 10 they took a final tour through the Long Island towns, meeting and lunching with Jacques Cortelyou (whose son presented the missionaries a hummingbird that he had impressively shot). In return for the elder Cortelyou's kindness during their sojourn, Dankaerts gifted him the copy of Pascal's *Pensées*.

Taking their leave, the duo headed directly north through the fields to Gowanus, not bothering to stick to the main roads. Arriving at the start of a new cycle of cornucopia, the Labadists found de Hart and his wife planting watermelons in some newly cleared, ever-fertile Gowanus land—"for water-melons must always have new ground, or the worms will destroy them," as Danckaerts warned in his journal. The foursome convened one last time in the de Hart house, where the couple displayed several pieces of rare Caribbean ambergris—a highly prized waxy gray substance found in the intestine of Sperm whales, used to make perfumes. This last meeting was surely a bittersweet good-bye—Danckaerts wrote many times about his affection for de Hart and his bountiful lands. "We said to them what we deemed proper for them," he wrote of his farewell, "and took our leave, reaching the city in good time."[45]

The Old Stone House

After the departure of the Labadists, Breuckelen grew in size and importance. The agricultural bounty of the lands supported a robust trade over the next two decades, and civic duties took on an increasing role in village life. Breuckelenites began holding elections annually in 1690 to choose commissioners for sanitation management, security, and property—jobs that had been informally performed before. During this period many previously established contracts were codified: In early November 1696, de Hart was finally awarded the patent for the purchase of his Gowanus land, originally belonging to William Adrianse Bennet, which he had been fighting to procure for years, the patent affirming that de Hart's land contained some 303 acres, upon which "he hath made considerable improvements." By 1698 the area population, including 65 slaves, had grown to 509 people.[46]

At the 1699 election, held on April 29, the chosen townsmen were officially charged with defending the boundaries, marking off the ownership of the empty lots, and, most important, instituting "laws and orders for the [best of] best of the inhabitants, and to raise a small tax to defray town charges." Although no change was made to the town's legal status, the result that Breuckelen became an official tax-collecting municipality affirmed its prominence among the other Long Island settlements. Two days later, de Hart's contemporary and Gowanus neighbor Claes Arents Vecht (also known as Nicholas Vecht) moved from the bustle of Hanover Square in Lower Manhattan to take up residence on his farmland, where he had completed one of the finest homes in the village.[47]

Rising from the base of the foothills that led eastward toward the future site of Prospect Park, the two-and-a-half-story Vecht Mansion was a paragon of luxury and stability. The lands were as lush as de Hart's, but closer to the village of Breuckelen and serviced by a bountiful freshwater spring—anecdotes about which appear in Brooklyn history well into the mid-nineteenth century. With stone walls "several feet thick" adorned with brass figures inscribed "1699," the dwelling boasted windows on either side of the front door and along the its back. The only stone structure in the area, the mansion dwarfed its neighboring dwellings.

Like de Hart's farm, Vecht's plantation, extending from Gowanus Creek, was long and narrow—designed to benefit from as much richly

A lithograph of the Vecht-Cortelyou Mansion printed in the first volume of Henry Stiles's *History of the City of Brooklyn* (1867).

diverse Gowanus land as possible: bay access was met by meadows perfect for grazing and planting, with the house in the foothills, where freshwater springs bubbled. Also, the home's height offered a great view of any approaching highwaymen or marauding natives. Unlike the other farms in Brooklyn, the de Hart and Vecht farms were surrounded by their own private woods, which gave easy access to timber, bark, and other important resources—other Brooklyn and Gowanus freeholders were allotted ten-acre plots in the woodlands south and west of the road to Flatbush, not nearly as convenient a source of firewood.[48]

The Vecht Mansion would survive for nearly two hundred years, brushing off revolutions and depressions to stand as the most ancient man-made landmark in Gowanus. It later became known as the Vecht-Cortelyou Mansion when Jacques Cortelyou—the great-great-great-grandson of the Utrecht-born settler and famed surveyor—purchased the house and part of the farm in 1790 for twenty-five hundred pounds. The original house was razed in 1897; half of the home had already been buried underground when area streets had been graded. The new structure was constructed in 1934 of stone and cement, including some original foundation stones. Today it is primarily known as the Old Stone House of Gowanus, a remnant of Brooklyn's long past that survives in Park Slope's Washington Park, between Third and Fifth Streets and Fourth and Fifth Avenues.[49]

After authorizing the collection of taxes in Brooklyn, in 1703 the Colonial Assembly, a locally elected body allowed by the British government, ordered a survey of "Broocklands improveable lands and meadows within fence," which found that greater Brooklyn comprised some 5,177 acres—200 of which belonged to de Hart (he had sold some of his property but was still the biggest landholder by this time).[50]

This survey initiated one of the earliest and crucial steps of Brooklyn development: On March 28, 1704, two important public highways were established by order of the colony's Assembly, "for the transportation of goods and the commodious passing of travelers." The first was named the "King's Highway" and eventually became Fulton Street, the main road in Brooklyn, running from the ferry landing eastward, past Jasper Danckaerts's church toward the town of Bedford, at the time a community separate from Brooklyn.

The second highway—eventually called Old Gowanus Road—was four rods wide (or sixty-six feet), with a fenced and gated path built specifically for transport, running from the old Flatbush Road (just before the toll gate leading out of Brooklyn) southward, on roughly the same path as today's Fifth Avenue, and then toward the Gowanus "mill neck." Also called Lubbertsen's Neck after its principal landowner, this swampy tract was known for its industry and shape: a narrow strip of land between Gowanus Creek and Wallabout Bay would be the easiest southern access to the peninsula hosting Brooklyn's original sites of settlement, with Red Hook at its westernmost point. The Old Gowanus Road passed by the lands maintained by the Brouwer family, ending at a public boat landing. Eventually, the road was extended to run westward along the line between the de Hart (or Bergen) farm and the Vecht farm, then continuing southward along the coastline.[51]

As Gowanus grain production increased, navigable public roads and landing sites for boats to transport this commodity became economically necessary and surely also gave the area inhabitants a dose of civic pride: while they had likely used these pathways already for their own livelihood (previously established in the vicinity had been the shorter Porte Road, which ran across the creek, between the two millponds, and separated the Brouwer farmland from Vecht's), the colonial government's public works had acknowledged their worth. Indeed, in 1709 the colonial government contracted yet another mill road at the northern border of the Vecht plantation, on land that had originally been held by Jan Evertsen Bout, who had gifted (or sold) this particular portion to Nicholas and Adam Brouwer Jr., sons of the first proprietor of Freeke's Mill. The two enterprising sons had dug a millpond by damming a branch of the Gowanus that same year and on it built the Yellow Mill (also known as the Lower Mill, and eventually Denton's Mill), at the northeast side of present-day First Street, between Second and Third Avenues. Their nearby house on Carroll Street stood until consumed by a fire in 1852.[52] "Both of these, mills, formerly known as Brouwer's were employed in the flouring business," wrote Stiles in the first volume of the *History of the City of Brooklyn*, "they buying the principal portion of the wheat raised in the county. Both Denton and Freeke had been merchants, were reputed to be rich, and were among the first in Brooklyn, who made use of coaches, or barouches."[53]

Denton's Mill and its accompanying pond played elementary roles in the story of Brooklyn's origins, but they also engendered what is possibly the most curious mode of transportation in Gowanus history: Nicholas Vecht's impressive mansion sat on a bank several feet from a salt meadow and about one hundred yards from navigable creek waters. Like his Dutch forebears, Vecht had dug a narrow canal leading to the creek directly from his kitchen door, but during low tide it was more like a mud channel that left his boat stuck—an inconvenience when he had fresh produce to sell in Manhattan. When Vecht saw his neighbors constructing a new mill with accompanying pond, he contracted with the Brouwers to provide some aquatic momentum from their new reservoir: After loading his boat with garden produce in the muddy channel, Vecht would sit down and raise his paddle up as a signal to an African servant (more likely a slave), who would raise a sluice gate. The waters filled a second channel leading to his doorstep, and the waters would float his boat. Old Vecht would then light up his pipe and sail down the creek, around Red Hook bound for Broad Street in Manhattan.[54]

For nearly two centuries these Brooklyn mills ground the flour used for local consumption and sale on Long Island and Manhattan. They were also significant Gowanus landmarks, providing an idyllic vision of the pastoral life that once defined Brooklyn. Teunis G. Bergen, the nineteenth descendent of an old Brooklyn family who long admired these elegant structures, wrote in 1868 that "in the old towns of Bushwick and Brooklyn the tide-mills and their placid ponds formed the most striking and characteristic features of the scenery. The sluggish streams where the lazy tide crept in its sinuous course among the

The original six towns of Kings County illustrated with historical notes and the homes of prominent Brooklynites, from a special tercentenary edition of the *Brooklyn Daily Eagle*, dated June 9, 1946. Brooklyn Collection. Courtesy of the Brooklyn Public Library and Newspapers.com.

reeds, were dammed at convenient points and when the ebb had lowered the surface below the flume sufficiently, the clatter of the simple machinery announced that the run of six hours had commenced. Ten of these tide mills were in use within the present limits of the city up to 1830, and several until within a few years."[55]

Extensive commercial activity, ongoing development around Gowanus Creek, and changes to its course demonstrated an ever-growing dependence of the locals for the services the waters provided. In 1744, almost a century after the first channel was dug, the state assembly passed an act to extend the ditch further at the expense of local landowners, allowing for more and larger boats to traverse. In addition to paying for the construction, residents and users of the canal were also bound to maintain a bridge that crossed the creek on the road leading south.

This improvement so eased the movement of boats past the treacherous shallows around Red Hook that in 1751 Gowanus descendants of the Vecht, Brouwer, and other founding clans raised £117 to buy a strip of meadow just east of the Van Dyke Mill, in Red Hook, to extend the ditch even further, deepening it to six feet and constructing alongside it a "foot-path, two foot and a half wide, to dragg or hall up their canoes or boats." Over the next quarter century, usage of the canal increased so much so that by March 1774—while revolutionary fervor bubbled across the colonies—New York's Colonial Assembly passed an act "empowering the people of Gowanus to widen the canal, keep it in order, and tax those who used it." Soon, however, the established order in the New World would be flipped upon its head in a political upheaval in which the Gowanus itself would play a significant role.

2

Bloody Waters (1776)

The Road to Gowanus

At two o'clock in the morning on August 27, 1776, an unfamiliar presence stirred William Howard from his slumber. Opening his eyes, the fourteen-year-old met the gaze of a British soldier. Howard quickly dressed and was led downstairs to the main room of the Rising Sun, his father's tavern. In the low-ceilinged room were two more British soldiers with bayonets fixed on the middle-aged tavern keeper, who was speaking to a man wearing civilian clothes, standing calmly at the bar and sipping a glass of liquor. The visitor spoke with Howard in a familiar manner, asking him detailed questions about the geography of the area as though such conversations were commonplace in the middle of the night in Brooklyn.

"I must have some one of you to show me over the Rockaway Path around the Pass," said the stranger.

"We belong to the other side, General, and can't serve you against our duty," replied the elder Howard.

"That is all right," the man returned. "Stick to your country, or stick to your principles, but Howard, you are my prisoner and you must guide my men over the hill." Howard attempted to object further but the man in the camlet cloak silenced him.

"You have no alternative," he warned. "If you refuse, I shall have you shot through the head."[1]

These forceful words marked no idle threat, for General William Howe, the commander-in-chief of the British army in North America, spoke them. At that moment he was accompanying one of three grand regiments, led by Major General Henry Clinton, whose mission was to seize control of Brooklyn from the forces of General George Washington. Clinton's quiet intimidation was especially effective thanks to the massive and eerily silent army stationed outside the tavern. An intimidating group comprising at least two companies of infantry, another company of dragoons (light mounted infantry), and grenadiers, the force numbered around ten thousand men and had at least fourteen pieces of artillery.

The British soldiers had begun a meandering trek at nine o'clock the previous evening, leaving their tents pitched by the village of Flatbush or the original Dutch settlement of 'T Vlacke Bos. Lieutenant Generals Hugh Percy and Charles Cornwallis, bringing in the heavier firepower and a reserve unit, followed Clinton's brigades of infantry and dragoons as they pressed eastward for nine miles past Flatlands (formerly Nieuw Amersfoort) to the village of New Lotts, where they turned a hard left northward to meet the chain of hills that runs along Long Island like the spine of a fish. The group had taken great pains to march as lightly as possible, using the cover of darkness and the soft grasses of fields and byways to mask their movement—Captain Cornelius Vanderveer, a Dutch inhabitant of Long Island, later wrote that he had witnessed the soldiers from his fence near Flatlands but could not hear them, even at a distance of barely one hundred feet. Howe had expected an American guard at Schoonmaker's Bridge—a narrow pass southwest of the present neighborhood of East New York—but finding none, he pressed northward across the fields from New Lotts to the base of the Bushwick Hills, which form the bor-

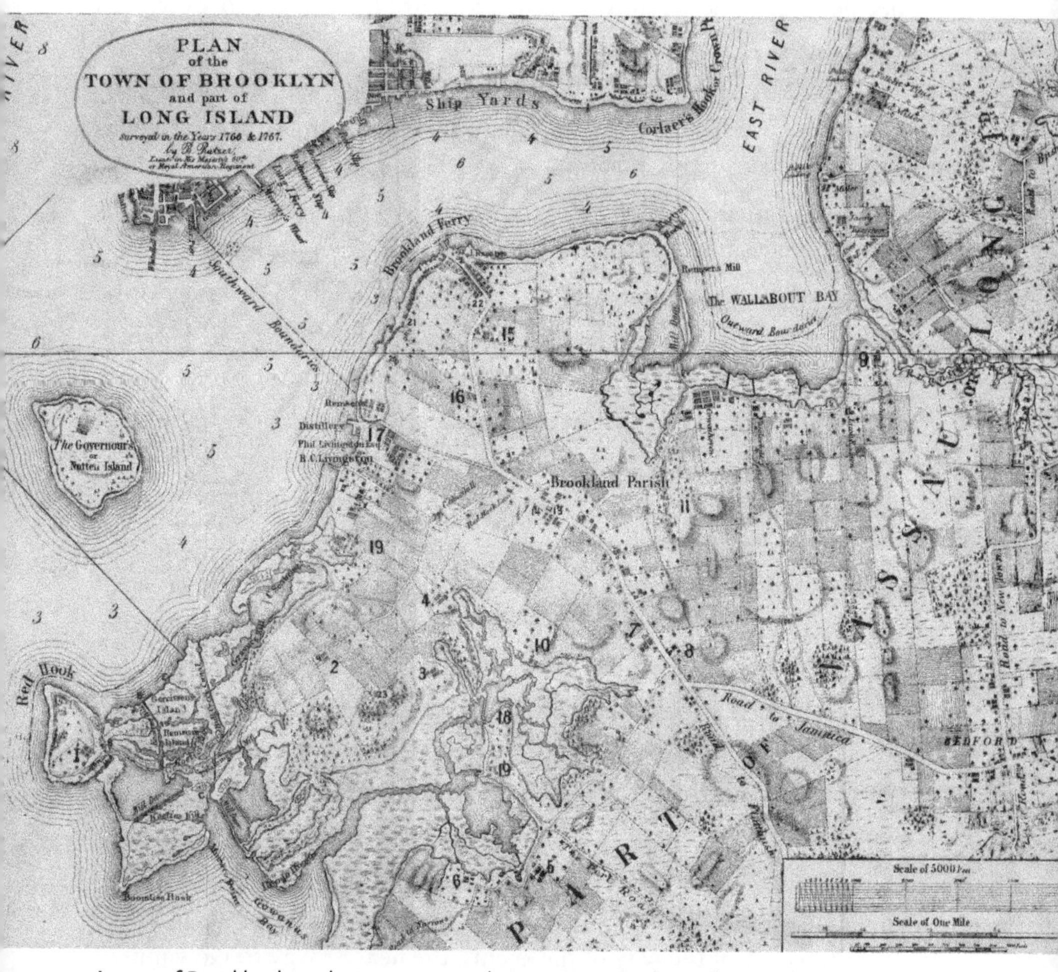

A map of Brooklyn based on surveys made in 1766–1767, drawn by British cartographer Bernard Ratzer. Courtesy of the New York Public Library.

der between Queens and Brooklyn and are now home to Evergreen Cemetery.[2]

After five hours of silent marching, the regiment had finally arrived at a low point in these hills, known as Jamaica Pass. It was here that they could access the road to the county of Queens and the village of Jamaica to the east, and to the west the Ferry Road or the King's Highway, present-day Fulton Street. Cleverly built near this vital crossroad was Howard's Rising Sun tavern, also known as Howard's Halfway House, since it stood between Brooklyn and Jamaica. (The structure existed well into the nineteenth century at the corner of Broadway and Jamaica Avenue, at the exit of the Jackie Robinson Parkway.) Here the regiment waited silently for merchant wagons to pass before Howe burst through the front door in his simple disguise, with gun-wielding soldiers in tow. The tavern sat at the entrance to a narrow and easily defended pathway through the hills, another leg of the route that Howe was certain the American forces would guard in anticipation of a sweeping attack. He thus sought out Howard's aid in search of the Rockaway Path, which bypassed Jamaica Road over the steep hills and would allow the British to avoid engaging or even alerting any patrols in the area. In another telling of his story (the younger Howard recounted the story many times throughout his life, with two slightly different versions published when he was well into his eighties), Howard recalled the general asking to be led "across these hills out of the way of the enemy, the nearest way to Gowanus."[3]

And so the two Howards led the British forces, following the path between their house and the horse shed. Behind them, the artillery men broke their silence for the first time, cutting down trees to clear the steep incline to allow the heavy guns, intended to besiege the American rebels, to pass; they used saws rather than axes, as the sound of chopping wood would have attracted American sentries. The rest of the forces maintained their quiet footfalls, and no alarm was raised. Once reaching the hills' apex, they descended upon the farm of James Pilling. Then, having evaded discovery by American forces, the company turned west and soon fell back on the Ferry (or Jamaica) Road in Ridgewood, Queens. Howe then released the two Howards back to the tavern, most likely with an escort to ensure their silence.

The pair arrived at the Rising Sun to find it surrounded by English soldiers, as guards had been posted around every home in the neighborhood to prevent any rebel sympathizers from alerting the American forces of the movement. The younger Howard recalled much later the odd scene of jubilant British soldiers who—clearly bored and anxious on the eve of a great battle—showed off their agility by taking turns running and pole-vaulting themselves onto the roof of the tavern house. The British guards "expressed the most unbounded astonishment on our return to the house at the unresisted progress of the army," he observed, but "were apparently without the slightest feeling of hatred or embittered feeling in their position as enemies . . . and we experienced nothing disagreeable from them during their stay."[4]

The Brooklyn Neck

With the American Revolution stirring across the Colonies, 1776 was an exciting year to be alive in New York. Despite the early victory at Bunker Hill, the British did not have the upper hand. New York City had been under the control of Patriot forces since the previous year, and the Provincial Congress now met at City Hall, only a few doors down from where the Royal Assembly convened (a rare occasion).[5]

Given its location, New York was of vital strategic importance to whoever controlled its ports, forts, and surrounding waterways. "As it is the nexus of the northern and southern Colonies," wrote John Adams (at the time a leading member of the Continental Congress) to George Washington in early January, "as a kind of key to the whole continent, as it is a passage to Canada, to the Great Lakes, and to all the Indian nations, no effort to secure it ought to be omitted." That month, Washington received reports that the British were planning a large naval expedition to a secret destination. It so happened that the

British objective was to regroup with a larger force in North Carolina, but fearing that Major General Clinton and his forces might arrive at any moment in New York, Washington requested additional troops from New Jersey to secure the port.[6]

Meanwhile, General Charles Lee, who held the same rank in the American army as Washington, was ordered to raise troops from loyal Patriots in Connecticut and oversee a fortification of the city.[7] Soon after his arrival, however, Lee determined that a complete defense of New York would be impossible. "What to do with the city," he wrote to Washington on February 19, "I own, puzzles me. It is so encircled with deep navigable waters, that whoever commands the sea must command the town."

Lee proposed that the army, if unable to protect the entire city, construct a system of defenses whose goal would be to prevent the British from maintaining a permanent hold. Securing the East River was integral to this plan—it would keep the British at bay and allow safe movement from Long Island to New York. In the same letter, Lee—who had arrived with 1,700 men in early February—also insisted upon the strategic importance of holding Long Island. "I wait for some more force to prepare a post or retrenched encampment on Long Island, opposite to the city, for 3000 men," he wrote. "This is, I think, a capital object; for, should the enemy take possession of New York, when Long Island is in our hands, they will find it almost impossible to subsist."[8]

On the other side of the East River, Brooklyn sat inconspicuously. The village that had grown up surrounding the old Dutch church consisted of little more than a few houses clustered together, while another similar grouping huddled near the ferry landing. Down the King's Highway eastward, the village of Bedford sat between the hills in a pass leading south toward Flatbush. To the north of Brooklyn was the settlement at the Wallabout; and finally there was Gowanus, "along the branch road skirting the bay." Aside from the occasional manor house, these limited settlements paled in comparison to the four thousand structures on the thriving tip of Manhattan. Kings County was home to idyllic beaches, soaring heights, and valleys dotted with settlements, a pastoral wonderland in comparison to the bustle of the city. Most of the inhabitants of the western edge of Long Island remained culturally Dutch, despite the transfer of New Amsterdam to the British in 1664, and had continued "to makes use of their customs and language in preference to English" throughout the eighteenth century.

Major Carl Leopold Baurmeister, a Hessian officer who would fight on the side of the British in New York, was quite fond of the people he met in Brooklyn. "The happiness of the inhabitants, whose ancestors were all Dutch, must have been great; genuine kindness and real abundance is everywhere; any thing worthless or going to ruin is nowhere to be perceived," he wrote. "The inhabited regions resemble the Westphalian peasant districts; upon separate farms the finest houses are built, which are planned and completed in the most elegant fashion. The furniture in them is in the best taste, nothing like which is to be seen with us, and besides so clean and neat, that altogether it surpasses every description." "The female sex is universally beautiful and delicately reared," he continued admiringly, "and is finely dressed in the latest European fashion, particularly in India laces, white cotton and silk gauzes; not one of these women but would consider driving a double team the easiest of work. They drive and ride out alone, having only a negro riding behind to accompany them. Near every dwelling-house negroes (their slaves) are settled, who cultivate the most fertile land, pasture the cattle, and do all the menial work."[9]

Long Island was the breadbasket of New York, as the British were well aware. A letter from an anonymous advisor to Admiral Richard Howe—head of the British naval forces in America and brother of William Howe, commander of the land forces—recommended Nassau County as "the only spot in America for carrying on the war with efficacy against the rebels. In this fertile Island the army could subsist without any succour from England or Ireland. It has a plain on it twenty-four miles long, which has a fertile country about it. Forming their camp on the above plain, they could in five or six days invade and reduce any of the Colonies at pleasure."[10] Immersed in traditional agricultural pursuits, Brooklynites were not opposed to British rule but generally neutral to it, and while at one time the British perceived the Dutch lack of patriotic fervor a strategic boon, the inevitable scourge of war would greatly disrupt their lives no matter what the cause.

In late February a regiment of 489 Patriot soldiers led by Colonel Jonathan Ward arrived in New York from Connecticut and soon set about building fortifications on the high points of the Long Island waterfront, complete with artillery. These held the dual purpose of keeping ships out of the East River and defending against a land attack from the hills in the opposite direction. Lee was appointed to command the Department of the South only a few weeks later, leaving in charge the recently promoted Brigadier General William Alexander, mostly known as Lord Stirling (he claimed to be the descendent of the Earl of Stirling, a long-dead Scot). The energetic leader quickly boosted the construction of defenses as the soldiers under his command swelled to about four thousand.[11]

On March 13 Stirling ordered that all New Yorkers were to participate every other day in the building of defenses, with their slaves working every day. The New York Provincial Congress hastily approved the order and directed the inhabitants of Kings County to do the same. The next day, from his base in Cambridge, Massachusetts, Washington wrote to Stirling that he believed the British were about to evacuate Boston and that he was "of opinion that New York is their place of destination. It is an object worthy of their attention."

As much as Brooklyn's diverse topography seemed an asset to the British, it also contained a naturally occurring line of defense for the Patriots. Prospect Range, a series of hills running northeast along the bay from New Utrecht (today's Bay Ridge) past the eastern shore of Gowanus and then along the spine of Long Island, rose sharply from forty to ninety feet in height—a perfect natural rampart for securing the Brooklyn Neck and Red Hook.[12]

The triangle of the original Brooklyn settlements remained the social and economic epicenter of the county—and would become Washington's interior stronghold. The hills were too steep for the heavy wheeled artillery of the day, while the thick trees and foliage made rapid troops movements largely impossible. The conditions provided also a battle arena more favorable to the American style of skirmish fighting in small bursts, as opposed to the open field battles preferred by the Europeans. Beyond the northwestern edge of the Prospect Range, referred to in maps and writings as the Heights of Guan or Gowanus Heights, lay the extensive marshland of the Gowanus Creek, a virtually impassable barrier protecting the inner fortifications around the town of Brooklyn.[13]

On March 17 the British abandoned Boston, where the occupation had become a drain on resources, and turned their eyes southward, confident of their ability to conquer the rebels in a face-to-face battle—General James Grant told Parliament famously that year that he could march across the continent with a force with just five thousand soldiers. The British planned to conquer the thriving port of New York and, having claimed the "key to the whole continent," to march the Loyalist forces north to meet the command of Major General Guy Carlton and his ten thousand men along the Hudson River, cutting off New England from the rest of the colonies. The Patriot forces soon left Boston, and Washington himself departed Cambridge on April 4, arriving in New York nine days later.[14]

Months of summer toil by the soldiers, citizens, and slaves in Brooklyn had produced an impressive and extensive defensive line. An imposing earthen wall towered on the heights just outside of the Brooklyn Neck, stretching a mile and a half from the head of Gowanus Creek to Wallabout Bay. With several redoubts, it provided an inner layer of defense for Brooklyn—allowing soldiers to guard the passes in the hills where the main roads gave access to the settlements of Kings County. Beyond these walls three main forts and two additional redoubts: By the head of the creek stood Fort Box, manned with four guns and controlling the Porte Road; to the northeast approximately three hundred rods (about three-quarters of a mile) stood the star-shaped, six-gun Fort Putnam (later renamed Fort Greene), with another circular battery three hundred feet farther along the ridge. Behind the main defensive wall stood Cobble Hill Fort (known as Corkscrew Fort, due to its circular road, or as Bergen Hill by the British forces), a three-gun fortification and important vantage point for following a battle; there were also gun batteries at Red Hook, and the aptly named Fort Defiance perched at the westernmost point of the peninsula. In addition to constructing the forts, the laborers had dug ditches and cut down all the foliage within one hundred yards of the defensive line to allow the defending troops clear shots. The marksmen would be ordered to hold their fire until the approaching force had crossed halfway through the ditch, marked by stacks of cut brushwood.[15]

The presence of the soldiers around Brooklyn was disconcerting to the local Dutch population, but not nearly as disruptive as it had been in Manhattan, where soldiers' excessive drinking and frequenting of prostitutes were widespread. In Brooklyn they quartered in bell-shaped tents with wooden floorboards, practically luxurious conditions, the satisfying and ample fare provided by the local Dutch farmers supplementing their food rations. But the young men in Kings County were not above mischief. They whiled away most of that spring and summer digging the fortifications and ditches, chopping down trees, and piling them as abatis (a common feature of fortifications, where whole trees are piled in a row with their sharpened branches pointing out toward attackers) at the Prospect Range. It was gruelingly hot and dirty work, and officers complained that they were unable to keep their men wearing clothes.

Most of the soldiers were not issued uniforms (the American forces were, famously with a few exceptions, very poorly equipped and encouraged to fight in frontiersman hunting shirts) and their limited supply of personal apparel was quickly worn out by the heavy work. The usual allowance of soap was also insufficient, such that General Nathanael Greene requested that Washington double the ration for those stationed in Brooklyn as "a piece of justice to the troops." There was little recreation beyond the natural habitat, which did afford the millponds of Gowanus Creek in which the soldiers could bathe. It was a privilege that not all the militia members respected: According to the orderly books of a Colonel William Henshaw, in mid-May some Gowanus inhabitants complained that several soldiers had taken to stripping naked and swimming, unabashed, in the "in the open View of the Women." Having bathed, they would scandalously run nude to their tents "with a design to insult & wound the Modesty of Female Decency."[16]

This may seem a harsh judgment to levy against bored and hard-worked young men, but the American officers were deadly serious about their cause and its sense of dignity (not to mention the danger of stirring any latent anti-Patriot sentiments), and so Henshaw was moved to act: "Tis with concern that the General finds himself under the disagreeable Necessity of expressing his disapprobation of such a Beastly Conduct, whoever has been so void of Shame as to act such an infamous part let them veil their past disgrace by their future good Behaviour, for they may depend upon it any new Instances of such scandalous Conduct will be punish'd with the utmost severity," he warned his troops.

> This is not meant to prohibit the Troops from going into the Water to bathe, but from going in, in improper places. Where is the Modesty Virtue & Sobriety of the New England People for which they have been remarkable? Is a good Character as a Soldier of no Value when it is esteem'd so great a Blessing as a Citizen? What a miserable Change from a Sober Virtuous & decent people into a loose disorderly and shameless sett of——. Is there no ambition left

> alive but that of appearing most abandon'd? Have the Troops no regard for the reputation of the Company or Regiment they belong to or the Colony from whence they came? Have the Troops come abroad for no other purpose but to render themselves obnoxious & Ridiculous?

Hoping to appeal to regional pride, he added, "Our Enemies have sought to fix a Stigma upon the New England People as being Rude & Barbarous in their Manners & Unprincipled in their Conduct. For Heavens sake dont let your Behaviour serve as an Example to confirm these Observations. The General flatters himself notwithstanding the Complaints that have been made the Offenders are but few, but he is determin'd those few shall not have it in their power to bring Disgrace upon the whole Brigade." As if the indecent exploits weren't enough, Henshaw also noted the Gowanusians' complaints of soldiers raiding their carefully planted oyster beds. "The Troops are forbid to touch any for the future under such curcumstances [*sic*]," he warned. "Is not the Crime of Indecency a sufficient Vice but Robbery must be added to it to qualify it."[17]

A Grand Regatta

As the march of war grew steadily closer, the city of New York was transformed. Women and children were scarcely seen on the streets, and houses and storefronts were shuttered. New troops arrived every day, some breaking into empty houses to use as sleeping quarters. In the eastern parts of Long Island, in Nassau and Suffolk Counties, Patriot regiments regularly raided and broke up Loyalist militias, confiscating weapons and imprisoning Tories. Leaders were compelled to swear declarations of allegiance toward the American cause or, at minimum, nonallegiance with the British.[18]

On June 25, the first wave of the British invasion sailed into New York Harbor and settled on Staten Island. General Howe (the late-night tavern visitor) commanded the force, boasting more than nine thousand troops on 130 ships. The fleet of Admiral Howe landed two weeks later with thirteen thousand soldiers and 150 ships.[19] Shortly after settling, the Howe brothers released a formal declaration across the regional towns with the help of Loyalist sympathizers, pardoning any individuals who had proclaimed allegiance "in the tumult and disorder of the times" to the rebel cause.[20]

But another declaration had already circulated through the colonies, one adopted by the Continental Congress on July 4, that had declared the thirteen independent of Great Britain, a new United States of America. On July 9, Washington ordered the New York City brigades to stand in a formation of hollow squares on their respective parade grounds to hear the full Declaration of Independence read "with an audible voice." A mob of Patriotic citizens then tore down a gilded statue of King George III on horseback that had been installed six years previous.[21]

In theory the Americans had quite a force to be reckoned with. The official number of troops promised to Washington by the Continental Congress counted around 23,000—but the list of actual enrollees never quite reached this number. As the humid summer heat descended on New York, there were just above 20,000 troops enrolled, but 4,000 of these were sick or otherwise unavailable. Some additional 3,150 recruits arrived in late July, but like most of the American forces they had no experience and lacked some of the most basic supplies. In mid-August the official complement of on-the-ground troops was 17,225, but only 13,557 were actually fit for service. Forces were thinly spread across New York, from Harlem Creek down to the Verrazano Narrows, with the largest concentration, about 5,500 men, stationed in Brooklyn along the fortified lines.[22]

With the 22,000 soldiers the British had landed with earlier in the summer, the opposing armies may not have been entirely unmatched—New York's defensive advantage gave reason for confidence to the Patriots. But the British received an additional influx of forces by August. On the first of the month Admiral Peter Parker, fresh from losing a battle at Charleston, South Carolina, arrived in New York Harbor with some forty damaged ships and about 3,000 soldiers, seething at their recent defeat. The combined force of thirty warships and four hundred transports (with an additional 10,000 sailors) topped off one of the largest expeditions in British military history. The final boost was a contingent of 8,000 Hessian mercenaries who had been traveling for more than three months (from the German principality of Hesse-Cassel) to aid the British in battle. In total, the combined forces of British, Hessian, and Loyalist troops (including some black militias from Virginia), and slave recruits from the West Indies (promised freedom for service), totaled around 32,000 trained soldiers. The Americans, mostly ill equipped and untrained, were certainly outnumbered, and their main advantage was their fight for freedom.[23]

The month of August grew increasingly tense around New York. In response to the unbridled drinking of nervous troops, Washington ordered all gin shops along Patriot lines closed on August 18. The peddlers who followed the camps were to limit their individual sales as well. Two days later Greene, the talented strategist in charge of the operations on Long Island, fell ill and had to be replaced with Major General John Sullivan, a man unfamiliar with the land and unknown to the Brooklyn troops. And finally, just before sunset on the 21st, a violent thunderstorm enveloped the skies of New York, raging for three hours. Ensigns W. W. De Peyster and Peter Vergereau, Captain Abraham Van Wyck, and an unnamed Connecticut soldier, all Patriots stationed in New York and Brooklyn, were struck and killed by lightning. For those superstitious among the Patriots, it was an inauspicious omen.[24]

But the morning of the 22 dawned clear and the waters of the bay lay calm, until, at daybreak, waters outside of the Narrows were broken by the British frigates *Phoenix* and *Rose*. These ships had been stationed around Staten Island for the previous month (a quick dash up the Hudson to attack some gun batteries notwithstanding), but on that day they sailed gracefully across the waters toward the western edge of Long Island, stopping about three hundred yards off the landing beach in Gravesend Bay, as scores of Patriot soldiers watched this progress from posts along the steep hills. A third frigate, the *Rainbow*, dropped anchor nearby, just off of Denyse's ferry landing. With guns loaded, the broad sides of the boats faced the shores and formed a protective corridor for what was to come.[25]

On Staten Island, the soldiers had been marching all night from their camp down to the shores of the hilly island. Before dawn, scores of soldiers had loaded onto seventy-five flat-bottomed transports, painted red and white, with hinged ramps in the front (and not unlike the landing craft infantry boats used at Normandy Beach during the Second World War). Replete with around fifty men each, crouched with their guns between their knees, the boats formed ten lines bow to stern. At around eight o'clock that morning the frigates exploded with noise and smoke as their cannons hurled volleys of hot iron at the coastline. Nearly a half hour of continuous hammering cleared the hills and trees of watchful Patriots, and the British sailors on all seventy-five transports began to row furiously toward their objective on the Brooklyn shore. "The day being remarkably fine," an anonymous British soldier later wrote in a letter home, "contributed towards the grandest Regatta you can imagine."[26]

According to most sources, within ten minutes of the first transport landing, the plains extending from Denyse's ferry landing toward the village of Flatbush were crowded with four thousand soldiers. Waves of British infantry came ashore wearing the standard red coats and tricorne hats, while Hessian grenadiers stood in strict formation in their blue uniforms with turned-back tails, topped with hats resembling a bishop's miter clad in metal, together with a smattering of Jaegers, or German rifle-bearing light infantry, wearing green uniforms and scarlet cuffs. Before noon eleven thousand more soldiers were deposited on the plains, as were supply wagons, horses for the mounted dragoons, and forty cannons. Two large galleys and eleven bateaux (heavy, flat-bottomed transports) aided the heftier parts of the operation. The Patriots stationed in the hills along the Narrows followed the swarm of ships, likely some with a degree of anxiety.[27] Had the rebels more artillery and resources, the landing might have been very different for the invading forces. "We were so near each other as to see every movement observed, them drawn up on the high ground ready to defend to the place of attack," the British soldier continued. "We saw them come down to their lines in Columns with great appearance of very detremin'd opposition."[28]

One of these columns, headed by Colonel Edward Hand, was a contingent of two hundred Pennsylvania riflemen. Colonel Hand had followed his enemy's movements since the transports had left Staten Island, and had ordered shots at the disembarking boats, but with little effect. Marching along to get a better view, Colonel Hand and his men discovered a party of British and Hessians moving, unknowingly, right toward their position. The group was most likely two battalions of light infantry commanded by Cornwallis under orders to examine the pass between the hills at Flatbush Road to see if it was occupied.

Intent on ambushing these soldiers, the riflemen waited, poised, but one trigger-happy, "imprudent fellow" fired too soon, alerting the infantry to the Patriot danger ahead. Their element of surprise now extinguished, Colonel Hand and his regiment retreated toward the road and the safety of the Flatbush Pass. Twenty of them went ahead of the pack to burn any nearby stocks of grain and stacks of hay and killing any stray cattle—to prevent the valuable supplies from falling into enemy hands. Meanwhile, Cornwallis and his forces returned to Flatbush to camp.[29]

After months of anticipation, Kings County had transformed from idyllic farmland into lawless wilderness. Days before the British had even left Staten Island, the roads leading out of Kings and toward Nassau County had been "blocked up with cows, horses, sheep, &c, which had been driven up during the night to escape the plunder of the British."[30] Houses and farms were now deserted, some with tables set with food as families had fled midmeal (popular stories recount how much edible food was discarded by the British invaders out of suspicion that it was poisoned). The white tents of the British and Hessians dotted the fields in the Flatlands and Flatbush, and clouds of smoke hung perpetually in the sky from cannons, gunshots, or the systematic burning of grain and other supplies. For three days after the enemy landing, the rebels carried out skirmishes and guerrilla attacks on the British and Hessian forces. A larger contingent of Colonel Hand's riflemen attacked the Hessian camp at Flatbush, only to be repelled again by the artillery.[31]

Although their efforts amounted to little more than intimidation, the Patriot skirmishing certainly boosted troop morale. Adjutant General Joseph Reed, one of Washington's top aides, wrote to his wife on August 24 that the officers and men were well behaved, and "the whole army is in better spirits than I have known it at any time . . . in the present temper of our men, the enemy would lose half their army in attempting to take it. While I am writing there is a heavy firing and clouds of smoke rising from that wood." That same day, another action saw Patriots torching the ancient homes of old Brooklyn families, such as that of Jeremiah Vanderbilt and Leffert Lefferts, since the Hessians had taken quarter in the dwellings. As it happened, Washington was on Long Island at that time and, having witnessed the razing of Patriot property, was more peeved than pleased. While the wanton destruction and violence might have been rousing for the soldiers, such disorganized thuggery was hardly part of an organized strategy. Perhaps worst of all, it was an undignified display in the face of their disciplined enemies.[32]

"Shameful it is to find that those men who have come hither in defence of the rights of mankind, should turn invaders of them, by destroying the substance of their friends," wrote Washington. "The distinction between a well-regulated army and a mob, is the good discipline and order of the former, and the licentious and disorderly behavior of the latter." Blaming the disorderly conduct on Sullivan's lack of experience, Washington had him replaced by General Israel Putnam, who, at fifty-eight, was the oldest general in Washington's command, and had been miserable stuck in Manhattan while battle brewed across the river. On the 25th the new appointee received word from Washington that the raids were "unmeaning and wasteful," and rendered their defense "contemptible in the eyes of the enemy."[33]

Washington had a point, but the Hessians were actually impressed with the American chutzpah. "[The rebels] have some very good marksmen," wrote one German officer, "but some of them have wretched guns, and most of them shoot crooked. But they are clever at hunter's wiles. They climb trees, they crawl forward on their bellies for one hundred and fifty paces, shoot, and go as quickly back again. They make themselves shelters of boughs, etc. But today they are much put out by our greencoats [Jaegers] for we don't let our fellows fire unless they can get good aim at a man, so that they dare not undertake anything more against us."[34] In fact, the American troops were probably simply daunted at the sheer size of the 21,000-man army under Howe's command. Washington had returned on the 26th to inspect the American defenses and the enemy line and was convinced of the risk—enough to send two additional regiments, Haslet's Delaware battalion and Smallwood's Marylanders, to Long Island. Well equipped with real uniforms, functioning muskets, and proper military training, these two battalions were by far the most battle-ready of the Patriot forces.

The fresh addition brought the total number of men fit for active duty to approximately seven thousand, and the reinforcements arrived not a moment too soon. As Washington was heading back to his New York headquarters, Howe was preparing his army to move. His objective was to conquer Brooklyn and its surrounding settlements, thus controlling the East River and the closest access to New York's primary suburbs. Protecting the narrow Brooklyn Neck was the Prospect Range, with its fortified walls and the impassable Gowanus Creek. But there were four roads that passed through the hills, along which the British could approach their target.[35]

Closest to the British camp was Martense's Lane, which led from New Utrecht, through a pass near the southern end of the present Green-Wood Cemetery to the coast road running along Gowanus Bay. The second was at Flatbush Pass, an opening farther to the northeast and right along the toll road between the towns of Brooklyn and Flatbush (the pass was, in a way, the demarcation between the two towns). This path would led through to the Porte Road and over the creek at Freeke's millpond. Forking off to the east, the third point of access was known as Bedford Pass, just a half mile south of the town of Bedford.

With his men arrayed for battle, Howe could practically taste his advantage: his forces outnumbered the Americans three to one, and General Henry Clinton, one of his commanding officers, determined that it would "not be a difficult matter to turn their left flank, which would either oblige them to risk an engagement or to retire under manifest disadvantage."[36] Howe planned to engage in a flanking maneuver—where a frontal attack is supplemented by more attacks on either side of the enemy—by splitting into three separate columns, surrounding and overwhelming the rebels to force a surrender.

Around nine o'clock on the evening of August 26, under the cover of darkness, the British and Hessian forces mobilized. Howe assigned General James Grant to march north to the narrows along the lower road at Martense's Lane with a complement of around seven thousand soldiers. Hessian commander Leopold Philip de Heister was to capture American attention at Flatbush Pass, while Clinton and the regiments of Percy and Cornwallis were to sneak the main attack body (with Howe in tow) through Jamaica Pass, as his intelligence reports claimed it had been left unguarded. The troops had been ordered to leave their tents pitched, unusual for a group of battalions on the move. In anticipation of a battle at any moment, Putnam had stationed about eight hundred Patriot soldiers at each of the passes, and along the breastwork regular postings of sentries who were to remain in constant communication with the forts and redoubts. A battery with several guns was placed at the centermost pass, at the Flatbush Turnpike, where Putnam expected the greatest action. It would prove to be a long night for the invading troops, to say nothing of the rebels.[37]

One of the first places that the Patriot soldiers took up guard was at the Red Lion Inn, right next to the entrance of Martense's Lane. Around 120 soldiers had been posted to the area when, around eleven o'clock, the sentries discovered two British soldiers poking through a nearby watermelon patch. They were likely a pair of scouts sent ahead of the advancing British forces—and had quite possibly never seen such fruit before, still on the vine. (Although more than a century had passed, the Red Lion was built in the same environs of Simon de Hart's watermelon patches in Gowanus, and in late August, the same time as Danckaerts's last meeting with de Hart, the watermelons were ripening at the end of the season.) The Patriot soldiers fired their rifles at the two scouts, who quickly retreated.[38]

These were the first shots in what would come to be known as the Battle of Brooklyn (sometimes called the Battle of Long Island), the largest engagement in the Revolutionary War in terms of both casualties and soldiers involved. Though many are not aware of its significance, including Brooklynites who live, work, and play on the battleground, it was the first battle the Continental Army fought as a declared independent nation, and its outcome would reveal much about the abilities of the American troops—their bravery foremost.

After the scouts dispersed, all was calm around the watermelon patch for the next two hours, but then British forces returned, this time with two to three hundred soldiers. Round, leaden bullets flew through the air, hitting trees and whistling past the Patriots' heads at alarming speeds. The Americans returned fire and resisted their enemy's attempts to surround them, but they ultimately retreated in great haste for the safety of their camps to sound the alarm of the inevitable onslaught. One officer and fifteen soldiers were left behind in the confusion.[39]

Over the hills and across the planes on the other side of Kings County, at this same late hour, another band of soldiers had just arrived at Jamaica Pass, the ten thousand men and fourteen pieces of artillery led by Clinton and his deputy, Lieutenant General Charles Cornwallis, all marching under the watchful eye of commander-in-chief Howe. The British troops had just captured five American sentries on horseback and taken them prisoner, and were in now in the process of waking up the innkeeper and his fourteen-year-old son at Howard's Halfway House. Although Howe impressed the Howards as guides to conduct his massive force over the Rockaway Path undetected, he was astonished to find that the Americans had left the Jamaica Pass unguarded, finding it "so incredible that so favorable a position for resisting his passage should not be occupied that he did not take the precaution of sending out his scouts to ascertain the fact."[40]

Clinton's forces were the key to the entire operation in Brooklyn. Howe knew the rebels did not expect the army to split and flank their troops, and never would have suspected their red-coated enemies to take the long march around the hills—so he planned to do just that. In the strategy devised by Clinton, the Patriots would soon be occupied fighting the smaller battalions at the Flatbush Pass and the Red Lion Inn, and eventually be pushed back against the fortified walls at Gowanus. At daybreak the rebels, already exhausted, would be overwhelmed by the stifling wave of ten thousand soldiers parading down the King's Highway, and ultimately forced to surrender. The plan was perfectly calculated, and the odds totally favored the British.

If Howe had realized that the five sentries on horseback would be the only resistance in the Jamaica Pass, however, he could have saved his army much time and trouble. While Howe's battalion was spilling over the Rockaway Path, British forces were roaming over the hills past the Red Lion Inn, the Patriot pickets having fled. General

Samuel Parsons, the brigadier on duty, witnessed this small invasion and attempted to regroup whatever defenses were around, then sent word back to Putnam's quarters. At the Patriot camp, Lord Stirling was awoken and personally ordered by Putnam to take two regiments and meet the enemy head-on. Gathering Haslet's and Smallwood's battalions, a combined total of about sixteen hundred men, Stirling marched along the Shore Road to the Narrows until first light (around six o'clock), about a half mile from the Red Lion Inn, where a bridge crossed a small offshoot of the Gowanus Creek, leading up from the bay into the marshland. There, Sterling met Colonel Samuel Atlee and his battalion of Pennsylvania musketeers, who pointed out the enemy moving barely in their sight beyond the trees. Stirling hastily concocted a plan to ambush the Brits, with Atlee's band positioned off the side of the road, crouched in the woods by the bridge. This motley group, all of whom were untrained and had no battle experience, surprised their enemy with several rounds of fire. Their boldness was commendable, but they could not hold back Grant's seven-thousand-soldier battalion from advancing over the creek. In anticipation, Stirling's two regiments had taken cover farther up the road, perched on a steep bluff that rose above the road to the edge of the bay.

Well known to the local Dutch as Blockje's Bergh (and sometimes Blockje's Barracks), this high cliff was advantageous for picking off approaching foes, especially those wearing bright red coats. In the dreadful moments as their enemy advanced, Stirling reminded his troops of Grant's boasting about his ability to conquer the whole continent. "Grant may have his 5,000 men with him now," Stirling said, "we are not so many—but I think we are enough to prevent his advancing further on his march than that mill-pond."[41]

For nearly two hours Stirling and his men exchanged fire with a regiment of British light infantry, who commandeered an orchard and some cover-providing hedges. The Americans had been ordered not to fire until the enemy was within 50 yards—perhaps realizing this, Grant's troops did not get closer than 150 yards. In response, the Americans set up field pieces and fired at the British anyway. Suddenly—perhaps overwhelmed by the artillery—the redcoats retreated to their main line. Meanwhile, during this initial bloodshed in the Battle of Brooklyn, Clinton's forces were sitting down for a quick breakfast. After their all-night march, Howe felt the soldiers deserved some respite. They were soon back on the road to Bedford, and had conquered the environs by eight thirty that morning. No longer in need of the subterfuge that accompanied the darkness of their march, the martial bands struck up their music, announcing their movement down Jamaica Road toward the Flatbush Turnpike.[42]

Back at Blockje's Bergh, the British had returned with their own artillery and were firing at the rebels while holding their line several hundred yards back. Their shells slammed down at incredible speeds, killing men instantly, and "now and then taking off a head." Several of the American officers later recalled that their untrained and outnumbered soldiers did not flinch at the onslaught of fire and the death surrounding them; they fired their own artillery in response to what appeared to be a deadly stalemate. To their credit, Stirling and his men believed they were holding the enemy at bay with their bravery. While this was not wholly untrue, Grant was simply following orders to not advance his troops until the signal had been made.

After losing their position by the creek bridge with Stirling, the regiment of troops led by Colonel Atlee, now not much more than three hundred strong, had snuck off through the woods toward a hill that would offer another vantage point, now known as Battle Hill in Green-Wood Cemetery and the highest natural point in Brooklyn. Some British soldiers reached it first, just barely, but were forced off again by the fierce advancement and utter resolve of Atlee's musketeers. After fleeing the hill, the Brits came around to attack several times, but Atlee's troops held them back while inflicting fairly serious damage. Cunning, if untrained, the scrappy Americans climbed trees and hid behind fences while exchanging fire in these tense moments. And while the Americans lost only three men at this particular battle, the British lost two officers and twenty-five soldiers and suffered nearly one hundred wounded—some of the highest casualty rates for the invaders that day.[43]

The Battle in Gowanus

Most confounding in the descending chaos was the behavior of the Hessians battalion, which, after daybreak, had advanced from their campsite toward the fortified Flatbush Pass, where about fifteen hundred soldiers were posted under Sullivan's command. Yet they did not attack, halting just barely close enough for the artillery in the breastwork to fire upon them. By nine o'clock Sullivan—who was well aware of Stirling's ongoing skirmish near the Gowanus road—had ridden through to reconnoiter at the Flatbush Pass, expecting the Hessians to attack at any moment. Instead, the banging of muskets and military drumming suddenly echoed through the hills, alerting anybody within a square mile to the arrival of Clinton's ten-thousand-man force of light infantry, dragoons, and guns, flanking to the back and left of Stirling's forces.

Clinton's noisy announcement, accompanied by a road visibly clogged with soldiers for the half mile between Brooklyn and Bedford, was a signal for Grant and the Hessians to attack with full force. The attacks by Grant's forces on the regiments near the bay, and the relative passivity of the Hessians, had been meant as distractions, while Clinton's main army flanked the Americans at Gowanus—surrounding on three sides the Patriot forces, outnumbered three to one, with practically no chance of victory. The head of the hammer had come down while the rebels believed Clinton's army was still resting back at the camp in the Flatlands.

What we know of the bloody chaos of the next few hours comes from the recollections of a diverse group of people with their own perceptions of time and events—reinterpreted by several generations of historians. Having arrived in the main arena in Gowanus, Clinton's light infantry began chasing down and firing upon the Patriot detachments that had begun a retreat from their posts along Jamaica Road, heading toward Putnam's camp in Brooklyn. Seeing this, Sullivan turned his force around and headed toward the British interlopers to the defense of his compatriots and in dismay at the assault. The five horseback sentries captured at Howard's Inn had been Sullivan's own (he had paid them fifty dollars out of his own pocket) and had failed to warn of the oncoming British. As Sullivan was meeting the British head-on in full-scale combat, the Hessians abandoned their idle post at the Flatbush Plains and were now pushing through the unguarded pass, a sea of green and scarlet uniforms spilling over the ridges (in perfect formation, somehow) as their drums announced their advance. Their sharpshooters led the attack, with the grenadiers and Jaegers not far behind; the musket-wielding ranks of de Heister kept up the rear. The British—mounted dragoons, grenadiers, and fiercely intimidating Scottish highlanders—slammed Sullivan's crew, attacking in full force. The air was alive with whizzing bullets, the smoke of muskets, and the explosion of grenades.[44]

Soldiers fell on both sides, blood staining equally the Americans' hunting shirts and the red uniforms of the British. Vastly outnumbered, the Americans turned back on their heels to retreat, only to fall onto advancing Hessian bayonets. Certainly, the Americans fought back—desperation and adrenalin likely rendered them as brutal as their foes. Within a few hours the pastoral countryside had been transformed into a killing field of unparalleled violence. A regiment of American riflemen were "mostly pierced by the bayonets to the trees," while Hessian, Americans, and British accounts all blame one another for escalating viciousness. "We took care to tell the Hessians that the rebels had resolved to give no quarter—to them in particular—which made them fight desperately, and put to death all that came into their hands," wrote one British officer. Another was slightly more humane: "The Americans fought bravely, and (to do them justice) could not be broken till they were greatly outnumbered. . . . We were greatly shocked at the massacre made by the Hessians and Highlanders, after victory was decided." A Hessian officer later insisted that Americans had instigated the killing within his ranks, as some had begged for surrender only to shoot their would-be captors as they approached—for the Germans, an extremely dishonorable practice. "The English did not give much quarter," wrote one Hessian colonel, "and continually incited our troops to do the same." "They were so much frightened," wrote Lieutenant Ruffer, referring to Patriot soldiers, "that they preferred being shot down to taking quarter, because their generals and officers had told them that they would be hanged."[45]

It appeared that all had been lost, and months of preparation had ended in failure. The Americans were by now very much aware that Howe's army had cut them off from their defensive line. The entire bay was alive with cannon fire, as the British ships attacked the gun batteries posted along the Brooklyn shores. British reinforcements were landing, enhancing their already overwhelming numbers, while the American complement slowly diminished. The most battered troops started to retreat, seeking whatever solace was left at Putnam's camp on the other side of the Patriot line protecting the Brooklyn Neck.

The area around the western banks of Gowanus Creek rapidly became the center of this battle, as the Americans were squeezed ever tightly back toward their defensive line. "I marched toward the ground occupied by our army, in the summit of the high ground in front of Gowanus, near the edge of the river, where the enemy were landing from their ships," Major William Popham recalled. "Many shots were exchanged between us and the enemy. . . . The whole bay was covered with the enemy's shipping. The firing continued all the time of the enemy's landing, and we lost several men." Being mistaken by a British commander for Hessians, Popham's men took the officer and his eighteen men prisoner. Popham continues,

> I was immediately ordered with a guard to convey them across the creek in our rear to our lines. On descending the high ground we

> reached a salt meadow, over which we passed, though not miry, yet very unfavorable to silk stockings and my over-clothes. . . . When we got to the creek, the bank of which was exceedingly muddy, we waded up to our waists. I got in after my people and prisoners, and an old canoe that had been split and incapable of floating except by the buoyancy of the wood, served to help those who wanted help to cross a deep hole in the creek, by pushing it across from the bank which it had reached. I had advanced so far into the mud, and was so fatigued with anxiety and exercise, that I sat down on the mud with the water up to my breast . . . in which situation I sat till my charge were all safely landed on the rear.[46]

Popham had found that the bridge previously spanning the head of Gowanus Creek, crossing Freeke's millpond, had been burned down by Colonel Ward. When his regiment of riflemen crossed the creek, Ward had thought that burning the bridge would prevent the invaders from reaching the Patriot safe haven. Instead it condemned many of his colleagues to an uncertain fate.

The overwhelmed Patriot forces were scrambling to escape across the Gowanus—those soldiers who found it impassable tried sneaking off in the woods, but were inevitably captured. The creek was simply the lesser of two evils. Confronting the terrible advance of Howe's forces, Stirling saw that "the only chance of escaping being all made prisoners, was to pass the [Gowanus] creek near the Yellow Mills."[47] "In order to render this the more practicable," he later wrote, "I found it absolutely necessary to attack a body of troops commanded by Lord Cornwallis, posted at the house near the Upper Mills."[48]

Since noon, Cornwallis's brigade had occupied the Old Stone House (Vecht Mansion), stocked with two small cannons. With its two-foot-thick stone walls and high vantage point, the structure was the perfect redoubt for launching an offensive into the Brooklyn Neck. Since holding a position there would too easily have allowed the British to pick off the escaping soldiers, Stirling's goal was to take the Old Stone House to cover the retreat of the remaining Patriot forces.

Putnam had thrown his most well-trained battalions into battle, leaving raw recruits behind in the Brooklyn defenses, and Stirling gathered for his purpose four companies of Smallwood's regiment, who would come to be known as the Maryland 400. Stirling's enthusiasm proved to be intoxicating for the soldiers in his charge. "He encouraged and animated our young with almost invincible resolution," Major Mordecai Gist, the commander under Stirling, later wrote. Stirling ordered all other troops to scramble back to Putnam's base camp through the creek. On the other side of the defensive line, Colonel Smallwood pleaded for Washington to send out a regiment to cover the retreat, but the general felt it would be too great a risk to put more men on the field. Still, he ordered two freshly arrived companies from New York, with two field pieces, down to the edge of the Gowanus waters on the defensive side to cover the retreat of his men.[49]

Stirling then launched his brave and foolhardy campaign. Advancing toward near certain death, the Marylanders assaulted in at least three waves, with guns firing from across the Gowanus to cover their movements. At one point, the British were forced from their position, until reinforcements regained the house, and more and more Marylanders lost their lives with each subsequent attack. While Stirling's troops were taking heavy losses, the retreating Patriot soldiers crossed the Gowanus as quickly as possible. Bullets struck the water as they fled. With recent steady rains, the Gowanus had already swelled to a considerable depth into the surrounding salt marsh, and at the hour of retreat the creek rose further with the incoming tide. Some soldiers drowned simply because they couldn't swim, while others were shot dead. Incredibly, the escaping soldiers were able to bring twenty-eight prisoners across the water.[50]

Joseph Plum Martin, a fifteen-year-old soldier, recounted the scene at Gowanus Creek in his diary:

> We overtook a small party of artillery here, dragging a heavy twelve pounder upon a field carriage, sinking half way into sandy soil.—They plead hard for some one to assist them to get on their piece; our officers paid no attention to their entreaties, but pressed forward towards a creek, where a large party of Americans and British were engaged. By the time we arrived, the enemy had driven our men into the creek, or rather mill pond, (the tide being up,) where such as could swim got across; those that could not swim, and could not procure any thing to buoy them up, sunk. The British having several field-pieces stationed by a brick house, were pouring the cannister and grape upon the Americans like a shower of hail; they would doubtless have done them much more damage than they did, but for the twelve pounder mentioned above; the men having gotten it within sufficient distance to reach them, and opening a fire upon them, soon obliged them to shift their quarters. There was in this action a regiment of Maryland troops (volunteers), all young men. When they came out of the water and mud to us, looking like water rats, it was truly a pitiful sight. Many of them were killed in the pond, and more were drowned. Some of us went into the water after the fall of the tide, and took out a number of the corpses and a great many arms that were sunk in the pond and creek.[51]

Finally, with the retreat of the Patriot troops nearly complete, Stirling sent the remaining Marylanders across the creek.[52] Across the Gowanus stood Washington and the other generals, watching the battle from a position atop a hill near where Henry and Pacific Streets intersect today. "Good God!" Washington cried out, wringing his hands. "What brave fellows I must this day lose!"[53] Their foes, however, stopped at the banks of the Gowanus and chased the Americans no further. The swampy morass seemed a death trap to the British and Hessians.

According to tradition, 256 soldiers of the Maryland 400 perished that day near or around Gowanus Creek in the defense of Brooklyn and were buried in a mass grave somewhere in the vicinity of Third Avenue between Seventh and Eighth Streets, not far from the present-day Canal. However, later research established a slightly smaller number of troops engaged and lowered the death toll to 144. Their sacrifice is all the more impressive considering the incredible odds against them.[54]

Amazingly, Stirling survived to see most of his men escape and determined that slipping between the lines to Fort Box or across the mill creek was impossible without being captured by the British. With the remnant of his command safe, Stirling turned his horse around and galloped toward the attacking Hessian battalion. He eluded capture by taking a hard turn around a hill, where he found his target, the Hessian commander Leopold de Heister. Dismounting, Stirling offered his sword in surrender. It was not yet two o'clock in the afternoon, and the battle effectively was over.[55]

A Critical Role

There is no mistaking that the Americans lost the Battle of Brooklyn. Of the approximately 7,000 troops on Long Island, 1,120 died or were taken prisoner, but this figure leaves out many companies for which there remains no documentation. Most likely the number of deaths was double this, while the British estimate of American casualties was upward of 3,000. The official list of British missing, dead, or wounded was only 349.

Historians have widely panned General Putnam as being poorly acquainted with the field of battle and enacting a pitiable strategy. Rather than focusing his troops in a single unit, he sent out the best soldiers to face indomitable numbers head-on, in small groups, keeping the straggling forces safely behind lines. Unlike Greene's more realistic tactic—holding points of defense for as long as possible and beating a hasty retreat once the enemy's troops overwhelmed—Putnam had his troops engage the enemy haphazardly, with no plan of retreat. In addition, he failed to maintain the night patrols ordered by his predecessors, which might have alarmed the Americans to the British advancement from the Jamaica Pass.

But the inexperienced Washington shares much of the blame for this outcome. In planning for the battle, he delegated strategy and planning first to Greene, then to Sullivan, and finally to Putnam. The number of troops Washington had stationed on Long Island was insufficient for the vast area they were expected to defend. The Battle of Brooklyn was Washington's first as chief army commander, and it was an unrealistic engagement whose tactics he had questioned until they were executed. Nonetheless, the loss forced Washington to reexamine his strategies and his understanding of the enemy, not to mention the execution of effective warfare. And the Hessian and British commanders were in awe of the bravery and ferocity of the Americans—the Battle of Brooklyn proved that neither they nor Washington would easily surrender.

A lithograph of Battle Pass, a key strategic point from the Battle of Brooklyn, in present-day Prospect Park. Originally printed in the first volume of Henry Stiles's *History of the City of Brooklyn* (1867).

The defensive topography of the Brooklyn Neck also played a significant role. Between Gowanus Creek and the fortified wall over the heights, the British and Hessian forces were at pains to push farther after defeating their enemies. They had marched and fought all night, many without food, and had more than a thousand rebel prisoners to process. Furthermore, as the last of the Marylanders were crossing the Neck, some thirteen hundred reinforcements arrived from New York—Joseph Plum Martin, the teenage soldier, among them. Although many companies of British soldiers sought to continue the attack, Howe didn't believe a head-on assault to be the best strategy. For the next two days, the British built redoubts and scattered fighting occurred between the two sides. Then on August 29, a massive rainstorm pounded Brooklyn, leaving soaked and freezing soldiers on both sides. The British, who had been hammering the lingering defenses with artillery, retreated to their tents from the pelting hailstones as nature seemed to ponder the future of American liberty.[56]

When the storm eased and the first light dawned, the American soldiers had seemingly vanished. Once again, young Martin is our witness to these extraordinary events. The previous evening, he and some fellow soldiers had snuck off in the incessant rain to find some dry straw to make beds, returning to find some secret plan afoot:

> I took a sheaf or two and returned as fast as I could to the regiment. When I arrived the men were all paraded to march off the ground; I left my wheat, seized my musket, and fell into the ranks. We were strictly enjoined not to speak, or even cough, while on the march. All orders were given from officer to officer, and communicated to the men in whispers. What such secrecy could mean we could not divine. We marched off in the same way we had come on the Island, forming various conjectures among ourselves as to our destination. Some were of opinion that we were to endeavor to get on the flank or in the rear of the enemy. Others, that we were going up the East River, to attack them in that quarter; but none, it seems, knew the

> right of the matter. We marched on, however, until we arrived at the ferry, where we immediately embarked on board the batteaux, and were conveyed safely to New-York, where we were landed about three o'clock in the morning, nothing against our inclinations.[57]

What actually occurred was a carefully organized and stealthily conducted evacuation of Brooklyn, the details of which were hidden from many of the commanding officers until the final minutes before the plan's execution. Washington knew that his forces stood too much to lose if the British cracked the Patriot defenses. Their ability to hold onto the East River was precarious at best (only the uncooperative winds were keeping the British fleet from dominating the harbor), and losing that corridor would be a disaster, separating the American troops. So through the night of August 29, appropriating every useful craft, Washington moved nearly nine thousand troops across the East River to Manhattan. Many of the thirteen hundred reinforcements were seasoned fishermen from New England, skilled at navigating the often-difficult waters. One of these determined soldiers made at least eleven back-and-forth trips across the river, around thirty miles of rowing, with the oars clad in cloth to stifle the splashing. In an incredible stroke of luck, according to some accounts a thick fog arose across the river during a break in the rain, shrouding the retreating American forces. Abandoning Brooklyn, the Patriots lost some ground, but the regrouping allowed Washington to enhance his strategy and defenses.[58]

Determining cause and effect in a battle, especially one two and a half centuries ago, is tricky business. Any number of factors might have changed the outcome of the Battle of Brooklyn: for example, had Washington ordered his reinforcements to Brooklyn earlier and sent them to battle, the fighting might have ended in stalemate. It is certain, however, that as a natural defense Gowanus Creek was a key strategic factor. It seems presumptuous to suggest that without Gowanus Creek, Washington's forces would have been overwhelmed and lost any hope of keeping New York under Patriot control. Even more presumptuous would be to suggest that such a loss might have affected the entire course of the Revolution. But it is fair to call that body of water an unsung hero of the Battle of Brooklyn—twice critical to the escape of Washington's army. More than Battle Pass, honored by several plaques tucked away in Prospect Park, the Gowanus waters bore witness to that bloody day in history, as have generations of Brooklynites since, none greater than Brooklyn bard Walt Whitman in "The Centenarian's Story":

> I tell not now the whole of the battle,
> But one brigade early in the forenoon order'd forward to engage the red-coats,
> Of that brigade I tell, and how steadily it march'd,
> And how long and well it stood confronting death.
>
> Who do you think that was marching steadily sternly confronting death?
> It was the brigade of the youngest men, two thousand strong,
> Rais'd in Virginia and Maryland, and most of them known personally to the General.
> Jauntily forward they went with quick step toward Gowanus' waters,
>
> Till of a sudden unlook'd for by defiles through the woods, gain'd at night,
> The British advancing, rounding in from the east, fiercely playing their guns,
> That brigade of the youngest was cut off and at the enemy's mercy.
> The General watch'd them from this hill,
>
> They made repeated desperate attempts to burst their environment,

Then drew close together, very compact, their flag flying in the middle,
But O from the hills how the cannon were thinning and thinning them!

It sickens me yet, that slaughter![59]

3

The Atlantic Docks and Basin (1812–1851)

The American Revolution changed the face of Kings County. Many families fled their homes, never to return, while houses that stood and orchards that had flourished were left smoldering. The aftermath of such destruction made room for growth—a newly free country played host to that newly American capacity for reinvention. New York remained a key to the continent and its port a commercial crossroads. Across the East River, the bustling settlement of Brooklyn soon followed suit.[1]

The southern settlements in Kings County were rebuilt much more slowly, retaining their rural identity and character. But as the new century turned, the settlements closer to the bustle—the Ferry, Brooklyn, Wallabout, Gowanus, and Red Hook—began to thrive (farther north and east, the towns of Williamsburg, Bedford, and Bushwick also grew at an impressive rate).

By 1800, around 2,400 people lived in town of Brooklyn, which included the clustered settlement along the Ferry Road and pastoral outer regions. This was barely a neighborhood compared to New York's 60,515 people, the most populous city in the nation. Ten years later, Manhattan would boast 96,000 inhabitants, but the city across the East River grew at an even faster rate. The environs of Brooklyn became a bucolic suburb for businessmen seeking respite from the bustle of everyday Manhattan. The establishment of regular steam ferry service in 1814 eased the daily commute, and within two years a village charter was declared, defining the new district as surrounding Red Hook Lane and Atlantic Avenue.

Finally there was some respect for Brooklyn as the trustees of this new village gained the authority to drain, fill, level, and generally improve roads and highways. Soon arrived markets, taverns, "slaughter-houses, houses of ill-fame, and nuisances generally" to regulate, and nine hundred new homes were built to house the growing population, more than seven thousand in the 1820s. The growing strength of this budding city was a source of pride to its people.[2]

By 1830 the population of Brooklyn had already doubled to fifteen thousand. Early industries had been established over the fruitful decade, including eight rope factories, four gin distilleries, two manufacturers of white lead paint, an iron furnace, two tanneries, and other "manufactories" making glass, chain cables, and glue. Amid all of the growth, the village government proved inadequate to its task of governance. There were more people arriving than dwellings available, and the village streets were spilling beyond the limits of the charter's boundaries.

Local landowners, many descended from the first Dutch settlers, began to see that their empty holdings were worth more divided into city lots than as farmland. While agriculture would remain an important commodity in Kings County through the nineteenth century, the growth spurts of this now-adolescent city could not be denied. A government uniting the village of Brooklyn and the surrounding town would fill the various needs, including uniform land regulation.

The people of Brooklyn also took regular issue with the looming presence of the city of New York. In what historian David Ment called a "basis of local chauvinism," Brooklynites retained a strong identity—their history and genealogy distinct from those of the folks across the river—which was most reflected in a desire for an independent city. While Brooklyn was a separate municipality from New York, the government of that city treated its younger sibling like just another ward—or the municipal designation given to different neighborhoods, mostly for voting purposes in the common council. One manifestation of this low regard was a conflict of transportation.

Being a properly chartered municipality, New York City controlled the ferry service, which included the right to permit new lines to serve portions of Brooklyn—a highly demanded service New York's trustees refused to create. This holdout was definitely tied into local politics, benefitting the New York owner of the steam ferry and his lucrative monopoly. In response, the village of Brooklyn flexed its municipal muscles and appealed to the State Legislature for a proper city charter; in 1834, the city of Brooklyn was formed.[3]

A Man Who Changed South Brooklyn

In the history of enterprising American capitalists, there are those who relied on education, family, and years of business experience to achieve great means. Others were scrappy, with few family connections but much inspiration in discovering opportunity. Colonel Daniel Richards, born March 5, 1792, at the village of Broadalbin in Upstate New York, was a scrappy one. He had a knack for timing, but also the confidence to invent new ideas and promote them all with the greatest enthusiasm. Richards would revolutionize the slumbering marshes of Red Hook and, in consequence, the Gowanus Creek and all of Brooklyn.

Before the Revolutionary War, Richards's native settlement was called Fonda's Bush, as it was close to the nearby town of Fonda (its founder, Douw Fonda, was a seventeenth-century Dutch settler). But a local of Scottish descent who disliked the foreign-sounding name had renamed the village "Broadalbin" following the Revolution. The surrounding area had originally been known as Caughnawaga, a Mohawk Indian settlement that translates to "place of the rapids," after the nearby Mohawk River. Caughnawaga was the seventeenth-century home of Kateri Tekakwitha, a young Indian woman and pious Catholic who was canonized in 2012 as the first Native American saint.[4]

Richards's father, also called Daniel, was the sixth-generation descendent of Thomas, a Puritan settler who had landed near Hartford, Connecticut, in the 1630s. After the Revolution, Daniel Richards Sr. moved with his wife Anna to Fonda's Bush, where they sired six children. After they had saved enough money, Daniel Sr. moved the family again, fifty miles west to a barely settled hamlet called Richfield, to open a tavern. His brother Samuel had a farm near Richfield with his wife and their eight children. Daniel Richards the younger grew to be an active member of early Richfield, working as a clerk in the country store and then joining the local militia the day he turned eighteen. He was immediately promoted to corporal.[5]

In 1812 at the age of twenty-two, Richards opened a produce business in the newly formed settlement called Monticello (not the much larger Monticello in Sullivan County), but his real skill for entrepreneurial savvy surfaced when he partnered with Horace Manley, a medical doctor and son of a local fur-trapping frontiersman in the wilds of Upstate New York. Dr. Manley and Richards, then young men born only a few years apart, knew each other from tiny Monticello. Both had worked in the community effort to build a regular postal service, as Richards was the first postmaster of Monticello in 1818, and Dr. Manley took the position several times through the next decade. In 1820, Dr. Manley purchased an acre of land known for a peculiar sulfur spring that emerged from under a white pine tree—the ground around it was always covered with powdery, tufaceous deposits associated with mineral springs. Various Indian legends spoke of the healing qualities of these waters, and Dr. Manley intended to profit from that local secret.[6]

According to Upstate New York folklore, in excavating the land to locate the source Manley unearthed an ancient pair of elk antlers as well as perfectly preserved ripe red plums and fresh-looking green leaves, all of which turned black upon exposure to oxygen. Another story tells that he had marked the site of a pine tree on the closest road with a pole brandishing a white handkerchief. One day the sight of it fluttering in the wind alarmed a countryman who was passing on horseback, which he mistook as a warning for smallpox. Holding his mouth and nose in hand, he galloped past the pole at great speed to avoid the fatal miasmas, only to accidentally catch a whiff of air "strongly impregnated with the fumes of the sulphur water." Checking his horse, he cried out in profound despair, "O God, I've catched it!"[7]

The success of the new mineral source, known as Manley Spring, was enormous. Within the first two years the doctor sold his plot to two businessmen for a hefty profit, and in 1822 he bought some adjacent land and built, with the help of Richards, the first bathhouse in the newly minted village of Richfield Springs. As co-owners, the two men were responsible for the growth of an entire community around this village—it is likely that Richards came up with the idea of building the modern bathhouse, as he later proved to be an innovative risk taker. Although details of their earnings are lost, both men made a small fortune from the venture. Dr. Manley spent the rest of his long life in Richfield Springs, where he became a prominent community leader and respected doctor, doling out the healing waters to tourists and locals who came to benefit from the mineral spas. Richards, eventually promoted to colonel in command of the 135th Regiment, was still involved in the business of produce and trade.

Just as his first fortune with Dr. Manley was solidifying, his other businesses probably also spiked a great deal with the opening of the Erie Canal in 1825. Only ten miles north of Richfield, , the canal lifted the towns of Herkimer and Ilion from rural obscurity. In the annals of New York City history, this great change also framed a decade of unparalleled growth in the commercial life of nascent Gotham. The Erie Canal was one of the greatest engineering marvels of the era: a man-made, navigable channel that flowed 363 miles from Albany to Buffalo along the Mohawk River, giving water access to every city and town near its shores from the Hudson River to the Great Lakes of the Midwest.

The western region of New York State exploded with activity and settlement. Rather suddenly, the cost of transportation to and from New York City from dropped from prohibitive to minimal. Food prices lowered as midwestern foodstuffs arrived faster and with less effort, while manufactured goods and farm equipment could be sent out toward the frontier with similar ease. The added boon of the Erie Canal solidified the port of New York as a key center of trade for the continent during the early nineteenth century. Furthermore, its popularity ignited a fit of canal building across the country, as the convenience and value of such waterways—and perhaps a budding desire to shape the land as the new Americans saw fit—became apparent.[8]

By July 1825, Richards's businesses were thriving, since he had the means to fatten up his six-year-old ox to a whopping 2,575 pounds (as proudly reported in one of the earliest issues of the *Western Recorder*, an extant Baptist publication published in Louisville, Kentucky). He also had an eight-year-old son, Delavan, born to his wife Betsey, who was by that time pregnant with their second child. Richards's daughter, named Betsey Greene after her mother, was born on February 17, 1826.

But this joyous occasion was marked by a tragedy that changed the fate of Richards—as well as Brooklyn and Gowanus, together. Less than a month after giving birth, Betsey Richards died. Likely the younger Betsey was named only after her mother passed away, as it was unusual to give a child a living parent's full name. She was "distinguished for her piety," wrote the *Recorder* at this sad story, and "her Christian walk and conversation shed light upon the circle of her acquaintances."[9]

It seems no coincidence that Richards soon abandoned his life in Upstate New York and turned to a place where opportunity lay: New York City. Like many who take the first plunge into big city life, Richards had been planning to return home: he wrote to his commanding officer in the 135th New York Regiment, General George Morrell on

April 13, 1827, requesting a year's leave from his position as colonel. But Richards never returned to live in Richfield. Before the end of that year Richards had installed himself in a room on 88 Pearl Street in Lower Manhattan, where he engaged in "produce commission and transportation." Likely he organized the bulk transport of vegetables and dry goods from his many sources in Upstate New York, along the Erie Canal, to the ports of Manhattan. Soon he would bring his son and infant daughter to New York.[10]

The improvements in transportation brought new international trade to New York, but also a deadly import: cholera. In 1832, Gotham was hit by an infamous epidemic that had spread across port cities from Bombay to Bordeaux for more than a decade. The rampant infection killed more than 3,000 people out of a population of 250,000, and it affected even the most obscure towns along the Erie Canal. At the time, people believed that cholera and dysentery were caused by miasmas—noxious, deadly fumes from decomposing matter that were believed to cause epidemics and spread disease. In that year Richards moved himself and his family to Brooklyn, possibly hoping to escape the worst of the epidemic.[11]

It was in this dynamic environment that Daniel Richards settled. He was a successful entrepreneur of decent means who had followed the call of New York City across the East River, to what many believed was a healthier Long Island countryside. In addition to vast fields and hills, there were many open tracts of Brooklyn dotting the waterfront. Richards had witnessed the Erie Canal transform his backwoods stomping grounds into a thriving and diverse economy, a model of nineteenth-century progress and innovation. During these early years of the industrial revolution, many successful and business-savvy opportunists saw that, as much as there was a need for new materials and ways to produce them, the key to financial success was transportation. The evolving systems of movement of goods or people created the best opportunity for business and trade.

From Wallabout Bay to the Ferry, private waterfront landowners had built warehouses and private docks, and now the city of Brooklyn was free to charter new ferry lines. Having already experience in the development of real estate in Richfield Springs, Richards knew to look for a niche to fill and the appropriate land upon which to build. Like other hungry developers of the time, his eyes fell upon the undeveloped marshland of Red Hook.

Until 1834 the brothers Matthias and Nicholas Van Dyke, scions of a venerable Dutch family, owned most of Red Hook (during the Revolutionary War, their father and grandfather were described as "staunch whigs and clever folks"). For nearly 150 years, the family mills had churned out flour and powdered ginger on the boggy peninsula, which was little more than a collection of hills surrounding a forty-seven-acre millpond. There were only six buildings on the island, and the brothers shared a house at the northeast corner of present-day Van Dyke and Van Brunt Streets, as well as two mills: the Ginger Mill belonged to Nicholas, while Matthias owned the Flour or Tide Mill.[12]

The southern portion of Red Hook had, however, "a high hill covered with locust, poplar, cedar, and sassafras trees," and to the west of this projection was Boompties Hoek or "tree-point" (and sometimes corrupted to Bombay Hook), famous for its oyster beds. Where others saw useless swamp and dilapidated mills, developers saw profits. And most passionate among them was Daniel Richards.

When Matthias died in 1834, a speedy land rush ensued as his heirs divided up the property, hoping to cash in on their swampy inheritance. Richards was one of the most prominent and vocal of these investors. Gathering a group of hopeful industrialists, he bought up the Van Dyke property in what was one of the first large-scale real estate development schemes in Brooklyn under the auspices of an organization known as the Red Hook Building Company.

In 1835, the tree-covered hill was cut down and used to fill up the millponds and marshes, leveling off the uneven land—kicking off the first in a series of topographical changes to Brooklyn's rolling landscape. Within the next two years a formal prospectus (a combination of informational pamphlet and business plan) was drawn up, the lengthy text within praising the merits of Red Hook's location. The prospectus offered company stock for a dollar per share, redeemable with a half-percent discount on Wall Street. Its objective was to presell cheap, easily constructed houses on the newly filled land, with a new ferry line running to Red Hook from Lower Manhattan.[13]

Although Richards's name appears on none of the surviving documents from the Red Hook Building Company, many secondary sources indicate him as the primary owner of land, and the great projector of early Red Hook. An 1838 communication to the Board of Directors from an anonymous "Stockholder" is strongly reminiscent of Richards's persuasive writing style, as seen in later documents. The passion with which this writer—"appointed to inquire 'as to the prospects of the company and the probable result to be anticipated form its operations'"—advocated the housing project could belong only to the former shop clerk from Fonda's Bush. Intended on being viewed by a wide audience, the communication speculated that land values in Red Hook would surely increase. It begins like a handbook of municipal facts, listing extensive information about Brooklyn's population growth and the value of lots around the waterfront. But soon afterward it evolves into nothing less than a flowery love letter to Brooklyn. Richards pushed strongly the rapid rate of development in Brooklyn, even greater than that in New York itself: "Either in the ratio or in the uniformity of increase for some periods commencing 25 years back, Brooklyn has outstripped every city in the state. May she not—nay, will she not continue to do so?" The stockholder repeated an argument favoring the nascent city's location and lack of disease compared to Manhattan settlements like Harlem, with "its facility of intercommunication, its beauty of situation, its pure and wholesome water and general salubrity and healthiness, [which] have already been alluded to."[14]

He also made the persuasive argument that New York's docks were already overwhelmed with traffic, and an upcoming expansion of the Erie Canal was bound to make it worse, and this was "to say nothing of foreign commerce, which already crowds the docks and water front warehouses of that city to a degree of inconvenience which is becoming intolerable." Furthermore, Brooklyn could not often accommodate the overflow from New York since most of the wharf space there was privately owned. The increasing appearance of big European steamships in the bay also could not be ignored. "They cannot, with convenience, intermix with the shipping at the crowded docks of New York," he insisted. "They require space. They must have coal yards and warehouses in the immediate vicinity of their docks. Where shall they go? Where can they go but to Brooklyn?"[15]

Perhaps most telling, the stockholder advised readers of the possibility of connecting the East River "across the Hook, with Gowanus bay, by converting a natural water course into an improved canal, easily constructed at moderate cost and for which the legislature have granted a charter." At this, he reveals a grand vision—a magnum opus in his mind: "Improve that part of Brooklyn, by regulating the streets, erecting stores and dwellings, and constructing docks and piers, and such are its advantages of position and access, that its lots cannot fail to command a population and a value," he wrote with passion. "If such be the facts, then, nothing is wanting to give value to the unimproved lands in Brooklyn, and to favour that more rapid increase in numbers, which it does not seem extravagant to predict, but a spirit of improvement and enterprise. . . . With such disclosures and facts as to the past, can there be any possibility of mistake in calculating the future?"[16]

Despite this swelling symphony to success, the Red Hook Building Company's plan fell flat. Nobody could be convinced to purchase prospective houses on a swamp in Red Hook, nor did the promised ferry line boost the neighborhood's profile. The failure likely had to do with timing: in 1835 the Second Great Fire of New York consumed many wooden buildings in Lower Manhattan, and then the Great Panic of 1837 spread across the country. Unperturbed, however, Richards refocused. He was still a significant property owner in the Sixth Ward—a district that encompassed Red Hook, mostly empty land. So he gathered together a group of nine directors—including his son, Delavan, twenty-two—and incorporated the Red Hook Cotton Manufacturing Company in 1839. He bequeathed to this company some eleven acres of land, spread across forty lots, "beginning at the northwesterly corner at a point adjoining a certain creek, called Gowanus Creek."

It was a valiant attempt, but it went nowhere, since by 1843 these lands were being called out for nonpayment of taxes in the *Brooklyn Daily Eagle*. The eleven acres, which the paper of record described as "at the easterly end of the water gate of the mill pond, belonging to the heirs of M & N Van Dyk," were also "colored red" and most important "one-half under water." It is clear that no significant development could possibly take place in that locality unless the waterfront was vastly improved and the flooded lands taken care of. But Richards was adaptable and probably could debate for hours with great passion and no sign of fatigue. Besides, his most salient point—that the overflow of commercial shipping in New York practically guaranteed good business, as long as there was a place for boats to dock—could hardly be argued with. With his housing development nixed and his cotton company never more than an idea on paper, building a new commercial dock became Richards's sole mission.[17]

Modernizing Red Hook

In September 1839, Richards hired Willard Day, a surveyor, to plan the modification of Red Hook's west coast to realize his vision. At Richards's own expense, Day measured the water depth at the South Ferry, established after the incorporation of the city of Brooklyn, all the way to Red Hook, taking soundings at right angles every fifty feet over the surface where the docks might potentially be set. The whole process, determining how much excavation would be necessary and where earth would have to be placed for grading the piers and lots, took two months. There was also the question of money, as Richards could not finance the oversize plan alone. He again set out to organize a stock company—one that had the right to build docks, piers, and warehouses along the Brooklyn waterfront—requiring a charter from the city legislature, and, most important, investors to make it all happen.[18]

Acting on a singular confidence and faith in his idea, Richards single-handedly petitioned the legislature, found investors, and incorporated his grand scheme: The Atlantic Dock Company, a corporation authorized with a working capital of a million dollars. Its purpose as legislated was to build "docks, bulkheads and piers" to form a boat basin that would "embrace a surface of 42 acres," in the Sixth Ward of Brooklyn, as Red Hook was officially designated at the time. On an original copy of his prospectus, Richards wrote in a sharply pointed, aggressive script that appeared to be in a terrible rush: "This prospectus was written, published, and distributed by Daniel Richards without aid from Any One—Also, projected the plan of the Atlantic Docks & Basin, and paid all the expences of the same, without aid, or recourse to anyone to reimburse, any part of the expense, D.R."[19]

It was a project of greater magnitude than any contemporary plan in Brooklyn and passed "with great persistence and by dint of personal energy and solicitation" in the State Legislature on May 6, 1840. As the primary organizer of this venture, a group of directors (likely the investors) was assembled, with Richards as secretary and James D. P. Ogden president (Ogden, a New York businessman with mercantile experience, was around the same age as Richards). The directors concluded that in order to achieve the massive scale envisioned, the Atlantic Docks would require deeper water then Richards's original plans. Again he appealed single-handedly to the legislature, this time to change the water line that had been established in 1836. His plea opened a second round of meetings, collecting signed contracts for additional land purchases, excavation, and dock work pending the passage of a yet another bill.

This was, however, met by a "powerful opposition by remonstrance" from Isaac Varian, mayor of New York, and also from New York's Common Council. Most likely the push-back was an attempt to stymie Brooklyn from supplanting any of New York's shipping revenue. Still, after two months of contest with his opponents, the new bill passed into a law on May 26, 1841. As a reward, Richards was appointed superintendent of works by the company's directors, and construction finally commenced on June 3. As head of the Atlantic Docks project, he struck the first blow of the sledgehammer at the groundbreaking—digging the first frame for one of the many massive blocks of granite that would soon dominate the skyline of previously empty marshlands.[20]

But for the next three years, a series of mishaps due to a negligent contractor left the project with only partially completed docks and no warehouses. Part of this was surely due to a lapse in Richards's leadership, but he can hardly be faulted: on April 4, less than two months before the water line bill had passed, his son Delavan died of unknown causes, the second great tragedy for Richards—and quite possibly the reason why construction suddenly faltered after years of focused effort. A new construction firm, Imlay, Townsend & Voorhees—a subcontractor hired to fill in the Red Hook millpond—was given control of the whole project. A silent partner in this firm was an experienced and wealthy entrepreneur, James S. T. Stranahan. In 1844, Stranahan managed to buy out a majority of the Atlantic Docks Company stockholders and became the company's de facto chief. Richards, now holding a small minority of shares, was in even less control of the establishment he had so keenly strived to construct.[21]

Although the reins of presidency remained in Ogden's hand for the time being, it was only under Stranahan's watch that the cornerstone of the first warehouse was laid on May 24. It was accompanied by a celebration and detailed speech of the company's history from Ogden. The warehouses were to be privately owned but administered by the dock company, and this first construction was for a businessman named Henry Grinnell.[22]

In a niche in the cornerstone of Grinnell's warehouse, the Atlantic Dock Company directors placed a number of documents: copies of the charter and prospectus of the company, a pamphlet describing the increase of commerce in New York, and the company's comparison of their work to the docks on the Thames (as well as the Liverpool Docks, the Bute Docks at Cardiff, the basins at Le Havre, Marseilles, Antwerp, and Albany); there was also a list of company officers, the names of contractors who built the docks and warehouses, and copies of thirteen newspapers that had been published that day. The festivities were not unwarranted: after that day, the Atlantic Docks changed not only the scale and shape of Red Hook but also its identity.[23]

For the next two years a group of five hundred immigrant men toiled in Red Hook to construct this monumental undertaking in modern shipping and warehousing. Most of the skilled laborers were Irish, but much of that force went on strike in April 1846, forcing D. S. Voorhees, one of Stranahan's partners, to call their bluff and hire unskilled Germans to complete the work. The strategy worked, since the Irish had little leverage and soon reached a compromise with the directors. The labor force was split evenly between Irish and German immigrants; the former group constructed docks at a wage of eighty cents per day, while the latter dredged the basin—using new steam-powered diggers—and received an additional five cents. According to the journalists of the *Brooklyn Daily Eagle*, the two groups competed with each other: supposedly, the ethnic division created an incentive for each group not to strike.

By the summer of 1846, thirty-two monumental granite storehouses on the dock had opened for business. Richards was the private

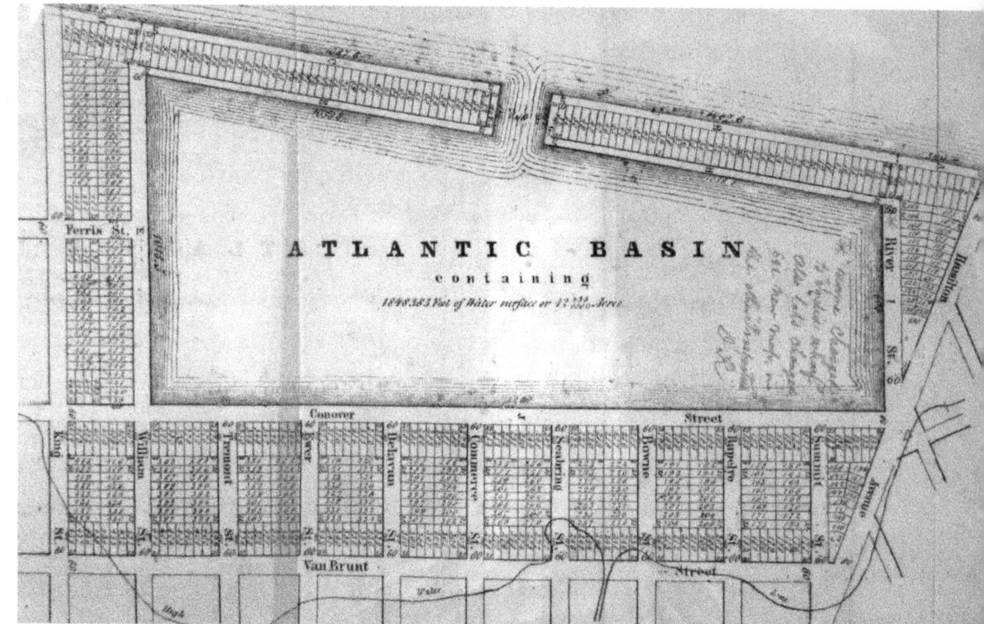

Daniel Richards's plan for the Atlantic Docks. His handwriting appears on the right side, indicating that River Street would have its "name changed to 'India wharf,' also lots changed, see new map in the other 'prospectus.' D. R." Courtesy of the Brooklyn Historical Society.

owner of several of the buildings, including the grandest: a four-story stone warehouse "fitted in a style superior to anything in this country," as the *Brooklyn Daily Eagle* (by then under the editorial watch of Walt Whitman) excitedly wrote, crowned with a "fancifully painted cupolas, upon which the 'stars and stripes' float upon the breeze." The first tenant, renting the two bottom stories, was the US government. Richards had spent the latter half of the 1840s scheming, building, and promoting the new business. He sent handwritten appeals to merchants and ship owners, informing them of the virtues of the state-of-the-art docking facilities with colorful maps and diagrams that proclaimed the basin's near proximity to Lower Manhattan. He wrote of the warehouses' two-foot-thick granite walls, which would protect perishables from the elements.[24]

Unlike the warehouses in Manhattan, these structures were right next to the wharves, which lowered cartage costs and wear on barrels. The achievement was revolutionary in New York. The landscape of Brooklyn had been morphed into a modern marvel of industry, and the docks and warehouses were immediately courted by all of the overflow boat traffic from New York. If Brooklyn was to be a international center of commerce, the Atlantic Docks would be the welcome mat. Still, as always, behind Richards's basic plan was something innovatory. He may not have been a major stockholder in the company he created from scratch, but he owned the biggest warehouse on its lots—and so he hatched a plan beyond storage space. In 1846 Richards began constructing by his warehouse a new state-of-the-art contraption that had first appeared in Buffalo only three years previous: the steam-powered grain elevator.[25]

Previously, the only method of hauling grain from boats employed by longshoremen, aided by ropes, pulleys, and pushcarts. The process, which could take days, had not been much improved upon since the Old Kingdom of Egypt. But a steam-powered grain elevator used engines and a bucket-type lift system to raise the grain to the higher level of a warehouse, moving approximately two thousand bushels an hour at a fraction of the cost. This invention transformed the movement and storage of grain in nineteenth-century shipping.

The new technology had been big news along the farming towns of the Erie Canal, and with Richards's push for innovation, his elevator was the third to be constructed in the United States and the first in New York Harbor. It was a wild success—not unlike railroads and other steam-powered inventions, the grain elevator helped define the beginning of America's industrial era. As an early adaptor, Richards had accomplished an amazing feat: within a few years, nearly all of the grain transactions in New York Harbor took place at the Atlantic Docks. For the second time in its history, Brooklyn—resting comfortably at the key to the whole continent—had become the epicenter

Daniel Richards's grain elevator at the Atlantic Docks. "A Scene at the Atlantic Docks Brooklyn." New York Public Library Digital Collections, 1861–ca. 1880. The Miriam and Ira D. Wallach Division of Art, Prints and Photographs: Print Collection, New York Public Library. Courtesy of the New York Public Library.

of regional grain trade. Most nineteenth-century sources remember Daniel Richards as the conceiver and projector of the Atlantic Docks and the owner of the first grain elevator in New York. For these things alone we can credit him with altering the course of Brooklyn history.[26]

Richards and the Gowanus Creek

In 1848, Richards was elected as an alderman to the Common Council of Brooklyn, representative of the Sixth Ward. A new ferry slip on Hamilton Avenue connected a company-run ferry to Whitehall Street in Manhattan, further solidifying Red Hook's status as a proper urban neighborhood (the service was taken over by the Union Ferry Company in New York once it proved to be self-sustaining). In March 1848, an editorial in the *Brooklyn Daily Eagle* praised the efforts of the Atlantic Dock Company, as though seeing the four-year-old development for the first time:

> The Atlantic Dock is truly a great, a magnificent work, and reflects the highest credit on those gentlemen who, ten years ago, had the sagacity to discover that the low grounds about Red Hook might be made to subserve the great purposes of commerce and the growth of our city, and the enterprise to carry into effect their Herculean scheme of encroachments and improvements in the very teeth of old Neptune. The splendid granite stores which have been erected along the front of Atlantic Dock . . . contain steam engines for the purpose of loading and unloading vessels and are so arranged that no cartage is required and very little hand labor. We learn that 400 feet of these stores on each side of the entrance to the great basin, making 800 feet in all, have been taken on a lease for a long number of years by the United States [government] and will be brought into immediate use under the warehousing system recently adopted by congress.

> The great basin, which covers some 40 acres, has been nearly filled with boats ever since the close of navigation, and many people make their winter quarters in them, and have service on Sunday in some floating chapel suited to the *floating* character of the population which may number a thousand or more. The people who live in these boats must have not only a church, but bakeries, grocers, rummeries &c. for the supply of their daily wants. The ferry which runs to New York from Hamilton Avenue is pretty well patronized, even now, and when the long rows of elegant buildings are completed, which are in course of construction, and peopled with *sleepers*, it will be quite a thoroughfare; and when the additional *thirty five* streets are opened and built up it will be decidedly a great ferry. In short we have no doubt that the *thirty five* streets asked to be opened by Mr. Richards will soon be wanted, and that a dense population will grow up in the vicinity of these docks, adding greatly to the wealth and beauty of our city, if not to its local spirit and individuality. We learn that an additional basin has been projected and that large calculations of advancement are made for the future. Well, gentlemen, go ahead. Your enterprise is worthy of the success which it has met.[27]

When Richards had planned the docks, ships had been known to wait up to two weeks in New York Harbor before off-loading, due to lack of space. Further delays in cartage and wharfing fees made shipping even costlier. But all of these headaches could now be avoided by docking in Red Hook. At the end of 1848, on an average day in November there were more than twenty large ships of one to three masts docked in the Atlantic Basin, and fifty more canal boats and barges; in storage there were at least two hundred thousand bushels of grain. With the growing network of American canals, barges were growing more popular and dependable with each passing year.[28]

By this time, Richards had grown into an established Brooklyn entrepreneur and politician, and after remarrying he had two more children, Elivra and Daniel Jr., and Betsey, his eldest daughter, married Henry Bradley in 1847. His business with Atlantic Docks secured him an enviable income. Richards Street, which runs along the western edge of Red Hook, is named after him. It intersects with Delavan Street, named for his deceased son, and Commerce Street, at its northern border. But with these streets nearing completion, he turned his attention to another idea he had had since moving to Brooklyn—the conundrum of Gowanus Creek.

The problem lay in the growth of the city at its banks. The population of Brooklyn was ever increasing—nearly one hundred thousand people by 1850—and the benefits of a growing civic population did not outshine the anxieties the growth caused. They were, as the *Brooklyn Daily Eagle* described in a September article, "all those evils to health, life, comfort, and morals, which are rife in this great city . . . the evils caused by accumulated refuse, slops, and filth of a large civilized community; which require sewers to carry them off and leave the air untainted."[29]

In addition to the pollution, progress necessitated more houses and stores. Diagrams of the city's streets had already been laid out, but some were little more than lines on a piece of paper. Red Hook was a prime example of how marshy land could be converted into useable urban space, and sitting directly to the east was the Gowanus. The creek had hosted boat traffic since colonization, and the local government, Dutch, British, or American, had approved many dredgings to allow easier boat access. That earliest example, dug by Dutch colonists, cut across the north of Red Hook and was visible well into the nineteenth century, until the Atlantic Docks construction removed it from the landscape.

There is no way that such changes escaped the watchful eye of the meticulous Richards. But while the Gowanus once provided oysters and important water access, the naturally occurring creek had reached a certain degree of obsolescence. It was too shallow for modern boats to navigate and no longer connected to the East River, and surrounding the estuary on either side for seventeen hundred acres was the indomitable salt marsh. With each rain, the meadows of the area were flooded for days—rendering the land effectively useless. This last factor made real estate development impossible, not to mention using it for shipping. The question that became prudent at this time, and indicated an important shift in thinking, was no longer how to utilize this flooding but how to stop it.

As a member of the legislature and the figurehead behind the Atlantic Docks, Richards rose to join the powerful Brooklyn elite. He was an active member of the Common Council Street Committee, devoted to the maintenance and construction of city walkways and roads. For Richards, a problem solver, the Gowanus Creek was a great challenge; the answer appeared to be staring him in the face. It couldn't function for shipping unless its banks were modernized, and the effort could not be taken unless the meadows were drained. Furthermore, as the *Eagle* pointed out, Brooklyn's growing populace needed sewers. In the winter of 1847, the Street Committee had appointed a talented engineer, Major David Bates Douglass, to conduct a survey on Gowanus Creek to determine if and how it could be improved to drain the meadows. Douglass was known in his field: in the 1820s he was the principal engineer of the Morris Canal, a technological marvel that crossed northern New Jersey from Jersey City to Phillipsburg using ingenious water-driven inclined planes to bypass the hills in the area. He was also, in the mid-1830s, the first principal engineer of the Croton Aqueduct, the large-scale city improvement project that brought clean drinking water to New York City from an upstate reservoir. Finally, in 1838 he drafted the early designs of the Green-Wood Cemetery, the idyllic Brooklyn landmark that changed modern civic cemetery design.[30]

Douglass and Richards were personally acquainted: the latter had solicited Douglass's written approval of the competence of Wil-

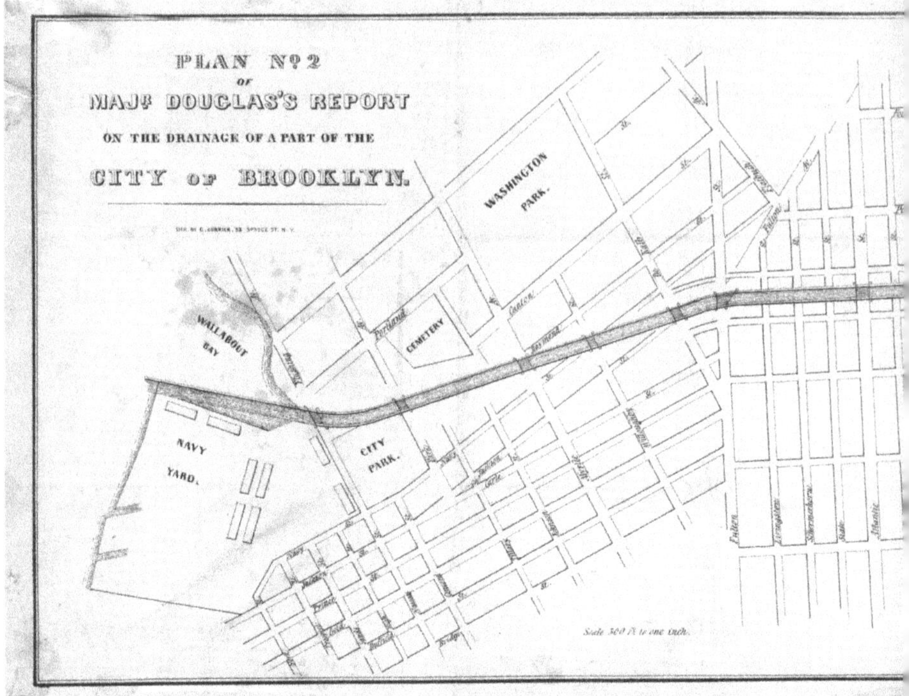

Colonel David Douglass's unexecuted 1847 plan for the Gowanus Canal, stretching from Gowanus Bay to Wallabout Bay. Courtesy of the New York Public Library.

lard Day, the surveyor who measured the water lines for the Atlantic Docks project, and the celebrity engineer's response appeared in the company's prospectus. It was likely Richards who called upon Douglass to take the first crack at the canal. Despite his obvious conviction for the idea, it likely was not Richards who conceived of using the canal for a drain, just as he did not engender the idea of using it for shipping. But considering his integral connection to the Atlantic Docks, his experience of the Erie Canal, and his commitment to Brooklyn's development, there were few men more qualified. It suited his interests and passions perfectly. Without a doubt, it became his personal project.

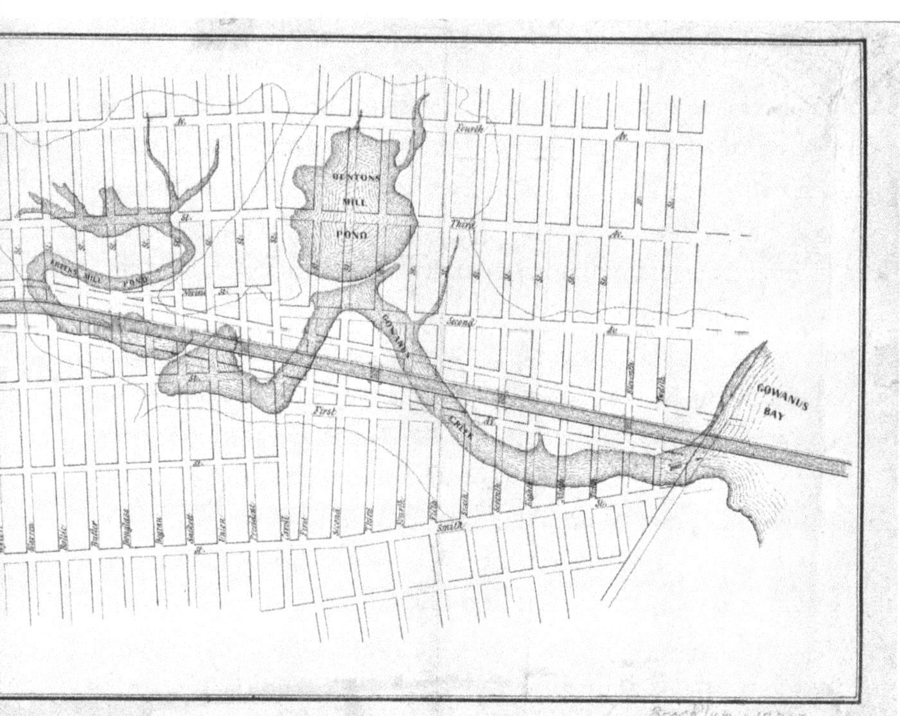

Douglass's sixteen-page report gave a detailed analysis of how to drain the Gowanus fields, with several options: First was to fill in the creek completely, at great expense, and create square lots for development, an idea popular among many local Brooklynites, who felt the healthiest solution was to eliminate the water. The creek could also be dug into a large basin into which the drains would empty, but the only current would derive from rising and falling flood tides. This "could not but carry somewhat of the matters received from the streets," according to Douglass, leaving street waste to sink to the bottom and, even with dredging, become "offensive" to anybody within smelling distance. As a solution to this, the engineer proposed two different designs for a self-cleaning canal that could be used as a drain for the fields, doubling as a dock for commercial use. He first proposed digging a long channel from Gowanus Bay to Wallabout Bay, passing major intersections and requiring a huge amount of land grading—both inconvenient and prohibitively expensive. The second design was a double canal, with parallel branches that connected like a straw folded in half. Gates and locks would be set in place to create the current necessary to flush out waste. "The canal in fact becomes a sort of river," Douglass wrote, "running, with a variable current indeed, but always *in the same direction*."[31]

Douglass was a brilliant engineer with warranted concerns about the pollution, but he was not a businessman. His estimated cost for the project was $366,740, approximately $100 million in twenty-first-century dollars. The meadows were not graded very high, probably to save labor costs, but that plan offered little room for wharves and even less opportunity for landowners to use the meadows as viable real estate. It offered sewers and drainage, but none of the capitalist impetus to effect change. Finally, the plan ignored the shape of the creek as it existed at the time and would have required even more digging and filling just to achieve the kind of symmetry a nineteenth-century engineer would admire.[32]

This plan did not inspire the legislature, likely because of its cost and clinical nature, which offered little reason for private financing. Richards, clearly unsatisfied but not defeated, again hired Willard Day as surveyor and conducted his own study of the creek. Less than two years later he released his own report and plan to the Street Committee, containing a design for a 100-foot-wide, 5,400-foot-long canal with walls four feet above the high water line, costing only $78,600. The design contained a number of private basins, all to be constructed by interested landowners, except for one public basin at the head of the canal (he admitted, at the end of the report, that this basin would bring the cost up to $86,223.30). This canal sported odd angles and bends and followed the path of the creek as it existed, so as to save money and time. Richards also included an extensive section on how the canal would be navigable to any number of barges and canal craft

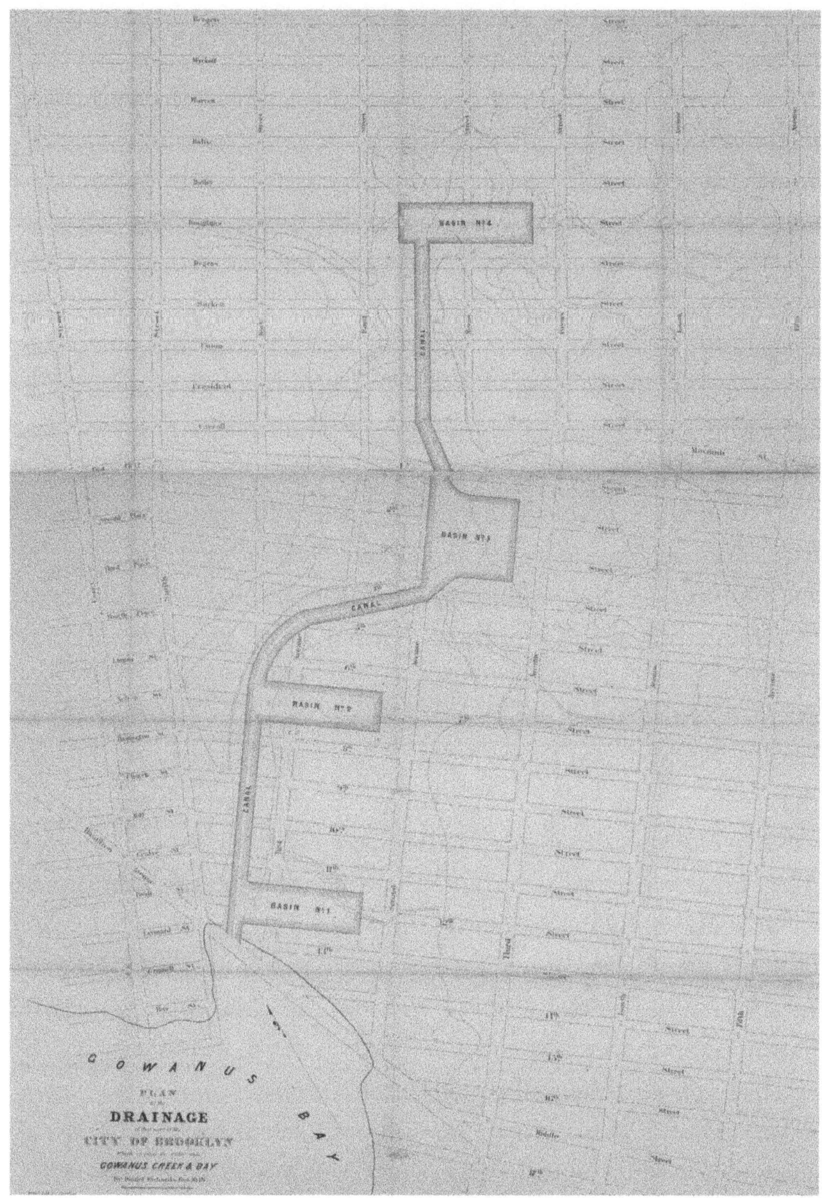

Daniel Richards's 1848 plan for the drainage of the Gowanus Canal. This design determined the shape of what would eventually become the present-day Gowanus. Courtesy of the New York Public Library.

popular in commercial shipping, which he felt that Brooklyn was lacking.

As always, Richards sold his idea with uncanny prescience: "The introduction of this class of shipping into this section of our city would cause to spring to life much new enterprise, and introduce a lively business along the line of the canal," he wrote. "The introduction of cheap warehouses sheds and yards, for storage and deposit of heavy coarse goods, as also lumber, coal, brick, stone and wood yards, as well as manufactories, all of which would cluster upon its banks, and it would, in due time, become a place of active business, at the same time serve as the best and cheapest mode of drainage to a large section of country that can now be suggested."[33]

Furthermore, Richards denied that the tidal movement was insufficient to maintain a clean canal. He believed that the tides and the depth of the bay would provide plenty of current to carry out the "mud, dirty water, and filth." In early 1849, only a few months later and with only mild resistance, the Common Council adopted his plan. The *Eagle* announced the specifics with great gusto. "A large navigable canal from Gowanus bay to Douglas street, through the centre of the meadows, into which the sewers from the elevated ground on either side, shall be emptied," the journalist wrote. "The great object to be attained in making this important work, is the removal of the marsh miasma which hangs about Prospect Hill and other portions of the city, making them liable to intermittent fevers and other diseases; and thus shutting them out from improvement."[34]

The *Eagle* also cheerfully predicted Richards's vision of the Gowanus neighborhood as "valuable for purposes of commerce and the mechanic arts," while filling in the creek, as proposed by some naysayers, would be the "height of folly." Creating a commercial canal—bringing their city a greater share of New York commerce—could only add to the "wealth and honor of Brooklyn."[35]

The Fall of Richards

In the complicated business of urban development, it is nearly impossible to proceed with any large-scale change or extensive work without offending someone. As often happens during exceptional growth, as Brooklyn experienced in the 1840s, real estate speculation ran rampant. The Atlantic Docks came to existence not solely due to the economic vision of Richards, but through his ability to sell that vision. The successful erection of the docks was a promise, an investment toward the future of Brooklyn that offered hope and, at times, great wealth. Following the early explosion of commerce, city officials hit the ground running and constructed roads and civic buildings—and also hired many city employees—with money the city government hadn't necessarily collected yet.

Francis B. Stryker, mayor of Brooklyn from 1846 to 1848, was a polarizing political figure during his two terms in office. The son of a butcher, Stryker was a prominent Whig whose campaign dubbed him the "poor man's friend." He is mostly remembered in a positive light, including his careful attention during several cholera outbreaks in Brooklyn (he is said to have visited many patients personally), and for increasing the police force in the growing city, making the streets safer and cleaner. The *Brooklyn Daily Advertiser,* a Whig-leaning publication, heaped great praise on the popular mayor throughout his term, much to the chagrin of the *Eagle*, which was critical of the local Whig establishment's financial mismanagement. In reference to the actions of Stryker and his fellow Whigs, the editors of Brooklyn's largest daily newspaper coined the term "Strykerism" to describe the particular combination of excess public spending, appropriation of public property, and shady civic contracts and kickbacks that proliferated during his terms. These accusations included excessive allocation of money to civic employees such as contractors, street cleaners, police officers, and night watchmen.

One widespread scandal described the local lamplighters using fish oil, instead of sperm whale oil, as fuel for street lamps—the former material was smelly, unreliable, and cheap, and its the supplier was likely taking a kickback. Many articles in the *Eagle* declared that the city was run as a large-scale municipal racket, a kickback machine that existed solely for enriching Brooklyn's prominent citizens. Taxes doubled under the Stryker administration, and a floating city debt of more than $83,000 appeared to provide the funding for various questionable improvements and overstuffed civic contracts. Daniel Richards was a devoted Whig and, while holding the precarious dual identity of alderman and developer, was accused of involvement in shady activities.[36]

Hints of mistrust surrounding Richards's practices surfaced around the time of Common Council elections of 1849. Mostly they focused around a street cleaning contract that he handed out which grossly overestimated the cost of dirt removal from a construction project (quite possibly the Brooklyn City Hall). "At the head of [the ticket for alderman in the Sixth Ward] is Ald. Richards with his head full of schemes for expending money and of apologies for the conduct of unfaithful officers," the *Eagle* columnist hissed on April 7. "It was he who went openly for taking the highest bids in giving out the contracts to the street cleaners and went into an elaborate argument to show that the contract, given to Roberts, could not be done for any less money. The work having been afterwards done for $7000 less than Richards' estimate shows pretty convincingly what the city will gain by his election." [37]

The writer returned with equal scorn on the April 9: "It seems that the financial schemes of Alderman Richards, his votes in favor of large appropriations, his speeches in behalf of all sorts of bubbles, his efforts to bestow money on contractors, street cleaners and everything else, have reacted against him in the sixth ward and that he cannot be *put through*, notwithstanding the large interests that he is supposed to control." Two days later, Richards lost the election. According to the *Brooklyn Advertiser*, "the Gowanus canal project killed Richards in the sixth ward." The Whigs, still present on the Common Council, were now reduced to a minority.[38]

When the 1850 elections approached the following year, the *Eagle* published an editorial claiming that the Whigs "look upon the city government as absolutely made for the benefit of contractors and speculators." This was directed entirely toward all political dealings that had dominated the Sixth Ward and environs, and much of the attention of Brooklyn's politicians. The previously useless lands, converted to a powerful tool for shipping and cornerstone for the new Brooklyn economy, seemed to be benefitting a select group, and not the city as a whole.

Dripping with sarcasm, the *Eagle* indicting local real estate honchos in their aspirations for political power, and one in particular:

> The Whigs have, in fact, nominated for Mayor the Atlantic Dock Company, with all of its speculations and collateral interests; including the Gowanus Canal, the Red Hook park, the Hamilton avenue opening, the cutting down of hills, the leveling up of vallies, the confiscating of lands for opening streets; in short the interests, general and particular, of the lot owners in a certain part of the Sixth ward. We might, for that matter, as well have had for mayor our worthy friend Daniel Richards, himself, who measured so accurately the dirt on Pacific street and calculated so nicely the cost of the Gowanus canal. The ticket appears to have been made by the Stryker Whigs for the benefit of speculators, contractors, and the b'hoys in general. . . . If the Whig ticket prevails we are to have the gambling operations of the Stryker politicians mixed up with the gambling operations in Red Hook lots and Atlantic Dock Bond. We are to have our city government converted into a great machine of speculation and conducted for the benefits of contractors and dealers in fancy lots.[39]

Certainly, the *Eagle*'s editors wanted all benefits that the development promised—jobs, increased commerce, improvements to health standards, and civic pride. But there was a school of hungry sharks swimming alongside Richards, many of whom were not above handing out shady contracts and enriching themselves by whatever means possible. Rapid growth brought anxiety to this once-small community, as they felt the power over the meadows and brooks that defined their landscape slipping away.

The mind-set of such capitalist scheming is in some capacity necessary for a major metropolis to succeed. Without that appetite for success, those flooded meadows and beaches would stagnate, dragging down Brooklyn's potential in the growing shadow of New York. Most sharks suffocate if they stop swimming, and devour anything they can while in motion. In the wake of the high scrutiny of election

"Daniel Richards," the only known portrait of him. The New York Public Library Digital Collections. The Miriam and Ira D. Wallach Division of Art, Prints and Photographs: Print Collection, New York Public Library. Courtesy of the New York Public Library.

season, Daniel Richards lost his momentum. Playing games with politics and money appears to have eclipsed his enthusiasm and initiative. The Atlantic Docks changed Brooklyn in a matter of years—nobody can deny this—but its success was dependent on an outside angel investor. This left Richards a minority player; although he was successful, he didn't learn from that experience. Instead he seems to have overstepped his boundaries and used his connections and position to dole out favors and cheat the system; he acted with impropriety, not humility.

Although Richards was able to secure the first legislation that authorized the digging of the Gowanus Canal—including the draining of seventeen hundred acres of meadows and the construction of wharves and docks (but not the emptying of city sewers into the canal)—following the election the project came to a screeching halt. Those landowners with fields prone to flooding were supposed be assessed for the cost of the project, but this idea was not met with enthusiasm. And though Richards was reelected to the Common Council and served again as alderman over the next two decades, he was never able to build a coalition of willing landowners to organize a singular canal project, nor could he acquire the legislation for a similar city organization. His popularity firmly plateaued, no longer could he muster the gestalt to propel his latest passion.[40]

One cannot help but admire the doggedness of this man: over the following years Richards had projected many new schemes and gotten involved in other real estate ventures, not just around Red Hook and Brooklyn, but farther south toward Yellow Hook and New Utrecht. But his final big plan was another boat basin in Red Hook, the Pacific Docks, in which he would finally be a principal stockholder. It was likely in response to the success of the Erie Basin, a project near his Atlantic Docks that had been completed by his real estate contemporary William Beard—another prominent Red Hook landowner and projector and likely rival. Although the two men were described as having worked together, Richards once sued

Beard in an attempt to stop a dock building project, possibly this very basin. Beard, who also had a street named after him in Red Hook, was the owner of expansive docks and an important figure in the real estate and commerce of Brooklyn during this period. His basin would become the final stop of the barge traffic from the Erie Canal—a commercial masterpiece.

Richards again toiled after his Pacific Docks project, repeating the process of securing petitions, raising funds, and obtaining the legislation to incorporate his company in 1857, all at his own expense. However, in this attempt he ran into another roadblock. The harbor commissioners objected to his plan and fought it at Albany. On a copy of the prospectus for the Pacific Dock Company in the Brooklyn Historical Society, Richards's handwriting—still pointed yet slightly weary—spells his disappointment: "All would have been built & completed if the Harbor Commissioners (also appointed by an Act of the Legislature) had not (wrongfully, I think) changed the water line at this point, which cut off more the one half of the water surface of the Basin; thereby distorting the intended improvement. D.R."[41]

Somehow undeterred, he devised yet another plan, this time to build a wide pier that extended across the bay. It would have created a grand basin at the mouth of the Gowanus Canal, designed for longer-term storage of boats, such as during the winter. Accompanying would be facilities for "long shore business trade." He again arranged the finances and found investors and brought his plan to Albany. This time, however, landowners along the Gowanus Canal and also along the bay fought his plan. They were concerned for their own interests—Richards's docks would have had first pick of all shipping business. And quite possibly they were fed up with his many attempts to re-create the Atlantic Docks, and this one seemed the most outrageous. It was certainly at a grander scale than any of his previous ventures. Their opposition was too great and Richards surrendered.[42]

The Promise of Commerce

The legacy of the Atlantic Docks was felt in Brooklyn forty years after their inception, as shown by an 1885 *Eagle* story about James T. Stranahan, the principal stockholder and president for more than thirty-five years. According to the *Eagle*, the docks were one of the most important places of interest in Brooklyn—among other virtues, the impressive granite warehouses framed a perfect view of New York Harbor and the many ships they hosted.

In his interview, Stranahan stated that by the 1880s his corporation had reclaimed one hundred acres of land from filling in the tidewater, and that fifteen thousand people lived in dwellings situated within a mile of the docks and warehouses—the result of Daniel Richards's thirty-five streets. A tenth of the seagoing vessels in New York landed in the Atlantic Basin, including two steamship lines running directly from Marseille and Hamburg. At least seven grain elevators were built, and, in addition to wheat products, the warehouses held large quantities of American commodities like tobacco, cotton, and sugar. Many of the bulkiest imports from other countries first landed in New York, and some passed exclusively through Brooklyn. At times this included steel and iron (before domestic industry produced its own), most of the salt imported to America, oranges and other Mediterranean fruits, and products like walking sticks and German-manufactured toys. At one point, all the coffee beans imported to New York landed first on the Atlantic Docks.[43]

Naturally, all of this commerce was a great contribution to Brooklyn's coffers. Stranahan claimed the Atlantic Docks, although hugely successful and integral to Brooklyn's economy, never provided him a significant profit. For the first twenty-five years, all of the company's profits had to be reinvested to "save it from embarrassment, and few of the original stockholders lived to receive a dividend." Over the course of its existence, he claimed, twice as much was paid out to the city in taxes as was paid as dividends to the company stockholders. If anyone profited off of the Atlantic Docks, it was the city of Brooklyn. "In fact, we have paid for more than 20 years the one-fiftieth part of the taxes of Brooklyn year by year," Stranahan said, "and my interest in the Atlantic Basin and docks is unfortunately for me so large that my share of the annual taxes of Brooklyn is about a one-hundredth part of the annual tax of the city."

In a characteristically New York kind of way, this remarkable and historic undertaking was already forgotten before the turn of the twentieth century. It had been the greatest scale venture and the first to host a steam-powered grain elevator. That first effort of a chain of modernizations defined Brooklyn's identity as a commercial city and set a standard for shipping that reverberated throughout the port of New York. And yet, in so many ways it was a labor of love. The *Eagle* reporter also asked Stranahan if it was true that, out of approximately six hundred thousand people living in Brooklyn by that time, only half knew where the Atlantic Basin sat or how grand it was. "No, not one in twenty," was his reply, and the proportion in the New York City even less.[44]

Just like the Atlantic Docks, Brooklyn nearly forgot about Daniel Richards and the indelible impact he made on the bustling city, never mind his leading role in the modernization of the port of New York. Not even an obituary exists for this elusive innovator, so he likely died in relative obscurity sometime around 1875. Richards was survived by his daughters, Betsey Greene and Elvira, and his son, Daniel Jr. Most details of his personal life are lost. Yet without Richards's efforts Brooklyn might have been a very different city. And while he was never directly involved with the Gowanus Canal after the 1850s, his initial vision and tireless actions planted a seed that would grow into one of the most infamous waterways in the industrialized world.

"In a very short time, the great want of New York will be *room, room, room*," wrote an *Eagle* soothsayer in February of 1851. That portion of Brooklyn "lying between the Gowanus Bay and Buttermilk

Channel . . . with the Atlantic Basin, the Pacific Basin, the Croton Basin, &c., on one side, and the Gowanus Canal on the other" would be the perfect new venue for "building up a great commercial interest." By opening the Atlantic Basin, the *Eagle* insisted, "the first great impulse has been communicated." Hope and excitement are palpable in the text. Finally, Brooklyn would no longer be overshadowed by its older sister, "the great centre which has swallowed up everything and we have been a mere appendage." When it became important enough to be "taxed and oppressed," residents believed that even New York had to recognize the smaller city's importance.

"At any rate we are satisfied of this one fact," the writer concluded, "that Brooklyn will be, in due time, a great commercial city."[45]

4

Sewers, Railroads, and the Castle on the Hill (1851–1857)

> The ancient mill which stood beside the old penny bridge, opposite Fisherman's Hall, and known as "Freeke's Mill," was last night burned down. For a number of years past nothing had been done by this mill, and it stood on the edge of the creek a crazy old skeleton, looking like a melancholy relic of olden times; and looking down at its decaying features, reflected in the waters of the creek, as if it had half a notion to drown itself. Some person, however, set it on fire last night, unless like the Phoenix, it collected a few stray beams of sunshine in the evening to light its own funeral pyre and expired in the aromatic flames. Peace be to its ashes. Its life not being insured, it has left Messrs. Brady and Fish to bewail its fate. The fire caused quite an illumination, and most have astonished the eels and crabs in the old creek, although we have not heard that any of the former were "frightened out of their skins."
>
> —*Brooklyn Daily Eagle*, April 4, 1851

The following February, less than a year after this monument of Gowanus agricultural legacy burned to the ground, the Street Committee of the Common Council voted in favor of a petition, by one "Charles Secor and others," to extend Bond Street to south to the bank of the Gowanus Canal. This was immediately followed by Alderman Lambert's motion to direct the commissioner of repairs and supplies to "cause a culvert across Bond street, to be built to carry off the surplus water," which was immediately adopted. He then added one more motion, asking the Street Committee to "examine and report on what streets in the south-western part of the city, it is necessary to build sewers, to carry off the surplus water," which also passed.[1]

This simple drain on Bond Street appears to be the first of its kind dug in Brooklyn, at least as reported in the newspapers. In response to the unending floodwaters plaguing that pesky corner of Brooklyn, other drainage sewers soon appeared. They serviced the flooded meadows around the vicinity of Smith, Sackett, and Bond Streets, near the head of the Gowanus Creek. Charged with "carry[ing] off the surplus water from a large section of the City in that vicinity," these independent storm drains were the earliest form of sewerage in Brooklyn. There must have been a noticeable change in some of the flooding meadows, since within a year of this improvement—in June 1853—landowner Edward Fiske began digging on his land what would eventually become the Gowanus Canal. He employed some forty to fifty Irish laborers to operate a powerful dredging machine—probably using the same steam dredgers that had dug the contours of the Atlantic Docks—to widen and deepen the channel and construct bulkheads and walls of wood pilings.[2]

There had been no shortage of construction work at this time for eager laborers. Thanks to an exploding population, in 1852 more than two thousand new homes were constructed in Brooklyn, where rents were 20 percent cheaper than in Manhattan. The *Eagle* screamed praise in particular for South Brooklyn, as the new neighborhood from Red Hook to the west bank of the Gowanus was dubbed, claiming it was "destined to be the Fifth Avenue of Brooklyn." South Brooklyn centered around the vicinity of the newly paved First Place, where "elegant marble and brownstone-fronted buildings were erected on the newly paved Carroll, Douglass, and President Streets." Farther south, the previously empty Hamilton Avenue boasted "the pleasant spectacle of whole blocks of beautiful brick houses of an elegant and substantial character," and by the Atlantic Docks stood "rows of dwelling houses, cotton manufactories, iron foundries, and institutions such as collect a useful population."

But even further, the *Eagle* insisted that the greatest improvement to the area would surely be the opening of the Gowanus Canal. That section of the city would be "thrown open to navigation with facilities for the erection of docks," and soon to follow would be lumberyards, brickyards, and markets. Property values would jump and a "new life be infused into the whole neighborhood." But at this time, while genteel houses (and outlying slums) burgeoned at the edges of South Brooklyn, the area called Gowanus—on the eastern side of the transmogrifying creek—had "all the pleasures and repose of a village, with the advantages of a metropolitan location; and for pure air, a magnificent view of the surrounding neighborhood, is not equaled by any other section of the city." Indeed, during long summer evenings pleasure-seeking Brooklynites would cross the aging bridges, passing over the saline, marshy waters to take strolls along the Gowanus banks, still "untraversed by streets and covered with shade trees." According to the *Eagle*'s more poetic descriptions, those pastures were like a wild public park on the edge of civilization, where the residents of growing South Brooklyn could act out a pastoral urban fantasy, benefitting lands essentially unchanged since colonial times.[3]

Even with the grand speculation in Brooklyn, the Gowanus Canal did not take shape for another decade. There was no unified, civic effort to develop the waterway—a complex engineering project such as this needed a singular plan and strong leadership. With the loss of a responsible projector, little was organized beyond the desires of individual landowners. The Common Council contributed little toward spearheading the construction, aside from voting for the tax assessment. As they found this difficult to collect, their hands were tied, if not from lack of funds, then from the limits of their power. None of the canal front was owned by the city, making its oversight difficult to organize, such that the bulkhead walls individual owners like Fiske had constructed were ineffective, allowing mud from the meadows to wash into the canal during rainstorms. This all choked the waterway so much that it became useless for navigation outside of high tide—the dense shantytowns nearby, and their growing number of inhabitants, were often in danger of floating away.

Then, in November 1854, the commissioner of repairs and supplies officially communicated to the Common Council that the Bond Street sewer was regularly clogged, which couldn't have helped move along the canal project. Soon afterward additional council votes allowed landlords to reduce their assessments by conducting more of the work themselves, but the work remained inconsistent and of poor quality. This canal project, now several years along, was failing. Its only hope of salvation would require some new blood: a powerful visionary with a vested interest in Brooklyn's future and—unlike Daniel Richards—a deep business sense (but mostly deeper pockets). This person would have to possess a divine level of patience and believe in the long-term value of the marshy lands. The project required someone who could stomach the thought of paying heavily into an investment, but mainly have faith—that immeasurable force, stronger than speculation or capitalist visions—in the success of this questionable plan.[4]

The Father of the Gowanus Canal

Edwin C. Litchfield, an attorney and son of a former carpenter turned US congressman, had moved to New York City from Albany in 1846. For the previous decade he had worked as a lawyer in the state capital, even serving a term as district attorney. By the time he arrived in Manhattan, ostensibly to start Litchfield and Tracy, his own private law practice, he was also on his way to becoming a railroad developer of exceptional wealth. As the new neighborhood of South Brooklyn was taking shape—the meadows drained and the canal first being dug—Litchfield began buying the old Dutch farms, some still owned by descendants of original settlers, on the outskirts of Brooklyn.

His older brother, Electus Bacchus, had moved to Manhattan in the 1840s from their hometown, Cazenovia, New York, to expand his mercantile business in the big city. Just like Daniel Richards, Electus had lived through the changes the Erie Canal brought to the economy of Upstate New York and attempted to make his living dealing in produce. For a decade, Electus operated a wholesale grocery at 60 Pearl Street in Lower Manhattan (only a few blocks from Daniel Richards's first address), as well as Litchfield & Co., a company that sold Sperm whale oil and candles. Meanwhile, increasingly throughout the 1840s, the studious Edwin found himself swept up the lucrative financial management of railroads. Being a successful legal figure in the centrally located state capital, he was likely attuned to a good deal of insider information in that burgeoning American industry.[5]

Indeed, when the state of Michigan sold its unfinished Michigan Southern Railroad in 1846 to an upstart engineering firm with no prior experience, Edwin C. Litchfield was the principal stockholder and treasurer (the firm's original name has been lost to history). That sale prompted him, along with his eldest brother Elisha Cleveland, to join Electus in his close proximity to the business world of Wall Street. By this point Edwin was married and had three children—Edward Hubbard, Henry Percy, and a girl, Frances Hubbard. Grace Denio, his last child, was born in Greenwich Village in 1849. Soon the Litchfield clan (not including the children) was united in a scheme to dominate the railroad industry, starting with the lines crossing Michigan and Indiana. Not a minute was wasted: soon after his promotion to president, by 1852 Edwin oversaw the completion of the Michigan Southern Railroad and, the following year, its merger with the North Indiana Railroad. Once the lines were linked, it was possible for a passenger to travel from New York to Chicago, with a few transfers along the way, entirely by rail. In other words, the Litchfields stitched together the first singular rail line to unite the northeastern corridor with the Midwest. Soon the enterprising brothers owned controlling interests in a number of vital railroad lines: Electus became the treasurer, then president of the consolidated Cleveland and Toledo Railroad, while Elisha Cleveland became a director of the Chicago and Rock Island line; the three later combined their interests in the Terre Haute and Alton Railroad. The development of such transportation often came with federal land grants, rewarding the growing family empire with sweeping tracts of undeveloped acreage in Ohio, Illinois, and Michigan alongside their railroads. They founded the town of Litchfield in Montgomery County, Illinois; another town called Litchfield, in Meeker County, Minnesota, was later named in their honor.[6]

A rail link to Chicago meant that the bounty of midwestern farms—grain, lumber, corn, and beef—could now be shipped quickly to the East Coast. Allowing cheaper food prices and an exploding market for modern transport, the growing rail industry would soon be caught up in investment mania, stoked mostly by investors from New York and abroad. In 1849 there were only about nine thousand miles of track nationwide; by 1860, there were more than thirty thousand.

Via his dealings, Litchfield soon embodied the archetype of a New York railroad mogul. Within a few years, he reinvented himself from an somewhat obscure Albany lawyer and district attorney to a high-powered businessman with a respectable fortune, living with his wife and children at 123 Waverly Place in fashionable Greenwich Village. Still under forty years old and exceedingly wealthy, Litchfield appears to have fallen in love. It's not quite clear how his eyes first fell upon the fields and historic hills of Brooklyn. Perhaps Stranahan, his classmate from Cazenovia Academy (and owner of the Atlantic Docks Company), had alerted him to the undeveloped but increasingly valuable lands across the East River. Considering the growth of commerce in the former idyllic cornucopia, every corner of Brooklyn was ripe for modern-day improvement. Perhaps just as the lands called out to the most brazen New World pioneers of the past, Brooklyn had caught Litchfield's attention. Or perhaps he, like Daniel Richards, was blessed with restless ambition and an eye for the value where others saw wasteland.[7]

However it came to pass, in this unique locality Litchfield saw a city of mounting commercial importance—where speculation could change the land values in a matter of days. He also saw the chance to build a legacy. Just like Red Hook the previous decade, in the late 1840s the land east of the Gowanus was barely settled save for some eighteenth-century farmhouses. But as did some *Eagle* journalists, Litchfield envisioned paved streets lined with houses of brick and stone, and busy canal wharves laden with commercial goods. There would be warehouses and lumberyards, active commercial spaces buzzing with workers who lived in nearby row houses. On his lands, Litchfield envisioned an American twist on an ancient idea: an English-style landed estate, but with the requisite castle overlooking a vibrant commercial district.

In 1852, brimming with cash from his railroad ventures, Litchfield bought 88 acres between the Gowanus marshes and the Flatbush Road from David Talmage, son of Thomas G. Talmage, a former mayor of Brooklyn. His second purchase was even greater: 150 acres from Jacques Cortelyou, a direct descendent of the early Dutch surveyor whose family had purchased the original Vecht plantation before the Revolutionary War. The head city clerk who officiated the sale happened to be Francis Stryker, the polarizing former mayor of Brooklyn who now enjoyed a cushy government post. This particular sale, which closed two days before Christmas 1852, included the Vecht-Cortelyou House—by then called the Old Stone House of Gowanus—which had stood on the historic, swampy lands since 1699. Strong as ever, the house was a monument of the Dutch roots of colonial Brooklyn and the bravery of Revolutionary War soldiers. There could be no coincidence in Litchfield's purchase of this particular property: it made him the owner of a tangible piece of his adopted city's history.

The Cortelyou deed comprised the equivalent of thirty city blocks, bounded by the projected First Street and Fifth Street, and from Tenth Avenue down to the Second Avenue—also the bed of the Gowanus Creek. That family owned other parcels in the area, spread out like disparate pieces of a puzzle, for which Litchfield paid approximately $150,000. He spent $100,000 more buying subsequent farms and lots, until he owned nearly a square mile of land east of the Gowanus Creek, stretching from today's First Street to Ninth Street, and from the edge of Prospect Park down to the canal.[8]

At the time much of this region was little more than swampy, flooded meadows with no roads. As Litchfield was ever the meticulous lawyer, every legal document in each of his purchases was recorded into an oversized, leather-bound ledger bearing his initials, residing today in perfect condition in the New York Historical Society archives. Beautifully rendered watercolor maps denote the plots of

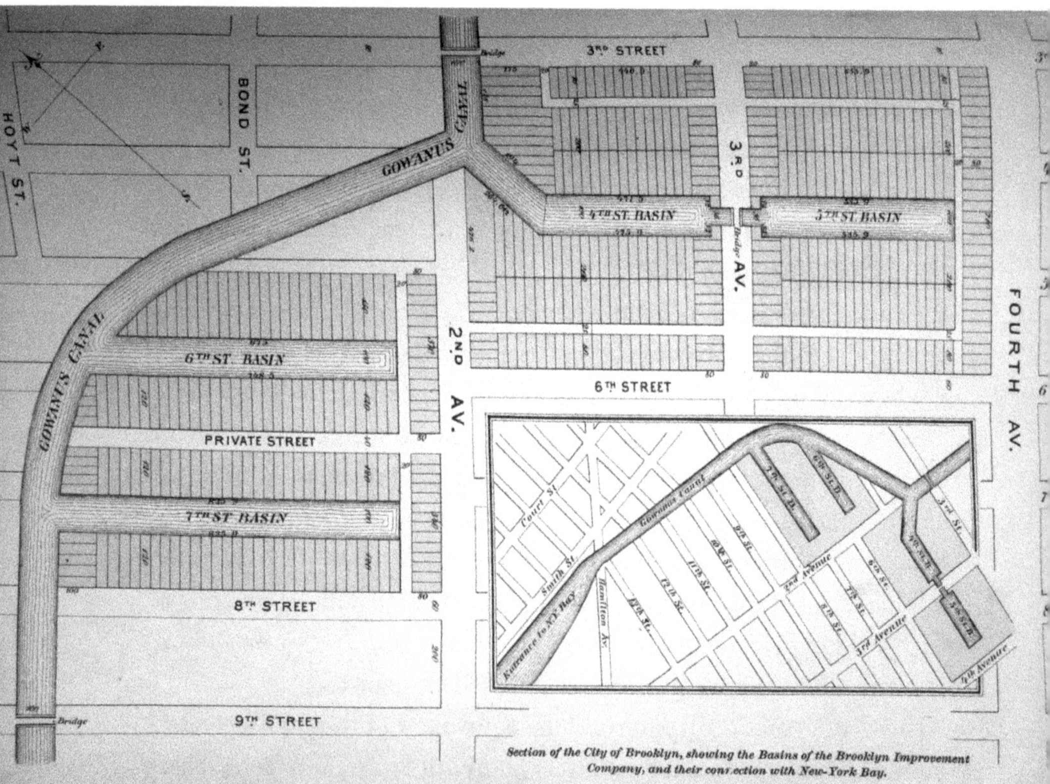

Edwin C. Litchfield's plan for the Gowanus Canal commercial district, undated. Litchfield Family Papers. Courtesy of the New York Historical Society.

land, divided among Litchfield's children, his wife, other family members, and business partners. Edwin's brother Electus had also invested in some Brooklyn real estate, but was more interested in developing local transportation: "The railroad mania appears to be still alive," insisted the *New York Times* in 1852, announcing petitions submitted by "E. B. Litchfield" to lay railway tracks on Montague Street and Myrtle Avenue—two main roads in the environs of central Brooklyn. The announcement also included his petition for the same kind of railways "from the Fulton and Montague Ferries to Third-avenue."

Although they each approached from different angles, the Litchfield brothers were moving toward the same goal of dominating Brooklyn's real estate. If Electus's railroad schemes worked according to plan, they would connect his brother's lands with the ferries to New York, hence exploiting the market at every possible angle. In their eyes, their Brooklyn holdings were bound to gain value: By the time of their arrival in the city, its population had swelled to ninety-seven thousand, representing a growth rate greater than that in New York City. According to later biographies published in the *Brooklyn Daily Eagle*, Litchfield's friends and business associates shook their heads at his foolishly extensive purchases—especially of empty lands whose future value was mere speculation. Most predicted that his hard-earned fortune would be "sunk here, before he could convert this wild upland and swampy meadow into paying property."

But Litchfield ignored their pessimism and pressed on, with the faith that the future of Brooklyn would "some day return a magnificent reward to the owner and investor." By the time of Litchfield's land purchases there was no singular effort to build the canal by the neighboring Gowanus proprietors—only the spot construction of rudimentary wharves and walls that were mostly unstable. Yet the arriviste Brooklynite had big plans, taking priority over canal construction: a great mansion fit for a feudal baron.[9]

Unlike Daniel Richards, who achieved his success via scrappy charisma, Edwin C. Litchfield found his fortune by virtue of his education and meticulous work ethic. Since youth he was especially studious, possessing grueling, Protestant principles likely passed down through six generations of god-fearing Anglo-Saxon American heritage. The scion of a large extended clan of Litchfields, he descended from a settler named Lawrence who arrived in 1634, probably from Kent, to found the town of Scituate, Massachusetts, with some original Mayflower stock from Plymouth (Litchfield remains a popular name in Scituate to this day). Lawrence's progeny spread through New England to Connecticut, and eventually Upstate New York; his ancestry can be traced back to fourteenth-century England.

Edwin, born on January 21, 1815, in Delphi Falls, New York, was the third of five brothers—after Electus and Elisha were the younger Erasmus Darwin and Egbert Delos (the former was simply called "Darwin" by the family, while Egbert died as a toddler). Despite condemning his children to a lifetime of misaddressed mail (the brothers were often confused in newspapers), the elder Litchfield patriarch, also called Elisha, was quite an example to follow. He rose from carpenter to mercantile businessman and eventually to officer in the War of 1812. When Edwin was two years old, Elisha was made the postmaster of Cazenovia, which led to a seat in the New York State Assembly (he was Speaker of the House in 1848) and eventually two terms in Congress. His first wife and mother to Edwin, Percy Tiffany, died in 1827. Elisha later married Lucy Savage Bacon, and together they produced four more children bearing their father's preferred naming scheme: Eliza Adeline, Emma Lucy, Edward Everett, and a second Egbert.

As an adolescent Edwin attended the Cazenovia Seminary—he was valedictorian of his class—and spent his free time on religion. Like so many young men of his generation in Upstate New York, he was swept up in the fervor of revivalist Christianity. While living in Delphi Falls, he attended nightly prayer meetings with his older brother Electus, at which he and the other "Dear Converts" would "sing and praise the Lord" and discuss the power of faith "in our own simple language."

"I feel it is a privilege that I have a friend that can I can communicate with," Edwin wrote to Electus, his closest brother, while studying at Hamilton College in 1831, "as both of us hope we have an interest in Christ." Ever the perfectionist with his younger siblings, he insisted that Electus help instruct the younger Erasmus Darwin in proper grammar and orthography, and push the oldest, Elisha, to repent from his meandering spiritual path. "Tell him to go to Christ, to trust in him, and commit his soul unto the hands of his maker," Edwin instructed. Years later, in Brooklyn, he would regularly worship in the Strong Place Baptist Church. The enterprising and precocious Litchfield graduated in 1832 with a bachelor's degree at only seventeen. By twenty he was practicing law in Albany. Standing just five feet eight inches tall with piercing blue eyes and a prominent nose, Litchfield spoke with the great confidence. He assumed the poise of those with pride in their pedigree and abilities. Litchfield was also fiscally conscious to a fault—even as a teenager he kept careful records of his possessions with a Protestant sense of entitlement. Well before he struck it rich as an adult, Litchfield kept strict notation of his worldly possessions that bordered on the obsessive.[10]

"You probably know that I have laid out but little expense as yet upon a room having purchased nothing but 2 chairs, shovel & tongs," he wrote to Electus from Hamilton College in 1831. "It will be necessary for me to get some things to write—table, desk, looking glass, &c&c. The first of these I have purchased of Brown for 15. I can get a desk in the village for $2 or $3, which I shall do unless I have contrary orders." Litchfield's passion for bulleted lists marks a great deal of his correspondence, which almost always pertained to the extensive business dealings that consumed his adult life. He found the time to court and marry Grace Hill Hubbard in 1841, herself the scion of a well-to-do Utica family (the partnership was successful for both sides, since Erasmus Darwin married Mary Smith Hubbard, Grace's sister, two years later). The father of these women, Thomas Hill Hubbard, was a Yale graduate and a founder of Hamilton College, Litchfield's alma mater.[11]

Grace Hill and the Rise of the Litchfields

In America of the mid-nineteenth century, wealth, like class and prestige, was not usually earned, but inherited. But Litchfield was a phenom, having created a small empire in one of the most successful new industries across the continent. He likely inherited the ambition of his father, who had socially elevated his name from humble beginnings to a respected congressman. Having achieved the necessary wealth to advance past his father's success, Edwin C. Litchfield's midlife project was to reinvent himself as a model of New World gentry. Being educated and enjoying intimate ties to state politics likely aided his plans, but neatly wrapping up the package was the obligatory Anglo-Saxon heritage, a genealogy stretching back to the earliest Puritan settlers of America and beyond. In buying the Gowanus property Litchfield hoped to secure the Yankee equivalent of an English-style landed estate: a manor house with a sprawling view across the valleys of Brooklyn, the lands producing a steady and impressive income for the lord and his progeny. But instead of agriculture, Litchfield would harvest American commerce and industry. His choice vista stretched well past the Gowanus, across the bay crowded with the masts of sailing vessels, steamship exhaust, tugs, and canal boats headed to and from New York. Looking down on all of this, the Litchfield Villa would be the crowning glory of a stature comparable to few in nineteenth-century America.

In 1853 only a few of original colonial roads led east of the Gowanus Creek, but Litchfield had already decided where his house would stand: atop the highest hill of the Prospect Range, on the edge of the former Cortelyou plantation. This locale was carefully thought out: the hills were the ideal location for a home with an impressive view of all of Brooklyn and New York City, including one of the oldest standing structures in Kings County. Beyond its age, the role of the Old Stone House during the Revolution forged a living historic link to America's foundation and one of earliest settlements in Brooklyn—most likely a point of pride for Litchfield.

Such choices of a detail-obsessed, calculating businessman were not made for immediate fiscal success. No matter that there was no conceivable method of making income from the near square mile of empty, swamp-ridden land. Litchfield was building a legacy that extended into politics and public life, which required careful planning and time. To build an imposing and fashionable residence to impress and entertain his moneyed peers, Litchfield turned to Alexander J. Davis, a celebrated architect in the prime of his career. Davis was most famous for his design of Lyndhurst, the sprawling Gothic Revival country house in Tarrytown, New York, built for former New York mayor William Paulding Jr. The mansion inspired a series of designs later dubbed Hudson River Gothic and would eventually be home to railroad mogul Jay Gould. Davis also conceived the neoclassical US Customs House on Wall Street in 1842, now known as Federal Hall National Memorial. But most relevant to Litchfield's desire for status was the fact that Davis's design of Winyah Hall, an Italianate-style villa in New Rochelle, had won first prize for architecture at the 1851 World's Fair in New York.[12]

Davis's early plans for the Litchfield Villa in 1853 included both Gothic and Italianate versions, but the latter style won out. Grace Hill, as the family called their dwelling in honor of Litchfield's wife, was to measure around five thousand square feet and sit 126 feet above sea level at the top of the Prospect Hills, between Third and Sixth Streets at the western side of Ninth Avenue (today's Prospect Park West). A stately entranceway would sit at the foot of a sixty-foot-tall square tower rising in contrast by a broader and shorter tower, much like Winyah Hall. Two statues of hunting hounds, seated on their haunches, would guard the entranceway. Although the house would eventually be filled with extensive statuary, these two dogs would be Litchfield's favorite on the whole estate. On either side of this impressive centerpiece would be two wings furnished with battlements, as well as "broad, luxurious piazzas and balconies and roof gardens."

Inside, intricate wood moldings and soaring plaster ceilings dominated the eye, naturally lit with skylights. Stained glass windows were installed in the upper stories—rare examples of pre–Civil War glasswork that survive to this day. There was no ballroom, but there was a game room and a theater. The dining room, library, and parlor rooms, all for entertaining guests, were decorated with intricate ceiling frescoes and sumptuous gilded cornices. From the grand bay windows were views of the whole of Brooklyn and beyond, New York Harbor. In the distance belched the smokestacks of Manhattan, monuments of nineteenth-century American progress. The bathrooms boasted hand-painted porcelain sinks, at least one of which survives to the present. His intention was to make Grace Hill a center of social life for Brooklyn and New York elite. After a year of planning, work commenced in June 1855.

"If you will call at my office at 12 noon today," Litchfield wrote to Davis in October of that year, "I will go with you to Brooklyn." This was likely their last in-person meeting before the villa was finished, as the following month the entire Litchfield clan embarked on a European tour. For the next two years, the railroad mogul kept close and regular correspondence with Davis from the major European capitals, discussing the details of individual room designs and material costs in meticulous, bullet-pointed letters.

"I am satisfied from your description to me that the white Canada marble mantelpiece—with cubic figures about 3 feet high—well sculptured for $550, may be bought for the parlor," Litchfield instructed from Paris in one of six finicky letters to Davis scrawled in hasty cursive, preserved today at the Avery Library of Architecture at Columbia University. "I await to hear from you what kind you find in New York suitable for Library & for Dining room and the prices. Please write me on this point as soon as may be that I hear from your letter before I get to Italy."[13]

While travelling Europe Litchfield bought furniture, statues, and sculptural marble accents—anything to suit the baronial atmosphere he wished to create. The surrounding landscape was to be as sumptuous as the house itself—Litchfield reportedly spent another $300,000 on landscaping and outdoor construction. Oak, cedar, fir, and elms trees already surrounded the property, while gardens and miniature groves were planted for pleasant walks and entertaining guests. Retaining the sensibility of a country home, there would be vegetable gardens and greenhouses filled with exotic plants, stables for horses and a coach house, a keeper's lodge, and even chicken coops and lodging for cows. No detail seems to have escaped Litchfield's eye, as he micromanaged Davis from Paris.

"And it is worth considering whether cows, chickens &c should not be provided for on the other side of the street. What think you?" he wrote to Davis in the summer of 1857. "Will there be danger of the chickens getting into the garden if kept close by? And will the cows (from their vicinity to the elevation where we desire to put the summer home) cause an offensive smell? I mainly suggest these points for consideration."[14]

Grace Hill was finished in October of that year, representing the height of Gilded Age opulence. A marble terrace hugged the exterior terracotta walls, while the finished interior boasted some thirty chambers, including a ground-floor bedroom for Mrs. Litchfield, who became disabled toward the end of the construction of the villa and could not walk, or barely so (one of the few available scraps of information on Grace Hill Litchfield is that she was "invalid").

Blue and white Minton encaustic tiles were imported from England to line the ground floor entry hall. This was another example of Litchfield's expressly American method of paying his way up the social ladder: Minton's was the leading English firm for such decorative finishes, a pinnacle of Victorian taste (while Grace Hill was being lined with Minton tiles, so was the floor the US Capitol in Washington, D.C.—most of the original ceramic flooring in both of these buildings survives today). Branching off of the main hallway, pilasters and columns with rococo finishes encircled the main drawing room—called the Gold Room—to form a colonnade terminating at grand bay windows. Gilded furniture formed an oval in the center of the room, encircling a white marble copy of *Dying Gaul* (a treasured statue in the annals of Roman antiquities). Suspended above it was a frosted and etched crystal chandelier.[15]

Perhaps the most unusual feature in Grace Hill was the second floor chamber with a high copula, covered by sliding doors that, once moved, revealed a hidden stage destined for private theatrical and musical performances. A door with a ticket window still sits at the entrance of this room. According to the *Eagle*, Litchfield's sons "Edward and his little brother [Henry], delighted in playing ghost to the fright of the uninitiated and timorous guest." The topmost floor mostly fell under the reign of servants, although the children's nursery was there and was hardly immune to Edward's mischief: In 1861 he carved a figure of a man wearing a suit and broad hat, marking E.H.L., his initials, and the year into the glass doors leading onto a small balcony. The window with the scratches remains, nonchalantly, in a room doubling as shabby office and storage space for the New York City Parks Department.[16]

The Litchfield Villa is Brooklyn's monument to the sumptuous character of the Gilded Age. It began with the mania of railroad construction, followed by an explosion of nationwide grain exports to more than $300 million a year, following Britain's repeal of its restrictive Corn Laws. Then the Crimean War, starting in 1854, cut off wheat supplies from the Ukraine and Poland—Europe's "breadbasket"—leading to even more American food exports. The war ended only two years later, but prices had inflated and midwestern farmers made grand investments in equipment and land to maximize production. The California Gold Rush also brought more currency to the American market, which helped stoke the railroad boom across the country.

Rail stocks became glamorous commodities, not just for Americans, but for foreign investors in Paris, London, and Amsterdam.

Doubtless, Litchfield's European tour had several goals: As a newly gilded American patriarch, the railroad mogul had a family to educate on the fineries of upper-class life. He was also searching to augment his cultural currency back in New York, furnishing his home with grandest touches of aristocratic European taste. Undoubtedly, he was also courting hopeful investors from that same echelon. Much like the construction of Grace Hill, on the Continent the railroad mogul was building a legacy. Despite the heavy expenditures on the house and grounds—a total of some $500,000, an enormous amount in pre–Civil War America—Litchfield was more concerned with the appearance of his building materials than their authenticity. In a sneering tone just a few years after his death, the *Eagle* called Litchfield's forty-year-old castle a "sham" because the faux iron doors were "just ordinary wood with wooden bolt heads and artistic paint." The exterior walls were "masquerading in brown stone mastic," since they were brick covered in stucco fashioned to look like brownstone.

As if Litchfield were not busy enough with his house, midwestern railroads, or European tours, he found the time to begin sowing his urban crop. Beginning in 1853, he graded and paved several city-mapped streets on his empty meadows using entirely his own money. Flushed with cash, the railroad mogul was spending with great abandon on roads what others did on stock trading or luxury goods. The first and most important was Third Street: up to that point there were no streets running the length of the Gowanus meadows that would connect his newly developing neighborhood to the rest of South Brooklyn.

Litchfield envisioned a picturesque road leading from the heart of South Brooklyn that crossed over the Gowanus Canal into a bustling warehouse and manufacturing district at Third Avenue. Climbing up the now smoothed-out slope, Third Street would widen at Fifth Avenue into the central commercial thoroughfare of his imagined estate, lined with stone buildings and upscale storefronts. It was not just a matter of pride, but a key piece of real estate success. Without decent transportation access, the Gowanus meadows would remain effectively worthless.

Although the Litchfield brothers' business offices were at 18 Williams Street in Manhattan—across from the celebrated restaurant Delmonico's (letters addressed to him sometimes indicated this fact to ensure their delivery)—Edwin's plan was to open a central Brooklyn location right at the crossroads of his projected village at the corner of Third Street and Fifth Avenue. Moving eastward, the street would give way to rows of impressive stone apartments, their value rising with the altitude. It would finally terminate, conveniently, at the entrance to his finished villa. To build a sturdy road from South Brooklyn, however, posed an engineering challenge. The elevation dropped significantly as the waterlogged meadows bowed toward the nascent Gowanus Canal. Once across the naturally occurring border, the grade of the land would still have to be elevated at least twenty feet above its actual level to keep a manageable slope—horses could be expected to fight gravity only so much.

Such a huge project was estimated to cost at least a quarter million dollars, along property that produced no income but was consuming itself in property taxes. Even a millionaire like Litchfield had balked at the expense—a true businessman obviously would not spend more of his own money building a public street than his own mansion, no matter how much perceived return. Thus, throughout the 1850s and nearly half a decade further, Third Street halted abruptly at the west side of Fifth Avenue. Envisioning more lots to develop and sell, Litchfield had improved other streets on his own dime: First Street up to Ninth Avenue, Fourth Street up to Eighth Avenue, and a small section of Second Street; he even raised the grade of Fourth Avenue across his properties from First to Ninth Streets.

In tandem with other surrounding landowners, the historic hills of the Battle of Brooklyn were cut down in the uplands, the resulting tons of earth used to fill in the lower-lying areas. Along with the construction of Grace Hill, the Gowanus landscape of the modern day finally began to take shape. The engineering prowess and will of nineteenth-century capitalism literally carved the landscape evenly to meet its needs, with the pick and hammer in Litchfield's hands. Between his land purchases, mansion, and early Brooklyn improvements, Litchfield had spent the previous decade shelling out nearly a million dollars, earned from the ballooning railroad economy. Then, as if perfectly timed to test his will, the greatest financial crisis in the history of the modern world erupted. It was three months before he was to move in to Grace Hill—the cement holding up the costly marble fixtures had barely dried. But a combination of rampant American speculation and a decline in European trade caused the great market crash, known as the Panic of 1857.

Litchfield had hardly been alone in his exploitation of the soaring economy—scores of American developers and investors had spent the 1850s cashing in on their good fortune. As the economy ballooned to untold heights in the middle of the decade, certain Wall Street investors began to feel anxious. One of these was Leonard Jerome, a wealthy Wall Street financier from an old New York family best remembered for siring Winston Churchill's mother, Jennie Jerome. The financier became increasingly opposed to the expanding bull market, and believed that the ballooning economy was unsustainable and unhealthy—that or he was trying to shift the favor of the markets so he could exploit the results. Either way, he started to correspond with John Bigelow, the owner of the *New York Evening Post* and an early adopter of the nascent Republican Party. Jerome fed Bigelow insider information, which led to the scathing and now-famous editorial, "A Growing Evil—Overspeculation." Published during the spring preceding the Panic, the piece criticized the supposedly "honest men" like lawyers and merchants for abandoning their careers to engage in the unsustainable hubbub on Wall Street.

Next, Jerome's pursued the ear of James Gordon Bennett, publisher of the *New York Herald*. By June, Bennett's paper became the pied piper of bearish investment, printing a series of homiletic editorials informed by Jerome's insider information. Bennett's essays condemned those benefitting from the bloated markets, and he pointed specifically at the Litchfields' Michigan Southern Railroad as a leading perpetrator. Adding to the intrigue, it appears that the *Herald* columns usually implicated "culprit" investors whose stocks Jerome had recently sold short. Whether the editorials were meant as benevolent advice or a highly dramatic investment scheme, the bear market champions persisted as signs of collapse loomed.

"Government spoliations, public defaulters, paper bubbles of all descriptions, a general scramble of western lands and town and city sites, millions of dollars, made or borrowed, expended in fine houses and gaudy furniture . . . are only a few among the many crying evils of the day," Bennet wrote in a June 27 editorial, as though pointing a finger at the Litchfields. Less than a month later, Edwin resigned as president of the Michigan Central, "in order to spend more time on personal matters." Soon the stock, of which Litchfield held a major stake, plunged along with the rest of the New York market. Four days later, Bennett smugly predicted that most major American railroads would be bankrupt before the next decade.[17]

Along with business stocks, commodity prices took a nosedive, setting the country into a full panic. Grain spiraled downward to a quarter of its original value—a heavy blow to Brooklyn's trade. Many of Litchfield's colleagues, who had also purchased Brooklyn land, dumped their holdings at a loss. Some predicted "louder than ever the ruin of their friend Litchfield." But despite the fear and confusion that ran through Wall Street and beyond, the now former railroad president would not budge. Perhaps to express his unmovable faith in Brooklyn's value, Litchfield refused to part with a single square inch of his real estate dream. Many spooked investors tried to rein in whatever cash they could, and "predicted louder than ever the ruin of their friend Litchfield," but he preferred to bide his time and endure the paper losses. This period of introspection possibly forced the de-

A portrait of Edwin C. Litchfield, undated. Author's personal collection.

posed mogul's attention toward something he could still control, the Gowanus lands.

Whatever his thinking, instead of backing down, Litchfield sold shares in practically every security he owned except for his greatest railroad holdings (he believed that transportation was bound to bounce back) to cover the taxes and expenses of his Brooklyn projects. The Panic and other crises would postpone major development for years, but they also refocused his attention. Litchfield and his brother Electus were not the types to so easily shed equity. The collapse of their young railroad plans had an important result: it turned their attention back toward the development of their adopted city.[18]

The Shanties of Gowanus

One April morning in 1856, a pair of horse-drawn carriages pulled away from the New York city inspector's office, heading to the Brooklyn ferry landing. In one carriage, a cadre of journalists from various local papers sat as they rumbled along the cobbled streets.

One was a reporter for the *New York Daily Times*, a rising star among the local broadsheets. Approaching its fifth year of publication, the newspaper would soon drop the "*Daily*" from its title. In the other carriage sat some members of the Tenement Committee of New York; all were bound for the notorious slums and shantytowns of the growing city across the East River. After safely crossing, they disembarked at the Fulton landing and walked to a brief visit at Brooklyn's City Hall. They continued south toward their first stop, a small cluster of huts squatting the western banks of the nascent Gowanus Canal—barely a mile away from Litchfield's sumptuous castle on Grace Hill.

Known as Darby's Patch, it was a miserable place where, at high tide, the Gowanus waters lapped at the doorways of the one-story, single-room shanties. Even worse, the area had just received rain, and one of the residents—almost all Irish immigrants—recalled to the journalists that they had stood on their beds and tables as the waters rushed over their packed-dirt floors. Pressing on from Darby's Patch, these Manhattan men—possibly dressed in three-piece suits, adorned with pocket watches and shiny cufflinks—headed south to their second stop, Gowanus Beach. This site by Hamilton Avenue and the creek had about sixty shacks, clustered together with no planning or logic, and no room for an open square of any kind, greater and more chaotic than Darby's Patch. The shacks were built on lots rented for twenty dollars a year from a Brooklyn landowner named Mr. Wood. At Gowanus Beach the reporters found a local woman whose furniture and floors were still wet with floodwaters.

But none of these slums compared to Tinkersville, a site named for those traditional wandering Irish metalworkers and utensil-menders who settled within its bounds. It was largest of these infamous Gowanus slums, sprawling toward Columbia Street and brushing the northeastern corner of the Atlantic Docks in Red Hook. Crisscrossed with "narrow and serpentine" lanes populated by slovenly drunks, Tinkersville had rickety shacks built of "likely stolen" wooden boards, according to the *Daily Times*. They formed a squat and uneven skyline, interrupted by stalls overflowing with the stink and din of cows and hogs.

Some of these poor shantytown Irish worked as street peddlers hawking "pure country milk" to the genteel populace of Brooklyn—but it was really drawn from sickly slum cows who grazed upon "swill from an adjoining distillery," as the *Daily Times* reporter exclaimed. "Even upon the Heights," higher-class Brooklynites believed they were "relishing the luscious draughts of the genuine Orange-County beverage."

There is something amusing about the idea of Gowanus cows, sustained on factory-derived slop, fulfilling the dairy needs of Brooklynites during this transitional period in the city's history. It would be another century and a half before supermarkets used buzzwords like "free range" and "locally sourced" to attract mindful urban consumers. Today, locally sourced Gowanus Milk would possibly do quite well in the local supermarkets of Brooklyn.[19]

Before Tinkersville was known by this colorful name, it was called Dowd's Island and "situated at the foot of Hicks Street, in Gowanus Inlet." Less of an island and more of a low hill surrounded by flooded salt marshes, the wretched spot was supposedly settled by Dowd, a tinker, around 1838. He dug a well and set up a shanty. Hearing of this settlement by word of mouth, other Manhattan "tinks"—as the nomadic men were also called—soon came to set up camp, and "tramped by day shouting out: 'Any kittles to mind'" ("any kettles to mend" in a stereotypical Irish brogue). The Penny Bridge at Hamilton Avenue, so called for the cost of its toll, was a sort of "annex" to the watery space. Dowd's Island was also a choice locale for catching wild ducks and snipe, and many a sportsman would come to these wetlands with bags in which to snag the fowl, if they were quick enough. For the less agile, the Gowanus Bay and Red Hook provided excellent sustenance. "As for fishing in the waters that surrounded the island and in Gingermill Creek, which ran from the foot of Columbia street into the bay, it could not be excelled," the *Eagle* wrote in 1888. "While mussels, clams and natural born oysters were so abundant that visitors looked upon those shell fish with contempt."[20]

Only after the "march of improvement filled up the watery waste and joined it to the main land" did Dowd's Island become Tinkersville. Once the Hamilton Avenue ferry arrived in Red Hook, many a stagecoach "did a thriving business" by picking up passengers arriving from Manhattan. But between the fishing and game and likely cheap booze, early Tinkersville was a leisure destination for Brooklyn's Irish. In his early life, Ned Harrigan—of the Vaudevillian stage duo "Harrigan and Hart," a defining and dominating act in early American musical theater—spent many an hour on Dowd's Island, when he wasn't toiling as a ship caulker.

"It was a fashion in those days and considered excellent sport for a downtowner," explained the *Eagle*, "who, being belated, after a day's fishing and seeing no boats handy, to seize on a fat swine and straddle the brute, who, to get rid of its rider and tormentor, always took to the water and swam for the main land, carrying its human cargo on its back. . . . It was a queer settlement, and the people who settled in that locality were more than queer."[21]

In 1845, Ireland's Great Famine pushed the most ambitious and desperate of peasants to seek a sustainable life in America. Following this, in 1848 a number of European revolutions were staged—known as the Spring of Nations, the agitation began in France, spreading to Germany, Poland, the Austrian Empire, and several other states—most of which failed. Further idealist farmers from the Young Irelander Rebellion were drawn to America, as were the middle-class German farmers and businessmen who had sought greater liberty and democracy in their native lands with disappointing results. For each of these groups, the United States held a special appeal. In 1850, more than 100,000 Irish immigrated to the New World, closely followed by 78,000 Germans. The following year, the number of Irish immigrants exploded to 221,000.[22]

The Gowanus slums peppering the southern districts of Brooklyn sprang from need. Jobs were abound for construction projects like the Atlantic Docks, and now the new residential and commercial districts south of Atlantic Street—including the Gowanus Canal waterfront. To live within walking distance of such jobs was the only option for poor laborers with no other mode of transport, and a guarantee of attendance for their employers. As always, where people slept greatly suggested class status—the wealthiest citizens lived in Brooklyn Heights, as the *Times* reporter insinuated above, and the poorest lived in backwaters like Gowanus and Tinkersville. Up until the early 1850s, small settlements like Darby's Patch dotted Gowanus Creek. Likely the dirtier, denser slums grew as developers took over the previously empty lands: According to the *Eagle*, only when Bond Street, which runs mostly parallel to the west bank of the canal, was graded and paved in 1851 were the "swarms of disreputable shanties" forced to clear off, their places "now occupied by substantial brick dwellings and an entirely different class of population."[23]

This largest immigrant group—with their particular modes of speech and Catholic customs, resided in similar Brooklyn enclaves with names like Irishtown, Kelsey's Alley, Slab City, and Young Dublin. They butted heads with the older cultural mainlines of Brooklyn, creating visible class divisions and a new layer of diversity. Certainly, the presence of the new Irish population bolstered Brooklyn's economic clout, but their great numbers also influenced the city's culture and politics. The Brooklyn *Advertiser*, the bombastic voice of the Whig Party in the growing city, displayed this frustration in 1852 by pointing a finger at local voters who would dare help elect for president the likes of Democrats such as James K. Polk or Franklin Pierce.

The Irish slums were "delightful retreats contain[ing] Pierce's constituents," the *Advertiser* claimed. "These are the scourings of other countries, who are totally ignorant of the principles upon which this republic derives her support."[24]

Part of the resentment was the power of immigrant politics. The highly established Whigs, and other conservative parties, were frustrated that a massive and arguably foreign population had summoned a singular voting advantage. But it was their own doing. Catholic immigrants were pushed toward the Democratic Party, not out of political leanings but because of many Protestant antagonists who were openly hostile to the newcomers—particularly, the nativist Know Nothing Party. According to this broad political movement of the mid-nineteenth century, Catholics, particularly the Irish, were infiltrating and poisoning the culture of America with their infidel religion. Politicians and Protestant religious leaders called for a more lengthy naturalization process to stymie the onslaught of Democratic votes. Class discomfort is a function of urban life in America, particularly in the New York City area. Unending immigration to this global crossroad remains. Even in Brooklyn during the nineteenth century, the population density made it hard to ignore the variety of cultures and all the issues such changes created.[25]

The Bond Street Sewer

At a Common Council meeting in late October 1856, Alderman Van Brunt offered a report in favor of allowing the sewer on Bond Street to drain into Gowanus Creek. This was the same culvert that sat at the end of Bond Street, but it had been backing up and was becoming a major nuisance—likely because the waters, tainted with effluvia from chamber pots and local cesspools, were collecting into stagnant pools on private land. The body voted to refer the matter to legal counsel to determine if the city had the right to do so.[26]

Modern sewerage was a dire need as the volume of waste increased along with the population. Previously, a system of cesspools served the city's disposal needs—alternately, there was the river or Gowanus Creek. But this was the industrial era, and working Americans and their modern cities deserved working sewers. Facing the mounting complaints of flooding across the city, the Water Board was upgraded into the Sewage Commission in the spring of 1857—one of the first public works group organized in the city of Brooklyn. A similar conversation among officials and engineers had been happening in major cities across the country. Boston had some rudimentary underground pipe system from the eighteenth century, but it needed improvements, and New York had been considering a more comprehensive plan since 1855. Philadelphia's chief engineer had just formally demanded a much more organized system.

The commission's first order of business was to hire talented railroad engineer Julius W. Adams to design a comprehensive sewerage plan. He spent the summer surveying some twenty-odd miles of eligible streets and drains. Perhaps a thrilling piece of civic history, the proposal Adams handed to the Brooklyn commission was the first design of a large-scale urban sewer system in the country. Chicago also lays a claim to this honor, but knowledge of Adams's work in Brooklyn was far wider spread among engineers. More than twenty years later, he authored a treatise, "Sewer and Drains for the Populous Districts," in which he quotes liberally from the original Brooklyn report. It became required reading for sewer engineers well into the twentieth century, and so thanks to this assignment historians remember Adams as a pioneer of modern-day American engineering.[27]

According to Adams's 1880 opus, simple drainage systems tend to grow around whatever naturally occurring streams can be found in small towns—a logical place to send unwanted rainwater. As population increases, the local authorities will usually deepen and then cover some part the local stream. Eventually more channels are dug, leading into the naturally conceived drain. This sort of "organic" system had developed in Brooklyn at various points around the Gowanus Creek, as Adams had surely observed during his time. But Adams's plans greatly expanded upon these extant systems, informed by his extensive surveys and experience with railroad engineering. In addition to water runoff, they were also designed to remove household waste. One of the quirks of his Brooklyn design was the use of a "combined" sewer, that is, one in which storm water runoff is collected in the same pipes as household sewage. In such a scheme, the offending contents would ultimately be shunted away via a long pipe to a sewer exit far from people's homes, ideally into a body of saltwater (rudimentary filtration systems existed at the time, but they were not terribly efficient or widely used). In consideration of how drainage grew in most settlements, the combined sewer was a matter of convention and convenience as compared to a "separate" system, with household and other waste lines running in separate pipes parallel to the street runoff. Some of Adams's engineering contemporaries felt that it was unwise to allow rainfall to flow off with raw sewage, but in his writings he dismissed this theory as "most impractical." The cost of a building separate system from scratch would be enormous, he believed, as it required twice the amount of drains in every building and pipes under every street. Citing London as an example—in 1857, the center of the industrialized world boasted the most sophisticated, large-scale sewers—Adams estimated that if the British government had created a dual-pipe system, it would have cost that city around twelve million dollars (several billion today). Hearing this estimate, Brooklyn's Sewer Commission, working with a limited budget, heartily agreed with Adams. The city would have a combined system with pipes leading into the East River at the foot of Wolcott Street, in Red Hook.[28]

There was another consideration Adams had to take into account: storm surges. The Northeast is known for short bursts of heavy rain—two or three inches in an hour—the kind that overwhelms a sewer system beyond its capacity. In these worst cases, the mixed contents of these pipes would back up into homes or overflow onto the streets. Before the advent of Brooklyn's drains, the marshlands of the Gowanus, the Wallabout, and Red Hook absorbed extreme floodwaters. But as the city became increasingly paved over, less open land was available to absorb the rain. As Adams wrote in 1880, even an expanded system could not be depended on to deal with the pesky upshot of unpredictable, high volume weather: "No system of sewage yet proposed in any city contemplates the removal of excessive storm-waters by means of the sewers . . . whilst the construction of sewers to meet the contingency would be attended with an enormous expense over the whole city, with in construction and repair, and prove of doubtful efficiency when suddenly called upon."[29] Still, there had to be an emergency outlet for truly massive storm runoff, and at best it would empty into a naturally occurring body of water. Adhering to these principles, Adams's plans called for this combined system to be connected to the easiest available exit: the Gowanus storm drains. During only the heaviest storms was the canal expected to absorb the overflow of combined sewage and rain. Just before the winter of 1860, the new Office of Sewer Commissioners announced that the new state-of-the-art system would finally open to serve that growing portion of the city by discarding waste and further draining the meadows.[30]

In hindsight, Adams's later success seems ironic: uniting the drains and sewers set quite a nasty precedent for cities—especially Brooklyn, and particularly at the Gowanus, which suffers from "combined sewage overflow" to the present day. We do know that these sewers were entirely too small because he readily acknowledged this fact and repeated it "as proof of the need of better knowledge of fundamental principles of design than he possessed in 1857." Plenty of circumstantial evidence suggests that observing the Gowanus area, and particularly the Bond Street sewer, influenced Adams's early template for the modern American sewer. The irksome proto-drain was often deemed responsible for area floods, and seems to have been a point of reference for Adams as he surveyed the Brooklyn landscape. Its legacy of never quite working correctly is a comedy of errors for Brooklyn[31]

Eventually the complaints grew so loud that the mayor requested the extension of the sewer directly into the creek. We know for certain that this connection was made, thanks to a dispute over the payment for its contractor, James McFarland, in the late summer of 1857. McFarland was promised $830 to lengthen the Bond Street sewer, work that the contractor said he faithfully completed. However because the contractor had not obtained a proper certificate, signed by the mayor and several higher authorities (as required by the Brooklyn City Charter), the city comptroller refused to release the funds. Not one to be slighted, McFarland turned to the local courts for justice and, with the power of Deputy Sheriff Perry, obtained a levy on all of the furniture in Brooklyn's City Hall for a sum of $882.

On the morning of September 24, Oakley and Wright, Sheriff's auctioneers, entered City Hall and proceeded to sell off the city's property, which drew quite a crowd. "Three desks, a safe, two closets, one case of drawer, a clock and a number of stools were successively sold at low prices" until the comptroller appeared with an edict from Judge Culver to temporarily halt the proceedings. Disappointed, the crowd slowly wandered away.[32]

Four years later, in March 1861, a man named Mr. Peters sued the city of Brooklyn for damages to his property in the vicinity of the Gowanus Creek—damages that echo through the Gowanus neighborhood today. It was Peters's fourth attempt to try the matter in court, and so the Law Committee of the Common Council brought it to the attention of the general audience of the legislature. Alderman Dayton, who knew nothing of the matter, suggested that they try to settle the matter with some kind of "advantageous arrangement," since it had to be "evident that a litigation so long pending could not be carried farther with any advantage to the city."

"If this case is tried," volunteered Alderman Green, "then I will again be called upon as witness. The damages were caused by the emptying of the Bond street sewer on the premises of plaintiff. The stench was so bad that it killed Mr. Peters' father-in-law, and injured the health of his wife. This property was valued at $5000, and is now so much injured from this cause, I would not take it as a present." Green then expounded the story, explaining that Peters had been unable to sell his property because of the sewage and ought to be compensated—although not "one cent more than he ought to have, but I would be for giving him that. If the claim was pressed against the city, the city would be beat."[33]

Mr. Peters's lawsuit is the first documented complaint of a foul stench arising from the Gowanus Canal and the nuisance of the Bond Street sewer. It would hardly be the last grievance, but this unfortunate side effect of progress marked a turning point in the identity of the canal toward a decidedly urban fate. This change was also visible in the increasing presence of poverty in the presence of wealth, another urban phenomenon: as the already-flooded Gowanus shanties were being inundated by raw sewage, less than a mile away Edwin Litchfield was moving into his opulent villa.

5

The Brooklyn Improvement Company (1858–1869)

One evening in October 1858, Egbert L. Viele, a civil engineer and veteran of the Mexican-American War, was as a dinner guest at Grace Hill. Standing at the grand bay windows in the dining room, Viele would have been able to see rolling hills, dotted with trees bursting with fall color. Past these unfurled an impressive vista of Brooklyn, then the grand bay teeming with ships and, in the distance, all of New York City. East of Litchfield's mansion lay a lush forest.

Barely a year had passed since the Litchfields had moved into their baronial Brooklyn villa, and everything was new. Gilded wall accents and polished mirrors sparkled with the flickering gaslight, sending shadows across the genteel European furniture in the sumptuous dining room, now set to host a grand dinner. Neoclassical marble statues by Hiram Powers, a famous Florence-based nineteenth-century American sculptor (his other well-to-do customers included several members of the Astor family), offset heavy furniture upholstered in satin and painted gold to match the wall accents. During his sojourn abroad Litchfield had become an avid art collector, finding a particular love for the austerity of Spanish baroque painters. He brought back original works by Velasquez and Murillo, hanging them in the dining and drawing rooms with the same meticulousness with which he conducted his business affairs. He had handpicked and positioned every adornment to lend character and class to his opulent castle.[1]

At his 1857 return Litchfield had launched a campaign with the Brooklyn Democratic Party and was nominated for a seat in Congress, in the second district—an attempt to follow in his father's footsteps. Doubtless Litchfield was full of pride—his was the grandest home in Brooklyn and an emerging nexus of elite social life. "These lands," Viele supposedly said, "would make an excellent park for Brooklyn."[2]

Previously the state engineer of New Jersey, Viele had just been named engineer-in-chief of a new project, called Central Park. It was a grand amenity that would change the city of New York forever, challenging the status quo of what one could do with urban space. Following years of land surveying and endless legislation, by 1858

"View of Site Chosen for Prospect Park." From the "First Annual Report of the Commissioners of Prospect Park" (1861).

the landscape architects Frederick Law Olmstead and Calvert Vaux had won a contest to design Central Park. Viele had been hired to carry out their wishes. At the time, such large-scale urban amenities were a favorite topic of conversation in the city across the river. The newspapers and power brokers of Manhattan had been preoccupied with the creation of a monumental public park befitting their expanding metropolis for much of the past decade. Before the Panic of 1857, waves of commercial success filled the city's coffers as it reached the stature of proper world capitals, like London or Paris. Each of these possessed emerald jewels of leisure like Hyde Park or the Bois de Boulogne; New York could not settle for less.

Not to be outdone by its elder sibling, Brooklyn followed suit. As was often the case, Brooklyn's stakeholders took a hint from the schemes transpiring across the river. Litchfield was clearly enthused

by the idea of a massive park in his backyard. Possibly, it was a welcome distraction for the businessman—he had lost the 1858 congressional election and then his father died in August 1859. There was surely a business connection in Litchfield's mind—even it its conceptual stages Central Park had encouraged major land speculation and development in Manhattan real estate. Other factors must have motivated the new magnate: the Panic of 1857 had drained the stocks of many overzealous investors, leaving even rich landholders like himself thirsting for liquidity. With Mount Prospect Park, the promising real estate tycoon had an opportunity to fill his coffers and increase the value of his holdings. Aside from quietly reeling from his losses of the past few years, Litchfield had another problem to address: what to do about Third Street. Within the unfinished road lay the unlocked potential for access and utility for his empty Gowanus marshlands. This park, he seems to have realized, could be the key.

As is often the case with New York real estate, it did not take too long for the local economy to rebound from the depths of depression. By 1859, New York and its environs were making a comeback, as was Litchfield, who had refused to jettison his railroad stocks. "Events justified his faith, and eventually the stocks he had retained went up, until what had been barely salable for one cent became worth one dollar or more, and trunk-fulls of paper, at one time scarce worth keeping as momentous of the past, became valuable and lucrative representatives of enormous values," the *Eagle* wrote admiringly. "The only effect of the depression of railroad securities in his case had been to postpone the period at which he could execute his projects for the improvement of his Brooklyn lands, but not to make him alter his intentions or despair of their ultimate fulfillment."[3]

One sign of a Brooklyn's economic recovery was the arrival of the Citizens' Gas-Light Company, a gas manufacturing plant. William P. Libby, owner and president, had purchased a big lot on the western shore of the Gowanus, bounded by Smith, Fourth, and Seventh Streets—near where Joseph Plumb Martin and other Revolutionary

War soldiers set up cannons to cover the final escape of the remaining Maryland 400. They broke ground in November 1859—it was likely the first modern industrial business to arrive on the nascent canal, such a big deal that even the *New York Times* covered it. "They will be the largest and most complete in the country, and by the 4th of July next the Company hope to be able to furnish 1,000,000 cubic feet of gas per day if necessary," the writer exclaimed. Gas delivery was a private business in the New York area, and companies like Citizens' Gas-Light did not operate simply to serve homeowners and small businesses. They sought big contracts, particularly for lighting public spaces. Brooklyn's growing grid needed streetlamps, and the company's future depended on the expansion of its biggest customer.[4]

Another sign of economic recovery following the depression was Litchfield's empowerment to seek legislation for his park. In the spring of 1860 the tycoon was stationed in Albany, as he wrote to a railroad colleague on April 6:

> I am a member of the third house of our State Legislature and shall be detained here yet for one or two weeks.
>
> I am giving attention to some local Bills—among others the city of Brooklyn & about establishing a large Park—in the immediate vicinity of my home. The bill has passed in one house and I think will pass the other, and if it becomes a law it will largely benefit my property: besides, the park will take $100,000 or $150,000 worth of my property which will have to be paid for by the city: so that, if this bill becomes a law, it will not be long before I can relieve you from any shivering on my account.[5]

The "third house of legislature" referenced by Litchfield was a somewhat cheeky euphemism for government lobbying. A successful businessman like Litchfield who enjoyed New York State political connections from both his father and father-in-law was perfectly suited to influence legislation. Less than two weeks later, on April 17, the legislature approved

Prospect Park. But there was another bill Litchfield had been particularly focused interested on: a new law that would create a special commission to improve the quality of Third Street in Brooklyn.

"Special commissions," as this type of semiautonomous civic body was dubbed, were groups of a half dozen or so influential politicians and businessmen with the initiative to lead necessary civic projects, armed with a healthy chunk of taxpayer-loaned capital to administer for the benefit of the whole city. The earliest example in Brooklyn was formed to create the city sewer system, an improvement nobody could argue with, and following that a commission was instituted to grade Hamilton Avenue from the canal to Third Avenue. That commission's work had been a windfall, improving access down at the bend of the old Gowanus neck and opening the road to New Utrecht and Yellow Hook for streetcars (although now people had taken to calling the latter "Bay Ridge," after yellow fever outbreaks gave the colorful word a bad association). Realizing the power of this new class of civic boon, Litchfield found the solution to his unfinished thoroughfare: such a grand amenity required an equally grand thoroughfare leading to it. In one trip to Albany, Litchfield secured the creation of a park that would increase the value of his property and with it a guaranteed and profitable sale of the undeveloped land. He had received the authority and budget, bequeathed by New York State, to oversee the construction of an entire road running from Smith Street in South Brooklyn, across and above the marshes, to his manor house on Ninth Avenue in the heights of Gowanus. Finally, his previously useless lots would have that basic and necessary access to create the genteel, multiuse neighborhood Litchfield envisioned.[6]

Following the passage of the park law, James S. T. Stranahan, millionaire owner of the Atlantic Docks, was named head commissioner. Stranahan, above all else, was terribly proud of Brooklyn and took his job very seriously. "While the great Central Park of New York, costing its millions of dollars, will, perhaps, in all time hold its superiority over any other which may be conceived or executed as a mere work of art," he began in the first report of the Parks Commission, "and while other cities may exhibit parks, ample in their extent and creditable for the good taste of their plans, the Prospect Park of the city of Brooklyn must always be conceded as the great natural park of the country; presenting the most majestic views of land and ocean, with panoramic changes more varied and beautiful than can be found within the boundaries of any city on this continent."[7]

The first hire of the Parks Commission was Egbert Viele as the chief engineer of the project. With Viele and Stranahan in his corner, Litchfield was virtually guaranteed influence over how this park would develop. With money raised through bonds, the city purchased great swaths of land from various owners, including several blocks of Litchfield's land at Tenth Avenue (and some lots owned by his brother Electus), stretching east and south to the border between the Brooklyn and Flatbush. In that first report, Viele proposed a park of rather obtuse design, bisected by Flatbush Avenue, but also with what appeared to be a large chunk removed: Starting at Ninth Avenue and Union Street, the park would run southward down to the corner of Litchfield's property at Third Street. The park would then take a sharp eastward turn, and then head southward to the corner of the proposed Tenth Avenue (which existed only on paper) and then south again, along the extreme edges of the Litchfield property, to the town line of Flatbush. "The primary object of the park [is] as a rural resort," expounded Viele in the report, "where the people of all classes, escaping from the glare, and glitter, and turmoil of the city, might find relief for the mind, and physical recreation." In Viele's design, Grace Hill's grounds composed a chunk of parkland that would remain private property, an ultimate privilege that no one else in Brooklyn would enjoy.[8]

Baseball and Ice Skates

While the Board of Aldermen voted to raise millions of dollars to manicure a park that resembled nature, the empty meadows of

Gowanus had served that purpose for locals, and not just for evening strolls: In 1855, an early amateur baseball club called the Brooklyn Excelsiors began to organize games on the empty meadows of the former Vecht plantation, then owned by Litchfield. They used the ancient stone house, still standing, as a clubhouse—often referring to it as "Washington's Headquarters," although the celebrated general never appears to have visited the structure. At this period, baseball was enjoying a mounting popularity across the country, but especially in New York, and even more so in South Brooklyn. Numerous clubs and amateur teams formed around various lots in this crèche of the development of America's favorite pastime.

The Excelsiors were a founding team of the National Association of Base Ball Players—the original governing body of the sport—although the Atlantics, Brooklyn's first professional team, would later eclipse them. Regular games were played as long as the fields weren't flooded, a frequent event at the Vecht plantation. During the winter, the ponds would freeze over for weeks at a time, but the cold hardly stifled a growing frenzy for outdoor recreation; soon enough, Brooklynites were ice-skating.

As with all popular fads in New York, this particular amenity begged to be monetized, and so in 1860 a budding entrepreneur named Oscar F. Oatman leased the frozen Vecht pond and house from Litchfield during the "useless" winter months. Under Oatman's auspices the colonial-era structure became the winter clubhouse for the Washington Skating Club, Brooklyn's first association of ice-skaters "of a first class character," as was advertised in the *Eagle*. Annual memberships cost a five dollars for men and included the right to two female guests at a time (additional female passes cost a dollar fifty). The pond was alternatively called Oatman's or Litchfield's Pond, but to most it was the Washington Pond. Excited to report on the sport, the *Eagle* followed the ice skating craze as it spread throughout Brooklyn. "Washington pond was flooded on Christmas Eve," the paper reported in 1861, "but the ice was unpleasantly rough from the effects of the recent snow." A pond on nearby Third Avenue was in the same poor condition: "A gentleman with two ladies fell through the ice and took their Christmas immersion without any material damage save a very decided shivering."[9]

Soon there were huge private skating ponds across Brooklyn, notably at Union Pond in Williamsburg (the town had been annexed by Brooklyn in 1855) and Capitoline Pond in the former village of Bedford. But thanks to Oatman's efforts, Washington Pond drew some of the biggest and most colorful crowds. He brought in bands to play popular music and organized carnivals and even elaborate ice masquerade balls: "Ten thousand people were attracted to the Washington pond on Monday, and what an odd scene it presented," the *Eagle* wrote after one such affair in February 1862. "Here is a fellow dressed as a Turk, skimming over the pond at a rate of a mile a minute. He dissipates all your previously conceived ideas of a Turk in an instant." Other gleeful skaters dressed as highway brigands and a dozen as stereotypical Irishmen, brandishing shillelaghs and bagpipes while gliding across the ice. Oatman soon brought ice sailboats and races to the pond, and the novelty was augmented further by backward and blindfolded races, some with hurdles and others with wheelbarrows. Skating lessons were advertised in the local dailies. Washington Pond became so popular that it had to be enlarged, then fenced in with the number of tickets severely limited.[10]

Most incredibly, the baseball fever that plagued Brooklyn during the summer soon extended to winter: local players replaced their cleats with skates and brought their game onto the ice of Washington Pond. The earliest recorded game of ice baseball in Brooklyn took place on February 4, 1861, between the Atlantics and the Charter Oaks, another local team. There were around twelve thousand shivering spectators in the crowd, which wrapped around Washington pond like a thick woolen scarf three people deep; women were outnumbered eight to one. According to the *Eagle* only a few players slipped and were brought "in connection with the ice," which was "a source of infinite merriment" to spectators. The Atlantics won, 36 to 27.[11]

The rules of ice baseball were essentially the same as for regular baseball but with certain concessions: there were only five innings and only ten players allowed on the field; the ball was painted bright red for greater visibility and was somewhat softer than a normal baseball. The bases were scratched into the ice, and players could overshoot them and still be safe, like with first base in a regular game. With different seasonal physics to work with, the best skaters soon grabbed the title of most valuable ice baseball players. While these ice sports proliferated all across the undeveloped lots of Brooklyn, so did Litchfield's development project, which ran right next to Washington Pond. With no railroad business to distract him, Litchfield was keenly focused on his Brooklyn holdings, and so the construction of Third Street began almost immediately after legislative approval. But yet again, national troubles would soon stifle big development in Brooklyn. Two months after the advent of ice baseball, the US Civil War broke out.

"The year 1861 was not a propitious year for carrying forward such improvements as are contemplated in the establishment of the Prospect Park," Stranahan wrote apologetically in that year's park report. "The commerce of the country suspended; the industry of the nation checked, and the hearts of the people crushed by a wicked attempt to destroy the benign government under which they lived and prospered, all public improvements became necessarily paralyzed."[12]

With the entire country at a loss for what to do, it seems fitting that the inanity of the ice baseball fad drew enormous crowds to every skating pond across Brooklyn. Perhaps surprisingly, the fad retained a steady fan base until the 1880s, but by 1865 the *Eagle* had grown impatient with the slapstick sport: "We hope we shall have no more ball games on ice," wrote one columnist, exasperatedly. "The ballplayers have their season and it is a long one; playing on skates is more tom foolery; it interferes with the rights of the ticket holders and creates dissatisfaction. . . . If any of the ball clubs want to make fools of themselves, let them go down to Coney Island and play a game on stilts."[13]

The Power of Special Commissions

As the end of the Civil War approached, construction in major cities gathered momentum. The improvements were certainly palpable in Gowanus: starting in 1864, Brooklynites no longer crossed the creek on a rickety wooden bridge, as Litchfield and his commission had constructed a modern iron pipe-truss bridge, suspended five feet above canal waters—the budget for this improvement was added much later, through a simple amendment to the state law. It boasted a modern swinging mechanism that rotated so masted ships could pass along the waterway, although only at high tide. A percussion of feet and horse-drawn streetcars soon led a symphony of urban growth as the Gowanus marshlands and hills became more accessible to the traffic of inner Brooklyn.

A short two years later, Litchfield finished construction on the first homes for sale on his gently sloping meadows: a block of twelve brownstone houses, three stories tall, including a basement and private yards, rising on Third Street directly east of Fifth Avenue. They were priced at around fifteen thousand each, aimed at an upper-middle-class market. A similar housing project sprouted on nearby Warren Street in 1866.

"These blocks, when completed," informed the *Eagle,* "will be worth over $400,000—quite an important increase in the taxable property of this city." As the final touches were added to his impressive brownstone facades, Litchfield—never resting—was busy incorporating a new business he hoped would become his magnum opus of real estate: the Brooklyn Improvement Company. Founded with the mission of developing his holdings along the Gowanus Canal, this corporation's first project was to build the private docks and wharves that would attract commerce and goods-laden barges to this corner of Brooklyn.[14]

The corporate directors included members of his family: his brothers Electus and Elisha, his brother-in-law Robert J. Hubbard, and his eldest son Edward—just twenty-one years old. The Brooklyn Improvement Company would be the vehicle by which Edwin inducted his son into the world of business. Other notable directors included Egbert Viele, now a decorated Civil War general, landowner Edward Fiske, and William P. Libby of Citizens' Gas-Light. After raising a hundred thousand dollars in stock sales, Litchfield assigned Brooklyn Improvement Company, or BIC, to manage the major tract of his land along the banks of the Gowanus.

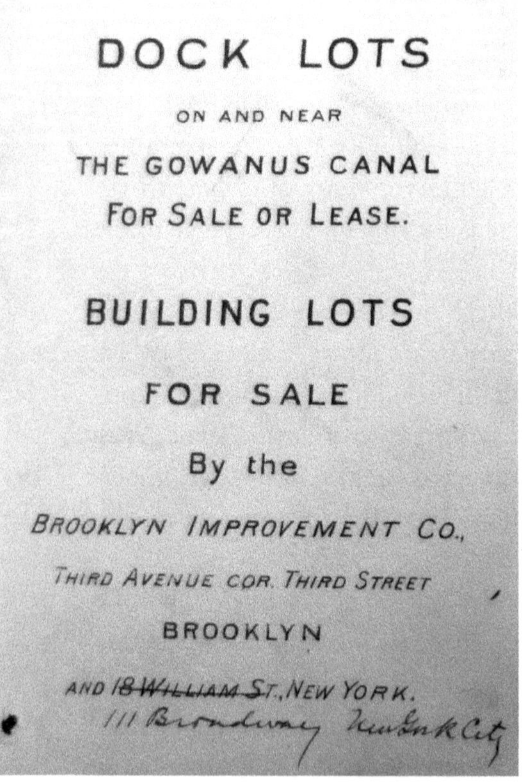

Undated portion of an advertisement for Brooklyn Improvement Company Lots, found in the Litchfield Family Papers. Courtesy of the New York Historical Society.

Only a few days after the BIC was incorporated, the New York State Legislature passed into law yet another civic improvement group: the Gowanus Canal Improvement Commission. Its purpose was to complete the long list of unfinished improvements necessary to create a viable commercial waterway along Gowanus Creek. This included dredging the creek bed so that it was deep enough for ships to navigate at low tide; building well-constructed walls that would not collapse and spill mud into the canal; and viable wharves along the twelve thousand feet of available space for barges to dock and unload their goods. The commissioners, who were all paid a modest salary, included several notable landowners: Martin Kalbfleisch, the mayor of Brooklyn, Thomas A. Gardiner, a state senator and the treasurer of Kings County, and also D. S. Voorhees, a local landowner and business partner of James S. T. Stranahan in the Atlantic Docks. Most tellingly, William P. Libby was also a founding member of the Gowanus Canal Improvement Commission.[15]

True, this was an overdue response to fifteen years of spotty, disorganized attempts to complete the vision of Daniel Richards. Yet years of vocal support from Brooklyn's newspapers and certain members of the Common Council had achieved very little for the canal as a whole. But the GCIC didn't emerge from a burst of sudden civic remorse; despite a decade of personal expenditures on street improvements across the empty Gowanus meadows, the Panic of 1857 had proven that even Litchfield could not engender his grand vision on his own dime. He had repeated the legislative song and dance of his Third Street Commission to lobby for the group's creation. Between the park, the roads, and building his palace, the railroad mogul had carefully prepared his investment for the private interest and speculation that would encourage such a commission into existence. Without his strong leadership or a comprehensive plan of action for that nascent part of Brooklyn, the Gowanus Canal construction efforts might have continued to flounder, mired in the mud forever.

The group received a bond of $175,000 from the city of Brooklyn, repayable at 7 percent interest over the next twenty years—once completed all landowners within two hundred feet of the canal would be assessed to pay for the loan. Just like with Third Street, the GCIC would bring much-needed momentum to the faltering project. It is no coincidence that the GCIC had essentially the same goals as the BIC—just on a larger scale. Mostly it completed the necessary improvements that other less resourceful landowners had failed to achieve. The commission had, in fact, united the area owners in an unprecedented way. In securing all that neither Daniel Richards nor the Brooklyn government had been able to muster, Litchfield had engendered the much-needed gestalt to awaken a two-headed creek monster. The line separating the goals of the GCIC the BIC was translucent, at best, as their relationship was complementary: Without full improvement of the canal on a larger scale, Litchfield's holdings would be useless. And without his private, economically viable interest to lead the way, the State Legislature might never have voted for the GCIC, nor the local government approved of it. Since Litchfield was a talented attorney, no paper trail connects him directly to the special commission. He had done the same with the Third Street Commission, and it probably would not have been prudent to draw too much attention to himself.

The injection of the GCIC's funds into the faltering project showed clear results. One year after the bill was passed, more than six hundred feet of the canal bed was deepened to navigable depths, and reinforced walls appeared on either side of the creek to restrain the mud and runoff. During the past decade, poorly constructed walls of piled wood had allowed muck to flow into the canal during storms, the runoff choking the Gowanus into a useless stream except at the peak of high tide. In late July 1867, the *Eagle* had plenty to say about the recent improvements:

> Hitherto, this canal has been regarded more in the light of an obstruction than a convenience, dividing two sections of the city, and through the requirements of navigation interrupting travel on two or three important lines, without yielding any adequate benefit in return because private enterprise would not combine to insure its complete improvement, and because capitalists did not seem to fully realize the great advantage its character as an inlet for vessels to this side of the warehouses would be to commerce of this section. . . .
>
> These property owners have taken steps to reclaim even the swamps, and use all the low lands that are situated in that neighborhood. They intent [*sic*] to construct a series of minor canals,

> extending at right angles to the main one, equal to it in width and depth, and terminating in large basins. Between these canals, and on the border of these basins, large warehouses are to be erected. . . .
>
> The main mover in private improvements is Edwin C. Litchfield, Esq.[16]

Only a few days after publishing the praiseful story, the *Eagle* published a counterpoint:

> While the canal may be of service for the purposes of trade, it is often a great obstruction to travel between the sections of the city it divides, and we think there ought to be some better regulation in regard to the opening of drawbridges. Two important railroad lines cross the canal, one at Ninth Street, the other Hamilton Avenue, which are but a brief distance apart. Often at the most busy time of the day, when he travel is greatest, the cars are delayed from half an hour to an hour at a time by the opening of the draw-bridges to let some vessel pass. The parties in charge of these crafts make no effort at expedition; lumbering canal barges come creeping along at a snail's pace, regardless of the sacrifice of time, valuable to others.[17]

The hasty arrival of canal-side businesses had brought a plethora of new boat traffic and an entirely new problem: the vessels could sail up the unfinished canal only at the peak of high tide, lest their boats run aground at the shallowest points. So many vessels would travel up the incomplete waterway that they would all clump at the bridges, waiting for the small window of time when they could safely traverse the full length of the Gowanus—too often these moments coincided with daily rush hour traffic. As many as twenty vessels could be waiting to pass upstream, and a similar number trying to get out, during the heaviest periods. The *Eagle* proposed various measures that would help to curtail the issue, such as limited hours for drawbridge openings and a minimum speed requirement for boats. In upholding the virtue of fair and balanced journalism, the editors published a letter in response to their editorial:

> To the Editor of the Brooklyn *Daily Eagle*:
> As I am one of those boatmen who go through the Hamilton avenue bridge at a "snail's pace" you will kindly excuse me for intruding on your valuable time in addressing my remarks to you, just to let you know what a very different view we of our craft take of things connected with the Gowanus canal.
>
> In the first place, you say that the bridge ought only to be opened at certain hours of the day. My dear sir, that is all we ask, for what would be the use of opening the bridge when the boats are aground? We only wish the bridge open when the three hours high tide allow our boats to float through.
>
> As for the "snail's pace," why the most of us own our own boats, and the quicker we get through the better for our pockets; and money, you know, Mr. Editor is the chief consideration with the boatmen under the bridge, as well as with the property holder on the other side of it. But a boat will not be driven like a horse and cart; it is against the nature of things.
>
> If the bridge was opened for every boat about the pass, it would cause a delay of about three minutes; but when the bridge keeper waits until he can let a dozen through at one time, it will necessarily delay the cars about one hour or more. The keeper, when finally ready to open the bridge cannot do so without help, and has to run among the boatmen to get some of them to help him, which those who are paid by the week will see him d—d before they do.
>
> After sundown and until 6 o'clock in the morning, he will not open the bridge for anyone, unless, as in my own case, you are able to coax the key away from him, so you can let yourself through when the tide is at its height in the night or early in the morning.
>
> Now Mr. Editor, I am on good terms with the bridge keepers, and do not so much blame them for their carelessness, as I under-

stand that they have to hand over one-half of their yearly pay as a slight token of their gratitude for favors bestowed. I only wish to give you an insight of things under the bridge, as they appear to,
Yours respectfully,

A BOATMAN ON THE GOWANUS CANAL.[18]

Speculation in South Brooklyn

Between the steam whistles of boats, the grunting of impatient animals, and the grumblings of irate commuters, life around the new bridges must have been deafening. Amid the cacophony, though, the Gowanus teemed with life like never before. Perched at his window in Grace Hill, Edwin C. Litchfield observed the bustle and smoke unfolding as his opus progressed.

Belgian paving stones of Third Street crept slowly toward his mansion, at night lit by lamps provided by his friend, Mr. Libby. Outside of New York, Litchfield's other ventures were prospering, from the now-expanding railroad empire to gypsum and coal mines and the considerable real estate he and his brothers acquired in the Midwest. For the first time in perhaps a decade, Litchfield's life was in order and his affairs stable, or so he thought. Prospect Park construction was now under way, having been revived thanks to the rebounding economy. Calvert Vaux and Frederick Olmstead, the venerated architects of Central Park, had been hired to rework their magic on the other side of the East River, scrutinizing Viele's plan. In their first report, published in 1866, the finicky Olmstead and Vaux declared that the lands originally purchased for the park were not sufficient to satisfy their vision for Brooklyn's pastoral pleasure gardens. In order to achieve required aesthetic precision, a "convenience of shape" and appropriate "amplitude of dimensions" were necessary—both of which were lacking in the current grounds.

This pastoralist philosophy was the basis for all of Olmstead and Vaux's park designs, the foundation of each meticulous decision: "It

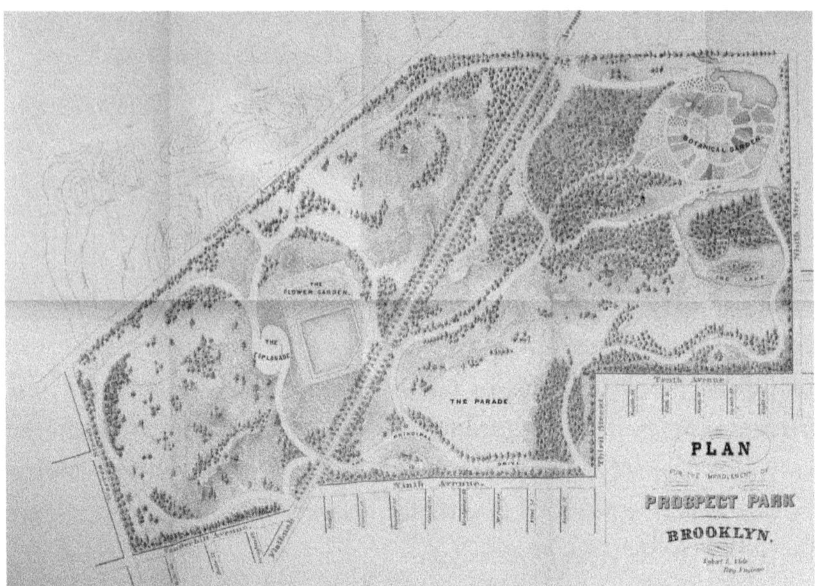

Egbert Viele's original plan for Prospect Park from 1861, which excludes the Litchfield Villa and surrounding property. "View of Site Chosen for Prospect Park." In "First Annual Report of the Commissioners of Prospect Park" (1861).

consists of combinations of trees, standing singly or in groups, casting their shadows over broad stretches of turf, or repeating their beauty by reflection upon the calm surface of pools," as the architects explained in their park report. At Central Park the execution of this goal, although elegant and simple, had proven to be complicated and expensive. These grand spaces had to unfold gradually, so that "the imagination of the visitor is thus led instinctively to form the idea that a broad expanse is opening before him." Without the proper buildup of Victorian anticipation, "the observer would take it all in at a glance, and if this were all he felt that he could look for, the result would be tantalizing rather than satisfactory."

First, Olmstead and Vaux wholly objected to the plan of Flatbush Avenue bisecting the park, claiming it "seriously interfered with the impressions of amplitude and continuous extent . . . and would always present a cramped, contracted and unsatisfactory appearance."

Trying to placate the desires of these temperamental artists must have been infuriating. Rather than plan around the bifurcated meadows, the men refused to make use of several huge tracts of land east of Flatbush. This left them with a smaller overall area for Prospect Park, quite the opposite effect they desired. Then the most incredible chutzpah: the designers objected to the remaining lands they did have to work with, because they were not enough. Their dissatisfaction focused on a particular spot, Tenth Avenue and Third Street:

> It is obvious that all that is required to form here a fair example of pastoral scenery is, first, an improvement of the turf, and, secondly,

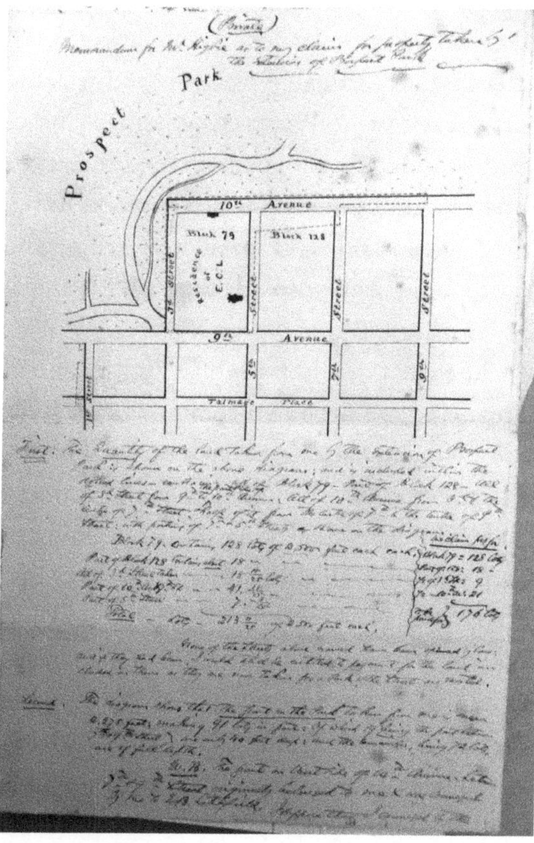

Map of the Litchfield property abutting a forthcoming Prospect Park, from a memorandum of Edwin C. Litchfield to his agent, July 1868. Litchfield Family Papers. Courtesy of the New York Historical Society.

> greater space, so that the observer may not see all the boundaries of free sunlight before him at a glance . . . [thus] we feel dissatisfied with the limits of the space we arc now regarding. It is evident at a glance, however, that if we do not restrict ourselves to the artificial boundary formerly fixed upon for the park, this space may readily be more than doubled in extent without encroaching upon any considerable natural elevation, and at a very moderate expense.

The "artificial boundary" Olmstead and Vaux sought to breach was a rectangular plot of ideal parkland that was occupied by the Litchfield Villa and its grounds. The only way Brooklyn's park commissioners could satisfy these fussy designers was to buy the Litchfield Estate. Olmstead insisted that the commissioners wouldn't regret the purchase, as it would also allow a vast improvement in the layout of all the park roads. That this particularly valuable piece of land was the missing piece of the puzzle, the answer to Prospect's missing symmetry, is not as ridiculous as it sounds. Even a layman could tell, after looking at Viele's initial designs, that Litchfield's house stood in the way of this park. Surely, Olmstead and Vaux predicted, selling the land east of Flatbush Avenue would neatly provide the cash for a new purchase of land.[19]

The pushy men clearly held a great deal of power: Central Park had been an international success, and the Brooklyn commissioners were quickly compelled to agree with their plans. A new proposal was immediately floated to the State Legislature, and, breaking from his loyalty to Litchfield, Stranahan defended the changes in a mid-March meeting of the New York State Senate Committee on Cities. "What the Commissioners want," he announced, "was to give the people a park worth of the name—a park that would be an ornament to the city. To do this, the proposed change was contemplated. I believe a great majority would favor it if they only understand the whole subject."

He then explained the architects' plans. After he finished, a man in the chamber stood up. "As a citizen of Brooklyn, I'd like to ask some questions," began the man, whose name was Mr. Gove. He pointed to a map highlighting the proposed park changes and turned to address Stranahan. "Who lives there?" he asked.

"Mr. Litchfield," replied the commissioner.

"Third Street was graded and paved at a cost of some $125,000," said Gove to the committee. "I think the city has done enough for Mr. Litchfield's property." A great discussion ensued, but nothing was decided.[20]

Litchfield was utterly opposed to the city buying his custom-designed home and gardens. Even the gas fixtures had been hand made for Grace Hill's gilded chambers. There was no point to being a real estate baron without owning a castle. But that's not how Brooklynites like Mr. Gove saw the story—they saw it as a means for Litchfield to collect more of their hard-earned tax dollars. The park extension became a hot topic of discussion in Albany and Brooklyn through the beginning of 1867. Middle-class taxpayers were opposed to selling the lands east of Flatbush, but not out of solidarity with their richest neighbor—they didn't believe that the Parks Commission had the right to act like a real estate agent. And certainly they didn't want to give any money to Litchfield.[21]

One year after the proposal was announced, a debate came to a head at a special joint session of City Affairs Committee in Albany that March. Those present included Frederick Olmstead, the park commissioners, senators and assemblymen from Kings County, and many others. "The land needed is extremely valuable for park purposes," Olmstead told the assembly, referring to the necessary breadth and picturesque views of the woodland that it would ultimately provide. "I would rather have ten acres of this plot than ten times that in any other direction."

Following this proclamation was an exhausting debate that ended in a compromise: Litchfield would agree to give up half of the block leading right up to the back of his castle. He would lose his stables and a conservatory, but the house itself and front lawn would remain intact for his use. All seemed fairly pleased at this, but after the meeting a powerful lobby from the new Ninth Ward in Brooklyn emerged. These landowners all had property abutting the parklands that Olmstead didn't want and were worried about the disastrous effect losing this park would have on their property values. With their opposition, the bill failed in an assembly vote.[22]

Once it appeared that Grace Hill was safe from the grasp of the city, Litchfield gathered his family and prepared for another long European tour. The time between the Great Panic and the Civil War had been extremely busy, and nearly a decade had passed since they had left the country. The now middle-aged railroad mogul seems to have believed that the Ninth Warders would fight any subsequent bills to take his land, and in the worst-case scenario his friends left in the commission fight the state. The trip may also have been a gift to Edward, his oldest son, now twenty-two years old and a recent graduate of the University of the City of New York (now New York University). Taking an academic note from his father, the younger Litchfield had ranked third in his class and presented a speech on the Napoleonic Wars during the grand ceremony.[23]

The Downside of Parks and Speculation

Now that Grace Hill was in order, the only thing left to keep Litchfield in New York was his stake in the Gowanus. Luckily, 1867 had been a very productive year, and the developments had moved very swiftly. Alongside the work of the Brooklyn Improvement Company, the city's engineers had built four thousand feet of stable canal bulkheads and deepened the channel using steam-powered dredging machines. The average depth was growing—from a functionally useless three feet—to a range of seven to twelve feet at low tide. At high tide the canal would be seventeen feet deep—creating eight times the working capacity compared to its unfinished state, the *Eagle* estimated. The land values had already doubled, even tripled. "Not only is this improvement of great importance as multiplying the facilities for landing bulky goods and materials in the city," the editors wrote, "but now it obviates the annoying and prolonged detention now experienced by city travel in crossing the canal bridges."

In addition to the improvements, the Gowanus Canal commissioners also promised to stop the pesky Bond Street sewer exit, which still had a tendency to "foul up and fill up the canal" with solid waste. In the future, streets would be drained only into the combined city sewers that exited out to the East River. The blocks adjacent to the Gowanus would have drains into the canal, but only for surface water, as only wharves and factories would occupy the land and—as sewer designer Julius W. Adams believed at the time—required no sewers.

Even with the problems of sediment and navigation, several high-volume businesses had grown alongside the Gowanus. Citizens' Gas-Light shipped in at least twenty thousand tons of coal every year for their manufacturing plant, while the Pennsylvania Coal Company—a neighboring business just south of the Ninth Street Bridge—brought in about eighteen thousand tons annually. Felt & German, another coal partnership, sold roughly the same amount. Building material and supply businesses also set up along the early wharves: the construction firm Morton & Canda, whose docks were by Carroll Street, brought in 150 barges loaded with brick within their first eight months of business. Watson & Poitinger, a lumberyard, had $180,000 in sales in 1867, which put them in only second place among a half dozen other Gowanus lumber companies. Litchfield's business promotion and legislative battles were certainly paying off—the canal wasn't even finished and new, successful businesses had been established around his properties at a surprising rate. Each of these businesses was beneficial to his scheme in some way: lumber, stone, and brick were needed to build his new homes and other developments, and fuel was needed for the construction equipment.[24]

With all of his holdings secure, Litchfield and his family departed sometime in the summer of 1867. He left Neil J. Higbie, his agent, in charge of all business affairs and had every copy of the *Brooklyn Daily Eagle* forwarded to his various addresses so that he might keep up with local news. It was through this medium that, almost a year into his European sojourn, Litchfield discovered that another park bill had been floated to take his house and grounds. In battling the decision, he wrote to all of his political contacts, but the State Legislature had taken due advantage of his absence. It was hardly a blessing to Litchfield, but there must have been some consolation in how desirable his land had become. "In the meantime, property adjoining the Park has greatly advanced in value and as the Litchfield property is benefitted more than any other—for to all intents and purposes it is within the Park—the value of the land has probably more than doubled, " the *Eagle* explained. "In 1865 they declared that they needed it; then it could probably have been purchased for $150,000; in 1866 they asked for it, and its value was then probably $300,000; in 1867 they again solicited power to purchase it, and its cost would at the time probably have been within $400,000."[25]

Speculation aside, the bill ultimately passed in April 1868. On the 11th of that month, Litchfield wrote from Paris to Higbie:

> Dear Sir,
> I have just rec'd your telegram saying "Park bill passed—takes all. Make contract with Wood." I understand this to mean that the bill my house & grounds are all taken. Ipso, you will not make the expenditures and improvements mentioned in my previous letters, that is you will not put storm drains in the house—nor have the plumbing overhauled—nor paint the roof, nor make the drain through the garden. In short, do nothing, except to have the house cleaned, and prepared for us to occupy as it is. Do this unless you hear from me to the contrary by telegram. I will write you again."[26]

True to his word, Litchfield corresponded regularly with Higbie, and in July he dictated detailed instructions in a ten-page memorandum, packed with meticulously numbered lists, bullet points, and sublists. Ever the lawyer, Litchfield had accepted that the law wasn't going to change and sought to gain as much compensation as possible from the situation:

> You must see to this: I must show the Commissioners that 3rd street property has a high value all the way down to the water.
>
> Lots of 3rd street range at prices \$3000–\$6000 per lot all the way down to 5th avenue, & are at \$5000 per lot on Gowanus Canal; while on 9th street you can price them at from \$300 to \$1500 up at heights at 7th or 8th avenue. Perhaps 3000 to 4000 above 8th ave. . . .
>
> In addition to the value of the lands taken, I think an allowance should be made to me for damages in taking my house. For example:
>
> Every carpet was made for the rooms, and will not fit any other rooms. So with mirrors—-and gas fixtures &c &c. You know it took 12 men to handle some of the large pieces of statuary. All that I shall be compelled to move and much of the furniture of the house will then be rendered valueless. I cannot of course specify <u>how much</u> this item should be: but it should be enough to cover the actual expenses of the operation & the probable loss of value in the function in consequence of being moved away.[27]

In regard to the actual value of the house and grounds themselves, Litchfield stressed the importance of buttering up the commissioners, so that they would see that the steadily increasing land values—plus the inflated costs of labor and materials—rendered the amount he deserved to be compensated much higher than the \$150,000 originally paid:

> You must be prepared with <u>proof</u> by good men as to values. This should be carefully made out in affidavits—so that if the Commissioners do not decide fairly, we can appeal.

> Finally: Let Scranton keep you fully supplied with the best cigars—and other things and have them on hand at your office, as well as at my house, that the gentlemen make your office their headquarters, free of cost as long as they choose—and make them comfortable when they are there.[28]

The city's unwavering quest to take Grace Hill over the past few years was not purely to benefit the public good. Local politics played a role, and hundreds of thousands of dollars in city loans were benefitting Litchfield-related projects. Brooklynites have long suspected that Litchfield wanted the buyout cash from selling his house, but his letters disprove that belief. The decision may indeed have been part of a grander waltz of political power. It's difficult to be certain, but it is quite a coincidence that as the city was acquiring his mansion, a local state senator pushed through a new law to shake down overbearing developers.

The Fall of Special Commissions

Henry C. Murphy was a born and bred Brooklynite who enjoyed a long political career in the service of his city, for which he felt deep love and pride. After founding the *Brooklyn Daily Eagle* in 1841 with Isaac Van Anden, Murphy was elected mayor. He served several terms in both houses of Congress, ran for a nomination in the 1852 Democratic primaries for president, and also served four years as ambassador to the Netherlands. He was obsessed with colonial history, and Murphy's greatest contributions to New York history are probably translating several early Dutch works into English, most importantly Jasper Danckaerts's *Journal of a Voyage to New York*.[29]

After returning to native soil around 1862, Murphy was elected to the New York State Senate, representing South Brooklyn. For several years he watched as the list of special commissions grew and lost patience as each was plagued with continuous delays and increasing budgets. The Third Street Commission had amended its legislation no fewer than six times since its creation, steadily augmenting the loan from the city. After 1860, a sort of urban gold rush had ensued when entrepreneurial Brooklynites discovered Litchfield's early successes with this "business model"—where special commissions could spearhead civic improvement and simultaneously boost property values, all holding cheap loans of taxpayer money and spending with little oversight. The most enterprising (or ruthless) commissioners, such as Litchfield, would then contract the improvements using their own construction companies—conveniently allocating cash payouts from the commission funds to their own private ventures (for example, Litchfield paid himself $22,000 for organizing the grading for Third Street). Soon there were special commissions to improve Bushwick, Atlantic, Fourth, and Bedford Avenues, and many others. Murphy decided that if left unchecked these ostensibly public organizations would quickly overwhelm the financial health of Brooklyn with debt. His eye on the mounting expenditures, Murphy determined to end the opaque and unregulated commissions.[30]

As it so happens, the same sentiment had been spreading in Brooklyn's Common Council, which had received many complaints from residents for running up their taxes. At their February meeting, a debate swirled around the room in City Hall, after the Brooklyn's attorneys proposed a bill that would transfer total control of all streets away from commissions and back to the aldermen. "There is little I wish to say as to the past working of these commissions," responded Alderman Whiting. "In some respects, hitherto, the city had derived benefit from them: but it could not be denied that the theory of vesting local authority in commissions is wrong and that the tendency was, already, and would be more and more as time passed, for the quality of the men who were appointed as commissioners to deteriorate."

"I am gratified to hear such sound doctrine," replied Alderman O'Keefe, who predicted that the burden of debt entailed by the commissions, once fully revealed to Brooklynites, would "make the people squeal." First, O'Keefe continued, there was the Prospect Park Commission, which through pure speculation "got up to enable owners of property in a certain quarter of the city to sell for two and three thousand dollars each, lots which five years ago would not fetch more that $250 per lot." He then listed a half dozen other commissions and how each landowner benefitted in various ways from the city cash. "Then there was the Third Street boulevard commission, designed to improve property which was hardly worth anything before, until this scheme got through at Albany for their benefit, and taking control of it out of the hands of the Common Council and the people, had placed lamps along their street only fifty feet apart," O'Keefe intoned. "This was a beautiful sight to look at, to be sure: but it was not quite so beautiful a prospect for the taxpayers of the rest of the city to pay for lighting three times as many lamps in proportion on Third St., merely to benefit Mr. Litchfield's vacant property as they had upon their own inhabited streets in other parts of the city."[31]

Considering these strong sentiments, it seems no coincidence that as the city acquired Grace Hill, Senator Murphy was pushing through an law that would close the Third Street Commission. It ordered that all work be finished by that September, and so the commissioners hastily completed the street, although in their final report they noted that heavy rains had recently damaged the paving stones at Third Street and Fourth Avenue. But since they no longer had the authority to have it repaved, they informed the Common Council with a wink that "as by the law, your honorable body can now have it done at the cost of the street."[32]

Not one to be left out of a conversation, the *Eagle* provided a decidedly split yet poetic sentiment on the outcome of still-transitory Gowanus lands:

> We do not dispute that the Third Street Commissioners have made an excellent street, quite a model in pavement, sidewalk and trees,

> and in the number of lamps far ahead of any other street that anybody ever saw. It shines like a comet's tail across the bleak expanse of the meadows at night. It is everything that is admirable to look at and useful to travel on . . . [but] the thickly studded lamps, giving their brilliant light amid the desolation of the swamp, illuminating the meadows more clearly than our best business thoroughfares are lighted, may be expected one by one to wash off into the seas of mud and marsh around them.[33]

Furthermore, the *Eagle* pointed out that if the same budget for developing the one-mile-long Third Street—now more than $250,000—was applied to all seven hundred miles of Brooklyn's roads, it would cost $14 million—enough to provide all of London with a dual-pipe sewer system, and certainly higher than the total assessed real estate value of Brooklyn.[34]

Litchfield was by no means defeated. He had gotten Third Street constructed exactly to his liking and convinced the city to foot some decent chunks of the bill and had already moved on to his next big project. Although he would soften up in his later years, at the age of fifty-three Litchfield was a hard and calculating businessman and had approached the personal loss of his home in his typically methodical manner. Being an ever-efficient attorney, in the same ten-page memorandum that instructed Higbie to furnish the park commissioners with cigars, Litchfield also provided detailed instructions about how to proceed with the Brooklyn Improvement Company developments:

> Whomever gets the contract for dredging out the Gowanus Canal can afford to deposit the surplus earth on my low ground for nothing.
>
> 1) Because from 2nd to 9th st my low ground is the nearest place where it is possible to deposit any large quantity

> 2) There is not any other low ground on the easterly side of the Gowanus Canal, where the surplus dredged from the Gowanus canal can be deposited (between 2nd and 9th street)
> 3) The contractor will get pay from the Canal Commission for dredging & removing the earth. All of the earth thus dredged from that part of the Gowanus Canal which is between 2 & 8th street will of course be deposited on my land.
>
> You must want that half of it, that is for half the width of Gowanus Canal belongs to me, as I own the ground & I object to it being placed elsewhere: and that part should be deposited on my ground without cost to me.[35]

Even while he sojourned in Paris, his thoughts were in Brooklyn and occupied with the minutia of where to deposit piles of Gowanus dirt. This phase of the project was serious business to Litchfield. Beyond from saving a few dollars in labor costs, the area between the canal and Fourth Avenue, from Third Street down to Ninth Street, was to be the Brooklyn Improvement Company's bustling commercial district. Filling in the ponds and creeks in that area meant creating stable land for warehouses and factories, the key to his real estate visions.

As it was, this marshland now resembled the Red Hook of two decades earlier, where several large hills had been cut down to make space for new constructions and also provide the fill to close up the forty-acre millpond. In the vicinity of Litchfield's grand plan were marshlands: frequently flooded, they were useless in the march of urban progress.

Naturally, the swampy lots on the east side of the Gowanus had their own ancient legacy: they marked the site of the fated crossing of Revolutionary War soldiers and the boat channel of Claes Vecht, builder of the Old Stone House. In this vicinity, around the plotted Fourth Street, was an offshoot of the Gowanus known as the Peter Staats-kill. Named after a founding Dutch colonist, the rivulet ran eastward toward Fourth Avenue and sat relatively unnoticed for nearly two hundred years. It could, quite possibly, also have been the freshwater stream that had once supplied the Vecht plantation with clean water. When Litchfield had begun acquiring his enclave of Brooklyn, he found that the surrounding parcels were not part of the Cortelyou estate, but a footnote in the lengthy real estate portfolio of a wealthy New York widow, Julia Gould Jerome. Her husband, Addison Jerome, had been an investor in Litchfield's Michigan and Southern Illinois Railroad and was also the brother of the financier—and Litchfield nemesis—Leonard Jerome, making Julia G. Jerome the great-aunt of Winston Churchill's mother. Mrs. Jerome sold her parcels around the Peter Staats-kill to Litchfield sometime after her husband's death in 1864. She had bequeathed to Litchfield a fundamental parcel of his commercial district scheme.[36]

Without proper drainage these marshy lands were useless, and the canal plans did not specify an eastward extension. But in his original 1848 designs, Daniel Richards had suggested that surrounding landowners would contract several private canal basins for their own use. Ostensibly they were to provide barges enough space to turn, but there was also no way to fully drain the surrounding fields without them. Richards had not highlighted this detail, probably to hold down construction costs. But now that the channel was a high-traffic zone, digging such basins made plenty of sense. A greater perimeter of the canal also meant more docks, and therefore the Brooklyn Improvement Company would collect greater wharfing fees. As Litchfield's special commissions and home were under fire, he had ordered the digging of the basin at Fourth Street that, at one hundred feet wide, would afford an additional fourteen hundred feet of wharf front. Just as the Gowanus Canal was designed to follow the shape of the original creek, the Brooklyn Improvement Company's private basin would follow the outlet of the Peter Staats-kill, as far as they could legally dig.

Senator Murphy, it turns out, was not wholly against Litchfield's plans: In February, five months after his commissions law officially transferred the control of Third Street away from private interests, Murphy introduced a bill that would authorize the Brooklyn Improvement Company to dig a branch canal across Third Avenue. A cutting, ten feet deep and forty feet wide, would traverse the thoroughfare, "over which a permanent iron bridge would be laid so travel of this street would not be obstructed." A branch canal would then be dug eastward from the bridge up to Fourth Avenue. Piping in, the *Eagle* called the bill "unobjectionable," as the extension would be "the quickest way to put the meadows to some useful purpose."[37]

Several weeks later, at a "numerously attended" meeting of the Improvement Association of the Eighth and Twenty-Second Wards, Higbie offered a detailed explanation of the plan as detailed in Murphy's law to a group of skeptical Brooklynites. Preempting one major objection that had begun to circulate, the agent assured them that the Brooklyn Improvement Company simply wanted to drain the meadows and had no intention of building a moving drawbridge across Third Avenue. If the basin were used for wharf purposes, he promised, it would be only for boats that could pass under a fixed bridge. But the crowd was not buying Higbie's pitch. "Considering the bill gave the Company much more extensive powers than this," retorted Mr. Spader, a former alderman, "if the measure is passed it will eventually result in bringing masted vessels above Third avenue and thus interrupt the travel on that street by a drawbridge like those on the canal below."

After Higbie departed, the real estate owners of the Improvement Association moved to send a remonstrance to the State Legislature, claiming that the improvements were "desired by but few, if any of the residents or real estate owners in said Wards, and is not required for the purposes of commerce and will greatly deteriorate in value the real estate in said wards."[38]

Two nights later, about 150 of these same property owners gathered at meeting hall on Fourth Avenue and Nineteenth Street to protest the bill. Speaking before the group, Joseph Wilson, another ex-alderman, claimed that the language of the bill "was only an attempt to delude the people into supposing that a drawbridge was not intended . . . [the company] were not going to excavate and pile and build warehouses between third and fourth avenues merely for a coal boat trade."

"Drawbridges have already kept South Brooklyn back more than anything else," Spader piped in. "The Gowanus Canal proper was being improved at the city's expense. What set of men could not get rich, if, like the Gowanus Canal wharf owners, they could get a law to compel the city to lend them a half on million dollars to improve their property with?"

To prove that even the city was on their side, Spader then read a letter from the sewer commissioner, detailing how the basin extension would require breaking apart a full block on Third Avenue—which had just recently been paved at no small expense. Most of all, it would require diverting a recently planned sewer main up to Fourth Avenue, which would be both inconvenient and undoubtedly injurious to the planned drainage.

After this Felix J. Duffy, another landowner, stood and claimed that the whole point of modernizing Third Avenue had been to give inhabitants a direct road to the Fulton Ferry so they could bypass the annoying bridges on Hamilton and Ninth Streets. The new bill proposed to "deprive the Eight Ward people of the sole benefit they expected," Duffy lamented.

"It is a scheme of fraud and villainy to injure the Eight Ward," declared Mr. Hinman, yet another ex-alderman. "It will depress and damage everyone else's property to benefit Mr. Litchfield and his associates. These canal basins will be mere mud-holes, generating malaria and disease, and they'll be no 'improvement' except for the undertaker."[39]

It was inevitable that Brooklyn's taxpayers would tire of Litchfield. The morning papers had just announced that they would be saddled with the cost of buying his land and house for the Prospect Park extension, to make a zoo and museum for the park. The commissioners had awarded the mogul $518,318.15—more than a third of the buyout budget—while an additional $500,000 went to his half-brother and sister-in-law, Egbert and Hannah Litchfield, for lands they owned directly south of Grace Hill. Leading up to this, Brooklynites had also covered the exorbitant expenses of Third Street, and now again for the Gowanus Canal—the source of all the traffic that plagued South Brooklyn. After all of this, Litchfield wanted to install another bridge. Sometimes, it takes only one extra drop of water to start a flood.[40]

Now mobilized, the Eighth Ward owners wrote to their congressmen protesting what they perceived as an opportunistic law. As it happened, 1868 was an election year for the State Senate, and so fearing the loss of constituent support, the Committee on Municipal Affairs unanimously voted against bringing Litchfield's basin bill to the senate floor. Soon afterward, Higbie announced that the basin plan was to be abandoned. The decision was a victory for the Eighth Ward, also because during that same session Murphy pushed through an act to shutter the Gowanus Canal Commission. It was by far the city's most expensive special project, with a budget soaring past $450,000. Murphy's bill was a carbon copy of his Third Street act and was happily received by his constituents and also the *Brooklyn Eagle*:[41]

> The GCC are simply a knot of private wharf-owners, half a dozen in number, whose very names no one can recollect without searching the records of legislation. It was, a the best, dubious whether this city ought to have loaned these gentlemen half a million dollars for improving their wharf property as they pleased, under their own management, but at the expense of taxpayers. However that policy was adopted, and the Canal and its bridges and navigation transferred from the power of the city to that of a few of the merchants who do business on its shores. Now, after half a dozen years spent in this way, Senator Murphy comes forward and says "Gentlemen, you have had time and money enough, given you by the city to finish whatever improvement you professed to design for this canal.

> We give you a year and a half more in which to finish your job, and then you must surrender it to the city, and begin to repay, by a local assessment, the money you have borrowed for your work."[42]

Written into the legislative act that authorized the BIC's very existence was the right to dig basins from the Gowanus Canal up to the border of Fourth Avenue—the act simply did not say anything about cutting into another road to do it. Ever the lawyer, Litchfield had desired, as the *Eagle* called it, "positive authority of law," to extend the basin, just to be sure. He saw this new law as a formality, or more likely a courtesy to South Brooklyn. Although he lost a battle, Litchfield would not give up. Instead he fell back on the original rights of incorporation act, positive authority or not, and instructed his agent to approach the sewer commissioners and again request that they divert the Third Avenue sewer around their canal project.[43]

Spader and the other Eighth Ward property owners were furious when word of Higbie's maneuvering got out and, in late June, published a formal resolution stating that the "renewed steps taken by Mr. Litchfield and the Brooklyn Improvement Company . . . after the agent of said so-called company had publicly announced that the measure had been abandoned, meets, as it deserves, our earnest condemnation and severest denunciation."

The Water Board attempted to settle the controversy by ignoring Litchfield's requests and rewarding a $186,000 sewer contract to a man named Van Winkle, who would begin work on Third Avenue in August. By officially commencing the civic work, Brooklyn's administration considered the bridge matter closed. "The history of former negotiations with Mr. Litchfield," the *Eagle* reminded in an editorial that same day, "proves that delay on matters in which his interest and the public's are involved, will be more to the advantage of the former than the latter. It is a sure thing that with a charter allowing him to make a canal to Fourth Avenue, Mr. Litchfield will eventually get a canal across Third Avenue."[44]

The *Eagle*'s soothsaying was wholly accurate, except that Mr. Litchfield did not wait much time at all. A fortnight later, a crew of one hundred pavement workers of the Brooklyn Improvement Company arrived unannounced at Third Avenue right by the former Peter Staats-kill. Armed with pickaxes, shovels, and crowbars, they proceeded to tear apart the fresh paving stones with gusto, which attracted quite a crowd. The ensuing drama was the biggest story in South Brooklyn for the final weeks of summer.

Hearing news of the unauthorized work, the mayor and street commissioner descended upon the scene and ordered the police to stop the work. Attending to his duty, Captain Stearns of Brooklyn's Forty-Fourth Precinct approached Isaac Delameter, the gang foreman, and ordered him to stop his men. Delameter, likely brandishing a heavy instrument, refused.

Although the details of the ensuing scuffle are lost to history, amid shouting and probably a few shoves, Captain Stearns of the Brooklyn Police arrested the foreman and jailed him, putting a temporary stop to the destruction. Nobody was reported hurt, but even the *New York Times* arrived in time to report on the raucous scene, interviewing local landowners who had cheered on the police as they stopped the operation. The unhappy Brooklynites complained to reporters that the basin would lower their property values by a half million dollars. Delameter posted bail the same day and was never formally charged with a crime. With admirable efficiency, that same day Higbie procured from Justice Tappan of the State Supreme Court an *ex parte* injunction—a court order that specifically ordered the city to cease their blockage of the BIC's digging work.

As if to drive the victory home, the next morning an additional fifty laborers joined the BIC breakdown gang at Third Avenue, provided by a Mr. John Bonesteel of the Nicolson Paving Company. This man of unparalleled nomenclature was happy to oblige; Bonesteel owned a sort of legally questionable monopoly, somehow having weaseled into the only license to lay Nicholson pavement in Brooklyn, and with his power came a flippant attitude toward authority, especially where streets were concerned.[45] He was, according to the *Eagle*, the "natural resort of anybody that wanted to get the best of the city."[46]

The resumed controversial work stoked unabated excitement among certain Brooklynites, as the *Eagle* reported:

> As the heat of the sun made itself felt the general discontent broke out in some quarters in open profanity. "Why, d—his eyes," said a prominent South Brooklyn politician of Radical tendencies, whose name is inseparably connected with the Navy Yard,[47] "if he digs his canal through th' avenue, we'll fill it up; if he builds a bridge, it will make South Brooklyn rise up in arms."
>
> Mr. E. C. Litchfield, who is to-day the most talked about man in that section of the city, is supposed to have been referred to. Similar threats of violence, but of a more serious character, were uttered in the Eighth Ward last night.[48]

Despite the subsequent fallout, the *Eagle* supported a compromise with Litchfield's plans, albeit not without some scolding:

> He acted very discourteously to the city, in not giving the authorities notice of his action. . . . Considering that his title to cut the street was a mere inference—correct, we think, but still disputable—and that people were known to feel strongly on the matter, it would have seemed that a decent respect for the opinions and feelings of the community as well as for the position of the city government as overseers and guardians of the street, should have impelled the canal makers to give notice to the municipal corporation and show their title before they began to cut. But instead of this the first notice the city had was in the actual prosecution of the work. Then at the order of the Mayor and acting Street Commissioner, impelled by request of the Eight Ward people, the police stopped the work. Instead of going to City Hall to explain, Mr. Litchfield went to a

> judge and got that easily obtained and almost invariable instrument of wrong, an *ex parte* injunction, ordering the city not to stop the cutting until a hearing had been had, which was fixed for a day distant enough to allow the whole job to be done before the city would have a chance to prove that Mr. Litchfield had no right to do it. . . . Probably Mr. Litchfield has enough in his act to warrant the cutting of the street and the Counsel, knowing that, did not wish to fight a losing battle; but still, Mr. Litchfield does not seem to have treated the city, nor [corporation counsel] De Witt, the objecting property owners and the executive city departments, with a reasonable degree of courtesy and confidence. If Mr. Litchfield has a good case, he should have had it before the city at the start; and if Mr. De Witt thinks so he should have so in Court, and not let the injunction stand unattacked and yet unexplained, until the canal cutting was finished.[49]

For weeks the controversy spread through the streets of Gowanus with most of the protest coming from property owners in the Eighth Ward, who lived on the cusp of the growing city of Brooklyn, and the market gardens of the area suburbs. William De Witt, corporation counsel for the city of Brooklyn, began the process of challenging the legality of the injunction. Of course, it was helpful to Litchfield that De Witt, in his post since 1869, was his friend and business associate, although the relationship was not public knowledge. The *Eagle*'s editors proclaimed that Litchfield could have peace with his neighbors if he would only write five lines for the *Eagle* over his own signature, pledging himself as a gentleman not to make or permit any attempt hereafter to change the fixed bridge into a swing bridge.[50]

Responding in the next day's paper, Higbie wrote that Litchfield had been out of New York for more than two months and that he, as the agent, personally and legally represented both the railroad mogul and the BIC in all business matters. He also pledged that there would never be a swing bridge, and that "if the city authorities think it will bind the stipulation more effectually, I will obtain Mr. Litchfield's signature to such stipulation as soon as a letter can reach him."[51]

Unmoved by Higbie's promises, the irate Gowanus residents expressed their dissatisfaction anywhere they could: in letters to various newspapers, on the street, and in public meetings. In what can only be described as a supportive, nonviolent mob, one evening around two hundred Gowanus property owners serenaded De Witt with a brass band in front of his home on Ninth Street near Fifth Avenue. Appearing at his window, De Witt gave a long speech thanking the mob for their support, but did not denounce the Brooklyn Improvement Company—instead he praised their efforts, but promised the ebullient crowd that he would ensure the company kept its promise about the bridge.[52]

Several evenings later, another "largely attended" meeting of property owners hosted some vocal critics of the Third Avenue plans, but the most enthusiastic remained John L. Spader, the de facto leader of the anti-BIC party of the Eighth Ward. "It has been suggested to him from various parties," Spader began, bringing silence to the room, "that the best thing the people of the Eighth and Twenty-second Wards could do in this matter would be to compromise with Mr. Litchfield. The Eagle ten days ago published an editorial article in which it was suggested that if the people did not now compromise with Mr. Litchfield, he might get his back up and put up just such a bridge as he pleased." The room was silent as the people considered this.

"To all of these suggestions, I have but one reply—and I guess that the feeling of the people is with me in it!" Spader said, his voice rising.

There was a pregnant pause as the owners awaited his response, and grinned when a glimmer appeared in his eye. "No surrender!" he cried, met with cheers from the crowd. "No compromise!" he yelled again. He finished over more cheering: "If Mr. Litchfield is right let him have all the law gives him, but we are determined to have our rights!"[53]

One week later, on August 19, Litchfield wrote a letter to the *Brooklyn Daily Eagle*: "I will pledge myself and the Company to never put up a swing bridge, or a moveable bridge of any kind, on Third Avenue. I will sign any paper or guarantee any bond that you make or agree to make, if that will be satisfactory. . . . I care not how strongly we are bound, for we do not want a swing bridge, and I have never contemplated putting one there."[54]

The letter was a strange victory for the Gowanusians of the Eight Ward, as the basin was ultimately finished and a nonmoving culvert installed. It was an equally strange concession for Litchfield who, being away during the summer, was able to dismiss the wishes of a whole community and the city government when the bridge controversy was out of his sight. But writing the letter proved to the public that he had indeed been aware of happenings on the ground in South Brooklyn; his dismissive tone betrays its significance only for that community. Even if Litchfield truly had no intention of building a swing bridge, the high-rolling emotional response was really about who controlled South Brooklyn's public spaces. Beyond what was printed in the *Brooklyn Eagle*'s pages, the anxieties expressed by local Brooklynites had built over the sudden and rapid changes to their community in a few short decades. On the shoulders of some remarkable advances clung an overwhelming amount of nuisance. Improved transportation brought needed fuel and goods, but also such noise and traffic that it seemed to render all progress essentially futile—particularly for the everyday commuter trying to live in the present.

The expansion of the city of Brooklyn and the commercial possibilities of the Gowanus Canal brought dreams of wealth and prestige to its businessmen and landowners. Yet every modern, urban convenience also ushered in problems and unwelcome changes. In the recent memories of any Brooklynite over the age of thirty, the Gowanus Creek had been a brackish stream, full of plant and animal life—fine for bathing and a convenient point of access for boats. For some, crossing its wooden bridges reminded people of the rural beauty enjoyed by their grandparents. But in a relatively short period, fueled by speculation and high-stakes investment, the creek had increasingly become an inconvenience, its charm polluted by the grinding gears of progress. The newly paved streets, lit by gaslights every fifty feet, surely indicated the direction Brooklyn was heading. But they led to empty, flooded lots—hardly an acceptable replacement for the meadows and ancient country roads that seemed to disappear from under the feet of Gowanus residents.

One vocal opponent of Litchfield, M. R. Toombs of the Eighth Ward, shared some thoughtful protests with the *Eagle* readership on August 13, the day after he attended that boisterous landowners meeting. Toombs claimed that the supposed improvement of the canal was nothing more than for the "pecuniary interest" of Litchfield, who needed the basin to raise the value of some fifteen hundred lots surrounding the proposed extension—without it, he would likely never profit. Furthermore, Toombs shared this about the conditions of the area: "The creek as it is now with its dirty, slimy, oily water, is a great nuisance. By its extension and enlargement this unhealthy stench will be increased, and the neighborhood full of frame houses, made double liable to great fires from the additional petroleum, wood, and lumber yards, and manufactories to be established on this basin. We are willing to suffer from the creek being where it is, but most decidedly object to having it extend further into our pleasant ward."[55]

6

Foul Odors and Foiled Plots (1870–1885)

As the *Brooklyn Daily Eagle* detailed in an 1870 column, "Changes of a Decade," that part of Brooklyn lying east of the Gowanus Creek had hosted a few buildings dating to the Revolutionary era—many still occupied by landowners of the ancient Dutch legacy. "Throughout the slope everything savored of 'ye olden time,' and while the farmer held the plough, cattle roamed about the slope," the *Eagle* waxed poetic, "and several old fashioned saw and grist mills, run by ponds still partially visible, converted trees into building material and grain into flour, to the profit of the merry miller and the convenience of the industrious husbandman."

But in ten short years, the story continued, the hills were leveled and trees uprooted, while ponds were filled and marshes remodeled into building lots. No other quarter of Brooklyn had transformed as dramatically as Gowanus, where paved streets ran alongside now hundreds of dwellings—from cottages to brownstone mansions and one-story frame offices to the "mammoth factory and mill." By 1870 the banks of the canal were littered with coal, lumber, and brick companies. Chemical works of various kinds had been established, as had textile mills and factories. Schooners, sloops, canal barges, and tugs filled the waterway, some using the now completed Fourth Street Basin of the Brooklyn Improvement Company. Despite the initial prosecution from the Eighth Ward owners, Litchfield's basin had proved itself a boon, for a time, ridding the area of some of the biggest marshes and bringing in more business. With the blessing of many community members, the Brooklyn Improvement Company began construction of new basins at Fifth and Eighth Streets.[1]

This rapid development and increasing land value breathed an unparalleled jolt of population into South Brooklyn: by 1872, this extended neighborhood had more than forty thousand inhabitants, about a tenth of the city population.[2] The explosion also raised questions about how healthy it was to live near former swampland. Fever from "ague," or malaria, was "an almost ever present disease even when [the Gowanus] was devoted to the grazing of cattle and the raising of market produce," according to the *New York Times*.

This reputation for disease had sent those seeking low rents and country air to New Jersey, rather than Brooklyn, for many years. But eventually those cities in the state west of the Hudson became too dense, and then Litchfield drained the marshlands. All of a sudden, it seemed, the Gowanus Highlands (still too early in its history to be Park Slope), with its cool breezes blowing in from the bay, was the most popular neighborhood in Brooklyn. "Market gardening gave way to additional extensions of streets, and building-lots took the place of grazing grounds," the *New York Times* wrote. "So eager were the people for purchasing and residence there while lots were low in price and building materials comparatively cheap, that scores of buildings were erected upon the lower levels where the lots were 'marshy' and 'very cheap,' and where to dig for a cellar was impossible without having the excavation fill with water almost as rapidly as the men could dig."

To rectify the flooding problems, many buildings erected nearest to the marshes simply did not have basements. The result was a "one-story city," as the *Eagle* called the area, since the land was still cheap enough for lower-class Brooklynites to build their own housing. Most confounding for the Victorian-era health experts were that outbreaks of diseases like malaria, dysentery, cholera, and smallpox in South Brooklyn occurred several blocks away from the canal—mostly up the hill, and not in the immediate vicinity of the stagnant waters. These conditions led well-meaning physicians to believe that the cool Gowanus breeze to the upland blocks carried miasmatic infections. This would explain why, by 1872, the cross section of Sixth Avenue and Middle Street (now Prospect Avenue) seemed an epicenter of disease—particularly one small house crammed with thirty-one people, all infected with smallpox. Of course dampness and miasmas were not responsible for the spread of disease. The most plausible cause for such epidemics, regardless of location, was commerce. With the sheer scale of people and goods that sailed into South Brooklyn from all over the globe, it would have been more surprising if infectious disease did not arise on a regular basis. Houses crammed full of people, mostly poor workers with limited hygiene, were petri dishes for infection.[3]

Whatever the cause, there was no stopping the spread of this second wave of commerce and industry in Brooklyn, as it was happening in cities across the country. Naturally, Edwin C. Litchfield had been quite busy: By the end of 1869, the BIC had erected more than sixty houses, the first ever for sale or rent on lots that would come to be known as Park Slope. The buildings were placed somewhere in the vicinity of Third Street and Fifth Avenue, and also leading up to Seventh Avenue and mainly marketed toward upper-middle-class professionals. Forty-four were handsome brownstone "mansions." The rest were fronted with brick, considered a lower-class material at that time. The value of Litchfield's lots—which had been "wholly useless and impassible in the hands of less enterprising owners," according to the *Eagle*—had quadrupled in ten years, even though most of them remained empty.

While this was great news for investors and local owners, the newly reassessed land value brought one of the two certainties of modern life: taxes. Litchfield's real estate tax bill in 1870 was a whopping thirty-five thousand dollars—tens of millions in today's money, and an immense sum for mostly undeveloped meadows that provided no income. It was a strange form of thank-you to the man that the *Eagle* heralded for "convert[ing] the portion below into a thriving commercial locality, adding immensely to the wealth and trade of the city as well as at last returning a tardy but ample interest on the vast amount of capital invested in the improvement of this part of South Brooklyn." He had already sunk more than a million dollars into all of the improvements, but he still had sold zero lots below Fifth Avenue, toward his hopeful cash cow, the Gowanus.[4]

Along the eastern banks of the canal, Litchfield owned 1,600 feet of frontage. The Brooklyn Improvement Company had spent a half million dollars building docks on his canal-side property, filling and grading the wharf up to 250 feet from the water. This had yielded at least one lease, for one of the largest lumber businesses in Brooklyn, owned by Mr. Bliss—but Litchfield needed more. He didn't have long to wait; by 1871, the Gowanus waterfront had replaced the East River as the great depot of Brooklyn's coal trade. Dozens of partnerships emerged, bearing names like Kelsey & Loughlin's, Deering & Hunts, and Nelson & Searls. Officially, their standard bituminous coal sold for $7.25 a ton. Doubtless, with the explosive growth of Brooklyn, it was easier to bring the loads of coal a mile inland to where it could be most efficiently distributed.[5]

Traffic and Commerce in New Gowanus

As the appointed keeper of the Hamilton Avenue Bridge, John Anglim was well known in South Brooklyn. His job was to maintain the vital bridge and, possessing the only key, open and close the swinging conveyance as traffic required. In the spring of 1871, however, many local pedestrians, train conductors, and boat captains made numerous complaints against him. They had too often been stuck in place, waiting for the bridge, sometimes for nearly forty-five minutes while Anglim was nowhere to be found.

"We pay the keeper $25 per mouth, and have done so for a long time, as an inducement to him to facilitate the passage of our cars," Thomas Sullivan, president of the Brooklyn City Railroad, told an *Eagle* reporter in mid-April. "Vessels are often very slow in going through, being poled or hauled by hand, and sometimes towed through by a steam tug not having power enough. By paying the keeper we thought to make him more careful and prompt than he otherwise would be, and that he would see that vessels were all ready to go through before he opened the draw."

A conductor on the Greenwood train line—which, in theory, crossed the Hamilton Street Bridge every fifteen minutes—believed that Anglim regularly collected bribes and "did pretty much as he pleased."

"Too often he left the bridge in charge of a boy, and often without any one in charge," he informed the *Eagle*. "When it was opened by some boatmen a few days since, and left open by them with no person on it, the conductors had to got a row-boat and get on the bridge and close it before their cars could pass." Eager to find out the truth, the fact-seeking *Eagle* reporter went down to the bridge to interview Anglim himself. But the keeper was nowhere to be found, so the reporter asked one of the various b'hoys hanging around the bridge, who directed him to a "small grocery store where drinking fluids form part of though stock in trade," on Hamilton Avenue by Court Street, just a few blocks away.[6] The store itself belonged to Anglim, it turned out, but the bridge keeper was not there either. Mrs. Anglim stood behind the counter.

"I think you'll find him down at the bridge, underneath, ironing it, for he said it worked hard and needed fixing," she told the reporter, who went back again to the bridge and, in frustration, yelled out "Anglim!" several times, which "only resulted in frightening the poor little fishes, who evidently took it for a threat against their lives."

This failed effort to locate the infamous key holder attracted the attention of a property owner across the canal, also a member of the new city-administered Gowanus Canal Commission. He would not give his name, but recalled that Anglim had been the bridge keeper before the city ran the canal but had been fired for "neglect of duty." The man was also "in the habit of using abusive language to boatmen who would not go up to his store and 'treat' before he opened the draw, and also that he would keep boats waiting and charge them wharfage."[7]

Although he had been fired, the bridge keeper had friends on the Board of Aldermen who quickly reappointed him. "He having once run for Alderman and got 400 or 500 votes, was considered a strong man in the Ward," the commissioner explained, "and more entitled to the berth of bridge-keeper than other men of less influence, who would be glad to have though place and attend to it faithfully for the salary. None of the bridges are what they should be, and the keepers are not beloved so much for their fitness as for their political influence. The most faithful of them all, Henry Hinges, was removed last January, to give place to a political appointee." Some quick fact checking at City Hall determined that in addition to the three hundred dollars he collected annually from the railroad company, Anglim received an annual salary of eight hundred from the city—"to say nothing of what perquisites captains of vessels and boatmen may pay him." Though some would have thought this a racket, Anglim would probably have called it his living. Decades of Gowanus traffic problems cannot be blamed upon one irresponsible cad, and one almost has to admire his shameless neglect and acceptance of kickbacks.[8]

Compared to other cities like Chicago, the bridge situation in Gowanus was fairly embarrassing. The bridges around the Chicago Loop opened in three to five minutes, and barges were always properly towed through by tugboats. This was due to an organized timing system that was not predicated on bribing the possibly alcoholic bridge keeper into doing his job. The growing traffic complaints were just a few among many indicators of Brooklyn's progress and its people grudgingly accepted their fate, along with many other transformations to the landscape.

With the arrival of the booming construction projects of the BIC and other developers, Gowanus became a destination for building

BUSY GOWANUS, WHERE THE COAL, LUMBER AND BUILDING MATERIALS OF HALF BROOKLYN ARE RECEIVED

A view of the "Busy Gowanus" from the *Brooklyn Daily Eagle*, dated April 1, 1906. Brooklyn Collection. Courtesy of the Brooklyn Public Library and Newspapers.com.

supplies needed for the new developments. Probably the most iconic of such businesses to settle on the canal was the New York and Long Island Coignet Stone Company. Its very first incarnation was the Coignet Agglomerate Company of the United States, and it originally occupied sixteen lots at the corner of Smith and Hamilton Streets around 1869. But by 1871 a considerable demand for its stone "engendered the necessity for a large new factory," reported the *Eagle* that March, "and accordingly one was begun on Third avenue, between Third and Sixth streets, the premises being located on either side of the Fourth street basin, but which extends to Gowanus Canal."

Coignet stone so popular because it was not stone at all but concrete—a particular blend of sand, lime, cement, water, and iron rein-

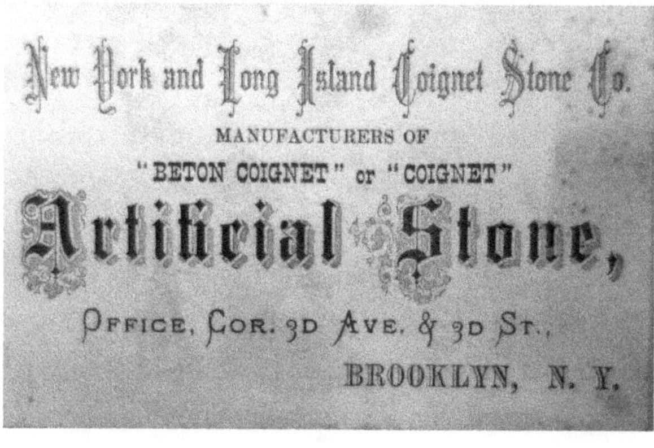

A business card of the Coignet Stone Company at Third Avenue and Third Street of Brooklyn, found in the Litchfield Family Papers. Courtesy of the New York Historical Society.

forcement invented by François Coignet, a French chemical engineer. Coignet's artificial stone cost half as much as the real thing and could be worked into any desired shape. In the 1850s this pioneering engineer had debuted his concrete blocks and molds to the French government as the building material of the future, and also one of "lost arts" of ancient Rome. Since the right combination of raw materials had been largely forgotten by the Middle Ages, a strong, usable concrete was a holy grail to nineteenth-century engineers. There were many inventors, particularly in France and England, who created similarly usable agglomerates, but none were as durable or weather-proof. During the ensuing decade, *beton-coignet* (as the product was known in France) changed the face of Europe.

At the 1867 Exposition Universelle de Paris (known as the World's Fair among Anglophones) a display of beton-coignet boasted its widespread application in numerous projects on their way to completion: the sewers of Odessa, Russia, and the docks of Bordeaux; the sidewalks of Lyon and the grand railroad bridge connecting that city to Marseilles; a 172-foot lighthouse in Port Said, Egypt, at the mouth of the Suez Canal, commissioned by Ismail the Magnificent, the Khedive of Egypt and Sudan who had studied at the Parisian military academy. In French the capital, approximately forty miles of beton-coignet sewer pipes were running under the streets, and eighty-seven miles of the iconic La Vanne aqueduct towered above the land. Even the very foundations and galleries of the World's Fair exposition building—erected temporarily for the event on the Champ-de-Mars—were constructed of beton-coignet.[9]

Some of these very impressed onlookers were a cadre enterprising American scientists and businessmen. They were so taken by Coignet's innovation that they imported the techniques and patents back home. Out of all the cities at their disposal to build a factory, these entrepreneurs chose Brooklyn—a national hotbed of the construction industry—and specifically right by the Gowanus Canal. The Long Island Coignet Stone Company, as it was renamed upon its flagship factory's construction, was one of the first firms in the United States to industrialize the production of concrete. The original Coignet manufactory could produce only enough material for one building facade in a single day, but the new works being constructed on the BIC basin soon would dwarf that operation:

> The [new] factory building is of mammoth dimensions, covering a full acre of ground, and being thirty-two feet in height. The building, now completed and occupied, contains machinery and material for manufacturing purposes. Among the machinery is a massive hydrostatic testing press, by which a crushing pressure of 120,000 pounds can be applied. The new works are capable of turning out fronts for ten ordinary houses per day, besides a large quantity of fine ornamental work, and will give constant employment to an average number of a hundred workmen.[10]

But the effect of beton-coignet in Brooklyn was fully realized in 1872, when an "elegant and substantial building," twenty-five by forty feet wide and two stories tall, arose next to the extensive works, at the southwest corner of Third Street and Third Avenue. Decorated in a late Italianate style, this new structure boasted ionic columns that flanked two elegant stairwells, leading up to twin porticos. Upon these neo-Greek structures sat triangular pediments, further recalling the classical features imitated by American architecture of this era. A special treatment rendered the cement a gray-white shade to resemble granite.[11]

The firm of William Field and Son designed this new Coignet Building with a dual purpose.[12] It would be the Coignet Stone Company offices, but also a flagship prototype of just how the material could be used. "The style of the exterior is very peculiar, combining excellent specimens of variety of architectural orders," the *Eagle* described.

> It is built entirely of the Coignet artificial granite shaded stone. It is two stories and a basement. The loft parapet adds to it the effect

> of almost a third story. The whole structure is a beautiful evidence of the work that can be turned out by that Company who are determined to have a standing specimen of how it will endure all extremes of heat and cold, frost, snow and rain. The smallest detail in the masonry is well defined and every design stands out in bold, striking relief. The edifice in the most select neighborhood would be a very attractive one, but located where it is, having nothing but wooden sheds and fences to contrast with it, stands out proudly and challenges the attention of all wayfarers.[13]

The Coignet Building was briefly a media darling: aside from mentions in newspapers like the *Brooklyn Sunday Review* and the *Eagle*, *Brooklyn Society Magazine* predicted that the edifice would become "an ornament to the city and will afford an opportunity of witnessing its beauty." The *American Commercial Times* declared the structure "handsome."[14]

By August 1873, at least forty-seven buildings in Brooklyn were being built with Coignet's imitation sandstone—populating stores and offices at well-to-do intersections like the junction of Flatbush and Atlantic Avenues and the mansions on Clinton Avenue. Beyond typical real estate, beton-coignet can be found still in New York City's neoclassical landmarks, including the Museum of Natural History, the Metropolitan Museum of Art, and the Cleft Ridge Span in Prospect Park. But perhaps most notable are the arches, columns, and traceries of the neo-Gothic Saint Patrick's Cathedral in Manhattan—the seat of the archbishop of the Roman Catholic Archdiocese of New York: "Fourteen teams are now daily engaged in transporting them from the works to the cathedral," wrote the *Eagle* in late August 1873. Throughout that lucrative year, forty tons of sand and nearly nine thousand barrels of Portland cement were delivered to the Coignet factory by way of the Gowanus. In turn, 765 building facades were shipped from the works, not including local deliveries made by truck or cart.[15]

François Coignet is considered the grandfather of modern-day concrete—at least by Norman Weiss, an associate professor of architecture and preservation at Columbia University who specializes in traditional building materials. Upon inspecting the Coignet Building in 2007, Weiss told the *Brooklyn Rail* that it was "the Rosetta Stone of pre-cast concrete in America." Weiss believed the odd and beautiful building, along with the Cleft Ridge Span in Prospect Park, to be a founding remnant of America's concrete industry. For unearthing that lost ancient art, Coignet was a "real hero."[16]

The Fall of Edwin C. Litchfield

In early 1873, the *Eagle* reported that Litchfield's lots around the Fourth Street Basin had grown to an estimated two million dollars in value—more than thirteen times his purchase price:[17] "Where the ground was the lowest, the mud the thickest, and water the deepest at high tide, now stand such buildings as these: Sulphur Works, a hat factory, numerous coal and lumber yards, and all kinds of building materials; the Coignet Stone Company, Asphalt Works, Chemical Works, Moulding and Planing Mills, Gas Works, Potter's Yard and an extensive oil refinery, from which oils are shipped, not only through this country but throughout foreign countries."[18] The commercial waterfront success of Brooklyn was of course not limited to the Gowanus. The entire coast, from Newtown Creek to our storied canal, was dominated by the booming industry of shipping and commerce. An estimated twenty thousand men labored on the city's docks, earning an average of twenty dollars a week—a respectable living wage at the time. In the face of its great neighbor, this remarkable achievement challenged a lasting social prejudice against Brooklyn. No longer, its residents proclaimed, was it a sleepy farming village or a bedroom community for Wall Street. Brooklyn had grown to the fourth largest metropolis in the nation and a center of industry. Scores of eager investors recognized the power of Brooklyn, focusing their efforts along its freshly cobbled streets. The city had a leg up on that other settlement across the river. "In New York every pound of cargo has to he transported over crowded, badly paved streets to the warehouse," the *Eagle* gloated. "In Brooklyn the unloading is done at the warehouse door. The advantage of these arrangements is apparent, and as a result of it, nearly all the Calcutta and South American trade of the port comes to Brooklyn; two-thirds of the coffee is delivered at our docks, and one-third of all the grain exported form this country to Europe passes through Brooklyn hands."[19]

It was a time of high profit and prosperity for Litchfield. His leases and sales were finally producing income, and he had achieved a magnificent feat in changing the face of Brooklyn. Edward, his oldest son, was married and now working in the family business. But rather than tending to his newly resplendent nest, Litchfield seemed in great haste to leave again. Part of his eagerness to depart was his health. He believed the European climate, and expensive water treatments, would help to treat some recurring ailment that he references (but never specified) in his letters home. He booked passage on the SS *Celtic*, a new 3,867-ton steamship of the White Star Line, for his wife, his

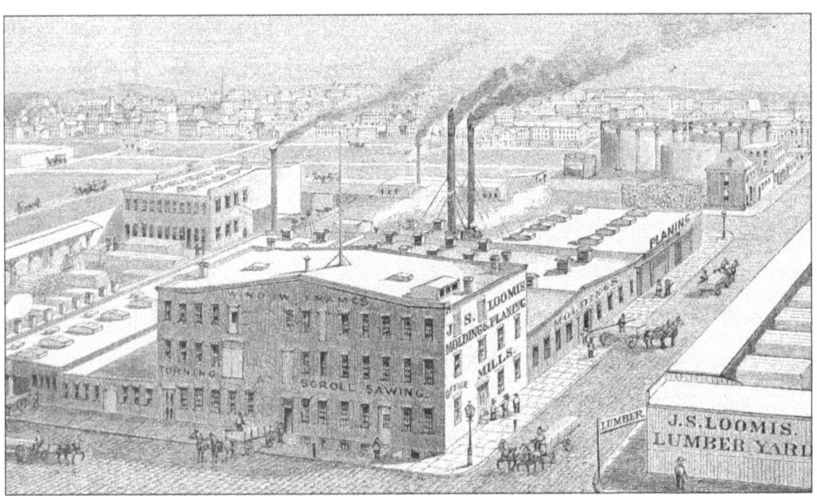

A molding and planing mill owned by John Sharp Loomis at Carroll and Nevins Streets, abutting the Gowanus Canal, ca. 1884. Henry Reed Stiles, *The Civil, Political, Professional and Ecclesiastical History, and Commercial and Industrial Record of the County of Kings and the City of Brooklyn* (New York: W. W. Munsell, 1884).

younger son Henry, who appears to have been mentally handicapped, and young Gracie. Frances, his elder daughter, had become Mrs. Turnbull and moved to Baltimore with her husband. On July 13, 1873, the great businessman and the family shipped out to Liverpool. This time he would leave behind twenty-eight-year-old Edward, whose wife had recently given birth, to manage the BIC and other affairs.

At this time, life in Europe was a fairly unstable compared to youthful America. France had been paying several years of war reparations to Germany following defeat in the Franco-Prussian War. England's shipping industry was suffering from complications that followed the opening of the Suez Canal. And most significantly, overspeculation had caused the Vienna Stock Exchange to crash that March. Banking houses across Europe were struggling to stay afloat. The nineteenth-century Pulitzer Prize–winning historian and industrialist James Ford Rhodes captured the American sentiment best around the time Litchfield was boarding the *Celtic*: "At that time it is not surprising that business men and bankers did not foresee what was coming. Prosperity was written all over the face of things. Manufacturers were busy, workmen in demand; streets and shops were crowded, and everywhere new buildings going up. Railroad earnings as compared with 1872 showed a gratifying increase. Prices of commodities were high, demand pretty good; everybody seemed to be making money and nobody suspected for a moment that he was living in a fool's paradise."[20] The failure of European banks strained business transactions across the world, especially the financing of American railroads—still the largest industry west of the Atlantic. Self-sponsoring their grand ventures was already difficult for American developers—interest rates had been growing since government had de facto adopted the gold standard in February 1873, and available credit was already stretched too thin.[21]

But all changed in the fall. At first Wall Street traders suffered through several drops in the market, causing some minor alarms. Then, "like a thunderbolt from a clear sky," on September 18 the colossal investment firm of Jay Cooke & Co.—a key financier of the

Civil War and primary investor of the "ill conceived" Northern Pacific Railroad—effectively declared bankruptcy. The news was a true shock to Wall Street, with pandemonium ensuing as stock prices immediately plunged: "The brokers stood perfectly thunderstruck for a moment, and then there was a general run to notify the different houses of Wall Street of the failure," wrote the *New York Times*. "The brokers surged out of the Exchange, stumbling pell mell over one another in general confusion and reached their offices in race horse time."[22]

The news shook the entire nation as banks began to collapse. The stock market closed for ten days, a record that has yet to be broken. Stuck in Europe, Litchfield was powerless to do anything as news of the turmoil buzzed along the wire services and filled European headlines. Then Murphy's Law came for the great projector at full force: On September 27, Edward sent a telegram to his parents in Berlin—it was the kind of message that curdles the hearts of switchboard operators: His son, Edwin's only grandson and firstborn of his eldest heir, had died. While the cause is unclear, the correspondence surrounding the tragedy provides some of the only surviving examples of Edwin Litchfield expressing profound emotion beyond a passion for business:

> Dearest Ned,
> We received this morning the telegram informing us of the death of your dear little boy, and I just sent a telegram to you conveying our deepest love and sympathy. No words can tell how deeply we feel this great affliction—great to us all, but so much greater to you the dear parents. The dear little child which we had all so much loved has been taken away, and it is hard to believe after our return he will not be there to greet us with his sweet little smile. I know how sad and dreary the world will seem to you after this loss of your little one—But our Heavenly Father knows how to temper the wind to the shorn lamb,[23] and he will support and sustain you in this great trial.

> Our hearts bleed for you and we feel that all we can say will only seem cold to that hot and overpowering grief which such an event calls for. You know our love for you and how gladly we would do anything in our power to comfort and to cheer you.[24]

In the same letter is one of the few surviving examples of Grace Hill Litchfield's voice:

> Oh my dear children, Ned & Maddie, how shall I express the sorrow which fills our hearts at the arrival of your telegram this morning. They ache for you with intensity, & also for us that we shall never see your precious little baby again.
>
> Oh that we could be with you, to mourn with you, if we could just comfort you. It is so hard to have the ocean between us at such a time.
>
> It is hard also to be obliged to wait for the slow mail, as more than two weeks must elapse before we can know anything but the bare, sad fact conveyed by the telegram. We do not even know where the darling died, whether you were still at Saratoga or whether you had reached your home.[25]

At the end of this tearful letter was a short note of sympathy, written in loopy, uneven handwriting by Henry. He was only two years younger than Edward, but the note reads like that of schoolchild. The next day, likely at a loss for what else to say, Litchfield wrote another long letter to his Ned, mostly addressing business matters: a $43,000 real estate loan, a possibility that Mr. Higbie was considering leaving his post at the BIC. "This must not be allowed," Litchfield instructed. "I count upon him remaining with us permanently—and it will be for his interest as well as ours." Halfway through the four scribbled pages he finally mentions economic turmoil: "I do not know how you have got along with the panic in New York. Of course, at such a time, it is inadvisable to sell securities except at a great sacrifice."

Finally, in closing the letter he mentioned again that he had received the awful telegram and responded by mail, "hopefully which you will have received."[26]

By mid-October, Litchfield finally had longer exchanges with Edward, and lamented over the details of his grandson's funeral. But even in the face of tragedy, he addressed the panic to dispense some fatherly advice:

> According to all that I have up to this time learned, from New York, I see that people are for the time being powerless to raise money—and I do not know as anything can be done except to wait. It is impossible to sell bonds at fair prices, and it will not do to throw them away. . . . Keep good courage—keep cool, remember that this panic, like all other things, will run its course . . . and after it is ended, property will remain, and credit will revive—and people who are really solvent, will, in the end, come out all right.[27]

But despite his own encouragements, the elder Litchfield hit bottom. As his health was faltering, his doctors and friends advised him not to leave Europe. Heartbroken, he wrote again to Ned, "All this has affected me and my head and I am really not fit to be in Wall Street." For Litchfield, such a confession was practically suicidal. By the next month, the great businessman's demeanor had improved. "I am very much pleased that you seem to be doing so well, and trying to so bravely to manage our affairs to the best abilities," he wrote to Edward. "The only possible school in which to learn to do business, and to do it well, is the actual doing of it—And you are now called upon to do our business—which just at this time, awaits in collecting in, as fast as may be, all that is coming due to us."[28]

He advised Edward to withhold as many payments as he could toward construction on the canal-front developments, likely in the hopes that workers would continue to labor under the promise of future payment. "This time will not last forever," wrote Litchfield, "and I predict that within six months money will be abundant in Wall Street and in other money centers. Then we may perhaps make sales of property." He insisted that he could probably not have done any better than his son in dealing with the panic, as "perhaps no one could avoid trouble under these circumstances."[29]

In the next letter, sent in late November, his acumen resurfaced: "All through the United States, I see in the paper, men are being discharged, and wages reduced. Our aim must be to reduce spending to the lowest possible point. All unnecessary employees must be discharged. Those whom it is necessary to retain must agree to a reduction of their pay. This is inevitable, and will happen all over the country . . . its effect will be, I presume, to reduce prices very generally."[30] But Murphy's Law had not quite finished with Litchfield: Two weeks before Christmas, he received a dispatch from Erasmus Darwin, informing him that Elisha Cleveland, their eldest brother, had died. He had been dangerously ill, but it was still a "very great shock" for Edwin to hear the news. "It was a great grief to me that I could not have seen him, and been with him, during his last days. But it was ordered otherwise—and I must submit," he lamented to Ned. Again, Litchfield plunged back into depression. "My own health made it impudent—possibly dangerous, for me to return," he wrote. "Even at this distance, my head feels keenly, and suffers greatly from all the American news. I do not think I have the strength to hear the [illegible] excitement of our actual New York business life." But to his credit, Litchfield had plenty of faith in his grieving son, assuring him, "The experience you will thus acquire will be of great service to you—and you will feel it becoming easier to you every day. Remember that doing businesses is nothing but affixing your best judgment to the decision of the various questions as they arise—and then taking the proper steps to carry out your decisions."[31]

There may be another reason Edwin C. Litchfield left the country so quickly during the height of prosperity, and stayed away during a time of great need. In March 1873, the great realtor began to receive letters signed by a mysterious "Ethan Allen." Most of the envelopes from this correspondence are marked "Private" and were directed to all of his various business addresses. Some contain no dates at all. One envelope was signed in 1874 with Litchfield's initials, including a note, "Some of the accompanying letters are without signature: others are signed 'E. Allen.' I do not know any person of that name. I have had other similar letters, which I have destroyed." But he did not destroy all of these letters, as numerous examples survive, often with varying handwriting and tone. With only the cryptic words of Ethan Allen (none of Litchfield's replies remain), a strange mystery is constructed around the railroad mogul's innermost personal life.

Many suggest planned meetings, like one of the first, from March 1873: "I can see you the 8th on the corner of 4th st east of no 14 at 12 o'clock." Another from the following December reads, "I think St Johns Park quite too conspicuous? You resided so many years at Waverly place it is not prudent to go in that vicinity. You forget that a public man like yourself would be remembered for years." Another letter from the same period reads, "I can see you in the immediate vicinity of No. 14 where you have visited so frequently on Monday 12 o'clock. There are urgent reasons and no other alternative. E.A." These anxious instructions and shadowy address beg the question of what Litchfield, or this writer was trying to accomplish. But soon, the intentions become clear from an undated note:[32]

> Mr. Litchfield,
> It is some time since you made progressions of rigard [*sic*] to business. . . . I was then ignorant of your true position, a young innocent girl. You took advantage of my confidence & used Strength to force me, and then when you could not reduce me to a life of infamy you took measures to injure me. I am ready for you now, indebted to you for a tarnished reputation. I can prove that I was badly tarnished by thinking you was what you represented yourself to be—an honorable man. No 14 is the only place where I will see you.[33]

Ethan Allen, if a real person, could have been a woman with whom Litchfield had an affair. The mysterious letters could also be part of a scheme to create a paper trail for later blackmail. Litchfield was, after all, a well-known, wealthy public figure, and the country was suffering from a debilitating economic depression. He could easily have been a target of scammers or political foes, and some of the more sinister notes were written in a different hand than others, usually with more spelling mistakes. But this kind of accusation was terribly serious, especially against such a wealthy and well-connected attorney, so it seems unlikely that this issue would have dragged on for so long unless there was some kind of damning evidence against him.

For decades these letters were tucked away in a folder the New York Historical Society, a miniscule slice of the extensive Litchfield Family Archive. Just why these letters survived is hard to fathom. Possibly the inclusion was an oversight, the rusty paperclips holding the letters together among the thousands of pages of surviving correspondences and ledgers. Perhaps Litchfield needed them as evidence, in case the matter shifted against his favor.

Allen's letters became more specific, particularly on January 12, 1874: "Will you endeavor to make out those Papers. I inferred from what you said that you would do so before leaving for Europe. Please direct to the same post-office you did in 1871 and oblige. Yours &c, E. Allen." These "papers" could have been money, but more likely the deed to some property. The specifics, quite purposefully, were never spelled out: "I cannot write more definitely," wrote Allen, "as you say your letters are often opened. I have refrained from any active steps because you did not think it prudent but the change has not met my anticipations."[34]

As that year dragged on, a beleaguered Litchfield waited for the warmth of spring and, supposedly, his ill health to improve before returning to New York. Back home, Ned faced the challenges of the economic downturn. His father passed the time visiting European capital cities. Despite the chaos and tragedy (and bubbling conspiracy) Edwin found time to visit Henry Poole & Co., a celebrated London tailor who founded the institution of Savile Row—a street still famous for bespoke suits. Poole rose to fame in the 1860s due to highbrow associations, mostly as the personal tailor of the Prince of Wales, the future King Edward VII. Edward—nicknamed Bertie—ordered the creation of a special dinner jacket, which, in America, is known as the tuxedo. In the 1870s, Poole's famous customers included William Waldorf Astor—cream of New York society, whose style the elder Litchfield often emulated.[35]

"It has occurred to me to me whether you might not like to have some clothes from Poole's made for you," Edwin wrote casually to Ned. "For example, if you want what are in America might call a frock coat suit—that is for all dress occasions, saving full evening dress, I could get it." The frock coat suit was a popular day garment in America, before the invention of the lounge suit. "I do not think that the cost here is more than half what it is in New York," he concluded, ever the businessman.[36]

Meanwhile, likely receiving no response as the elder Litchfield was abroad, Ethan Allen's tone became increasingly melodramatic. "You can go where I direct you or I will make everything public," the writer warned. "You had better take other measures or I will tell all about the relations. You can go till you see me where you said you would not comply with my request although you knew what I asked was right & reasonable. You have had amusement. I can turn the cards & give you what you did not look for."[37]

By early 1875, Litchfield had finally returned home. A letter from Allen dated March 29 reveals that Allen was indeed a real person, as Litchfield wrote a note on the back of the envelope: "Monday morning—Le meme jour j'ai rencontré dans la rue par accident." This rough French translates as, "The same day I met in the street, by accident." Here is the best and only proof that Litchfield knew the mysterious person—the only reason why he would have written himself a vaguely coded message. For the remainder of 1875, Allen—at least the one with more feminine handwriting—became angrier in tone as her meeting was continuously postponed: "A man who will pass himself off for a single man because his wife is an invalid, & when detected in the act will take advantage of his position & threaten the helpless, is beneath contempt," Allen wrote.

Litchfield must have challenged these accusations, for Allen continued to write, incredulously, "Your wife became your wife under adverse circumstances did she? It is a pity that when an invalid she could not have made it more widely known that you were shackled. You have pursued your course of villainy long enough." Subsequent correspondence mentioned Litchfield promising Allen a house, but the writer claimed it was no compensation (and had heard that the mogul had no right to dispose of the property, wherever it was). A final note remains from the end of November 1875:[38]

> You know as well as I do that I can expose you, but you have realized in my helplessness it will not do. Your presents are all preserved, and unless you do your duty everything else will be exposed. You came in the dark, your wife an invalid as I learned long after I made your acquaintance. Came with all the freedom of a single man first friendship, then affection. What right has a married man to speak of regard to a single woman, none.
>
> Relieing on my isolated position you passed yourself off as a single man when I wished you to attend to what I had entrusted you with, you began to talk about your irreproachable reputation. Your power to injure anyone. You can use your powers, employ all your miscreants I will do first what I told you I would make your name hissed at. Where you are honorable, I am ready for you. Your Catholic friends will not, cannot protect you. The word shall be down with the protestant ruffian. Who gives his means secretly to uphold the Catholicks but his vote goes for the republican. You wish you was a foreigner don't you. How many times have you said it?[39]

The threats of the mysterious Ethan Allen, whether wronged lover or political conspirator, seem to have gone mostly unfulfilled. Yet the lengthy episode offers more insight into Litchfield's private life than any other source, and also a taste of the importance of identity and affiliation in Brooklyn's politics. Through his career in real estate, Litchfield had navigated the intricacies of the local power bases and integrated himself into the cream of Brooklyn's society, but ultimately he was disappointed. Litchfield's upbringing, wealth, and influence should have landed him a post in some legislature, but he was never elected to office. Some later news stories suggest that his wife's invalidity and thus failure to make Grace Hill a social center of Brooklyn were responsible for his inability to move up. Or perhaps, as Ethan Allen suggests, he had relied on the Democratic political machine and its powerful Catholic base to help his projects thrive, and perhaps made favors to them—a difficult game to win. There are other routes to political success, but Litchfield faltered. His business practices were sometimes unstable and, at worst, unethical. In short, he had a reputation, which the mysterious Ethan Allen may have contributed to, albeit nothing scandalous enough to end up in the papers.

Mostly, these letters illustrate a strong opposition to Litchfield's success. From everyday citizens to high-powered politicians, many were rooting against this great fixture of Brooklyn life during its industrial heyday. Tomes have been written about the minutia of Brooklyn's political life during the Gilded Age: David McCullough's excellent *Great Bridge* explores the construction of the Brooklyn Bridge. He includes the integral involvement of familiar Brooklyn figures like the venerable and successful James S. T. Stranahan and the great political reformers Henry C. Murphy and Seth Low, mayors of Brooklyn and New York. But Litchfield is not at all remembered like these men, despite being a member of their circles. He was one of the largest landowners and taxpayers of Brooklyn, and the grand projector of the Gowanus Canal. He was a member of the Historical Society, the Mercantile Library, and every important venue for a well-to-do

Brooklynite. Yet his name appears usually as no more than a footnote in most of the city's histories.

It would be quite a poetic liberty to offer up Ethan Allen as a symbol of the misfortune and poor choices that prevented Litchfield from achieving the great legacy he desired. For all of his success, his end was not happy: At the onset of what would be known as the Long Depression—which persisted for longer than the Great Depression of the 1930s—he lost his grandson and brother. During this period he was often ill, and his daughter Gracie was also regularly afflicted with various unnamed ailments. His wife, being handicapped, had been unable to serve as social maven of Grace Hill. This fact seems to have shorted his ability to network and entertain—often key to a successful political career—before his barge could float among the cruising vessels of Brooklyn's political elite. Tack on a disabled adult son, and Litchfield experienced plenty of disappointment, frustration, and loneliness. Even the blackmailer Allen declared rather pityingly in one letter that Litchfield seemed to be a stranger in his own home. To build up power and prestige in a place like New York is a complicated and exhausting business. Against all odds, after thirty years of effort, it seems this visionary businessman had seen quite enough.

Sewers, Taxes, and Decay

"A Stench in the Nostrils of South Brooklyn," called out an *Eagle* headline in April 1876, reporting that the regular dumping of ash and "other offensive materials"—sometimes a thousand barrels a day—had left stagnant, polluted ponds between Third and Fourth Avenues, from Second to Tenth Streets—all Litchfield properties. As the great projector's personal life crumbled, a tangible decline in the public sphere had also begun. As the grades of certain plots rose high above other undeveloped sections, former Gowanus wetlands had been cut off from the tidal creek, leaving foul, "mismanaged" swamps.

A particularly visible culprit, though not a pond, was Litchfield's Fourth Street Basin: "Waters are becoming more and more obnoxious every year, sides of docks are encrusted with filth, and carcasses float there for weeks," as the *Eagle* reported. "It is nothing but a perfect cesspool," Colonel Helmstreet, a Gowanus landowner, told the paper. "Day after I have seen the same carcasses floating in the water by the half-dozen."[40]

The following month a meeting of the Health Committee of the Board of Aldermen was called to order at City Hall. Residents of South Brooklyn gathered to voice their grievances in regard to the conditions along Third Avenue in Gowanus. Mr. Brower, a resident, claimed that the intolerable stench from an area pond was driving people from the neighborhood. "Tenants who took up house on first of May were giving them up and moving away," he claimed. Brower explained that the Board of Health had turned to the Common Council, which assigned a measly hundred dollars to "abate that great nuisance"—barely enough to pay an inspector to simply discuss the situation. A plan was contrived to pump the offensive water from the pond and fill it with dirt—but it had yet to be voted upon. The next man to speak was Dr. Agrippa Nelson Bell, editor of the *Sanitarian*—the first significant US public health journal, dated to 1873. Dr. Bell was one of the leading experts of sanitation during this period and also a Brooklynite, living on Clinton Street in Cobble Hill.

"I have always understood that the city possessed bodies with legislative powers who could remedy these difficulties," he said, "and they would be criminally negligent if they failed to do so." He proceeded to read a list of statistics showing that the area had four times as many deaths from preventable diseases than from the worst smallpox epidemics, concluding that "from these facts, the Board of Health would be justified in calling for extraordinary resources."[41]

The board, in fact, had been collecting several years of data for their own report on the issue. Dr. Raymond, the superintendent, walked the Gowanus Canal banks himself during this time, his lively comments published in an 1876 Brooklyn medical journal:

> Go with me to the foot of Bond Street, where one of the largest sewers in the city discharges its contents. Here are the feces and urine of not far from forty thousand people, a city in itself: as large as Paterson; larger than Dayton, Ohio, and Nashville, Tenn.; the feces annually amounting to two thousand tons, and the urine to one hundred and sixty thousand barrels! Look at the map of the city and see where this mass of filth is discharged. Is it out in the bay, where the tide can carry it faraway to the ocean, where air and water may oxidize it and render it innocuous? Is it in a swift-running stream, that hurries it on to the sea so rapidly that the pure spring water has not time to become contaminated?
>
> No; it is into a large, open sewer, called the Gowanus Canal, which receives not only what the Bond Street sewer brings it, but also what comes through several smaller ones. In it there is no current; the tide rises and falls, it is true, but so slowly that everything which is poured into it sinks to the bottom, and is constantly added to till the sewer's mouth threatens to be obstructed or navigation is impeded, and then the dredge is set to work. Every low water the sun pours down its rays on this heap of filth, gases are generated, rise to the surface, are carried off by the winds, and our mortality tables show us the results in the deaths from fecal diseases.[42]

In August 1877, the contents of this report finally surfaced in the pages of the *Eagle*, under some very damning headlines: "Very Vile: The Disgusting Condition of the Gowanus Canal." Underlining the paper's postulation that the canal was in "really shocking condition" were some alarming statistics: 9,187 pounds of feces and 10,682 gallons of urine were expelled into the canal, on average, every day. "Cumulatively, that came out to 1,676 tons of solid waste and 63,600 hogsheads per year."

According to the *Eagle*, during the sewer system construction, the great demand for drainage required that the densest quarters of Brooklyn be completed before the huge exit mains in the outlying parts of the city. Temporary outlets, like those along the Gowanus, were used instead, but the time had long passed to finish this work properly.

"The Gowanus Canal is nothing more nor less than an open sewer," Dr. Raymond told the *Eagle* in an interview. "The whole surface of the water is agitated from the human excrement and other filth at the bottom, and, when they reach the surface, break, diffusing the noisome vapors far and wide. No sewer should be permitted to discharge into this canal, and I would most earnestly recommend that the Board give this matter their consideration at the earliest possible moment."[43]

The noxious overflow continued, and in February 1878 some Gowanus property owners petitioned the city to dredge the canal near Sackett and Degraw Streets, since it had become unnavigable, making business impossible. The city engineer, Mr. Demerritt, estimated it would cost $130 to remove the piles of sewage and waste, but also that "he did not think it was the duty of the city to do the work for the expressed benefit of property owners."[44]

A week later, the *Eagle* published a response from an intrepid reader with the initials J. C. B. His dissertation-length letter on the legal history of the Gowanus Canal's origin is the most complete and detailed ever to have been published. He stresses repeatedly that the canal's construction was funded by assessments from local property owners, and not technically any expenditures from the city's coffers. Certainly, Brooklyn city bonds had provided the cash to fund the labor, but the private owners were paying these back over a twenty-year period. Most importantly, J. C. B. pointed out in exacting detail that the laws creating the canal allowed for only surface drainage to enter the canal, and those acts "expressly left out and no authority given to empty sewers or sewerage into the canal" by any private owners or the city of Brooklyn. He suggested taking a glance at the "very excellent map" of Colonel Julius Adams that illustrated the exact location of Brooklyn's sewers and the extent of their drainage:

> It will also show that the Bond street sewer, one of the longest of the city, was to have been built, not to empty as it does now into the canal, but to have continued down along the west side of the canal to the corner of Hamilton avenue and Lorraine street, through the latter to Walcott street and through this to its foot, emptying into NY Bay.
>
> These citations show that no authority was ever given the city to use the canal for its own purposes for anything save surface drainage, and it necessarily follows that whenever the city has gone beyond this it has exceeded its powers and benefitted itself at private expense.
>
> This canal, built at the expense of property owners at its bank, is made an open sewer for a large portion of the city, which has borne no part of the burden of its construction. The failure to construct the Bond Street sewer according to the plan has saved the city several millions of dollars, and yet does not, as the report of the Board of Health shows, answer the purpose for which it was commenced, because being incomplete it does not do the work it was intended to do.[45]

J. C. B. was either a well-informed landowner or a man unusually obsessed with the ancient waterway and its origins (an affliction that the author is all too familiar with). But his point that sewage had no legal right to be ejected into the Gowanus remains relevant today. The story of ever-mounting health problems, also impeding navigation and befouling the air of the entire neighborhood, only grew in 1878. In October, the *New York Times* called the canal "a nuisance, emitting a malaria that has caused many deaths."[46]

In November a sizeable delegation of South Brooklyn property owners gathered in City Hall to urge Mayor Howell to adopt a measure to abate the nuisance (those present included William P. Libby and Cornelius J. Bergen, the latter a senior member of that venerable clan of Brooklyn landowners). As J. C. B. had suggested, they proposed an extension of the Bond Street sewer out to Wolcott Street, at an approximate cost of $140,000. The mayor conceded that the sewer had to be taken care of but, naturally, was "opposed to having it done as a general charge on the city." He encouraged the men to get legislation passed that would collect private landowner assessments to pay for a new sewer.

By the end of January 1879, such a bill was finally introduced to the State Legislature and subsequently passed. It proposed to extend the Bond Street sewer to a permanent outlet into the East River, paid for by district assessments. After this was completed, the final clause of the bill determined that "no sewerage or anything but pure water shall be run into said canal," and any person violating this be guilty of misdemeanor and liable for up to a two-thousand-dollar fine, six months imprisonment, or both. "This means a radical change," the *Eagle* concluded.[47]

It could not come soon enough for some Brooklynites. In the summer of 1880, a self-described engineer and inventor named H. S. Maxim wrote to the *Eagle* that the Gowanus remained so "dreadfully filthy" with organic material that it was in a state of constant fermentation, such that "the quantity of foul gasses given off is so great that the water appears to boil in some places." He proposed digging another smaller canal, with a system of locks that would help to flush out the worst of the canal pollution. Ironically, his system closely resembled the original Gowanus proposal by Major David Douglass in 1847—it had been rejected as unnecessary and too costly.[48]

The passage of a new sewer law was just one indicator of the changing economic tide. A wave of optimism swept across Brooklyn's lands, otherwise the city would never have bothered to address the costly Gowanus concerns. The most important project on the city's agenda was the Brooklyn Bridge, which was finally nearing completion after a decade of construction. This now-iconic conveyance spelled one thing to Brooklyn's real estate holders: recovery. During the downturn the city's property values had remained flat, and owners of large tracts of undeveloped lots had let their holdings go unregulated and unrented. Darby's Patch, the pulsing Irish slum that had long grown near the Gowanus, was regarded as an eyesore and detriment to the city. As the economic panic subsided, Brooklyn became ravenous for new revenue, and calculated new valuations for the many empty lots. Immediately the legislature began a hot new pursuit: back taxes.

The city had assessed Edwin C. Litchfield, along with all Gowanus property owners, for funds to pay for the new sewer construction. But it didn't stop there—the powers that be began a complete overhaul of Brooklyn's tax system. While investigating endless bookkeeping records, the assessors discovered that many of Brooklyn's top landowners owed years of unpaid arrears. Litchfield, who had the most holdings of all, had not paid a dime on his still undeveloped lands (large tracts between Seventh and Ninth Avenues) since 1872. The distraction of the Long Depression, some high-powered connections, and local prestige allowed this to oversight continue for years. William De Witt, the city's corporation counsel throughout the 1870s, was a friend and associate of the Litchfields (after retiring from his long-held position in 1883, he formed a law firm with Charles Tracy, a former law partner of Edwin's who had served as a judge in the Court of Appeals). Considering the Litchfields' great wealth and the fact that BIC had been such a driving force of Brooklyn real estate after the Civil War, the family had forever garnered special treatment. Of course, they were not alone in this; many other landowners had withheld tax payments. But the Litchfields were too big to pass under the radar.[49]

The city determined that collection time was nigh: the arrears for taxes and water rates (regardless of whether the properties had plumbing) had amounted to many thousands of dollars, sometimes greater than the actual value of the land itself. Even further, the Board of Assessors calculated enormous new estimates for the value of Brooklyn property: in 1879, an unfinished canal-side lot belonging to the BIC was estimated to be worth $2,600; in 1880 it was valued at $10,000. Litchfield, his family, and the Brooklyn Improvement Company owned several thousand lots, and were slapped with an arrears notice for almost $950,000.

This amount, which included a decade's worth of interest as high as 12 percent, was the largest tax bill the city had ever handed out. It would have been a fifth of Brooklyn's operating budget for the year—the cost of funding both the Police and Park Departments, with money to spare. With this sum Litchfield could have handed a one-dollar bill to each citizen of Brooklyn and still had enough to pay the rent on his mansion for a year. It would be tens if not hundreds of millions of dollars today.

He should have been outraged, but by this point Litchfield the elder appears to have given up. Grace, his wife, had died in the fall of 1881. He was sixty-six years old, and usually in ill health. Living a European life, such as partaking in water cures in the south of France, was preferable to struggling with money and politics in Brooklyn. He left the grand business dealings entirely to Edward, who went to the assessor's office to pay the first installment of the arrears. But the younger Litchfield, showing great moxie, brought only half the money—refusing to pay for the ballooning interest. In response the Board of Assessors refused the payment entirely and put a lien on his property. Edward rebutted by suing the city for passing an illegal assessment law. The matter went to civil court, and in 1882 the judge ruled in Edward's favor, as such a "gross discrepancy [in land value] must have sprung from an error of the assessing officers." The board appealed, and a legal battle ensued. For two years the board updated the arrears law, and the value of Litchfield's property was increased again by at least 10 percent—including the developed properties, now producing an inflated income that they taxed with no abandon.[50]

"I have opened negotiations direct with the enemy," wrote Edward, finally, to his ailing father in April 1883, "for a treaty of peace & mutual burying of the hatchet in our long war against taxes, etc. in Brooklyn." The family business was under heavy fire, as the city had collected from the Litchfields hundreds of thousands in income tax and was still litigating to collect the arrears. At the advice of a Brooklyn judge, Edward made plans to call upon Seth Low—the new Republican mayor of Brooklyn. This new chief had been the privileged son of a shipping merchant who made a fortune importing silks and tea from China. His grandfather was an early mayor of Brooklyn, when it was still only a village. Low was unusually honest for a politician, and is remembered as a tax reformer who reduced the city's debt. He was also closely involved with the construction of the Brooklyn Bridge, and would go on to serve as the second mayor of the consolidated New York City in 1902 (Brooklyn united with New York into a single municipality in 1898). This reasonable new mayor, if anybody, could stand up for a mutually beneficial settlement in the face of the Board of Assessors.

As recounted in a detailed letter to his father, at five o'clock the evening of April 5, 1883, Edward met with Low in his home in Brooklyn Heights. The mayor was very friendly and engaging, and then "opened fire" by suggesting that the Litchfields give up the baronial Grace Hill. It would help Gracie, Edward's younger sister, Low reasoned, who was often in ill health. Although it may seem unrelated, that the family still occupied the Prospect Park mansion was another source of resentment for Brooklyn's leaders. Both the land and the home belonged to the city, yet the family enjoyed the privilege of living there for a measly twenty-five hundred dollars a year. Low's suggestion was veiled political advice, but Edward soon drove the conversation toward settling the arrears problem.

"It is time to close out the matter finally," Low agreed. The mayor repeated the recent law that had been passed that year, which dictated that landowners like the Litchfields could either pay in bulk all of the taxes for 60 percent of the new value of their lands, or attempt to reason again with the Board of Assessors and their interest charges. "We are probably more heavily invested than any body else," Edward complained to Low. "The valuations of our property are so enormous, so outrageous, so excessive that the amounts involved were so great that we would have to stop and consider if it were safe to throw so much into the bottomless abyss of Brooklyn Property." Furthermore, Edward continued, the assessors were prejudiced, one having said to his face during their most recent meeting "it was no use to reduce Litchfields' valuations as he would not pay his taxes anyway." But that was not so, Edward exclaimed, as they were in fact already heavy taxpayers, who had paid over half a million dollars in hard cash into the city treasury that year. "We have done enough," he said, and then whipped out a paper with new, lower values for his undeveloped lands that he declared more reasonable.

"Since I entered my father's office ten years ago," continued the cunning young businessman, "up to the present day we have not had an offer to buy a lot for cash between Seventh and Ninth Avenues. Now, if it was a business matter or a railroad litigation I would make a cash offer and clean up the whole business, and make the whole property tax producing." Seth Low's eyes glistened in the lamplight, pausing at the end of this speech. "It would be difficult to arrange under the law, but I take pleasure in the idea of closing the whole manner," the mayor agreed. He then conceded that he knew the prejudice existed, and tried to control it, but would be very glad to settle with the Litchfields. Low believed that if they did so, then the other landowners and the assessors would settle and the arrears question would be at an end. Brooklyn would have plenty of cash to operate with—and the mayor's political career would greatly benefit.

Using reduced valuations, discounts, and the sort of specious real estate voodoo that drives New York's great economic engine to this day, Edward concocted a full-cash offer—$375,000. "Of course," he wrote to his father, "I am not at all sure that anything like this scheme would work . . . nous verrons: courage, mes amis, le diable est mort (on dit)!"[51]

Although the arrears matter would ultimately not be settled for a number of years, Edward wrote to his father several times in April and May sounding confident and jovial—once to recount the opening of the Brooklyn Bridge, which he believed would help the real estate situation ("The celebration was the greatest thing of the kind ever had in Brooklyn. . . . I did not attempt to fight my way up in through the crowd, contenting myself to seeing the procession over the bridge, the salute from the fleet of six men-of-war & watching the crowd"), and also to give him a business update:

> I suppose you are now settled in Paris and giving the tailor great anxiety, literally "fits" about your summer wardrobe. I do not think we need worry about the arrears matter, nor ought we to pay much under the present law. If real estate never becomes saleable we had better keep our money: if ever does become active we could afford to pay the arrears out of the profits. There are some pieces, however, we ought to settle, such as the middle of the ball ground,[52] as it is now leased for 5 years.[53]

Most likely the city backed off because, after 1883, Edward began paying taxes again after the decade-long break. But there was no rest for the young businessman, for in September the Prospect Park Commission sent him into another tailspin. Edward was away in Wyoming on a hunting trip, and his father was on an extended European sojourn, and the commissioners had waited years for new offices and announced they would no longer renew the family's lease on Grace Hill, which was expiring at the end of the year. "It is a very very sad undertaking that lies before me & I came home from the hunt with a very heavy heart to carry it out," Edward wrote to his father. "As requested the statuary it shall be all packed as directed, dogs and all, you bet."

He began the process of moving by getting an expert from the Metropolitan Museum of Art in New York to handle with the statues. Edward soon wrote to his father again: "In the face of the enemy, as we are here & continuously under fire, it is pleasant to have a little diversion and amusement, even if it takes the form of exterminating innocent and amiable grizzly bears from the face of the earth." The younger Litchfield had become entranced with hunting and proceeded to list his trophies from Wyoming, which had just arrived in New York: an antelope, some elk, three black-tail deer, several black bears, and nine grizzly bears. The noble beasts were huge, one ten feet long and nine hundred pounds. All had been shipped back stuffed and mounted—but Edward now lacked a house in which to display them. He planned to move his family into a smaller mansion in Brooklyn Heights.[54]

Yet the great railroad family was not the only one in Brooklyn being kicked out on the street: At the end of September, three police officers went on a tour of Darby's Patch to inform several hundred Gowanus inhabitants they would have to leave their shacks within two weeks. The slum had formed on the estate of Margaretta Remsen, a recently deceased scion of an old New York family, and the city had foreclosed on her property. There was plenty of colorful resistance as the police knocked on doors: One "dumpy, fat Irishwoman," as the *Eagle* described, once realizing that her visitor was a sheriff, cried out "O, begad, I'll have nothing to do with yer at all!" and slammed the door in his face. "Indade, I can't understand a word you say," her shanty-dwelling neighbor quipped. "I have got the malarial favor so bad I can't listen to yer." The last squatters were evicted in mid-November. Many resisted: a man stood in his doorway clutching an axe and a carving knife, while another scrambled to find ancient lease documents. But eventually the entire slum was emptied—one resident, Mary Waters, claimed she lived on the estate for thirty-five years.[55]

Meanwhile, through the early winter Edward was busy emptying out Grace Hill—they had to vacate their home of more than twenty-five years by January 13, 1884. Most frustratingly, in mid-December a park police officer had ordered Edward not to remove the sculpture of the hunting hounds guarding the doors of the mansion—he claimed that the Litchfields might not have the right to remove them. "On hearing this I gave orders to hasten the boxing of the dogs & to have a wagon there early the next morning to take them away," Edward wrote. "That afternoon however they sent around a written order 'authorizing him to remove' our dogs! Why did they not give him permission to remove our furniture! I removed them the next morning before they could change their minds." The Litchfields' extensive library was also inventoried, packed in boxes, and moved from Grace Hill to the Coignet Building on Third Avenue and Third Street. All of the expensive mirrors and paintings were stored there as well. The statuary would be stored temporarily in a small building next door. John Farell, live-in building caretaker, would watch over the expensive objects. The BIC had taken over the Coignet Building as a second office when the concrete works had gone out of business. "It is an awfully sad task removing all these things," Edward wrote to his father, "and I feel as if when I get through I would never want to be back at Grace Hill again."[56]

On July 25, 1885, Edwin C. Litchfield died in Aix-les-Bains, in the south of France. He was seventy years old. In August the great projector's body was shipped back to New York, where he was laid to rest in the family plot in Green-Wood Cemetery next to Grace Hubbard Hill Litchfield, his wife. After the appropriate mourning period, the Brooklyn Improvement Company board met on September 12, 1885, and resolved that Edward H. Litchfield would be elected the new president to fill the vacancy left by his father. On motion, the board also empowered the company to "bring suits against the city of Brooklyn for damages caused by reasons of the running of sewers into the Gowanus Canal."[57]

7

Industry, Identity, and Violence in Gowanus (1885–1898)

John Walsh was the watchman on duty at the Citizens' Gas-Light Company the night a destructive cyclone hit the city of Brooklyn. It was just after seven o'clock on January 9, 1889, when the massive windstorm swept across the city, tearing down signs and breaking windows. The gale blew with such strength that streetcars were blown off of their tracks.

One had been crossing the Gowanus Canal at Hamilton Avenue, near Citizens' Gas-Light, at Smith Street and Fifth Street. It overturned, spilling its passengers onto the bridge, dangerously close to the frigid waters below. As the winds howled around his wooden guardhouse, Walsh noticed a light coming from somewhere in the yard. It barely illuminated the three massive holding tanks in the yard, the largest of which was fifty feet tall and contained a half million cubic feet of gas. The cyclone was just then passing overhead.

At that moment, without warning, the largest tank exploded. A tremor shook the streets and foundations of Brooklyn almost a mile in every direction; the deafening sound reached even farther. Soon following was the crashing din of several tons of iron tumbling back to earth. Waves rippled across already agitated Gowanus Canal, lapping the bulkhead walls.

The tall fence surrounding the yard was a shattered memory, while sheets of flame engulfed Fifth Street and shot up into the sky. All of the streetlamps and house lights in much of South Brooklyn were extinguished as the blaze rapidly consumed their fuel source. From a distance, the contrast of the suddenly dark neighborhood was all the more shocking as burning gas lit up the evening sky, visible for miles around. Several minutes passed, and Walsh, somehow still alive, emerged from the wreckage and ran to the surviving tank that was closest to the blaze. This one was half the size of the former behemoth that lay in mangled pieces across the yard, and gas was leaking from its seams. His own life an afterthought, the watchman heaved against the escape valve wheel on the side of the huge iron cylinder. A pronounced hiss announced its opening as the gas safely discharged into the ground. Walsh breathed a sigh of relief. Seven minutes had passed since the first inferno began. Just then, the tank farthest from the blaze exploded. Another volley of iron columns and trusses went flying through the air, crashing to the ground just as the firefighters arrived to tackle the inferno—luckily, on the opposite side of the yard.

"The scene in the gas company's yard was chaotic," wrote the *Brooklyn Daily Eagle* the following day. "The 10 great cast-iron cylindrical columns, two and one-half feet in diameter, were broken in pieces and blown into the street like so many needles. The heavy iron plate roof had been thrown off the tank, and the entire apparatus lay in a heap on the ground. The fence lay flat on the ground. Scattered here and there, over sidewalk and roadway, were heavy iron beams and girders."

Panic had ensued in all of the shanties and tenement houses that surrounded the gasworks after the first explosion. Every window around Fifth and Smith Streets had been shattered and front doors were torn from their hinges. The rough furniture, hewn by its working-class owners, had splintered at the force of the explosion.

Noxious gas fumes and fire spread through the buildings on Fifth Street. Jeremiah and John Dugan, residents of number 15, barely got their elderly mother out of a rear window before flames consumed the building. A man named John Tierney fainted from the escaping gas fumes but was revived in the nick of time, although his son suffered serious burns on his face and hands. A woman named Rose Duffy suffered bleeding cuts from the broken glass. One family, including eleven children, escaped while their home burned to the ground. The authorities never determined quite what caused the explosion. They hypothesized that the destructive wind—which razed dozens of buildings across Brooklyn—had knocked over the heavy iron cover.[1]

One month after the Citizens' Gas-Light explosion, a hundred workmen gathered around a curious brass machine at the New York Cream of Tartar Factory on Ninth Street and the Gowanus. Standing next to the two and half foot contraption perched on a wooden platform was Edward Oliver, one factory worker who lived in Astoria, Queens. The device was a new centrifuge, invented by a man named Samuel S. Hepworth, designed to dry the tartaric acid crystals needed in the manufacture of cream of tartar, a key ingredient in baking powder. In powder form this chemical had a myriad of other nineteenth-century household uses, such as solvents for cleaning porcelain and metals and removing rust.

Already familiar with the centrifuge, Oliver switched on the machine and, under the hum of the spinning mechanism, began to explain how it worked. Just as the internal chamber reached full speed there was a terrific bang, and the machine exploded. Particles of brass and iron bolts flew in every direction, smashing panes of glass fifty feet away. Six men were knocked to the floor, most of them covered in blood. Emil Weber, the foreman, and Robert King, an eighteen-year-old workman, were dead—the tops of their heads entirely blown off by flying machine parts. Through some miracle Oliver had been knocked unconscious but received no serious injuries, while other workmen were not so lucky: Charles Bradshaw suffered serious wounds in one thigh, Peter Zwitzowitsch fractured a leg, and Charles Meyers's face was torn by a flying piece of brass and his eyes scalded by the harsh chemicals. The police were not notified of the explosion at the cream of tartar factory until a full day after the incident occurred; reporters were denied explanations by factory leadership, only that the matter "concerned the company alone." Found at their homes, the injured workers refused to be interviewed as they had "been instructed to say nothing" by their bosses, according to the *Eagle*. Drs. Schroeder and Bayliss, brought in by the company owners to attend to the injured workers, also "refused to have anything more to do with the case," according to the *Eagle*. The two were regularly employed by the Royal Baking Powder Company—the owner of New York Tartar Company—to attend to workers, and were likely paid to keep silent. Still, the story eventually made its way to the intrepid *Eagle* reporter, who made sure to show the extent of trouble the owners went to to keep the story under wraps.[2]

At the end of the nineteenth century, the Gowanus neighborhood—extending for several blocks around the busy industrial waterway—had become one of the densest industrial quarters of Brooklyn. Since the opening of Citizens' Gas-Light, two other manufactured gas plants had opened in the area, leading to the dubbing of Gowanus as "the Gashouse District," an appellation that persisted well into the next century. Furthermore, three-quarters of all exports and imports in the port of New York were being handled in Brooklyn. These included exotic commodities from all over the world, such as sulfur, iron, coconuts, tobacco, cork, tar, rock salt, Italian marble, camphor, bamboo, and hemp. Of America's coffee, 90 percent was shipped in from Manila or Maracaibo to Brooklyn warehouses. In 1887 alone, more than a million tons of sugar and fifteen million pounds of crude rubber were shipped through the city's docks—nearly 90 percent of the whole country's supply.[3]

New methods of producing and refining these raw materials were invented every day, providing countless new opportunities for work—

especially to immigrants and their children—and products to sell. But while daily innovations provided greater and cheaper comforts for America's growing class of thrifty consumers, the new technologies brought about a gruesome number of new ways to injure people. The peril of factory work in this era was hardly limited to adult men, as women and children worked and suffered in these hazardous workplaces as well. Three days before the gas-plant explosion, thirty-year-old Minnie Ward was at work at Planet Mills, a textile plant on President Street and Bond, one block from the Gowanus Canal. The factory specialized in carpets and mats woven of jute and hemp—cheap natural fibers widely bought by the growing middle class. While Ms. Ward operated one of the massive steam-powered looms that morning, a piece of her clothing was caught in the shafting mechanism. The unfortunate woman was lifted in the air and thrown around for several rotations of the apparatus before the other workers were able to shut it off. An examining doctor declared that she had suffered internal injuries, and several friends had to help get to her home in Red Hook.[4]

While few nineteenth-century factory could be considered safe by today's standards, weaving mills had a particular capacity for injuring workers. The industrial-grade looms spun and bound fibers together at alarming speeds to attain the latest standards of production. In one 1882 incident, a Planet Mills employee man named Kearns had the job of guiding raw jute into the rollers of a "carding machine," which would remove the useless hard refuse at the ends of the plant. While doing his job Kearns's left hand was inadvertently pulled into the mechanism, cutting off one of his fingers and leaving a grotesque scar on his palm. He sued his employers for ten thousand dollars, but the presiding judge declared there was no evidence of the owner's fault, and "it did not appear that the plaintiff was not himself guilty of contributory negligence."[5]

As remains the case today, rich business owners often had the advantage over their employees of high-priced lawyers—if not also greedy judges. But workers were not always at a disadvantage: In December 1885, a young boy named Michael Ryan was working the rollers at Planet Mills when the machine caught one of his hands and pinched off the ends of every finger. He sued in a case that was heard before the New York State Supreme Court. "The defense claimed the boy was negligent and had been cautioned as to how he operated the machine," the *Eagle* reported, "but the counsel for the plaintiff argued that the defendants had no right to employ a lad about a dangerous piece of machinery." The jury awarded young Ryan—his age was not published, but he was probably not older than fourteen—a verdict of $250.[6]

Just one week later, seventeen-year-old Gowanus resident Ellen Judge got her right hand caught in the Planet Mills machinery, with two fingers requiring amputation. One month later a "bobbin girl" named Julia Foy was cleaning an active bobbin frame when her right hand also got stuck, crushing three fingers. Likely inspired by Michael Ryan, Ms. Foy sued her employers for ten thousand dollars in the circuit court. While the owners attempted to show that the frames were stopped for five minutes every week for such maintenance, other bobbin girls testified that five minutes was not enough time to complete the task, and the foreman regularly saw them cleaning the machines while they were in motion.[7]

Entrepreneurs and factory owners did little to protect their workers from peril. The Triangle Shirtwaist Fire, the historic tragedy in which more than 140 garment workers died in a Manhattan sweatshop—elevating worker safety conditions to a national concern—would not occur for twenty-five years. Case in point, several months after the explosions at Citizens' Gas-Light and New York Tartar, Planet Mills suffered a massive fire, causing half a million dollars worth of damage. Nearly three hundred women and young girls were working after midnight on April 12, 1889, as an unusual amount of business "having called for the pushing of work day and night," according to the *Eagle*, when flames broke out on the first floor. The conflagration quickly spread, as "immense heaps of lumber about the factory fed the flames and added to the grandeur of the scene." Hearing the alarms, the terrified workers dashed for the stairs, but were driven back by clouds of smoke. They took to the fire escapes, crowding at the windows as the air grew thick and noxious.

Although the workers were lucky to even have such an escape available, a foolish designer had placed the escapes directly above a deep areaway (those sunken stairwells along certain prewar buildings that allow outside access to basements). It would have been a fall of twenty feet from the bottom of the escape to the concrete floor of the areaway. Literally hundreds of women, "nearly crazy with fright," clung to the precarious iron bars as flames devoured the mill behind them. Directly across from Planet Mills sat a row of tenements housing most of the workers and their families, now jolted awake by the chaos. A large crowd quickly gathered, some screaming out the names of their loved ones in panic. Officer Sheedy of the Third Precinct soon arrived and recruited two men, Frank Martin and a Mr. McGarry, to tear the woodwork from the side of a truck and raise it to the fire escape, creating a rough wooden slide. Two reporters on the scene, Mr. Marvin and Mr. Fitzgerald, held it in place as "the girls rolled down the incline pell mell."

Minutes after the last of the women hit the Gowanus soil, the boiler exploded in the basement and part of the building tumbled in. Against all odds, the casualties announced were just a few bruises, since all of the women and young girls were accounted for. James Piggot, a clerk in the city's Building Department, later declared to the *Eagle* that he had inspected the building earlier in the year and suggested that the two flights of escape stairs be placed outside the building, "which the owners cheerfully did." Without a shred of irony, Piggot's department had considered the structure "one of the safest in the city," which he believed was verified by the successful escape of the two-hundred plus women. Aghast at the "speed and fury of destruction in South Brooklyn" that evening, an *Eagle* editorialist was not inclined to agree with Mr. Piggot. "Any particular building in which 300 busy women and girls are crowded is really a 'tinder box'—even if it is not swept out of existence in an hour with the convenient aid of thoughtful piled up timber," the writer argued. "At this day there is no excuse for failure to make great industrial buildings reasonably fireproof. . . . For example, a systematic and successful movement to make the places where men, women, and children labor safe and wholesome would accomplish more for 'the working classes' and all other classes than centuries of agitation to tax private ownership of land out of existence." While clearing out the debris to rebuild the factory two months later, some workers discovered a few charred human bones. They were declared the remains of Hugh McNerney, a fifty-five-year-old engineer and the only casualty of the fire. He lived at 233 Hoyt Street with his daughters Mamie and Susie, who had worked alongside him at the mill.[8]

The setting of industrial Gowanus provided for another kind of violent activity: In June 1884, two youths working at Planet Mills were asked to fetch the same pushcart that had been left on the sidewalk outside. Walter Henry, who was only sixteen and small for his age, got to it before John Fitzgerald, a much bigger twenty-one-year-old. Despite Fitzgerald's clear physical advantage, Henry refused to surrender his prize, and so the older youth punched the younger several times and threatened worse. In response, the teenage Henry unsheathed a long and especially sharp knife—used in the mill for cutting thick canvas—and plunged the blade into the left side of his older opponent's chest. The skimpy youth fled immediately and the wounded Fitzgerald was soon rushed to the Long Island College Hospital, where he died the next day. After being captured Henry claimed that, fearing bad treatment due to his diminutive size, it was not the first time he had used the knife in self-defense.[9]

Such anecdotes were commonplace and regularly circulated in Gowanus, revealing the character of an era that had, in the space of a few decades, grown accustomed to stories of violence in a now-industrial setting. Several days after Fitzgerald's murder, Planet Mills' employees enjoyed a company picnic at Schuetzen Park in New Jersey, a pleasant outing without any incident of note. Nonetheless, two weeks later a rumor began to circulate in "that portion of South Brooklyn bounded by Baltic street, Eleventh Street, the Gowanus canal and Dennet place," as mapped out by the *Eagle*, that a young employee named Rose who attended the picnic never came home and her body had been found in a nearby clump of woods. Her parents supposedly did not inform the police to avoid notoriety and attention. Investigating the story, an *Eagle* reporter visited the Planet Mills office, where a clerk volunteered that a piece of clothing belonging to Rose McNierney, one of the employees, had been found in the Gowanus Canal. She was, however, at work upstairs.

"No reporter can see Miss McNierney, she is busy!" declared John Rutherford, the mill superintendent in a mad and excited manner. He refused to divulge the young woman's address, so the reporter consulted the local directory and soon after arrived at the residence of a Mrs. Michael McNierney, at 395 Baltic Street in South Brooklyn. It was the wrong Mrs. McNierney, unfortunately, but the woman still had plenty to say on the matter. "The poor girl was shot dead and then killed with a knife and had all of her fingers cut off," she explained, and then insisted on leading the reporter up a rickety staircase to her neighbor, Mrs. Murray, who knew the whole story.

"You're always telling everything I tell you, ain't you now?" was Mrs. Murray's salutation, and then the two began to bicker until it got so heated that the unwilling informer seized a heavy ladle on the table, at which time the reporter quickly excused himself. Further inquiries proved that every Gowanus resident had his or her own version of the gruesome event, and only after combing through the miniscule Dennet Place, Luqueer Street, and Nelson Street was the proper McNierney home found—next door to the Smith Street Glass Works. Rose, a pretty and entirely alive seventeen-year-old, answered the door, but her mother quickly appeared to explain the issue. This particular string of gossip had been relayed to her by "a lump of a girl and some old woman" who had arrived at the door a few days after the company picnic. Her "Rosey," apparently, had been found drowned in the Gowanus and her corpse was lying on the Third Street Dock.

"I didn't feel frightened because I knew Rosey was in the house ironin' all afternoon," Mrs. McNierney explained, but it made little difference. Half the neighborhood had already heard the story and arrived in droves at her doorstep to pay their respects—including some nuns from the local Catholic school and even Father O'Boylan from St. Mary Star of the Sea (he claimed to have come to shame the gossip mongers). "Ever since wherever I go I be stopped and asked about it until I'm nearly crazy," Mrs. McNierney complained, once she completed the lengthy tale. The reporter lucked out, in the end, and was finally allowed to accompany young Rose back to work at Planet Mills.

"Do you know," she said, "I think that two kittens that were found drowned at the foot of Eleventh street is the foundation of all the rumors?"

"How that could be?" the reporter asked.

"Well, I have a dress of a peculiar pattern that is well known down here and the stuff the kittens were wrapped in was just like my dress," Rose explained. "Someone recognized it and said it was part of my dress, and the story went around. The people down here are terrible gossips."[10]

Nature in Industrial Gowanus

Aside from knife fights, fires, lost extremities, and rumors, the same flooding that has characterized Gowanus throughout its history continued to plague the neighborhood of Planet Mills. Unlike the operose Dutch colonists, who used the flooding to their advantage, nineteenth-century urban expansion and the reality of industrial life had made such adaptations impossible. These floods had gotten worse following the closure of the Bond Street sewer. That "fix"—blocking out the oldest drain in the city—was supposed to halt the raw sewage problem in the canal. It did reduce the sewage flow into the canal, but at the price of much greater flooding in the surrounding streets. The resulting floods indicate an important truth of the Gowanus Canal: no matter how it might be modified, the Gowanus remains the site of a wetland at one of the lowest elevations in Brooklyn—a collection point of a grand watershed. Only the monumental, astronomically expensive effort of engineering could change this fact of geography, and so during the greatest rainstorms, swelling tidewaters fill the main and lateral sewer pipes. Once these are full, the waters fill area basements—a fact of nineteenth-century life that continues today.

The drain to Wolcott Street that had been dug to replace the Bond Street sewer couldn't handle the volume of water that New York experiences, never mind the power of gravity. Meanwhile, raw sewage

HERE THEY ARE, FISHING AT GOWANUS CANAL.

A group of young men fishing in the Gowanus Canal, taken by the *Brooklyn Daily Eagle*, dated April 5, 1912. Brooklyn Collection. Courtesy of the Brooklyn Public Library and Newspapers.com.

still flowed into the canal through several other outfalls, and years of waste had piled up at the exits. Local landowners were furious that the city had allowed their neighborhood, with all the flooding, to continue as a shallow cesspool.

In 1886, Gowanus waterfront landowners John J. Hill and James L. Morgan sued Brooklyn for twenty thousand dollars for blocking up the bottom of the canal with sewage from the infamous Bond Street exit. The troublesome overflow had been closed for around two years, but that hardly addressed the huge pile of waste that had been left behind, untouched and stinking. Before the state Supreme Court, the men argued that their 622 feet of dock frontage on the canal had been rendered practically worthless—their witnesses claimed that the Gowanus was so filled up "that laden boats could not reach their docks."

One Gowanus pilot testified that he frequently found the canal unnavigable. In his cross-examination, the pilot described how the propellers of his boat churned up clumps of tar from the bottom of the canal. In the city's defense, corporation counsel Almet F. Jenks argued that if the waterway was choked up it was because of the nearby creosote works or Citizens' Gas-Light plant, not the sewer. The production of creosote, a chemical preservative distilled from coal tar, was a natural progression in new Gowanus industry, since the raw material from which it was derived was in healthy supply from the manufactured gas plants. Despite being a heavily toxic carcinogen, coal tar has myriad applications that were reflected in nineteenth-century American industry—from pavement sealing to medical uses, like treatment of dandruff, psoriasis, and even headaches (since the 1980s, coal tar's dangerous side effects have led to its substitution with less harmful alternatives in many household products).

At any rate, two months after the trial, Jenks sent to the mayor his annual Law Department report, which included the results of the case. Justice Cullon ruled in favor of the city: "I regard this as a most satisfactory result," wrote Jenks in the report, "inasmuch as a recovery by the plaintiff would undoubtedly led to the institution of many actions by other owners of land along the canal."[11]

Jenks was unintentionally prescient on the issue, but such victories against the city had already unfolded in other parts of Brooklyn. The whole of the waterfront from Williamsburg to Red Hook was dominated by shipping and industry. At the northernmost part sat Newtown Creek, Brooklyn's other industrial canal that serves as the natural border of Queens County, at the tip of Greenpoint. Quite similar in origin to the Gowanus, Newtown Creek is bigger and just as disgusting: in addition to raw sewage, this "turbid and oleaginous torrent," as the *Eagle* described it, was polluted by various slaughterhouses, oil refineries, bone-boiling establishments, fertilizer plants, and "and other industrial nosegays." Its home, Williamsburg, also suffered regular floods, and local inhabitants had led the way in filing lawsuits against the city.

The pollution was so pronounced that toward the end of an especially pungent Brooklyn summer in 1887, the *Eagle* published one of its pithy editorials, "Brooklyn Outrivaling Cologne," which opened by referring to Brooklyn as "a center of evil odors" among all the cities of the Union. "How is it that Brooklyn, of all cities in this Republic, should be selected as the haunt of smells—evil, unsanitary superabundant smells?" the writer complained. "The State Board has earned the gratitude of the Brooklyn public by holding a session here and doing something to abate the swill milk evil, and if it would detail two or three representatives to this city to test the fluids sold under the name of milk from tramp wagons and in corner groceries, it would in time break up the evil of skimming, water, and adulterating milk. If it can give us pure milk can it not give us pure air?"

"South Brooklyn has lately permitted itself to be lured by a foolish ambition into an attempt to outrival Newtown Creek—a hopeless attempt, by the way—and being deficient in piggeries and fertilizer works it took to flooding the tenement cellars and drowning the rag and bone collections of the Neapolitans who live there," he continued.

"Failing to arrive at any solution of the imposing problem, the Mayor, the Fire Commissioner, the Health Commissioner and the Sewer Director went to the scene of the moisture and found innumerable children wading about the cellars and first floors of the neighborhood. Those that were not wading were shaking with malaria. The whole district exhaled a wild and furious smell. One Italian was ordered to bring his rags up out of the wet, and it was then announced, 'action would be taken.'"[12]

In October, another *Eagle* editorial recalled that when the Bond Street sewer was being closed, the chief city engineer had proposed a giant sewer main to run along Greene Avenue to replace it, projected to cost a prohibitive one million dollars. The large-scale work would have been the most efficient tactic to alleviate Brooklyn's two worst flood zones, all at once. But the "political economists" of the Board of Aldermen—mainly Michael J. Coffey, a leading Brooklyn democrat who had served in both houses of the State Legislature —rejected the plan and its price tag. Instead, the aldermen had kept up their Brooklyn tradition of ignoring the instructions of engineers and gave engineer Robert Van Buren (who was descended from President Martin Van Buren) a little more than two hundred thousand to contrive several makeshift relief sewers.

"He knew it would serve the purpose very incompletely and has done so," wrote the *Eagle*, sympathetic to Van Buren's woes. "If the means to carry off the water was insufficient, other and sufficient means should be supplied. Any man forehanded enough to secure for himself a dwelling place and intelligent enough to go into it when it rained could not fail, reasoning by analogy upon a grade above idiocy, to reach this conclusion." The Brooklyn government's stingy behavior was a sharp contrast with the situation of the 1860s, when haphazard expenditure on "public" works of speculative importance such as major road projects in unsettled parts of the city were rampant, as long as certain wealthy landowners deemed them valuable. Many of those improvements had since suffered damage, thanks to shifting land grades and post facto utility installations, and were now being neglected. "Unfortunately for the city," the *Eagle* editorial concluded, "when extravagant and anticipative outlays of this sort was stopped and 'retrenchment' became as urgent and indiscriminating a cry as 'enterprise' had been, things needing to be done immediately were put off also."[13]

Aside from the fear of disease and the inconvenience, the mismanagement was embarrassing for Brooklynites. After nearly a half century of wild expansion, the country's third most populous city still suffered crippling floods when it rained. Again, our storied canal neighborhood was not alone in this affliction. One infamous locale during the 1880s was the junction of the former North Second and Ninth Streets in Williamsburg, now called Metropolitan and Rodney Streets, respectively. This intersection sat at the head of the former Bushwick Creek, a marshy and long-vanished estuary that reached a mile inland to the present-day Williamsburg neighborhood, toward the seventeenth-century Dutch settlement of Boswyck. When it rained, the basements of area houses would flood to the surface; streetcar passengers had to stand on their seats to avoid the water while passing over Ninth Street. Before long, irritated Brooklynites sued their city for negligence.[14]

In his 1887 report, Van Buren suggested that the city reopen the sewage-spewing Bond Street overflows to quell the floods. If that didn't work, sewer relief lines would have to be constructed, but the engineer was worried about the flooding from Sackett Street. "I find a great deal of trouble owing to the sewer being too low," he wrote, and went to express his desire to construct a new sewer at a higher grade—but his budget would be limited more than ever. It was a precarious game for Brooklyn's government to play with the health and sanitation of a thriving city. "The measure is imperfect," the *Eagle* concluded, "but it is urgent and will have to be repeated until the penny wise and pound foolish method of transiting the business of a great city is abandoned." Within two months about a dozen residents of the flooded parts of Bond, Baltic, and Sackett Streets sued the city for nearly twenty thousand dollars in further compensation, this time for damage cause by floods.[15]

As was typical of aldermen, the deliberation over Van Buren's plan carried on for months. By January 1889, more than fifty residents had sued, now for more than triple the original amount sought. Finally the elected officials agreed upon a plan, this time to build a second Bond Street relief branch, on Baltic Street. But the complaints and various lawsuits from local residents had caught the attention of the New York State Board of Health, and in the summer of 1889, a special commission was gathered to review all of the conditions at the Gowanus, led by Dr. John Griffin, Brooklyn's health commissioner. This Gowanus Canal Commission took surveys and interviewed local residents over several months, presenting a lengthy report that fall.[16] The results were quite drastic:

> We are led to decide that the filling or closing up of the Gowanus Canal is the best means of its improvement or betterment. . . . Beyond question this so-called canal is a private waterway, not more than 560 feet of property along either side of its banks, exclusive of the bridge property, belonging to the public. Further, it is incontestable that, while the canal is a source of great profit to less than 100 persons, firms or corporations who enjoy a monopoly of its ownership, it is detrimental to health, obstructive to traffic, and an injury in its present condition to real estate values throughout South Brooklyn.

The report also pointed out that four sewers still emptied into the canal, and "a large number of water closets . . . [since] the canal has at all times at least a population of 500 human beings, besides numbers of animals, with hundreds of persons employed in and about it, for whom only sewage directly into it is provided." The commissioners also included a petition signed by three thousand regular passengers of the streetcar line along Jay, Smith, and Ninth Streets (originally drawn by horses, the path would eventually rise above the bridges to become one part of the IND Culver Line, now known as the F Train). They complained that the opening of the Hamilton Avenue and Ninth Street bridges regularly worsened the morning rush hour commute. P. H. Flynn, a real estate dealer, recalled in testimony a twenty-minute delay at Hamilton Avenue that scared off a potential wealthy client from New York: "My prospective customer did not want to cross the bridge, but left the car with the remark that property located on the other side of a body of water like the canal and which delayed travel to such an extent was not worth investing in."

The commission also identified the worst polluting businesses: the Fulton Municipal Gas Works (at Nevins and Sackett Streets abutting the canal), one unnamed starch works, a dye company, a lime kiln, and the New York Cream of Tartar Company. However, in the eye of the public none of these "agencies of nuisances" came close to that of the city itself—not only for allowing the sewers to dump in the Gowanus, but for permitting those companies to their discharge their refuse into the canal, usually at night. Furthermore, the commissioners informed, "on the last occasion of our inspections, the carcasses of at least a dozen animals were seen to float on its surface."

The report estimated that the whole fill-in proposal, which included purchasing several million dollars worth of private canal-side property, would cost the city at least ten million. An alternative improvement plan was also presented, almost as an afterthought. It suggested a repair of the many rotting wooden bulkheads and dredging the canal down to the hard bottom, cleaning out all of the gunk and refuse. Finally, a "flushing gate and conduit for the cleaning of the canal may appear necessary hereafter." The cost of these alternative improvements was estimated to be at least five hundred thousand dollars. Perhaps unsurprisingly, the Gowanus Canal Commission was quickly disbanded after the report was published.[17]

But the damage was already done: In February 1893, George H. Deitsch, a state assemblyman, proposed a bill to close the canal, backed by the thousands of signatures of local discontents. "At no time," claimed the *New York Times*, "have more than sixty-four firms and individuals opposed such a thing. Yet the sixty-four have always triumphed, They have factories along the canal and fill the water with foul-smelling stuff, but they make large sums of money every year, and do not hesitate, it is said, to spend some of it among a certain class of thrifty legislations."[18]

The most vocal opponents of the closing were indeed entrepreneurs and landowners such as Edward H. Litchfield, whose businesses depended on the Gowanus waters. Their main argument against filling the canal included the major cost and that it would disrupt yet another massive project, the Greene Avenue sewer main. The largest outlet of the Greene Avenue project, which was intended to drain portions of Clinton Hill, Fort Greene, and Fourth Avenue, was at the head of the Gowanus—and comprised more than double the area drained by the original Gowanus Creek. In addition to solving the problem of an extensive "flood district," in Brooklyn, the waters were intended serve the dual purpose of flushing out the foulest of debris floating in the stagnant canal. It was not a bad plan, per se, but these protesting businessmen were likely more concerned about fiscal than civic health. The same week that they spoke out against filling in the canal, the Philadelphia and Reading Railroad went bankrupt—the first sign of the impending financial crisis known as the Panic of 1893. Much like its predecessor exactly two decades earlier, this financial depression was not the ideal economic environment to fund civic projects.[19]

South Brooklyn Mythology

Daily life in Gowanus clearly did not play out only in sewer planning meetings. Rather, the docks, yards, and factories along the canal drove Brooklyn's economy. Longshoremen strained their muscles daily to unload cargo, and the sweat of carpenters mixed with sawdust in lumberyards as the city continued to expand. Factory workers counted their extremities before clocking out at night. Yet many skilled laborers considered their lives to be prosperous and enjoyed more free time and spending money than agricultural workers or untrained construction workers. For recreation, one of the most popular activities among the Brooklynites was baseball. For more then thirty years, amateur and professional games had been played all across the city, especially in South Brooklyn—and in particular the area around Gowanus.

"The base ball fever has broken out with redoubled force in South Brooklyn," the *Eagle* wrote in April of 1891. "All the vacant lots in the vicinity of the Gowanus canal were crowded yesterday with contending teams and spectators. Hundreds of people assembled on the Twelfth ward flats in the afternoon expecting to witness the game announced between the Nassaus and the Fultons. The latter, for the second time this year, failed to materialize, however and the crowd was not backward in expressing its disappointment."[20]

A story of one such match was published in August 1892, in which a gang of nine Gowanusians formed a baseball team under to sponsorship from one Mr. Mulgrew, who owned a rather infamous pub somewhere in the neighborhood. He had provided uniforms, oversized shirts, and knickerbockers that sat "very close to the shoe tops of the different wearers, but then the Gowanusians are not, as a general thing, very particular," according to Maurice McLoughlin, the *Eagle* writer. This gang sat around drinking "washtubs" of beer provided by Mr. Mulgrew's bar, waiting for the "Sons of Rest," the rival team that was walking down from Williamsburg in the midday heat. The cockiest player, Slob McTerrigan, gave some "sound advice about the manner in which they were to sail forth to conquer 'de mugs from Butchtown' (this being the name by which Williamsburg is known in Gowanus)." The nine were joined by a number of "'heelers' or 'scrappers' to 'pile on' in case there should be any disagreement between the members of the opposing nines: and if a game by any accident should happen to proceed without a hitch the 'heelers' return home quite disgusted."

Soon quite a crowd had gathered, including the "entire kid population of Gowanus," mostly to poke fun at Mr. Mulgrew's ill-fitting team uniforms. The game quickly began, with one Jigsy McDuff as pitcher. After a near score by the Williamsburg team, McDuff struck out the other players, and so the home team came to bat. Slob McTerrigan, a hulking brute, was the first up for Gowanus, scrunching his face so as to strike "terror into the gizzards of all the onlookers." He approached home plate, appropriately marked by a cobblestone.

"One strike!" yelled the umpire as McTerrigan swung at the teaser in vain. The second ball was an inshoot, catching the giant off guard and striking him "fairly amidships." He howled in pain, and, ignoring the umpire's yell of "Take yer base!" marched up to the little pitcher, threatening him with the heavy bat.

"Wot did yer wanter do, kill me?" he asked. A crowd gathered as the game finally became interesting.

"Aw dat wuz only an accident," said the pitcher through his grin.

"Well maybe dis is an accident of de same kind," said Slob, poking the smaller man in the stomach with his wooden instrument. "I'll show youse dat youse can't come no funny business over us, see?"

At that, the pitcher jumped in the air and landed several right hooks in Slob's face. Mulgrew's team then jumped the pitcher and "'engaged in the great tough game of piling on,' which consisted of throwing themselves into the thick of the fight and following the Irishman's advice of hitting a head wherever they saw one."

With the fantastic colloquialisms and exaggerated Brooklyn accents, this story is fiction, but it represents an important greater truth—by this era, Gowanus had taken on the role of a defining cultural benchmark of working-class Brooklyn. The full account in its colorful and verbose glory was published in a *Brooklyn Daily Eagle* column called "Eaglets," a sort of proto-comics page (printed images were too expensive for a daily newspapers in this era) of funny poems and one-liners. The writer, Maurice McLoughlin, was a Brooklyn humorist familiar with the Irish quarters of his native city. His comical stories were published weekly starting in 1891, in an aptly titled series called "The Gowanusians." Without a break, for 133 consecutive weeks the *Eagle* published McLoughlin's stories, following the slapstick adventures of stereotypical Irish families with names like the Mulgrews, the O'Dooleys, the McSniffigans, and characters like Slob McTerrigan. It would be a disservice to omit the end of McLoughlin's baseball tale: "Then a small boy watching the riot saw a policeman and shouted 'Cheese it' and the whole mob scattered in different directions. The national game has received a severe setback in Gowanus from which it will not recover for some time."[21]

The "Eaglets" column was a trove of nineteenth-century popular entertainment, in a style lost to—or inherited by—radio shows and eventually cinema and television. Stories about urban life, from baseball games to the street chatter of "ethnic" neighborhoods of one of America's largest cities, had great appeal to the American public. Readers enjoyed narrative tours of African American quarters or immigrant populations like the Irish, Germans, Chinese, and Italians (to name a few). These were not just Brooklyn audiences: since the Civil War, the *Eagle* had a "Circulation Larger than any other Evening Paper Published in the United States," or so its masthead boasted, and its pages were circulated nationally. Although certainly the local paper of record, the *Eagle* was a widely distributed evening paper, and Gowanus was its oft-mentioned center of commerce and industry—unsavory, seedy, but ultimately at the forefront of business and culture. The comical and unselfconscious characters were recognizable to a greater public. This platform elevated McLoughlin's stories from mere fiction to the stuff of urban mythology. McLoughlin gained inspiration while strolling the streets of Gowanus, considering the architecture and eavesdropping on local chatter to capture that particular character of neighborhood folk. In his writing, a truth emerges amid his humor:

> Gowanusians have one great advantage over the residents of some of the higher toned parts of Brooklyn. That advantage consists

> in the fact that the majority of houses in that peculiar section of our beautiful city are but one story high. Of course some of the Gowanus streets boast of high stoop, two story and basement brick houses, and some even have an occasional brown stone edifice which rises to the dignity of two and a half or three stories, but the section of the famous neighborhood of which this story treats, and in which reside the McBrannigans, O'Dooley's and Mulgrews, consists mainly of the humbler class of dwellings, which, though not exactly shanties, are still not palaces.
>
> The advantage of living in a one-story house is very apparently on a warm day. There are no stairs to climb and consequently no distressful groanings from the female members of the families on account of that dreadful complaint, palpitation of the heart, which is so common among the women of the "upper ten" who live in four story mansions. The principal advantage of living on the ground floor is that, when it is very warm in the house one can easily slip out and get a breath of fresh air.
>
> That is what makes Gowanus such a sociable place and that is why I have been able to report so many pleasant sidewalk conversations between the neighbors, who, if they were shut up in those prison like abodes of brick and stone, which so many of our streets are lined, would probably remain unacquainted with one another during their whole lives.

Following this introduction, McLoughlin recounts such an conversation between three Gowanusians, Mrs. McSniffigan (the contractor's wife, "who lives in a more pretentious house than her neighbors but who is not very stuck up on that account"), Mrs. McBrannigan, and Mrs. O'Dooley, on a sweltering August morning in front of one of these small buildings. A stereotypical Chinese man walks by the trio, "dressed in the usual loose fitting garments and carrying a small fan which he fluttered industriously . . . he had the temerity to smile and say something which sounded like 'belly hot.'"

"Well well, is there any bounds to the impiddince o' thim yalla divils? Phwhat business is it of ours if his ould belly is hot," complained Mrs. O'Dooley, setting off a ridiculous conversation about the morals of such foreign devils. Of course, to the contemporary eye, these stories read as insensitive and off-color, if not purely racist. This was a period of American history when minstrel shows and all various iterations of such "racial" humor were widespread and wholly acceptable—especially in a column purely focused on lampooning Irish Americans. McLoughlin is himself guilty of writing and performing a minstrel character, a black preacher called Reverend Plink Plunk who delivered "a wealth of humor and homely philosophy."

But McLoughlin extended his satirical pen to the many types of Gowanus inhabitants beyond the Irish or African American, such as a matronly German, Mrs. Dinkelbecker. In one story, this long-suffering woman has a tussle with a billy goat belonging to Mrs. O'Dooley—she grabs his tail and bashes him over the head with a stick after catching him gobbling down a choice morsel from her clothesline. A fight between Mrs. Dinkelbecker and the goat's owner soon transpired:

"Vot does your coat mean by shvallerin my husband's new vite shirt," she demanded, setting off an inappropriately hilarious argument in which she threatens to kill the goat if she cannot retrieve the sixty-three cents she had paid for the shirt.

"See here Limberger," Mrs. O'Dooley yelled in reply, "I was living in Gowanus when you an' yer Budweiser husband were over in Germany digging in the fields."

Through its satire, "The Gowanusians" opens a window onto nineteenth-century views of the identity of the "lace curtain Irish," a term aimed at Irish Americans of the era, usually of the second generation, who had risen above the stereotypical shanty dwellers and attempted to adopt a more assimilated and middle-class lifestyle (and misplaced disdain for newcomers). These stories became madly popular among Brooklynites, such that McLoughlin was regularly invited to local church socials, balls, and charity events to present selections from his work in an exaggerated Irish brogue, to the delight of these well-to-do audiences. In 1894 he published an entire book of his Gowanusian columns and received high praise for his "Hibernian Humor" from the *Eagle*:

> Here the author expresses his gratitude to his own, as the Irish race as a nationality "can so heartily laugh at themselves when fairly and funnily put into print, without extenuation and with nothing set down in malice." Certainly that pioneer portion of Brooklyn celebrated in "The Gowanusians" to which the commerce and the general comfort and luxury of the city are so much indebted, has had its uninviting features not little irradiated by Mr. McLoughlin's characteristic pictures of the life of its denizens as it runs, Erin like, to fun under whatever circumstances.[22]

McLoughlin's work is proof that Gowanus had developed a character of its own and a reputation that extended beyond Brooklyn. But a place cannot boast a true and proper mythology without an authentic expression through poetry and music. Stories can be told and repeated, but songs are sung on streets, bars, and social gatherings. They are best when a particularly salt-of-the-earth type of local celebrity composes them. Michael J. Shay, also known as the Gas Drip Bard, was such a man who gained a great deal of popularity for his natural wit and skill with words. Among his many compositions was the "Gowanus Canal in Song," published by the *Eagle* in 1898:

> Away down town, where the atmosphere is hazy
> From the smoke of the factories ascending to the sky,
> The smells, Oh! so horrid, would almost set you crazy,
> But I'm told in that neighborhood the people seldom die.
> Way up on the "Slope" all the people are complaining;
> From the foul scented odors their health is quickly waning,

And the smoke from the soft coal their linen it is staining
When the wind blows that way from the Gowanus Canal.

Chorus:
When the wind blows east, when the wind blows west,
Or when it's from the north or south, you never get rest;
In summer or in winter, in the spring or in the fall,
You breathe the same old odors from the Gowanus Canawl.

Verse:
In famed "Darby's Patch," oh that muddy stream it rises,
And down to sweet Gowanus Bay it rushes with a roar;
Where barges, canal boats and schooners of all sizes
Are unloaded by Tom Hanley, the jolly stevedore.
The girls down there are so winsome and so pretty,
And the boys there are healthy; if not handsome, they're witty;
Oh you all know Farrell—he's Mayor of "Slab city"
He's thriving on the odors from Gowanus Canal

Chorus.
The Irish and Dutch, Scandinavian and Negro,
The Hebrew and the Chinaman, all jumbled in a batch;
The Scotch and the English, the Swede and wicked Dago—
A great conglomeration living down in Darby's Patch.
They're used to the smell; sure, cologne they never carry;
But a stranger would die if a short while there should tarry;
You can all get a job now from Councilman McGarry.
To disinfect the odors of Gowanus Canal.[23]

Shay was born in a village called Kilvemnon, a parish of Mullinahone in County Tipperary, Ireland. In 1863 he immigrated to Brooklyn with his father, at the age of six. After skipping years of school to play hockey, upon turning eighteen he got a job at the Brooklyn Union Gas

Company, soon maintaining a hundred gas drips across the city. His job was to pump out the water that condenses in the gas pipes, which he performed dutifully for more than fifty years ("Whole neighborhoods might be left in darkness if I neglected my work, so you see it is a very responsible position," he once explained in an interview). At some point, he began composing poems and songs, eventually self-publishing them in a hand-bound manuscript, which he sent to the *Brooklyn Daily Eagle* editors.

Their response was highly enthusiastic. These tunes, which Shay composed to be accompanied by banjo, were popular among *Eagle* readers, and the editors were happy to publish them. Shay claimed he never intended to make a career from his writing—beyond amusing his friends and improving his signature—but during his lifetime he composed and published dozens, if not hundreds of songs pertaining to city life in Brooklyn. These were mostly homages to his gas worker colleagues, commentary on local politics and consolidation with New York (he was opposed), and depictions of the conditions on the Gowanus Canal.[24]

Much like McLoughlin, at the turn of the century Shay was invited to perform his songs in front of many live audiences, church socials, and company picnics of Brooklyn Union Gas. His songs encapsulate the attitude of Brooklynites of this era, when the Gowanus was a necessary and celebrated nuisance, but also where the workingmen of this storied neighborhood could be celebrities—local heroes of their race and class. The canal was no mere obscure cesspool but, for better or worse, an integral seam across the fabric of Brooklyn. It boasted popular images full of personality, local characters and heroes to worship, and the songs of a bard to immortalize these moments in time.

There is a hint of nostalgia in one of Shay's works (along with a dose of Irish pride), "Down Where They Make the Gas," published in 1899 and later performed at the Brooklyn Gas Employee's "smoker"—an informal social gathering attended by three hundred of Shay's colleagues. Here is a small excerpt:

> Way down in old Gowanus, Slab City and Darby's Patch,
> Where squatters lived in years gone by, all jumbled in a batch.
> The frisky goat he roamed at will and chewed the verdant grass.
> But 'tis years ago since any grew, down where they make the gas;
> The odors of old Barren's Isle, ain't in it with the smell
> That rises from the old canal. I guess you know it well;
> The air is full of microbes, just hold your breath and pass,
> Or you'll get asphyxiated, sure, down where they make the gas.
> . . . Carlin, Connors, Claney, Cooley, Corridan and Rose
> Mulvihill, Hoban, Nolan, Gibbons, Keeley, Lynch and Bowers:
> Barret, Barry, Kenny Cotley, Farrell, Crane and Grace,
> These gashouse men, you may be sure, are of the Irish race![25]

The Gowanus Canal's most distant mythology evokes Lenape tribes, flooded tide mills, Revolutionary War battles, and now-abandoned industries—the titans of Gowanus past. But the contemporary, twentieth-century legends still alive in the minds of neighborhood residents are of crime and violence. Of course, stories of attempted drownings, stabbings, robberies, and suicides at the banks of the canal stretch back into the mid-nineteenth century. But probably the first in-depth argument of a criminal element around the Gowanus Canal was published in the *Brooklyn Daily Eagle* in March 1887, "On East Baltic Street: A Pessimistic View of the Physiognomy of a Thoroughfare" (other subheadlines throughout the story included "Criminal Suggestions of Gowanus Canal" and "A Possible Confederation of Thieves"). "If ever the Police Department has a rogue's gallery of streets," wrote the columnist E. R. G., "we may be certain that East Baltic Street from Hoyt to Nevins will be represented. There is not the least doubt in my mind that this is due to the proximity of the Gowanus Canal. The police of this city are morally certain that in the neighborhood of this detestable plague spot are scores of houses where stolen goods are concealed. But it does not seem to have entered into the heads of those who control the department that the choice of such a locality is due to the facility which the schooners and canal barges give for the transference of plunder from one point to another."

"The proceeds of robberies from other sections," he extrapolated further, "are brought by innocent lumber schooners and sloops laden with bricks and barges filled with tobacco bales, to this unfortunate city, to be disposed of in New York or here; and the insolent and motiveless burglaries which have terrorized our citizens and made one weeping widow are the consequences of the congregating at this one point of thieves, robbers and burglars from many regions." The opinionated columnist had spent the previous twelve months "narrowly scrutinizing" the people who worked around the canal, and truly believed that there was a "complete confederation of criminals, whose headquarters are here in Brooklyn, in the immediate neighborhood of the Gowanus Canal." A "large percentage" of the laboring men on barges and yards were allied with criminals, if not breaking the law themselves, they "wink at it," harboring criminals and giving passages to "men who are at odds with justice."

E. R. G. did not offer any particular evidence or crime statistics to support his theories, but instead took an eastward stroll along Baltic Street, two blocks north of the canal, and described what he saw. Starting at Court Street, he found the class of houses and the streets quite respectable and clean as he marched toward Smith Street. But once passing this thoroughfare and walking toward Hoyt Street "we descend the hill literally as well as figuratively yet the houses here are the abode of poor people, and of vicious ones." The houses were meager and ill kept, the surrounding streets and yards full of "filth and garbage." The whole neighborhood plagued by "juvenile bandits who lurk around." This unfortunate trend worsened as he passed above the head of the canal, past Bond Street, then Nevins—until he arrived at a curious short block, a break in the grid running from Baltic to Butler Street, called Cleveland Place.

It was still in an unpleasant location ("not to put too fine a point on it, is only just outside the jaws of the lion, being between Nevins street and Third avenue"), but in much better condition its surrounding blocks. There were two dozen cozy, two-story cottages with basements "very much on the order of those built in Philadelphia for this class of occupants, but neater and more artistic." High fences kept out the riffraff, and in the center of the little street lay a "refreshing strip of green turf."

Like all odd corners of cities, Cleveland Place had a story. Local landlords had built the houses intending to rent them for twenty-five dollars a month, but the first tenants were of the "tough variety," according to the *Eagle* and had to be evicted. To "tempt a better class," the landlords tried lowering the rent to eighteen dollars but the newcomers were even worse than the previous. In response, they tried an entirely new strategy: "Finally the projectors kicked out all the white rowdies, raised their rents to the normal figure, $25 a month, and announced that the row would be reserved for colored people of the utmost respectability," the columnist explained. "This plan succeeded, and the occupants are such refined people, such thorough ladies and gentlemen that though the women are nut brown maidens and the men have more or less coffee in their complexions one feels instinctively that they are more akin to us than the ruffians of the Gowanus Canal and its neighborhood."

It should come as little surprise that poor white inhabitants of the blocks surrounding Cleveland Place resented a wealthier and higher class African American enclave—just as it is unsurprising that the writers of white-owned newspapers, even as widely circulated as the *Eagle*, assumed that none of their readers were black (a problem that persists in American media today). These inhabitants, mostly journalists, clergymen, and restaurateurs, were regularly the subjects of racist verbal abuse by their neighbors. Conversely, those same poor whites supposedly had no qualms about schmoozing with working-class black Brooklynites—a whole row of houses between Third and Fourth Avenues on Baltic Street represented another African American enclave. But according to the *Eagle*, the young men of both races would hang out on the street and gamble, "pitching pennies in the most amicable style and cursing each other with the good humored fervor of true fraternal feeling."

Despite the warm activity of the community on the street, E. R. G. was disheartened by the suggestively clad young women (i.e., with hair down to their waist and a bare arm or leg) who hung around these gamblers as these "lower-class" behaviors spelled out a "cousinship with crime." But, he asserted, it had nothing to do with poverty itself: the fault lay with the Gowanus Canal, "uncontrolled, unwatched and utterly neglected by the authorities," breeding the vice that made the area "morally pestilential."[26]

The next month, our opinionated flaneur published another account of street life, following the fallen grandeur of Union Street and again condemning the "Unfavorable Effect of the Gowanus Canal," and its "hateful, malignant destiny." This time E. R. G. began by exploring the Italian community that had settled on the western edge of Union Street, in Red Hook at Columbia Street. With the same severity of his Baltic Street column, the writer criticized the dirty-faced Italian children and their swarthy mothers. "Are you a business man requiring unskilled labor and have you a blind unreasoning hatred against the Irish?" he quipped.

> Make your way straight to the western end of Union street and see a *padrone* and hire gangs of Italians. So long as you satisfy their *padrone* you will satisfy them, but if you do not, the matters may go ill with you, for these men carry knives as certainly as wasps have their stings, and use them as readily and as unscrupulously. Never before has the American power of assimilation been put to so tremendous a test as now, and there are wise men who doubt if it will be able to accomplish its work of turning these men from the Heel of the Italian Boot into American citizens. If it is done at all it will be through the Irish, with whom the Italians manifest a desire to be on friendly terms.

E. R. B.'s street-level ethnography of Brooklyn catalogues, without intent, a particularly late nineteenth-century anxiety over this new wave of immigrants—a sentiment shared by many so-called "native-born" Americans. His April column is an early long-form account of large immigrant Italian settlement of Brooklyn, revealing the growth of a large community from an epicenter on Columbia Street to well past the Gowanus Canal. But the Italians were not the only recently settled nationality: thousands had arrived from Poland, Austria, Hungary, and Russia, including significant numbers of Jews. Yet again the microscope of Gowanus functions as a window into the past anxieties of urban change, both ethnic and geographic: As the *Eagle* columnist took downhill trips into the Gowanus region, his final judgment was that, as a source of pollution and social pestilence, the canal should be filled in—just not with the "wires of crinoline hoopskirts, tomato cans and dead cats" of decades past.[27]

8

Strikes, Moonshine, and Mobs (1902–1949)

One of the most debilitating strikes of the early twentieth century was the Great Anthracite Coal Strike of 1902, in which nearly 150,000 Pennsylvania coal miners tossed their picks and shovels in a union protest of long hours and low wages.

There had been coal worker strikes only a few years before, but anthracite coal, or hard coal, was unique, burning cleaner and longer than bituminous coal (the linen-staining "soft coal" of Michael J. Shay's song) and was owned by a "natural monopoly," as it could be found in only fewer than a half dozen counties concentrated in northeastern Pennsylvania. But the owners of these mines had saved huge stockpiles of anthracite, which they used to control market prices during times of oversupply. The enormous power these owners wielded seems improbable, but before oil and electricity were readily available sources of energy, coal was the only option for most of the country. The strike began in May, but grew into a months-long standoff as the stockpiles slowly dwindled.[1]

By October, nights were getting cooler and there was no coal to buy at all, and people were growing desperate. They looked for any kind fuel to burn, including their own furniture. In Brooklyn, the poorer classes scoured every square inch of coal yards and gas plants, anywhere there might be stray briquettes of coal lying around. As reported by the *Eagle*, some locals found another source of accidentally discarded fuel:

> Mining for coal in the Gowanus canal is one of the latest developments of the coal famine. The mining is done with rakes such as are used in fishing for clams and oysters and quite a lot of coal has been secured by men in rowboats.
>
> Nothing can exceed the determination of the Italians of the Hamilton avenue section to secure all the fuel possible in the shape of driftwood. Owing to the reconstruction of the north and south piers of the Atlantic Dock, the water there, about the time of high tide, contains large quantities of yellow pine and pile beads that have been cut off by the dock builders. It is not unusual to see string pieces fifty or sixty feet in length, sometimes with a lot of timbers attached. . . . Formerly no one would go to the trouble of fishing for a water-soaked log. Now nothing escapes the harpooners, even though the log should be covered with barnacles and eaten to a shell by borers.[2]

Nationally, the coal shortage crisis grew so dire that President Theodore Roosevelt intervened, calling an unprecedented meeting of representatives in government, labor, and management of the coal business in early October. He had no real authority to interfere with the strike, but he pleaded for compromise, if only for the good of the country. After 163 days, the United Mine Workers ended their strike on October 23, 1902. It was just one of scores of widespread union actions that marked the early twentieth century. These associations were partially religious in nature—the Catholic Church, particularly Pope Leo XIII, was an important supporter of workingmen's unions and the labor movement in America.[3]

On the local level, there were many reasons to get involved with unions: defending laborers' rights, fighting for fair wages, and simply belonging to an organization of one's peers. Yet politics was another reason. Great power could be found in the ability to mobilize groups of like-minded individuals, and early twentieth century Gowanus provides an example as such, misguided though it might have been. In April 1903, five hundred workers from the eight asphalt companies in New York City went on general strike. Out of solidarity, five hundred workers from similar fields (portable engineers, blue stone cutters, curb setters, and pavers) joined the protest. It had all begun in January, when the Asphalt Workers' Union had sent a new schedule to their employers that included a wage scale, an eight-hour workday, and preferential employment for union men. But the owners refused the terms, and meetings with arbitrators dragged on through the spring. Finally, the union reps decided they had had enough and flexed their muscles. For a long month, nary a sidewalk or road was repaired in New York.

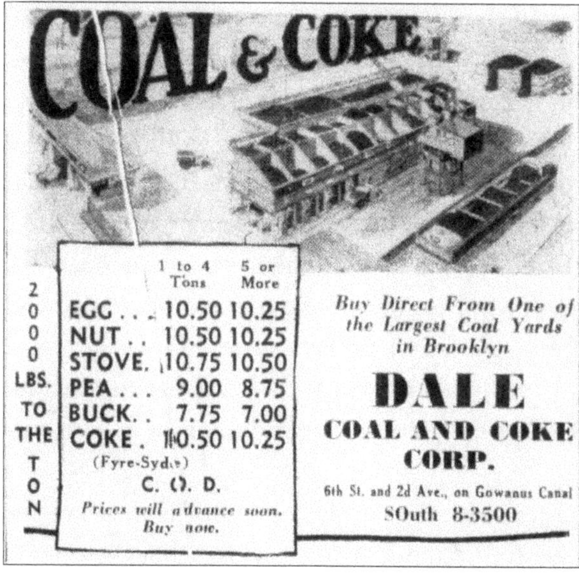

A 1934 advertisement in the *Brooklyn Daily Eagle* for a coal yard and depicting a barge on the Gowanus Canal. Brooklyn Collection. Courtesy of the Brooklyn Public Library and Newspapers.com.

Finally, the company owners settled with the union, and asphalt layers returned to work in the beginning of May, at least in theory. On May 4, the day after most workers had returned to their posts, some men from an asphalt plant on 113th Street and Lenox Avenue struck again, aggravating negotiations and quickly ending the shaky truce. Negotiations would have to start all over again. Although this strike appears to have been the result of a simple misunderstanding, rogue protests quickly spread throughout the city—perhaps most colorfully in the Gowanus area of Brooklyn: At seven o'clock the morning of May 11, an "angry mob" of three hundred Italian laborers marched through the Gowanus Canal district and halted at Douglass Street and Third Avenue, where a number of men were paving the sidewalk. The president of their "association" demanded that the pavers stop working and started a shoving match. The police arrived and arrested three Italians, breaking up the mob "before any severe assault had been committed."

However the workers regrouped and continued south, arriving at the Uvalde Asphalt Plant on Third Avenue and Sixth Streets. There was a "lively fight" as they attempted to shut down the factory, although none of the workers would comply, but the police again had to intervene. The mob quickly moved on to harassing a paving crew on Seventh Avenue. Then they turned back toward Third Avenue and Third Street, ending up at the doors of the Brooklyn Alcatraz Asphalt Company. Some workers fled, fearing the "vengeance of the mob," but the dogged police soon caught up with the rioters. By noon, work had resumed as normal. Mr. McCoy, manager of the plant, claimed his workers made good pay, $1.75 to $2.50 a day (a decent wage in 1903). "We do not propose to have these men, or their leader Lawrence, who formerly was a contractor, tell us how to run our business."[4]

Riots and fights between factions of Brooklyn's men were not the invention of immigrant Italians, but rather a legacy that these newest groups had inherited. Gangs of violent young boys were inherent in the DNA of South Brooklyn, and some were the stuff of legends. Since the early days of the nineteenth century, rambunctious children of a certain class ruled the streets, roaming alleyways and dominating street corners. They got into daily scuffles over trivial, ridiculous matters such as a stolen hat or a game of marbles scattered into the dust by a swift kick. In response, the offended boys would gather their clans and arm themselves with pockets of pebbles, bean shooters, or sling shots fashioned from the tops of an old shoes, which "when swung over your head a few times, could deliver half a brick with the accuracy of a bullet." Then the young toughs would confront their enemies at open war, flinging rocks and skirmishing until sundown—when they could run home to dinner, unless a cop came to break it up first.

According to one account, in the mid-1800s the entire male population of South Brooklyn under the age of thirty was divided into four "great clans," whose territories extended to all of the neighborhoods in the borough of Brooklyn. The largest of these clans, the Roosters, was centered in the densely populated South Brooklyn, itself divided into many smaller factions constantly at war with each other. The divisions generally lay between the different slums, such as the Patchers (from Darby's Patch) and Slab Cityers, from the slum in the vicinity of Bond and Fifth Streets. But chief among the Rooster clan were the Pointers and the Creekers, the gangs with the largest followings. These two groups are the most often cited in the annals of South Brooklyn's early "gang" history. The former's styling referred to the home territory of Red Hook Point—the westernmost portion of the eponymous neighborhood whose borders were roughly south of Hamilton Avenue and west of Columbia Street—while the latter was named for Gowanus Creek.

A pervasive story is of a Creeker venturing into a Pointer's territory. The local boys would surround the unfortunate Creeker and ask "do you like cake, or pie?" If he answered cake (which he inevitably would, as it was code for "Creeker"), the Pointers would pummel the unlucky kid, which was still better than dirtying his reputation by lying about his gang associations. It was wholly unfair to Creekers who wanted to swim in the municipal pool at Red Hook or Pointers who wanted to go to a baseball game in Gowanus. Boys who attended schools on the wrong side of their respective territories were harassed and beaten so often that at least one teacher would chaperon the students on their walk home. Only during larger-scale battles—where kids from completely different sections of town, like the Forty Acres clan of Irishtown, by the Navy Yard—would the Roosters actually band together and fight the interlopers. These wars, although not terribly serious, would remain active for years, the "jealousies and distrusts arising from them would cling to the actors in them long after the serious work of life had been entered upon." Jobs, family, even political appointments and elections in nineteenth-century Brooklyn could arguably be determined through one's association with a group.

The genesis of these regional conflicts dates to well before the 1860s, springing from rivalries passed down from the different companies of Brooklyn's volunteer fire service. These gangs of working-class men were based in different neighborhoods and competed in fighting the city's numerous fires. Special commendations and new equipment were handed out based on the volunteers' performance heroism. The rewards were meant to encourage high performance and efficiency, but consequently stoked "jealousies existing between the different sections of the city" that filtered down to the youngest of street kids. By the last decade of the nineteenth century, however, the flow of once epic battles slowed to a trickle. By the turn of the new century the legendary turf wars had almost completely disappeared. The volunteer fire service was eventually disbanded, cutting off the root of all of the discord. Vacant lots that had been ignored for decades, favored battlegrounds of these boys, were being built up thanks to the increasing value of Brooklyn's industry. These obliterated both the primary reason for a street war (to protect one's turf) and the arenas in which to fight. Finally, the establishment of city playgrounds and the common school system removed scrappy, slingshot-wielding youths from the street, forcing them to interact and meet each other in a more egalitarian setting. The animosities eventually melted, and the Pointers and Creekers silently agreed on a truce. This was quite agreeable for most Brooklynites, as "it made it possible for a citizen to take his wife or children for an airing without danger of having an eye knocked out or a skull fractured."[5]

According to one *Eagle* story, the "closest approximation" to these ancient Brooklyn rivalries took place in the spring of 1890, a skirmish between "a dozen men from the Italian colony on President Street near 4th avenue, and about an equal number of Americans and Irish boys from Third Avenue." Whole bricks and pieces of brownstone or cobble were lobbed along with curses in "all the dialects of Italy" and the "choicest tenth ward English." Little damage was done, and in that way it resembled the battles of decades past—up to a certain point: the engagement took a sharp turn because the "one sided and bloodless duel did not suit the Italians," and so one of that gang pulled out a gun and began to shoot, wounding a little boy in the leg. Officer John Clancy of the Brooklyn police then broke up the engagement. The story, though teetering toward racist, marks the transitional period of Brooklyn's history in which one established brand of local hoodlum seems to be replaced for a decidedly foreign one. It speaks more to the local perception of changing times and populace than to the nature of one group as more violent than another.

The Sewer Problem, Continued

Following the asphalt riots of spring, the summer of 1903 proved equally tumultuous for Gowanus Canal's drains: at the end of June, a massive rainstorm had totally overwhelmed the Greene Avenue sewer main, creating such high pressure that "heavy manhole covers were hurled into the air and geysers formed in the openings." The worst flooding concentrated around Fourth Avenue and St. Mark's Place, near the head of the canal. The dangerous malfunction was attributed to the fact that the outlet into the canal, through which the Greene Avenue sewer emptied, was smaller than the actual sewer pipe it serviced. A further relief output had been planned but never built due to "lack of funds."[6]

"Nothing but storm water was intended to enter this relief sewer," wrote Charles F. Breitzke—a promising young engineering student in the Sanitary Research Laboratory at MIT—about the Greene Street sewer main, "but, whether by accident or design, it is now flowing during dry weather and is discharging sewage into the canal." In 1906, Breitzke published an undergraduate thesis examining the conditions of the Gowanus Canal, including a possible remedy to the nuisance. He had been studying the waterway for nearly three years,

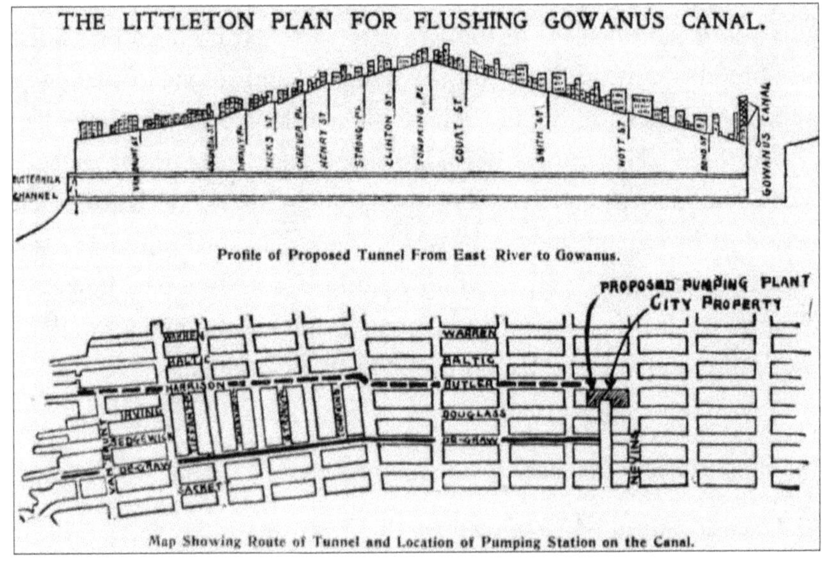

Early plan for the Gowanus Canal flushing tunnel, ca. January 1905. Courtesy of the Brooklyn Public Library.

and the report was so well received among the academic community that his work was published in a prominent technology journal. So many of the city's sewers dumped untreated wastewater directly into the harbor that the government could no longer ignore the growing waste problem. Health officials on several tiers of government feared one of New York's greatest assets, the huge protected bay, had become a breeding ground for dangerous bacteria. Besides, pollution was terrible for business, the lifeblood of New York. In an effort to stem a public crisis, the State Legislature created the New York Bay Pollution Commission to assess the problem, just as Breitzke was beginning his research. Several years of surveys, experiments, and testing ensued.

According to the commission's 1908 report (which liberally quoted Breitzke's findings), the Gowanus Canal was among the most polluted areas in the entire harbor. The scientists used the number of bacteria in the water to determine where the worst of the sewage was concentrated: a count of more than 10,000 per cubic centimeter of seawater would constitute "heavy pollution," while more than 100,0000 would "represent truly offensive conditions." Testing revealed that some parts of the Gowanus Canal contained 625,000 bacteria per cubic centimeter (for a further a point of comparison, in present-day New York State, legally swimmable water cannot contain more than 24 bacteria per cubic centimeter). There was also observable evidence of concern: in 1905, an outbreak of typhoid fever on Long Island had been traced to oysters and clams that had grown in New York City limits. After centuries as a local gastronomic delicacy, the famed New York oyster would have to permanently retire. Because of this rampant pollution, they were simply too dangerous to eat.

Breitzke's statistics also speak for themselves: the sewage pollution levels of the canal were almost fifty times those of the harbor, and the water in the canal was estimated to be 25 percent sewage. "Practically all the plants along the canal discharge directly into it," he wrote, "but the amount of sewage from these is small when compared with that contributed by the city sewers. Not only is the discharge of the sewers greater than that of the factories, but its amount and its offensive character are shown by the bad condition of that part of the canal into which it discharges." He was also quite vivid in his description of the water, generally describing it as "black, warm, and foul." No fish had been caught for years in the waterway, and there was no flow. At least eighty vessels a day entered the canal at its entrance, about a quarter of them towed along its full length.

The lower half of the canal had patches of "brown and yellow oily substances," particularly around the infamous Bond Street sewer (despite many protests, the ancient culprit had been reopened in the late 1890s after too many putrid street floods engulfed the neighborhood). This foul-looking sheen "spread out in thick layers on the water surface and seem to gather up all the other floating debris, such as waste paper, fecal matter, melon rinds, banana skins, kitchen refuse, tin cans, broken boxes, coal dust, and other matter." But the worst culprit was the exit at the head of the canal, where the Green Avenue main spewed filth. Even during dry weather there was a continual flow of "waste paper, hair, and other sewage stuff. White scum covers the water surface in front of its outlet. Slaughterhouses drain into this sewer, for at times large quantities of blood are discharged. On wash days suds are in abundance."[7]

With the failure of the Greene Avenue Sewer to clean the canal (or drain the streets, for that matter) the state was insistent on cleaning up the harbor. Money was earmarked for a new "high-tech" flushing tunnel that would use propellers to force unpolluted water into the stagnant cesspool. The channel would extend under Columbia Street, drawing water from the Buttermilk Channel, the short waterway in the East River between Brooklyn and Governor's Island (although it also could pump water in the opposite direction, an option that engendered a separate political battle). Construction began immediately in 1906 and continued for five years, with mounting

Jennie Haviland, "Miss Gowanus," at the opening ceremony of the Gowanus Canal flushing tunnel. *Brooklyn Daily Eagle*, June 21, 1911. Brooklyn Collection. Courtesy of the Brooklyn Public Library and Newspapers.com.

public excitement as the city promised to purify the canal and get rid of the smell.

Just before noon on June 22, 1911, crowds surrounding the flushing mechanism's housing, a red brick structure on Douglass Street at the head of the canal. Even the *New York Times* reported the grand celebration:[8]

> In gala attire, all South Brooklyn took a holiday yesterday to celebrate its long-looked-for emancipation from the evil smells given forth by the murky waters of Gowanus Canal. The day marked the opening of the tunnel which the municipality has built at a cost of nearly $1,000,000 to flush and cleanse the much-used water-

> way. . . . The ceremonies consisted of formally placing the pumping plant in operation, a parade of decorated craft through the canal and along the bay front, an inspection of the Fourth Avenue subway work, and a big procession of business vehicles through the principal streets of the district. . . . Factories, coal pockets, docks, and bridges along the canal and most of the business houses and dwellings in South Brooklyn were decorated with flags and bunting in honor of the occasion, and great crowds watched the parade of boats and that of wagons and trucks.[9]

Williams Jay Gaynor, the mayor, and Lewis H. Pound, commissioner of public works, flipped the large switch to set the works in motion. Cheers erupted and flashbulbs exploded as Mayor Gaynor waved to the crowd and another procession of boats. He soon turned and walked to his waiting car when nine-year-old Jennie Haviland, daughter of the commodore of the parading fleet, called out his name and handed the mayor a bunch of white lilies. Having been crowned "Miss Gowanus," Jeanne was to usher in the new era for the neighborhood, and did so by tossing some of her lilies into the canal, "as an earnest of the purity of its waters that is to be."

Later on in the festivities, the mayor found himself standing at a luncheon sponsored by a grain company (which owned a massive warehouse at the mouth of the Gowanus), giving a long-winded speech about the commerce of Brooklyn and its superior docks compared to Manhattan. "What would we be here without it?" he asked. "The Gowanus Canal is one of the greatest assets in the City of New York. Efforts to purify it have been frustrated by the city government in permitting sewers to be emptied into it. I counted sixteen of the sewer holes opening into the canal near its head to-day, and I was told that there were sixteen more down the line. I used to walk around the canal when I was Judge: I did not only start to walk when I became Mayor, you know. I would often board vessels in the canal to see what was going on in the world. Even Gowanus is some part of the rest of the world."[10]

MACHINERY INSTALLED TO FREE THE GOWANUS CANAL OF FILTH.

The Pumping Station for the Gowanus Canal Flushing Plant.

WORK of installing the machinery which will pump the accumulated refuse from the bed of the Gowanus Canal is proceeding now with considerable speed, and by spring it is expected the great flushing system will be ready for operation. The work of purifying the canal will devolve largely upon a suction pump. This will be driven by a 400-horse power alternating current electrical motor. This motor will drive a 9-foot turbine wheel set in a double-ended tunnel, through which the mud will be sucked by the action of the great wheel. The 9-foot turbine wheel is to be coupled directly by a horizontal shaft to the motor set in a pit of such depth that the main shaft comes to the same elevation as the center line of the tunnel through which the waters of the canal are to be drawn. The capacity of the pump is 80,000 cubic feet per minute, enough to change the entire contents of the canal three times a day, working the pumps at intervals. At the ebb of the tide it is planned to run the machinery, when the dirt-impregnated waters of the canal will be floated down the East River into the bay. Clean water from the harbor will flow in to take the place of that displaced by the pumping.

At the present time the house which is to hold the pumping machinery is entirely inclosed, and the machinery itself is arriving and is almost ready to be set in place. Owing to the weight of some of the parts, this operation itself involves several unique mechanical problems. The total cost of the work will be about $800,000, of which a little more than $717,000 is to be spent on the tunnel. Two valve gates will approximate a cost of $11,000, the motor pit and appurtenances, $24,500

Pit in the Pumping Station which is to hold the turbine; and part of the machinery.

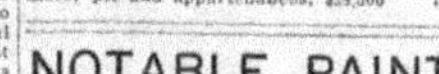

NOTABLE PAINT

Pa

IT was not so very long ago that some young men, with a good deal of experience in selecting works of art and in putting them in an attractive way before the public, determined that a good place for an art gallery was on Fulton street, in what used to be a rather uptown location. That was in the Bedford section, and they selected a place on the first floor in a handsome exterior near

Pumping station of the Gowanus Canal flushing tunnel. *Brooklyn Daily Eagle*, February 17, 1911. Brooklyn Collection. Courtesy of the Brooklyn Public Library and Newspapers.com

Bootleggers and Gangs of Gowanus

One of the children who undoubtedly took part in the Gowanus flushing tunnel festivities was Alphonse "Al" Capone, one of the most infamous gangsters in American history (his most celebrated nickname, "Scarface," was never uttered to his face). He was born on January 17, 1899, to Neapolitan immigrants Gabriele—a barber—and Teresina Capone on 95 Navy Street, near the Brooklyn Navy Yard. When Alphonse was ten the Capones moved to 21 Garfield Place in South Brooklyn, two blocks from the Gowanus Canal, just as the tunnel was opening. Capone attended school until the age of fourteen, when he was expelled for spotty attendance and, apparently, striking a teaching that scolded him.[11]

As the hulking youth matured on Brooklyn's streets, so did stories of New York's nascent crime syndicates: "Fifty-Four Killed or Injured by Black Hand since June 1" screamed an October 1905 headline of the *New York Herald*. Under it lay a long list of murders, bombings, and arsons committed by men with Italian names, "no matter whether there is a Black Hand, a Mafia, or not." The writer, Broughten Brandenberg, was an expert on immigration and crime who had authored a book, *Our Imported Criminals*. He was quick to point out that "the great list of murders and outrage does not reflect on Italians as a people," and also that often it was other Italians who were the first victims of organized crime. Out of more than thirty violent crimes he detailed, three were in Brooklyn, and one particular case involved a "Vincenzo Capaldo of Carroll Street," who was "threatened by the Black Hand and asked to leave money in an old coat at Third street and Gowanus Canal." The police placed the coat full of marked bills on the designated spot, but the mobsters grabbed it and vanished before anybody could react. Soon afterward, a destructive fire raged through Capaldo's Carroll Street tenement, one block east of the canal.[12]

The popular association of the Gowanus neighborhood with crime and hooliganism is as strong as its association with bad smells and pollution: the stories lean heavily on legends of the Italian Mafia, but this idealized ethnic gang was not the only dominant party in Brooklyn. A legendary collective of Irish gangsters known as the White Hand supposedly controlled most of the illegal business on Brooklyn's docks during the early twentieth century. The newspaper accounts describe the White Hand as a loose affiliation of hoodlums who hung out around the Gowanus Canal, particularly in the vicinity of Bond, Butler, and Baltic Streets. One of the first mentions of this motley group is from 1905, in a piece about a hard-drinking teenage "tomboy" named Ellen Hardiman, who had "prodigious strength for a girl." "Nel" was known for regularly assaulting adult men and could carry an iron cook stove on her back. Another story of the same street corner from 1907 details a twenty-three-year-old named Charles Ward, who attacked a cop with his own club (the officer had tried to confiscate a suspicious-looking bag full of lead pipes).[13]

With its reputation for crime, Gowanus was also no stranger to the production of illicit spirits. Considering that thousands of sailors, salesmen, and merchants were crawling around the wooden docks stained by polluted water in the early twentieth century, Gowanus was destined for bootlegging. On Carroll Street between Nevins Street and Third Avenue, steps from Al Capone's childhood home and a block from the canal, a no-frills, Neapolitan-owned restaurant called Angelo's Tavern opened in 1906. At the height of Prohibition, owners Angelo and Filomena Montemarano famously sold home-brewed beer on the premises—there was even a chute installed to drop bottles into the basement in the event of a police raid.[14]

But as early as 1902, Brooklyn police had tracked down and seized a moonshine still that had installed at Smith Street and Ninth Street. The operation was a partnership of three Jewish Brooklynites, David B. Rothstein, Nathan Bluestone, and Bernard Brodsky. Their illegal still, at the time the largest of its kind in Brooklyn, consisted of a three-story wooden building that purported to be a grocery store, although the only product for sale was sugar. Inside Rothstein housed his wife and six children, along with two large boilers According to the *Eagle*, the distillers didn't even use corn, but "bought sugar by the barrel to convert it into alcohol," and would hide the 150-proof spirit in paint cans kept in a storefront on nearby Third Avenue and Thirteenth Street (cleverly disguised as a paint store to operate as a front for distributing the white-colored liquor). The still, which produced approximately fifty barrels of high-quality spirit a week "exclusively for the Hebrews of the city," sold the cans for a dollar fifty per gallon.[15]

The association with bootleggers and violent crime takes on a particular flavor in Gowanus, especially when one considers the story of John Romanelli: On an August afternoon in 1915, eight-year-old Tony Scudo was playing with some neighborhood friends at the end of Second Street at the Gowanus Canal. They had made a game of taking chunks of loose paving stones and tossing them into the stagnant water. These heavy pieces of infrastructure, Belgian blocks, could be found all around Brooklyn and New York City in general—they supposedly arrived in American port cities in large numbers as discarded ship ballast, and eventually were used to pave the roads and sidewalks. At some point, young Tony pried loose an especially large stone and struggled under its weight carrying it to the banks of the canal. With great effort he heaved it into the water and was rewarded with a satisfying splash. But he had no chance to savor the moment; the momentum he had mustered threw the young boy off balance and he tumbled into the murky canal. Tony's small companions ran to spread the alarm while some laborers on a nearby brick barge dove after his sinking body.

News of the accident quickly spread and a crowd gathered along the canal shore as the search continued for far too long. Among the present were Tony Scudo's distraught parents and two undertakers: Gaetano Mangino, whose office was on Union Street between Fourth and Fifth Avenues, and John Romanelli, his business rival. The latter, whose office was on Third Avenue and President Street, was infamous in the neighborhood as the unofficial mayor of Brooklyn's Little Italy. Romanelli watched as Tony Naparano, the Scudos' next-door neighbor, retrieved the young boy's body and gave it to his mournful parents, who passed it off to Mangino. Romanelli was furious: the high-profile tragedy had happened on his turf, while his rival's office was several blocks farther from the Gowanus. In response, he verbally threatened the rival undertaker.

Later that evening, Romanelli gathered a group of young toughs at his office, intending to go search for his rival and procure the rights to bury poor Tony Scudo. But the undertaker didn't have very far to look: Mangino had assembled his own posse in order to address the threats head-on. One of Mangino's runners, Vincent Gianelli, walked right up to Romanelli's storefront, pulled out a pistol, and fired a shot; the bullet barely grazing the unofficial mayor's forehead. It's not clear whether any words had been exchanged, but as Gianelli ran away, Romanelli and his crew grabbed guns from their office and rushed outside, right into their rival clan. Volleys of bullets were fired into the suddenly crowded neighborhood, and a bloody battle ensued. Upward of 150 young men were swept into the brawl, crouching behind doors and small columns while taking shots like two armies of Neapolitan snipers.

An apparently fearless crowd of onlookers filled the streets, blocking the entire avenue from a supposedly safe distance. Police reinforcements were called, and it took the officers an hour to fight through the dense crowd and put an end to the violence. By the time they had regained control, Mangino lay on the sidewalk, bleeding to death. He had been shot in the stomach and ribs and stabbed twice. Not far away was Romanelli, who suffered only minor injuries but was still sent to the hospital. Gianelli, curiously, had turned himself into the police at the first opportunity, while his boss Mangino was not expected to survive. After being treated, Romanelli was arrested along his son Dominick and his son-in-law, for carrying concealed weapons.[16]

Nearly five years later, days before Christmas 1919, a strange epidemic had spread across New England: More than sixty people had died after drinking some kind of tainted "whiskey" in Hartford, Connecticut, and Chicopee, Massachusetts, among other locales. Many more had reported debilitating sickness and attacks of blindness. Several similar cases soon emerged in New York. Some police investigation determined that the offending beverage was not whiskey at all but methanol, or wood alcohol—a highly toxic chemical used as antifreeze or a stabilizer in formaldehyde. Consuming two teaspoons of wood alcohol in its purest form can destroy a human optic nerve; four more can be fatal.

Two days before the New Year, the New York City Police Department arrested six men in connection with the sale of the deadly spirits, including Adolph Paranelli, a New York City wine and liquor dealer, Dell'Omo Amadeo and Luigi Puga—partners in two Mott Street grocery stores, in the heart of Manhattan's Little Italy—and John Romanelli, the Gowanus undertaker and a "well known neighborhood politician," according to the *New York Times*. The police had traced the origin of at least seven barrels of pure wood alcohol falsely advertised as whiskey to Romanelli's garage. According to Paranelli's testimony, a saloon keeper from Hartford named Nathan Salzberg had asked the liquor dealer to procure him some whiskey to sell in Connecticut. Paranelli put in the necessary calls and was passed around from a Mott Street grocery owner to a Brooklyn druggist who referred him to Romanelli. The undertaker had a special permit to buy wood alcohol to use in embalming fluid, and he sent the seven barrels to Paranelli's office on Bleecker Street. From here they were distributed to various buyers, who were informed that the drink was whiskey. Salzberg, who was tried for manslaughter in Connecticut, paid $4,800 for three barrels, or about $50 per gallon of the deadly booze.

Just six months prior the US Congress had passed the Wartime Prohibition Act—a precursor to the Eighteenth Amendment. The measure threatened to ruin the businesses of entrepreneurs like Paranelli by making illegal the sale of any beverages containing more than 2.75 percent alcohol. For each barrel the liquor dealer had received a $150 commission, but instead of relishing the sale, his name appeared in local newspapers as being part of the deadly conspiracy. He soon turned himself in to Colonel Porter, head officer of the New York Custom House. "The manufacture and sale of liquor from nonbeverage alcohol since wartime prohibition became operative has constituted the greatest get-rich-quick scheme that the Internal Revenue Department has ever had to cope with," Porter told the *New York Times*. "There is more moonshine whisky being made in New York City than in all parts of the country combined."[17]

As Prohibition entered the 1920s at full steam, so did the shipping industry in Brooklyn: "The Gowanus Canal is one of the dirtiest, one of the shortest and one of the most important waterways in the world," boasted an article in the *New York Times*. "It is estimated that more than $100,000,000 worth of materials will pass through it in 1922." While only one and a quarter million tons of freight had moved through the New York State Barge Canal (successor to the Erie Canal, more than 500 miles long) in 1921, upward of two million tons had moved through the 1.8-mile-long Gowanus, "without any worth-while charge to the city." Maintaining the Barge Canal, however, had cost New York State three million dollars.[18]

It was in this heated environment that Al Capone cut his teeth as a gangster. Although the *Brooklyn Eagle* claimed that the street gangs of Brooklyn's youth had disappeared, they seem to have been replaced with something more violent. But the names like Pointers and Creekers, lived on; new gangs, like the South Brooklyn Boys, who dealt in much more serious crimes than throwing rocks, were formed. According to William Balsamo, a former dockworker and grandson of a founding Brooklyn Mafia leader Batista Balsamo, "Capone learned all there was to know about extortion and slugging and the rest on the banks of the Gowanus Canal." Brooklyn's waterfront districts were already "crawling with crime" and every conceivable scam: gambling, smuggling, cargo theft, prostitution muggings, labor rackets, extortion (particularly hitting the stevedore companies) and opium dealing.[19]

During this era, increasingly powerful Italian gangs wanted a larger piece of the action, but the White Hand controlled most of the illegal business on Brooklyn's docks. According to Robert Schoenberg, a detailed researcher of organized crime in New York, the loosely affiliated Irish gang had organized chiefly as a reaction to the threat of the Black Hand, which the newspapers would dub any Italian criminal activity. This is partially a misnomer—"Black Hand" technically refers to the particular methods of extortion practiced by these gangs—and it was loaded with racist overtones. Still, the sinister imagery of the *mano nera* brought fear and power that the Italians exploited, and so Irish gangsters organized their crew under famed leaders like "Dinny" Meehan and his lieutenant, "Wild" Bill Lovett. The latter was an elfin-looking man, only five foot seven and 140 pounds, but he was so widely feared across the Brooklyn waterfront that he never bothered traveling with a bodyguard. During the height of the White Hand's control of the Brooklyn docks, Capone was running with various Italian neighborhood thugs. He joined a Manhattan youth gang, the Forty Thieves Juniors, allowing him to progress into the notorious Five Points gang—a precursor to the modern-day New York Mafia. Impressed with Capone's budding reputation, a Brooklyn crime boss and skilled extortionist named Frankie Yale decided to mentor the young brute.[20]

Although more devoted to business than brawling, Capone could also be a ruthless hothead and an efficient murderer. According to a tale recounted by William Balsamo, one evening during Holy Week in 1917, Capone came with three other wise guys to a neighborhood craps game that Frankie Yale ran in an apartment over a garage on Third Avenue and Fourteenth Street. One newcomer to the craps game was Anthony Perratta, a native Italian who had arrived without an invitation and was now having entirely too much good luck. On Yale's orders, Capone and another thug waited for the gamblers to filter out into the chill of early spring. He hid in the shadows in the back of the hallway and pounced on Perratta, then shot him in the center of his chest. Capone and crew loaded the body into a car and drove to the end of Degraw Street and Nevins Street, where tall grass was along the Gowanus Canal. After a few minutes of heavy lifting, Perratta's corpse joined, according to Balsamo, "the skeletal remains of innumerable murder victims."[21]

Capone was a ruthless enforcer and efficient collector, and so Yale's partnership with the violent twenty-year-old proved lucrative—that is, until one afternoon in early 1919. Capone was at Fulton Slip Inn near the Navy Yard, taking a drink break from his collections around Pier 4, when a White Hander named Arthur "Criss-Cross" Finnegan walked through the door. There are a few accounts of how the altercation began—one version includes that the Irish gangster, being especially drunk, accidentally pissed on Capone at the urinal. But by all accounts, at some point Finnegan began to pick on the hulking, ham-fisted Italian. After Finnegan shouted some racist epithet, Capone promptly thrashed him within an inch of his life. Finnegan had been low in the ranks of the White Hand, and when word of Finnegan's mangled face got back to "Wild" Bill, half of Brooklyn's criminals likely felt sorry for Capone. Perhaps ironically, he had just married a young Irish girl named Mae Coughlin after she gave birth their son, Albert "Sonny" Capone. The wedding ceremony was in St. Mary Star of the Sea church, on Court Street. Capone had responsibilities now, and Yale was afraid of losing his most efficient earner. To protect his protégé, Yale sent Capone to Chicago in 1919.[22]

In April 1920, Dinny Meehan was shot in the head five times while in bed with his wife, at 452 Warren Street, just a few blocks from the head of the Gowanus Canal. Some underworld mythology attributed the killing to Frankie Yale, although other accounts attribute it to an intragang revenge killing, as Meehan had supposedly double-crossed a colleague. Months later, on December 9, 1920, a forty-six-year-old Brooklyn police officer named Daniel Grennan finished his beat from

Smith Street to the Gowanus Canal, clocking out at his station at four in the afternoon. Heading home to an early supper, he stopped at the butcher shop of Joseph Travero on Fourth Place, where he asked to leave his revolver until his next duty shift at eight o'clock. He was never seen alive again. The next day the police sent out a confidential alarm, but news of Grennan's disappearance leaked to the press.

"Fear Missing Policeman Is Victim of 'White Hand Gang,'" the headlines read, as Margaret, Grennan's wife, told reporters that when he was assigned to the Gowanus beat, it was "infested with gangsters and gunmen of the worst type." Apparently the stalwart cop had quickly arrested several members of the White Hand, if only to show he meant business. Following some tips, the authorities dredged the Gowanus to search for a body, but turned up nothing. On March 4, 1921, Captain John Grabshaw of the Standard Oil lighter was docked at First Street when he switched on the propellers of his vessel. The motion disturbed something in the murky Gowanus water, and then a bloated body floated to the surface. It was Grennan's corpse, still wearing his uniform and badge from the afternoon he had stopped at the butcher.[23]

As in the years past, bodies turned up around the Gowanus, but the difference between the 1920s and 1930s and previous eras was the manner in which they were found. In the past, most bodies appeared to be the victims of alcohol or suicide—these were mutilated. In August 1923 the captain of a coal barge docked at the foot of Second Avenue (at the entrance of Edwin C. Litchfield's Fourth Street Basin) spotted a corpse floating on the water, wrapped in burlap sacks and tied around the waist with window sash cords. A blunt weapon had smashed the right side of his skull and jawbone. Although he had been underwater for two weeks, the body was still wearing an expensive gray suit with fourteen one-dollar bills in his pocket.[24]

Gruesome murders occurred in or around the canal periodically over the following decades. One famous case, in April 1936, a body wrapped in a soiled white bedspread and a rough burlap bag was pulled from the Gowanus Canal at the foot of Bond Street. It was Tony Gubitosi, "21-year-old petty racketeer of 290 Third Avenue," who had been missing since January. He had been stabbed five times in the heart, and his skull was fractured. In August of that year, a lumber worker was leaving his yard when he spotted a trunk lying in an empty lot at Percival and Court Streets, one block from the Gowanus Canal. Curious, he pushed through the tall grass to investigate. He cut through the yards of clothesline, opened the trunk, and saw a body "stuffed inside the trunk and trussed, Jack-knife fashion, with clothes line which eras wound tightly around the wrists and ankles and then drawn around the neck and knotted several times." Twenty detectives of the Brooklyn Homicide Squad arrived on the scene, confused that the killers hadn't dumped the body into the canal. Perhaps, the police hypothesized, they saw a car approaching and abandoned the trunk before they could complete the task. The detectives later found that the victim had been stabbed forty-eight times with an ice pick, mostly in his heart. They identified him as William Hessler, a low level criminal who had been arrested for kidnapping and attempted extortion, but was never convicted.[25]

After Frankie Yale's numerous attempts on his life, "Wild" Bill Lovett was finally executed sometime around November 1, 1923, in a longshoremen's dive, the Dock Loaders' Club. He had apparently been drinking heavily, and fallen asleep in a back room. His body was discovered, skull smashed in, by a patrolling policeman at eight thirty in the morning—Balsamo, ever the conspiracy weaver, claims that Yale ordered the killing after he received the hot tip about the slumbering White Hand boss. He was replaced by his brother-in-law, the final dangerous leader of the White Hand, Richard "Peg Leg" Longergan. Unlike his previous boss, Peg Leg always traveled with a crew of henchmen, and was a dangerous man who wanted nothing more than too eliminate Frankie Yale.

His chance would come in 1925, at the Adonis Social Club, a private speakeasy and restaurant on Twentieth Street and Third Avenue in southern Gowanus, where Yale held an annual Christmas stag party. Peg Leg intended to deal with the Italian problem once and for all by heading a strike at the Adonis late in the evening. According to most accounts, a White Hander named Eddie Lynch, seeking to defect, tipped Yale off to the plot. Supposedly Yale phoned in a favor to Al Capone, who came in from Chicago for Christmas.[26]

By the time Peg Leg and his crew of five men arrived at the Adonis, it was already two in the morning on December 26, but the Christmas party was still raging. Yale was nowhere to be found, and there were no active Black Handers they recognized in the dining room, so they sat. Capone, whom most White Handers had never seen in person—supposedly stood behind the bar pouring drinks. From his station he could see clearly the table full of White Handers, and he remained quiet and cool. The waiter (and Al Capone's cousin), Sylvester Agoglia, played dumb, pretending not to recognize the White Hand boss. Supposedly, Peg Leg asked where Frankie Yale was, and he said he didn't know. This was the moment. Capone hit the light switch, and more than twenty shots were fired in the darkness. The remaining civilians screamed and ran for cover against the walls. After an eternity of a minute, the lights came back on. One of Peg Leg's henchmen lay dead, the rest had bolted out the front door (or crawled, as Jimmy Hart managed to escape with bullets in his hip and leg). Peg Leg's corpse, his brain filled with two bullets, was crumpled at the foot of a cheap piano, lying in a pile of ragtime and jazz music sheets. A copy of "She's My Baby" still sat in the piano's rack.[27]

Police arrested the surviving White Handers, Agoglia, and Capone, among other witnesses to the crime (Capone was listed as a "bouncer and supposed Chicago gunman"). All were released without charges. The White Hand organization would crumble after this paralyzing attack. With the elimination of the final head of Irish operation, the Black Hand finally took control of Brooklyn's docks and warehouse rackets. Under leaders like Frankie Yale and his associates from the Five Points gang—especially the brothers Vincenzo and Philip Mangano—a lucrative criminal business empire would thrive. Many of New York's wise guys settled in South Brooklyn, buying houses on President and Henry Streets, running numbers, opening social clubs and bars, or hosting gambling parlors. The 1920s would prove to be a gold mine, and would provide an education.[28]

Gowanus Grit

Before March 13, 1928, John McGibney was just an unemployed ironworker in Gowanus. He was hanging around the docks at the foot of Court Street, probably hoping to score a bit of work, when he noticed a spout of water fly up into the air, right at the mouth of the Gowanus Canal. He realized, soon enough, that the spouting was coming from a small whale, possibly a baby. McGibney and three other jobless laborers, Harry Dolan, Henry Steele, and William Lynch, borrowed a motorboat to further investigate. They saw that the whale was "bleeding from a large wound near its fin and that it was feebly lashing the water with a bruised tail." The water spouting from its nostrils was also clearly tainted with blood. Using a length of steel cable they had brought along in the boat, the men prepared a noose and tied it to the creature's tail.

They began to tow it to shore, with Dolan wielding the boathook "with a professional whaler's flourish." Once they reached Clinton Street, a second noose was thrown around the whale's head, and "enlisting the help of a dozen men," the suddenly employed band of amateur whalers attempted to lug the mammal ashore. Just as they were about to heave, the whale began thrashing around with such savage force that the men had no choice but to drop the cables. "For fifteen minutes," the *New York Times* story concluded, "the monster churned the waters of the basin in its death throes. Seagoing tugboats near the water were rocked by the commotion. Then the whale became still." The day after the capture, Dr. George G. Goodwin—associate curator of mammals at the American Museum of Natural History—

arrived on the scene to identify the creature. It was, indeed a baby sperm whale, eighteen feet long and two tons. Dr. Goodwin loaded the carcass into the truck that would deliver the whale to its final destination, an exhibition of marine animal skeletons in the institution's Oceanic Hall. He rewarded the ironworkers fifty dollars (about six hundred today) for their struggles.[29]

"Brooklyn's Own Whale Sold to Science for a Mere $50" read the *Eagle*'s headline the following day. The violent battle had become instant legend, spreading across Brooklyn's saloons and docks, with journalists from the *New York Times* and every other daily newspaper arriving on the scene to see the whale firsthand. Across the city dozens of versions of the story were recounted, the whale probably growing larger at each telling. Articles relating the unfortunate mammal appeared for the rest of the week.[30]

It is no wonder that the whale's violent thrashings disturbed nearby tugboats, as the Gowanus Bay was awfully crowded in 1928. More than twenty-six thousand barges, boats and other vessels would pass under the Hamilton Street bridge, the unofficial entrance of this ancient boat channel—at the height of its career. Nearly fifty different industrial firms and warehouse businesses could be found along the banks of the canal: lumber, sand, and stone yards, gas manufacturing and coal processing plants, ice houses, chemical dye factories, concrete works, and tile factories—and these were just the legitimate businesses. The largest asphalt plant in the world had been erected at its mouth. But within a year, the foundations began to crumble. After the 1929 stock market crash businesses atrophied and families were left destitute. The Great Depression washed over the United States and the whole world, sending the new decade into decline and infamy. By 1931 approximately fifteen million people, a quarter of the nation's workforce, were unemployed.[31]

On March 22, 1933, Roosevelt signed the Cullen-Harrison Act, which legalized the sale of beer and other low-alcohol beverages. It was the beginning of the end of Prohibition, and the Mafia-controlled bootlegging operations were poised for change. Going legitimate, while lowering profits, was not considered a loss for the Brooklyn Mafia. Such businesses still brought in income, and provided cover for other illicit activities. The Michel Brewing Company on Bond and Fourth Streets, for example, had survived Prohibition by producing "near beer," a brew with very low alcohol content that was common during the 1930s. Often near beers were later injected with higher grade alcohol, or the brewing plants had illicit corners where higher-alcohol beer was produced. On July 3, 1933, a grand explosion and fire erupted in the brewing plant. It was not a pre–Independence Day fireworks test—Roosevelt's laws had just allowed for expansion of the brewery's operations, and a crew of riggers had been moving two sixteen-ton condensers to make room for increased production.

The first was dropped off without a hitch, but while moving the second the riggers snapped a two-and-a-half-inch ammonia pipe. The room filled with fumes as sixteen men scrambled for the exit, and there was a deafening bang. "The flames that followed the explosion climbed through the three floors above and spread into an unused icing plant next door," reported the *New York Times*. "The firemen, aided by the fireboats William J. Gaynor and Zophar Mills, which came alongside the brewery in an inlet of the Gowanus Canal, maintained a sheet of water on the firewall separating the engine house from the brew house and saved the latter building from damage."

The only man hurt in the explosion was Peter De Vito, who ran the company's trucking and had been in the main building at the wrong moment. He suffered a fractured shoulder and injuries to one leg. His presence speaks quite a bit about what kind of business the brewery had been: De Vito was a well-known criminal in Brooklyn who had a large trucking business but moonlighted as a strikebreaker. He once received a huge sum, about a half million dollars, to cart in armies of thugs and end strikes on well-known corporations like Standard Oil and the American Can Company. Although De Vito had also been indicted for his involvement in illicit bootlegging businesses in Jamaica, Queens, his downfall came from tax evasion. In 1929 he paid $223.65 in taxes on a reported net income of $14,275, when he really earned upward of $300,000. While an IRS inspector, Charles Keveney, was conducting the audit, De Vito informed him that he was "boss in Kings and Queens and boss of your boss." De Vito also said that he was friends with Al Capone and that "if income tax agents made too much trouble they might be taken for a ride." Upon his arrest, the police found two pistols hanging off the strike master's bedpost, one of which had no license.[32]

A month before the brewery fire, and less than a mile away, government employees had discovered an even better-kept secret: "A corner of the old 'Stone House of Gowanus' was unearthed," reported the *New York Times*, "twelve feet below the ground surface, and about 100 feet southwest of Fifth Avenue and Third Street" by excavators of the Brooklyn Park's Department. Historical and civic organizations had been searching for the famous seventeenth-century building for years. They had pieced together accounts from "several old residents of the area" who remembered seeing the house as young boys, and clues from a century-old painting that belonged to Brooklyn resident Robert S. Cortelyou, whose ancestors had once owned the house. The house was depicted on a bluff overlooking Denton's millpond and the Gowanus Creek. But in 1897 "the entire slope from Prospect Park West to the canal was graded to provide for city streets, and the house virtually disappeared." Having discovered this piece of American history, the Parks Department planned to restore the house to its original condition, reconstructed as a memorial on a new city park.[33]

In mid-September, an area of Gowanus to the south of the new viaduct began to reek strongly of alcohol. The odor was eventually traced to one building, 44 Thirteenth Street, at Second Avenue, which was subsequently raided by a joint operation of the Justice Department and Brooklyn police. They found a newly installed twenty-thousand-gallon liquor still, but made no arrests as the entire crew had escaped through the back doors. There was other brand-new equipment worth an estimated $150,000. "The condition of the equipment and the fact that parts of the plant were still under construction indicated, according to the police, that the still was being installed by bootleggers to meet the demand for liquor expected to result from the imminent repeal of the Eighteenth Amendment," wrote the *New York Times*. Doubtlessly, criminal money funded the expensive operation. Soon after, on December 5, the Twenty-First Amendment was ratified, ending the thirteen-year ban on spirits. Despite the end of Prohibition, organized crime persisted. Poverty continued to squeeze the soul of the nation, and the violence became increasingly vicious in the inner city—and Gowanus was no exception.[34]

Legitimate business on the Gowanus, like along all of America's industrial waterways, declined in the years of the Great Depression. There is little hard information on the exact cause, but several factors were at play: Marine access to the canal had diminished, partially due to the decades of sediment that had settled at the bottom, but also because commercial ships had grown in size and berth, making the Gowanus a decreasingly convenient place to dock. Depression-era urban development and construction were almost completely static, suffocated by the lack of capital to invest in new commercial buildings and homes. This decreased demand for brick, lumber, and other building materials, all vital Gowanus industries.[35]

Other changes were due to progress and innovation: Electric light bulbs were the new the standard for lighting homes—formerly the bread and butter of manufactured gas companies. Coal was used less as heating fuel as oil became increasingly available. Advancements like these coincided with greater use of trucks and highways in shipping and commerce. There was also less citywide demand for hay and grain as horses had been almost entirely displaced.

These changes had a ruinous effect on the formerly thriving Gowanus. Crime and the rank odor of sewage would not so easily recede, but after centuries of thriving commercial activity the Gowanus was headed toward abandon. It had been a gradual process, but the neighborhood was all the more derelict due to the criminal presence. Yet the city was not ignorant of the suffering neighborhood. Like many of New York's struggling communities in the 1930s, the Gowanus and Red Hook areas were pegged for urban revitalization. The figurehead of this recovery movement was Robert Moses—the authoritarian city planner immortalized in Robert Caro's celebrated tome of power and money in civic society, *The Power Broker*.

While wearing many hats during his long trajectory in development, Moses began his career overseeing the creation of large public works in New York, mostly state highways and parks. He served a year as the New York secretary of state. In New York City he served as commissioner of both the Parks and City Planning Departments, and was also chairman of the Triborough Bridge Authority. The latter of these positions gave him practically unbridled development power, as he controlled millions in toll revenues over which the city government held no authority. In the 1930s he began a grand scheme of highway construction across the city, meant to connect Manhattan to the outer boroughs and suburbs.

One progressive infrastructure plan that had been floating around since the 1920s was a car tunnel that would travel under the East River to South Brooklyn. Following the onset of the Depression, city officials believed this car access from the Battery in Lower Manhattan to Hamilton Avenue, right by the Gowanus, would aid revitalization in South Brooklyn and across the river. Mayor Fiorello La Guardia also knew that the drained city coffers couldn't support any large-scale projects; New York could not build the tunnel without Moses. He had access to millions of dollars in toll revenues. But for his own reasons, mostly his own visibility and the promise of higher revenue, Moses wanted the construction to be a bridge, and he pushed heavily to change the plan. He faced opposition from the business and political powers in the city—even the public generally disagreed with Moses, not wanting to further alter the landscape of the harbor. In the meantime, he was also involved with several parkway projects across

Long Island—foreshadowing the growth of American suburbs—with a particular portion running along the shore at Sheepshead Bay, between Brooklyn and Queens. It would become the Belt Parkway, and it needed a connection to Manhattan. This missing link, for which construction began in 1939, was called the Gowanus Parkway after the historic region it would bifurcate.[36]

The elevated highway was constructed along the original Third Avenue El line, running twenty-six blocks toward Bay Ridge, in a neighborhood called Sunset Park. It is an early example of Moses's penchant for bulldozing through vibrant neighborhoods. Third Avenue was an active thoroughfare, the core of Sunset Park. It had never been particularly beautiful, but was clean, safe, and full of stores, restaurants, and theaters; even at night there was pedestrian traffic. It was certainly poor, but crime was concentrated along the waterfront past Second Avenue. Place the shadow-casting highway there, the residents pleaded. But Moses made sure the highway was set for Third Avenue because the original El structure was still intact, eliminating the need for a new right-of-way. Furthermore, Sunset Park wasn't worth saving, he insisted. It was a "slum." The new parkway was constructed down Third Avenue. The sides of the structure stood too close to the buildings. It casted shadows double the width of the El, and Third Avenue became always gloomy and damp. More than hundred stores were closed, and twelve hundred families were evicted from their homes, knocked down to build access ramps. In its later years, the former pedestrian thoroughfare would be associated with sex shops and prostitutes. "If Third Avenue was the heart of the neighborhood," wrote Caro, "Moses tore it out."[37]

There were very few occasions in Moses's decades of service when he did not get his way. But on July 17, 1939—just as Gowanus Parkway construction had begun—his bridge plan was vetoed, an ordered handed down from President Roosevelt via Harry Woodring, the secretary of war. Supposedly the structure would be an added barrier to the Brooklyn Navy Yard and could also be vulnerable to attack during a potential war (even though there were already two other bridges in the bay). The decision was just as much a check in a grander political battle at play, as Moses had intense rivalries with both President Roosevelt and Mayor La Guardia. City planners dusted off their cursory tunnel plans and rushed them to completion in time for federal review. On October 29, 1940, Roosevelt was standing at the corner of Van Brunt Street and Hamilton Avenue. "I feel like saying today 'at last,' because for some time there would be a dispute as to whether we would cross the East River," said the president. His short speech explained that choosing an appropriate project had been a question "that mere laymen couldn't decide," and that ultimately building a tunnel versus a bridge would be "safer for America and all its cities." A few words later he "pulled a cord attached to the whistle of a steam shovel," which signaled to Louis Cappola, the operator, to drop the great steel bucket and take the first bite of earth that would become the Brooklyn-Battery Tunnel.[38]

That the president himself kicked off this ceremony is a testament to the national significance of New York, both economically—an improvement of the city's fiscal health would be a good litmus test for the recovering country—and strategically, as the possibility of war loomed oversees. But it is odd to imagine one of America's most celebrated leaders standing in the most notorious section of New York Harbor, gloating over his winning a turf war with Robert Moses just steps from the mouth of the Gowanus Canal.

In 1940, that part of Hamilton Avenue, along the Gowanus and the Erie Basin, was "a favorite hangout of longshoremen, prisoners on parole, and pirates." According to a Depression-era writer named Dorothy Bennett, locals called it "the Jungle," with "its countless saloons, its old hotels, and, according to report, its houses of ill fame." Bennett, known as "Dotty" to her friends, was also an assistant curator at the planetarium at New York's Museum of Natural History. In 1940 she published *Sold to the Ladies!*, an account of how she and girlfriends Ruhe and Gibby purchased a dirty old welding barge on the Gowanus Canal for $160 and turned it into a houseboat-cum-summer getaway.

"'It's no place for ladies,' the policeman had warned us about Gowanus Canal that first day," Dotty began, and launched into an engaging first-person narrative of how her crew of recent college graduates gutted and restored the filthy, oil-soaked barge. Written in a lively and cheerful demeanor, her book presented an idealized modern-day gentrification narrative of the Gowanus Canal neighborhood. To expedite the process of removing a carpet of rusty nails from the floors and the ends of broken pipes from the ceilings, these women convinced their modern and sophisticated friends to lend a hand in renovating the shockingly viable forty-foot barge, renamed it the *Barnacle* (this being ironic, since the Gowanus water was "so filthy that no

3 Girls Bought a Gowanus Barge, Turned Life Into a Salty Adventure

Brooklyn Cop Said 'It's No Place for Ladies,' But Dot, Gibby, Ruhe Loved It

HEFFERNAN Says:

FEATURES BROOKLYN EAGLE

EARS TO THE GROUND

By CLIFFORD EVANS

Dorothy "Dotty" Bennett, with friends Ruhe and Gibby, renovators of the Gowanus barge *Barnacle*. *Brooklyn Daily Eagle*, June 13, 1940. Brooklyn Collection. Courtesy of the Brooklyn Public Library and Newspapers.com.

marine growth can survive"—barge captains were said to sail into the waters simply to keep their hulls clean of barnacles, shipworms and, jellyfish). In the process of their restoration, the charming and modern twentysomething single women befriended a number of Gowanus sailors, tug captains, and junkies (then a term for marine scrap collectors, a Depression-era occupation) who generously aided the young professionals in their scheme, offering gifts and repair advice.

These locals assured the ladies that barge was completely seaworthy—each of the tanks and capstans was worth at least double what the women had paid for the whole barge. Amused by the moxie of these young professionals, the junkies gifted them old cable spools to serve as coffee tables and a sea chest with rope handles. "Our Gowanus helpers were in a constant state of perplexity over our friends," Dotty wrote. "They marveled that we could get a nursery school teacher and a planning engineer in a department store to tar the roof, a coal salesman and a sculptor to work out of the same can of paint with a dog fancier and a psychologist." One couple, "Don and Dorothy, artist friends from Greenwich Village, as poor as the rest of us," arrived one day in a taxi with a young dalmatian on a leash.

"It beats hell the way you get all these aristocrats to work for you," exclaimed one Gowanus neighbor, named Terry. Perplexed, Ruhe tried to explain to Terry that she and her compatriots were hardly upper-crust snobs, but working folks. "Well, they're aristocrats, all right," he insisted. "They brought caviar today, and only aristocrats eat caviar. Anybody knows that." Over the course of a year, the women outfitted the large cabin with bunks and furniture, enough to make it a livable home. When the summer arrived, they moved into the barge to complete the final touches. "Our living on the Gowanus worried some of our friends, but we felt perfectly safe," Dotty wrote. "Every man nearby was a self-appointed watchman. Just because of the neighborhood, every neighbor we knew seemed to feel personally responsible for us, though many of them constituted the very element of whom our friends were most afraid." Once their new home was complete,

Dotty, Ruhe, and Gibby sailed the *Barnacle* around the harbor, spending time at the South Street Seaport, eventually chugging up into the Long Island Sound. They docked at Manhasset Bay, and used the barge as a weekend and summer getaway. They stayed there for three years, once returning to Gowanus to find some cement brushes and other barge gear (there was nowhere else in the city to find that particular item). Dotty soon found Al, a junkie with a big yard full of scrap. He remembered Dotty as one of the barge ladies and gave her six brushes, as well as a new scraper and marlin spike (a tool used in marine rope work). "Why you couldn't *pay* me for it!" exclaimed Al, sincerely upset when Dotty inquired about the prices. He refused to take anything but some information about the barge and life on Long Island Sound. "The Gowanus had not changed," Dotty wrote. "The same generous interest that we had met before was still characteristic of our old friends."[39]

In a manner of speaking, the era of the Second World War kept the canal industry unnaturally afloat. When the *Barnacle* ladies bought their barge in the mid-1930s, the slips were empty, almost devoid of activity. But upon Dotty's return, four years later, she discovered a resurgence of business, formerly abandoned warehouses bulging with supplies. Dozens of barges docked on the Gowanus's piers. But even this activity represented only a third of the traffic the Gowanus enjoyed during the late 1920s. Highway systems were developing across the country—no longer would industry need inner-city waterways to transport and receive goods.[40]

Manufacturing firms closed their doors or moved to less cramped locations outside of the urban jungle, now easily accessed by car and truck. Low-risk postwar loans gave the newly rising middle class a chance to escape the grit of the inner city for ideally manicured suburbs, and they did so in rising numbers. The postwar opportunities for young couples were better than those their parents had: for the middle class, there were plenty of office jobs with good wages and subsidized educational opportunities for returning soldiers. Although postwar America proved to be a prosperous time of growth, urban economies across the country were not rebounding—the future, and the new American dream, was a home with a backyard and a thirty-year mortgage. Inside cities, however, poverty and racial tensions were on the rise—those robust working-class quarters became decayed and all the more sinister.[41]

Joseph Mitchell, an American writer and luminary of the *New Yorker*, is celebrated for his lyrical portraits of odd and marginal characters, particularly in his home city of New York. In his heyday, Mitchell's celebrated profiles captured the ethos of the changing city, giving a voice to the many fascinating layers of class and ethnicity hiding in odd pockets of the urban landscape. One of his most famous accounts, "The Mohawks in High Steel," was published in 1949. In the midst of the neighborhood's decline, Mitchell captured life in a colony of Native American immigrants from Canada who had settled in Brooklyn, in a neighborhood called North Gowanus, "an old, sleepy, shabby neighborhood that lies between the head of the Gowanus Canal and the Borough Hall shopping district."

Aside from their heritage, these men were unique for their tendency to work in steel and iron construction work, particularly on bridges and skyscrapers. They had attained a legendary status for showing no fear of heights, often working as riveters, the most dangerous task in the business. Many had worked on the Empire State Building. This particular tribe called itself Caughnawaga, and for three centuries its people had been settled in a Catholic reservation outside of Montreal—one of the earliest reservations in the Americas. Little Caughnawagas had also flourished in Detroit and Buffalo. But the original Caughnawaga "village" had been a traditional settlement in Mohawk region of Upstate New York, near Fonda and Broadalbin—almost too coincidentally, the birthplace of a Gowanus grandfather, Daniel Richards.

Although the Caughnawaga formed a small colony in Brooklyn, their presence was strong enough that "all the grocery stores in North

Gowanus, even the little Italian ones" stocked the brand of cornmeal the women preferred to use in making Indian boiled broad, or *ka-na-ta-rok*. The Nevins Bar & Grill, a snug and plain establishment at 75 Nevins Street, was the central Caughnawaga hangout. It was, according to Mitchell, "one of the oldest saloons in Brooklyn. It was opened in 1888, when North Gowanus was still an Irish enclave, and was originally called Connelly's Abbey. Irish customers still call it the Abbey." Most Caughnawaga proved dour and adverse to conversation, but one famously garrulous regular, the squat and barrel-chested Orvis Diabo, recounted hours of stories to Mitchell about the history of his tribe and its particular livelihood. He was fifty-four years old and his Indian name, O-Ron-ia-ke-te, translated as He Carries the Sky, and like many of his fellow tribesmen, Diabo had been traveling between the reservation and Brooklyn for at least twenty years. Although even he could not say why the first Caughnawagas chose North Gowanus (most likely, the rent was cheapest there), they had always preferred the more village-like Brooklyn, joining its local unions. "I enjoy New York," he told Mitchell, while sitting in the Nevins. "The people are as high-strung as rats and the air is too gritty, but I enjoy it."[42]

9

The Fall of South Brooklyn and the Brownstone Revolution (1950–1981)

"Yep, things have certainly changed along the old creek," confirmed Captain James Kirk of the tugboat *Hugh Bond* in 1949. A seventy-four-year-old "grizzled port captain and dean of the Gowanus tug admirals," he had been piloting tugs on the canal for fifty years for the Gowanus Towing Company and had memories of stinking garbage and kids bathing in the funky waters.

In Kirk's youth, the canal was so crowded, a tug would enter at the foot of Smith Street at sunrise and wouldn't arrive at Butler Street (the terminus) until noon. A 1905 story from the *Eagle* reveals that the captain once found the body of drowned man wearing a full cutaway suit in the canal, by Thirteenth Street. At the time of the interview Kirk's boat, the *Hugh Bond*, had been named for a nearly mythical tug captain who had founded of the Gowanus Towing Company and ruled the waterway in the late nineteenth century.[1]

Schooners used to fight for right-of-way along the canal, explained Harry F. Pearsall, president of the Gowanus Towing Company in a 1950 interview, but now they were as "scarce as a horse-drawn wagon on the streets." For seventy-five years his company had operated tugboats, and had long been the central dispatcher for traffic up and down the waterway. But now the trucking industry competed heavily with the barges of Gowanus.[2]

At the beginning of the Second World War, approximately eighteen thousand vessels entered the Gowanus Canal annually, a marked drop from the heyday of the late 1920s. By the early 1950s, the number plunged again to ten thousand; by the 1960s, so much boat traffic had been lost that the Army Corps of Engineers did not bother to gather statistics at all. While the flushing tunnel continued operating steadily through this period, the constant inflow of wastewater and silt and a relative lack of dredging took its toll on the decreasingly important waterway. Around 1960, the propeller-drive shaft of the tunnel broke entirely. According to neighborhood legend, a disgruntled city employee dropped a manhole cover into the works, disabling the mechanism entirely. For the next thirty years, the Gowanus waters remained stagnant and stunk up the neighborhood in a manner that hadn't been witnessed since the turn of the twentieth century. Abandoned, the once world-famous canal was left to rot, and the people in its vicinity left to breathe the fumes.[3]

Only in such a rank space of urban decay, where midcentury neglect left the inner cities to their own devices, could free theater of violent crime play out unabated. For it was at this time that the most infamous

Photograph by Jules Geller from the interior of the Gowanus Towing Company. *Brooklyn Daily Eagle*, June 25, 1949. Brooklyn Collection. Courtesy of the Brooklyn Public Library and Newspapers.com.

of street battles and gangbanger fights erupted in a violent gang war that proved true the mythology of the Gowanus as a base for organized crime. It began with a Sicilian don, Giuseppe "Joe" Profaci, a founding boss of New York's Five Families. He was a contemporary of the Mangano clan and for twenty years ruled parts of Brooklyn, making millions from extortion, protection rackets, and gambling.

During the 1950s, he began an expansion of his gambling operations into certain parts of South Brooklyn, a neighborhood on the brink of fiscal decline. But he unknowingly impeded on the territory of Sam DeCavalcante, a New Jersey boss who ran gambling in the same part of Brooklyn, and disputes erupted among their capos. In order to prevent bloodshed, the two bosses met in Profaci's hunting lodge in New Jersey and sat cordially throughout a fine dinner, never discussing the issue at hand until the meal was over—and only as if it was the most

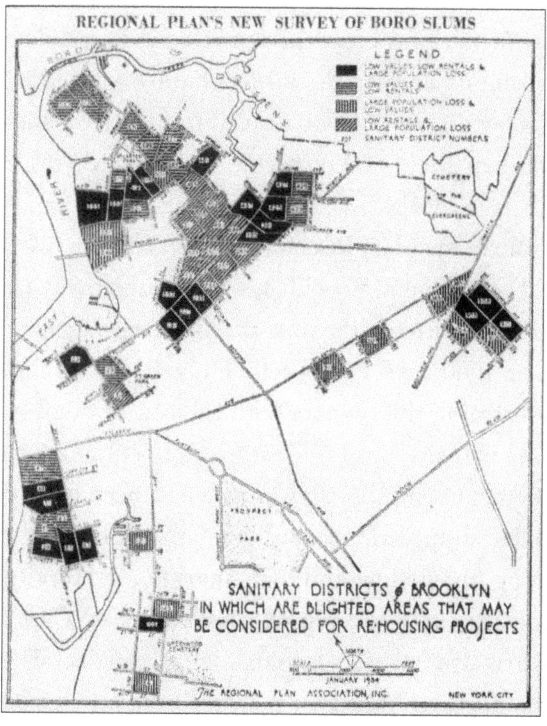

A 1934 map of Brooklyn's "blighted" areas that illustrates the decline of South Brooklyn, in particular the areas surrounding the Gowanus. Courtesy of the Brooklyn Public Library.

trivial matter. A solution was soon reached: "the Gowanus Canal which bisected the area in question was designated as the demarcation line between the two groups." The next day the word was passed down to the troops and open conflict successfully avoided.[4]

Had the negotiations failed, the next course of action would have been to involve the famed Mafia Commission, which dealt with interfamily disputes. Only the most serious of infractions required such high-level arbitration, which was both embarrassing and potentially harmful to a family's image in terms of power and control. But Profaci was not universally loved in his whole family, nor did they think much of his being a stickler for tradition. The aging despot still taxed each of his subordinates twenty-five dollars a month and demanded huge percentages from every gambling venture, illicit loan, and hijacking—whereas in other families some of these contributions were voluntary. Most of all they deplored his nepotism. Profaci handed out favors and jobs to old friends and longtime associates, leaving only the slightest taste for the younger members of his crew—as tradition dictated. The most motivated and disgruntled crew in the Profaci family was led by the Gallo brothers, Lawrence (Larry) Gallo, a quiet, round-faced man in his thirties, Joseph (Crazy Joey) Gallo, his skinny, unpredictable younger brother, and Albert (Kid Blast) Gallo, the youngest and handsomest one. They had a fourth member, Joseph (Joe Jelly) Giorelli, who was short and fat. All had grown up in Brooklyn, working their way up into the ranks of organized crime from the time they were teenagers.[5]

The Gallos had built up their own racket selling jukeboxes to bars and restaurants—strong-arming the owners who refused to comply. They even organized a repairman's union—Teamster's Local 266—to further the extortion scheme. Crazy Joey's nickname had been earned through his ruthlessness. He supposedly kept a lion named Cleo in the basement, and would drag his victims and loan-sharking debtors to the top of the stairs, and then toss the big feline some meat; Cleo's roars were effective in scaring the debtors into making payments.[6] The favored hangout of the Gallos was Monte's Venetian Room on Carroll

Street—once known as Angelo's Tavern and still owned by the Montemarano family, but they changed the name in the 1930s after an inspiring trip to Venice (and a tongue-in-cheek reference to the Gowanus). Legend dictates that in the early 1960s, when life for the Gallo brothers was getting hot, Frank Sinatra, Sammy Davis Jr., and other members of the Rat Pack would host post-Copacabana parties and impromptu concerts in the restaurant. For years Monte's hosted high-profile visitors, such as Leona Helmsley, James Caan, Danny Aiello, and Hedy Lamarr.[7]

The Gallo brothers took orders from a capo named "Frankie Shots" Abbatemarco, who ran some extensive gambling operations in Brooklyn. For his own reasons, in 1959 Profaci ordered the Gallos to kill Abbatemarco. They had no problem carrying out the hit, but were incensed when their former capo's gambling interests were divided among Profaci's contemporaries, leaving no taste for the Gallos. Crazy Joey was furious. He began to recruit other young toughs he knew from the neighborhood, formulating a plan to overthrow Profaci and take over his lucrative rackets. Together the brothers, plus Joe Jelly and several other associates, pulled off a daring kidnap of five senior members of Profaci family in February 1961. They nabbed the don's brother, Joseph Magliocco, his brother-in-law, and capo Joseph Colombo. The only person they didn't get was Joe Profaci himself, who managed to escape. They held the hostages for two weeks in Red Hook, and then released them on Profaci's promise that grievances would be heard. John Scimone, one of the hostages, claimed he also had grown tired of Profaci's tactics and offered to help the Gallos.

But Crazy Joey, full of rage, refused to sit down with the Profacis until the don pledged him a hundred thousand dollars as a gesture of goodwill. The issue was serious enough that they called upon the Council of the Five Families to weigh in on the matter. After a sit-down, the council deemed the conflict to be an "intra-family" issue, and that nobody else should be involved in the decision making. During this tense, months-long period of no compromise, Joe Profaci was quietly wooing back many members of the Gallo brothers' rebel army—promising money and opportunity to return to his good graces.

In August, Scimone conspired a meeting with Larry Gallo at the Sahara Lounge, a supper club on Utica Avenue, to discuss the faltering negotiations. It was empty, save for the bartender. After several minutes at the bar, Scimone went to the bathroom, leaving Larry alone in the smoky darkness. Suddenly, two hands appeared in the darkness and wrapped a garotte around Larry's neck, cutting off his air supply. The man demanded to know where Joey was, but the suffocating Gallo brother refused to talk. The cord got tighter until Larry's motor functions started to falter, and he pissed and defecated into his pants. They didn't kill him, however—a police officer happened to walk into the bar, and Larry's attackers scrammed. Besides, Profaci wanted the Crazy Joey dead, and killing Larry would only drive the upstart deeper into his hole. Although just barely escaped death, Larry later refused to identify his attackers to the police—as that would have violated the *omertà*, the code of silence all "made men" in the Mafia swore to uphold. But the next day Joe Jelly went missing—and was never heard from again.[8]

Realizing that the Profacis meant business, the remaining Gallo crew went into hiding, barricading themselves in their tenement on President Street, in Red Hook. Crazy Joey, frustrated and antsy at being sequestered in a dusty tenement, was always urging Larry to go out gun slinging in Brooklyn. They were, after all, at war. He took the risk of visiting Manhattan in the open, going to Greenwich Village and taking his wife dancing. Over the next few years at least a dozen men were wounded or killed during the conflict, and many of them within a few blocks of the Gowanus Canal. On October 4, 1961, Joseph Magnasco, a Gallo man, was shot to death at the southwest corner of Union Street and Fourth Avenue. One month later, Crazy Joey was sentenced to seven years in prison for federal tax fraud, but the violence persisted: on December 11, Larry Carna, another Gallo man, was wounded in a drive by shooting in front of 511 President Street, at the corner of the Third Avenue. Even after Joe Profaci died of cancer in the summer of 1962, battles continued when the Gallo clan refused to accept the new Profaci underboss, Joseph Magliocco. Meanwhile, the other New York families were rattled by the level of publicity and media coverage of their "personal" problems, and hoped the fire would burn itself out.[9]

At seven o'clock on the morning of May 19, 1963, Carmine "Snake" Persico and Alphonse D'Ambrosio, Profaci men, were driving up Bond Street. As they passed Degraw Street, a green truck pulled up alongside their car and unloaded at least six shots from a twenty-two-caliber rifle. Persico was hit in the mouth, hand, and shoulder, D'Ambrosio also suffered two wounds, but somehow none were fatal. Persico was a particularly sweet target for the Gallos—he had been one of their original recruits for taking down the Profaci autocracy, but the old Sicilian boss enticed him back with promises of shared power. Persico was the mysterious strangler of Larry Gallo at the Sahara Lounge, and his nickname, "Snake," was supposedly bequeathed by the Gallos after learning of his betrayal. Later that evening, seventeen Gallo soldiers, including brothers Larry and Albert Gallo, were arrested by police for possession of firearms and silencers.[10]

While the Gallo-Profaci conflict would come to an end in the mid-1960s, the battles waged across New York, and in South Brooklyn particularly, left a profound impact on the image of the Gowanus Canal and its environs. Although the Italian community had laid its roots in Brooklyn before there was even a concept of a Mafia, the association between the canal, crime, and this community had been solidified since before the turn of the century.[11]

The Invention of Carroll Gardens

One morning in 1975, Salvatore "Buddy" Scotto Jr. was sitting at a desk in his funeral home on First Place and the corner of Court Street when the phone unexpectedly rang. Although he was busy, the forty-six-year-old funeral director and native Brooklynite picked up the receiver. "Mr. Scotto?" asked a voice. "Yes, this is Mr. Scotto, but I can't talk," he said flatly. He was a tall, often serious-looking man with a dark, thick head of hair and olive complexion. "No wait a minute Mr. Scotto. The Vice President would like to talk to you."

Speechless, he heard a click and a pause. "Hello Sal, this is the Vice President," spoke the voice of Nelson Rockefeller, calling Scotto by a name that almost nobody used. "I'm kind of disappointed that you're not going to support the President, Sal. And I thought I'd call you and ask you about it."

Before Rockefeller was appointed by President Gerald Ford as vice president in 1974 he had been the wealthy scion of one of America's richest families (his grandfather was John D. Rockefeller Sr.) and served as governor of New York since 1959. Scotto, a Brooklyn small business owner and neighborhood activist, had never imagined speaking to the man when he was Governor Rockefeller—let alone Vice President Rockefeller. But without his realizing it, Scotto had been long ready for this conversation and kept his cool. "Listen Governor, we've got problems," Scotto began, launching into a conversation he'd had many times before. "We've got that stinking Gowanus Canal that we're going to lose a $458 million project for because the city is in bankruptcy now and cannot afford to come up with its share, and nobody gives a damn about it. We have Fulton Mall that's halfway done and stopped cold and not going any further. We've got a Brooklyn waterfront that's falling apart. I don't see why the hell I oughta support anybody."

"Well, what are you talking about, this canal?" asked Rockefeller, and the two spent a half hour discussing one of America's most polluted and neglected waterways. They also talked about the disappearing jobs for longshoremen and the wavering livelihoods of his Italian American neighbors—the many woes of 1970s Brooklyn. Days after this chat, Scotto was packing a bag to go down to Washington, D.C., to meet with the vice president. Joining him would be the pastor of St. Mary Star of the Sea, his local church, and Don Moore, president of the Brooklyn Chamber of Commerce at the time.

Just weeks before Rockefeller called his funeral parlor, Scotto was simply a community activist and neighborhood leader. But that year he made at least fifteen trips to Washington to discuss the future of his dying borough; during one such excursion, he recalls, Betty Ford served him a cocktail. Rockefeller promised him results on finishing the Fulton Street Mall—a commercial rejuvenation project for a mostly vacant and dangerous avenue, one of the oldest in Brooklyn—and congressional funds to finish up the multimillion-dollar Red Hook sewage treatment plant. The latter, Scotto insisted, would help to put an end the eternal downpour of raw sewage into the Gowanus Canal. "All I had to do was go to Kansas City, Missouri," Scotto says. "I never even heard of it! What do I know, I was just this guy from the neighborhood."[12]

There were good reasons for Nelson Rockefeller to be concerned with Missouri's largest city, and the relatively unknown Brooklyn community leader. The former was the chosen site for the 1976 Republic National Convention, where Gerald Ford planned to secure his base for his first proper election. Meanwhile, Scotto had just been "overwhelmingly" elected as a local Republican delegate, running at the encouragement of a district leader in Brooklyn, Frank Gargiulo, in 1975. When Scotto showed up to the delegate's meeting in Downtown Brooklyn, the local GOP leaders were viciously fighting over whether they would support Ford in the primaries. Rockefeller, by then on Ford's ticket, was the head of the Republican Party in New York State, but some were insistent on backing the upstart Ronald Reagan for nomination. Bewildered, Scotto had refused to commit to either one, which unknowingly placed him in a unique position. The race for nomination was a close one, and the Ford administration was doing everything in its power to court the undecided delegates.[13]

"Buddy," as most Brooklynites knew the funeral director, was born in 1928 and grew up in the neighborhood once known as Red Hook, in South Brooklyn. His grandparents were Sicilian immigrants who landed in the early twentieth century, but unlike most of their *paisan* neighbors working the docks, his family grew into one successful entrepreneurs. Scotto's parents, Pasquale and Rose, ran a successful funeral parlor and import business that chiefly dealt in wine. The latter took a sharp hit during Prohibition, so they opened movie theaters, at least four on Court Street alone. Scotto's family was better off than most, avoiding the destitution and other common inner-city afflictions of that era. Growing up on the streets of 1940s Red Hook or Gowanus (the border being rather fluid), Scotto observed as the middle-class flight to the suburbs and other postwar changes squeezed the neighborhood into a poverty-ridden shell of its former self.

Many of the Italians and Irish who could afford to escape did so in droves. Meanwhile, before the end of World War II nearly two million African Americans had migrated to the Northeast in search of industrial jobs. Most headed to major cities—as did a number of Puerto Ricans, half a million immigrating to New York before 1960. Many of these newcomers settled in pockets around Red Hook, Gowanus, and Park Slope. Racial tensions grew as neighborhood demographics became more diverse. Scotto recalls rivalries he and Italian neighbors felt with all groups when they were young. Just like with the gangs of Gowanus past, the close quarters often led to heightened tension and fights—this time along racial, not geographic, divides. By the 1960s, institutionalized racism determined the fiscal value of Brooklyn's neighborhoods, at least according to banks and real estate brokers—in a practice known as redlining, the latter refused to offer mortgages on properties in "high-risk" neighborhoods, a poor euphemism for non-white areas. The arrival of working-class African Americans further encouraged many white families not to settle in cities (in many cases, middle-class African Americans also abandoned the inner city, a with similar fear of encroaching poverty), and the failure of city governments to revitalize the neglected infrastructure further pushed people to the "suburban fringe." Only the older households remained, while the young families escaped to their manicured suburban dreams.[14]

Throughout the 1950s and 1960s, South Brooklyn's legacy of commercial grandeur faded, replaced by seedy, abandoned waterfronts, street gangs, and Mafia wars. Scotto went to college locally and then joined the National Guard; his unit served a four-month rotation in Korea. Following that he served three years of active military duty, and then eight more in the reserves.

After he retired from the service in 1963, Scotto saw how much farther his stomping grounds of Red Hook and South Brooklyn had degraded: Many of his cousins and friends had left; storefronts stood shuttered and buildings half empty. Even at that time, Scotto had plans to get married and flee. Decades later he becomes sheepish when admitting that he was embarrassed by his native neighborhood, and particularly by the Gowanus Canal. "This place was for the poor," he has said in numerous interviews. He bought a home in Bay Ridge—still Brooklyn, but a more suburban area of a higher class than the inner-city dregs of Red Hook. But stronger than economic downturn or the fear of inner city implosion were Scotto's indignant Sicilian parents. They still ran the funeral home and owned real estate in the neighborhood. Despite Buddy's pleading in 1964, they refused to leave South Brooklyn. This is where they had raised their child and gleaned their livelihood, and their name was well known in the community. "They said they didn't want to live with 'those people,'" Scotto explained, referring to white Protestant suburbanites.[15]

The evolution a city neighborhoods is nuanced and complex. Even in the worst periods of decline, the tipping point of renewal is often waiting in the vestibule, ready to emerge. A most pertinent example is the venerable upscale neighborhood of nearby Brooklyn Heights, which had steadily lost middle-class residents starting in the 1920s—the nascent years of American suburban. To the dismay of those upper-crust white residents who stayed, many of the previously moneyed Brooklyn Heights owners sold their one-family homes as separated rooming houses. Working-class Irish and Italians moved into these converted dwellings, and by the 1940s only a few blocks of high-rent housing existed near Montague Street, the main thoroughfare. The small pocket of the remaining white middle- and upper-middle-class families brushed elbows with the newer working-class "white ethnics," Puerto Ricans, and African American arrivals.[16]

Following the Second World War, however, a small wave of adventurous middle-class creative types began renting some of the cheap rooming houses and dilapidated brownstones of Brooklyn Heights. These "colonizers" were mostly artists, writers, and some white-collar professionals, streaming in from increasingly modernist Manhattan. Longing for a different urban setting, they embarked on a mission to restore the neglected, human-scaled buildings of their adopted borough. Among the most famous of these "neo-Dutch" settlers was Truman Capote, who moved to Brooklyn Heights in 1957. While much of the borough was dingy and gray to Capote's eye (the imposing modernist megaliths, Concord Village and the Civic Center of Downtown Brooklyn, had recently been erected and dominated the eastern skyline), Brooklyn Heights recalled a charming Victorian past, with its carriage houses, low-scale brick buildings, and quaint shops. The contrast from the sterile lines of midcentury, international-style architecture was refreshing to these Manhattan and (sometimes) suburban transplants. They were "brave pioneers bringing brooms and buckets of paint," Capote wrote in his memoir, "urban ambitious young couples, by and large middle-rung in their Doctor-Lawyer-Wall Street-Whatever careers, eager to restore to the Heights its shattered qualities of circumspect, comfortable charm."

In his detailed history, *The Invention of Brownstone Brooklyn*, Suleiman Osman describes this postindustrial "rediscovery" of the Heights and other brownstone neighborhoods, which became a "birthplace of a new romantic urban ideal" Capote and his peers, recasting the "townhouses, waterfront piers, and industrial lofts as sources of anti-bureaucratic authenticity." Their refusal to align with the zeitgeist of their modernist contemporaries would grow to Brooklyn's "Brownstone" movement—not only did they cast a prototype for the borough's future gentrification before the term was even invented, they also "forged an alternative to the dominant modernist ideology of the 1950s and developed a distinctly urban (or anti-suburban) identity for the new middle class." Soon, as increasing numbers of Brooklyn enthusiasts arrived, the purchase and restoration of red brick townhouses and venerable brownstone buildings became a regular discussion in the real estate pages.[17]

Pockets of "brownstoner" enclaves budded and spread, passing the demarcation line of Atlantic Avenue, where the street life was even more diverse: the storefronts were Lebanese and Syrian Arab markets and spice stalls, bodegas with signs only in Spanish. The pedestrians were local working-class Italians and Puerto Rican émigrés. Farther south, under a veneer of postwar neglect, were cheap brownstones ripe for the taking, in one of the oldest neighborhoods of the original city of Brooklyn. As their movement spread, the newcomers fought to protect their adopted Victorian surroundings from any "out of place" corporate development.

The Brooklyn Heights Association had been established in the 1930s to preserve the character of the once-wealthy enclave, experienced a swell of new membership. But the settlers south of Atlantic Avenue had entered a new frontier, no longer Brooklyn Heights. They were adherents to Jane Jacobs–style principles of urban development—particularly the value of mixed-income, mixed-use neighborhoods and "human-scale" buildings that did not blot out large portions of sky. In the spirit of such ideals, in the late 1950s new settlers named their colony "Cobble Hill," inspired by the Cobble Hill Fort—also known as the "Corkscrew Fort" where George Washington stood during the Battle of Brooklyn. They established the Cobble Hill Association, indicating the blocks that extended south of Brooklyn Heights, bordered by Court, Hicks, and Degraw Streets and proudly announced in local newspapers "with a romantic 19th century heritage that is being reawakened." Faced with unwanted developments, the white-collar inhabitants organized rallies, letter-writing campaigns and petitions that the city government couldn't ignore. Their efforts prevented a chain grocery store from moving into an empty lot on an otherwise picturesque block, and got the city to build a small park instead. To the east, past Smith Street, the North Gowanus of Joseph Mitchell was redubbed Boerum Hill in 1964, mostly through the efforts of one brownstoner named Helen Buckler, who anticipated a similar flurry of middle-class settlement (ironically, that area never had a hill).[18]

Scotto witnessed the neighborhood leaders emerging in these budding enclaves, and how curious it was these groups moved to city neighborhoods, instead of out to the country like most of those who were financially able at the time. "We didn't know what to call them at first," Scotto later told the *New York Times*, "so we called them 'beatniks.'" But he was inspired by their activism, and so along with other Italian neighborhood contemporaries in their forties—including Joe Cardillo, Josephine Taranto, Prudence Cangiano—met and discussed the many issues plaguing their native streets: youth violence, its effect on local schools, the growing presence drugs and dealing, and landscaping of treeless blocks. Bound together by their causes, this group desired a name like the associations in the fancier blocks to the north, as Red Hook and Gowanus held the stigma of violent crime and poverty. Lying between the thoroughfares of the neighborhood, Court and Smith Streets, was the once-elegant Carroll Park, which ran alongside Carroll Street—also the name of the IND subway stop. This area was particular among other Brownstone neighborhoods for its wide streets flanked with carefully tended front-yard gardens, often flanked by statues of saints or the Virgin Mary. The group decided on the "Carroll Gardens Association," and dubbed a wholesome new name for one of Brooklyn's oldest neighborhoods. Unlike the other associations, the CGA was made up of neighborhood natives. Real estate agents began listing "Carroll Gardens" on their business cards, and the name soon stuck.[19]

Scotto and his allies originally made a pact to be purely civic group, not to get involved in local politics. Mostly they were registered Democrats, and there was already a local political organization present in South Brooklyn. One of the main foci spearheaded by Scotto was to clean up the Gowanus Canal; out of all the plagues creeping through the community, the waterway's disgusting conditions gave a bad name to the Italian Americans, Scotto felt. "Where the hell were our people?" he has often asked. But it was naive, Scotto later said, to assume that they could operate a campaign for civic improvement wholly outside of local politics. But the founding members of the CGA would not step on the toes of the regular Democratic organizations, and some even supposedly received subtle threats of violence from the Local 1814, the Mafia-controlled longshoreman union ("The fish stinks from the head," an anonymous union member warned Scotto's father over the phone one evening).

Soon, all of the original members of the nascent community group had abandoned Scotto. However, by the end of the 1960s a cadre of twentysomething Italians from the community—including Joe Bruno, Mike Pesce, Sal Ferrioli, and Eileen Dugan (all of whom would lead successful careers in local politics and law)—joined the CGA, along with several of the new "beatniks," or brownstoners. All were imbued with activist ideals of the era, and shared Scotto's enthusiasm for environmental cleanup. They didn't care about which politicians held power, but simply wanted to improve their community, adopted or otherwise. The CGA pursued efforts including a tree-planting campaign and a neighborhood watch. But the youthful group soon got involved with the Independent Neighborhood Democrats, a recent challenger to the mainline Democratic organization. The young activists were against the Vietnam War and considered Buddy—a retired Army veteran who had no love for conflict—as an ally for their cause. They used the antiwar fracturing among area Democrats to call attention to their own group and push for new programs to improve the deteriorating neighborhood.[20]

As it so happened John Lindsay, the Republican mayor of New York, took a particular interest in Scotto's group, as he sought to outplay the regular Brooklyn Democrats as he approached the end of his first term. That political body had done little to save the working-class neighborhood from economic failure, or at least that's how the conditions appeared to many of the residents. Although most of the

CGA members were brownstoners and not the native Italian members of the community, their added punch attracted the attention of City Hall. Lindsay became a strong ally, Scotto said, "as he recognized us as a group that was at odds with the existing power structure. So he and his people gave us a tremendous amount of help." The CGA was able to raise thousands of dollars from neighborhood landlords and tenants for their revitalization project. They planted more than four hundred trees, and in 1968 CGA secured the funding for a day care center and a senior center—with the help of Mayor Lindsay and the Congress of Italian American Organizations (another community group that Scotto established, known as CIAO). Soon Carroll Gardens and the work of its association were featured in the *Village Voice* and the *New York Times*, the effort a "model for local development." But what Scotto and his group sought for the canal was something bigger—a sewage treatment plant to put a stop to the noxious overflow that continued to plague the canal.[21]

While lobbying for this major work, in 1968 Scotto's group hired Richard Kaplan, an architect, to draft a plan to redevelop the canal area and to act as a community advisor. Invigorated by this sudden community interest, the City Planning Commission of New York moved "with all due and deliberate speed" with a plan of their own, which began by promising the new sewage treatment plant. No longer would they dump raw sewage into the canal, the city claimed—except for approximately ten times a year, due to the old plumbing. "And the city is building the new plant without the capacity to treat the volume of water a heavy rainstorm will dump—it would be too expensive to build a plant with such a capacity," wrote Stephanie de Pue, of the *Village Voice*, on the issue. "So whenever there's a heavy rain (remember last summer?) they plan to bypass the plant and dump sewage into the canal. Also, they say that it would be too expensive to separate the storm system and the sewage system, and that the Gowanus is the natural low point and drain for the entire South Brooklyn peninsula—that they couldn't make the water go anywhere else without enormous expense."[22]

It was the same song of the city government echoing through history: "We simply cannot afford to fix this." The community, as usual, wanted to hear something better. They urged the city to consider more studies, and see how much it really cost to permanently fix the ancient plumbing. They wanted a recreation area near the canal. "The city has a marvelous way of imposing its problems, financial and otherwise, on the communities that it deals with," continued de Pue. "I suspect that one of the problems the committee faces is that the city is not whole-hearted in its desire to see the canal cleaned up. The key to the problems of the entire area lies in the fact that the canal is presently zoned for industrial use, and how are you going to keep the public from demanding non-industrial land usage if you make it pleasant? Walt Whitman once praised the beauty of the Gowanus, but William Bendix has long since made it into a national joke.[23] Such are the rewards of letting the politicians do it," de Pue lamented.

The Department of City Planning had calculated that the Gowanus still held about eleven thousand jobs in manufacturing and industry, and a revitalized South Brooklyn could support double that amount. In all of New York, almost no lots greater than a few acres were available for manufacturing and similar businesses, but in Gowanus there were 110 available acres of unused industrial land—more if abandoned warehouses were taken custody by the city. "In its Master Plan," de Pue explained, "the city emphasizes the necessity of redeveloping, not losing industrially zoned land."

As though in response to this claim, Scotto took the journalists from the *Village Voice* and the *New York Times* on a tour on the banks of the Gowanus. "Here we are 30 minutes from the heart of Manhattan, and what do we have? A miserable, stinking parking lot," Scotto told the *New York Times* in 1969. The canal was "flanked by vacant buildings, small factories, parking lots, storage yard, and crumbling pilings. Only about three barges a week now make their way under the narrow drawbridges through the garbage-strewn water."

Scotto wondered aloud just how the city proposed to get new industry in the area if it hadn't yet.

In Kaplan's plan, local industry would be limited to only the eastern, or Park Slope, side of the canal. After some unspecified cleanup, the western banks would become "the scenic focal point of publicly assisted housing." In leading this tour, Scotto effectively declared his lifelong campaign—to clean the Gowanus, and fill its banks with new housing developments. Within this goal was to preserve the Italian American population that defined Carroll Gardens, whose territory was increasingly encroached upon by young urban explorers—the very people he teamed up with to bring attention to the ailing neighborhood. The construction and investment in the community could only be positive, he reasoned.[24]

"In 10 or 15 years, this area will be the vital, professional, upper-middle-class center of New York, housing the families the city desperately wants and needs to keep," de Pue concluded. "It represents a fantastic resource to the city. Here Nouveau Brooklyn will rise from the slums."[25]

The Promise of Decay and Renewal

The 1970s proved to be a transformative decade for South Brooklyn. While New York City slowly fell into bankruptcy, crime and drugs became increasingly visible on the streets. Yet pockets of brownstoners trickled into certain blocks and avenues in Park Slope, Fort Greene, and Carroll Gardens. Members of the CGA set up an office at 445 Court Street, just south of Third Street and blocks from the Gowanus, and in 1970 the younger activists convinced Scotto to run for Congress against incumbent John Rooney. Although Scotto advocated the various renewal projects, the sewage treatment plant, and the battle against the drug trade on the streets—he handed out hundreds of pins reading "Fight Organized Crime" to longshoremen and neighborhood youths—he never served in any legislative body.

However his name rallied many Carroll Gardens inhabitants to vote, particularly the remaining Italian Americans, proving he had a bloc of community favor at his disposal.[26]

Meanwhile, the afflicted neighborhood began appearing in headlines: "Cleaner Gowanus Canal Looms," wrote the *New York Times* in July 1972, highlighting a US Army Corps of Engineers' proposed plan to remove some sixty thousand cubic yards of polluted sludge from the bottom of the canal. The story included an interview with William Van Pelt, the latest president of the still-extant Gowanus Towing Company, whose fleet of ships had been reduced two—a fifth of their complement in 1950s—that made fewer than a dozen trips a week up and down the decayed waterway. Despite the CGA's success in engaging the city government, securing federal support for cleaning up the Gowanus had proven difficult. In April 1973, Donald Elliott, the former chairman of New York's City Planning Commission, had a disappointing meeting with the Army Corps of Engineers in Washington, D.C. Elliott was charged with leading the Gowanus Canal Redevelopment Committee and had traveled to the capital with seven other members to plead for a federally funded dredging of the waterway. The corps "rejected flatly" the requests, as they "did not believe that the economic benefits to be derived from dredging equaled the cost." Furthermore, even if he did somehow prove economic feasibility, and Congress passed a law allowing it to take place, President Richard Nixon "would refuse to permit the dredging to be done."[27]

Yet as the stench of stagnant pollution continued to waft over Carroll Gardens, the wretched conditions couldn't change the draw of cheap rents, pushing "settlement" farther south and then east toward the waterfront. But the Gowanus neighborhood, particularly east of Bond Street, was not known for brownstones or townhouses. Surrounding the "Lavender Lake" were odd one-story structures, sprawling warehouses, former horse stables, abandoned or underused factories—all unique, but not the charming Victorian fantasy townhouses of the purely residential streets. Instead artists, artisans, and assorted creative types—denizens of Greenwich Village and the industrial streets of SoHo—saw beauty in the raw and unusual architecture and even the stinking glory of the canal. The area was still dangerous, of course, but so were many corners of New York during the worst of the 1970s nadir. The edgy, postindustrial grit of Gowanus appealed to artists seeking studio space, where the cheap warehouse space was abundant. The water was a unique landscape to photograph and paint. There was something pleasant the new arrivals saw in the Gowanus—compared to the soaring high-rise jungle of Manhattan, the low-scale hodgepodge of brick warehouses made room for broad views of the sky. Furthermore, the houses nearby were dirt cheap.

This last fact was the major attraction for Linda and Joseph Mariano, an artist couple who immigrated to Gowanus from Greenwich Village in 1974. They were just barely in their thirties, both painters who worked as teachers—Joseph taught high school physics, and Linda instructed art to students of all ages. Also an adept of knitwear and textiles, Linda later published a book of her own weaving patterns and designs. With a tight budget and broad imagination, the Marianos dreamed of a large, open space to live in, with an art studio and a room for their two-year-old daughter, a backyard as an added bonus. After a long search through some dodgy corners of Brooklyn, the Marianos found a three-story brownstone on President Street near the corner of Bond Street. Clearly a fixer-upper, it was across from the former Planet Mills weaving establishment and one block from the Gowanus Canal. The asking price was only ten thousand—suspiciously low even then—yet they had plenty of trouble securing a mortgage. After more months of searching, only one small bank in Queens thought it prudent to lend for a home in such a degraded area.

"It was edgy," Linda, by this time around sixty-seven years old, recalled in 2010, above the great wooden table in her kitchen, cozy and cluttered with newspapers and kitschy objects. Linda's petite frame and tufts of hair haphazardly piled onto her head barely contain a woman of almost shocking energy, paired with timeless chutzpah.

"You couldn't park your car outside without someone breaking the window or stealing your hubcaps!" she finished, grinning. Surrounding her was thirty years of eclectic decor—funky tiles, and painted cabinets; mismatched doors framed around stained glass widows, kitschy picture frames with family members and artwork of all kinds (the work of her grandchildren was particularly featured). Over the course of her adult life in Brooklyn, Linda and Joseph restored each door, cabinet handle, and missing tile with found objects—either saved from the street or the result of rummaging through secondhand stores. They were the archetypal 1970s brownstoners, fixing up their adopted homes with care and patience, indigently bohemian in the face of a home surrounded by crime and delinquency. The new settlers of Gowanus had to have a taste for the unusual and offbeat—who else would live at edge of a heavily polluted canal? One of Linda's favorite activities has always been pounding the Brooklyn pavement, discovering new sites and familiar corners.

For decades she crossed the canal at Union Street to reach her teaching jobs in Park Slope, scouring the streets for clues of the industrial past along the way. The Union Street bridge was her closest access to Park Slope, and on the north side she would pass an abandoned two-story warehouse, covered in graffiti. Once upon a time it was home to Thomas Paulson & Son, a brass foundry, built around the end of World War II. Linda loved the odd building and felt increasingly attached over the years, recalling bygone industrial days as she crossed the reeking water. There were many other old buildings to appreciate: a soaring Romanesque revival structure on Third Avenue, the Coignet Stone Company Building (also called the Brooklyn Improvement Company Building), former horse stables. Like most of the residents of Gowanus, new and old, she knew little about the true conditions of the canal, only that it was especially polluted.[28]

In 1974, the year that Linda moved to Gowanus, Buddy Scotto had convinced some microbiologists from the New York City Community College to bring their students to the Gowanus and test water samples for bacteria. What they found was frightening: typhoid, cholera, dysentery, and tuberculosis organisms—and as New York City became increasingly bankrupt the promised sewage treatment plant seemed ever further away. Lawsuits between the federal government and the city held the project in limbo—that is, until Scotto (who had temporarily changed sides to the Republican Party) got elected as a delegate for the Republican National Convention. After his many conversations with Vice President Rockefeller, Scotto bartered his delegate vote for a promise of federal funding. In February 1975, the New York City Department of Environmental Protection took the first step in the "massive pollution control program," and dredged part of the canal for the first time since 1949, removing some twenty thousand cubic yards of sludge. Finally, digging for the interceptor sewer began in October. The whole project—including the Red Hook Sewage Treatment Plan curiously located in the Navy Yard—would take twelve years to complete, but it was a huge victory: not only for the Gowanus Canal, but for Scotto and his network of organizations. Increasingly, the man from Red Hook was known as the "Mayor of Carroll Gardens."[29]

In September 1977, Scotto took a winding boat ride on the "foul and flotsam-littered canal" with a *New York Times* reporter and some key members of local government: Representative Frederick W. Richmond, the canal region's congressional replacement for John J. Rooney (and one of its wealthiest members), and Eckardt C. Beck, regional administrator of the Federal Environmental Protection Agency. They passed piles of abandoned cars and empty warehouses. "There is no reason why this property along here shouldn't really have value and attraction," Scotto commented. "The canal has all kind of potential." The excursion, clearly organized for the press, was meant to hype the upcoming release of the preliminary findings of an $8.1 million federal water pollution study—one that Richmond helped to secure for the Gowanus. The study would also inform on "spurring residential and industrial redevelopment adjacent to the canal" Richmond made sure to add.

"It will be up to the community," Beck later interjected, "to decide the residential, commercial and recreational future of the area once the canal is cleaned up after the Red Hook Interceptor Sewage Plant is built and in operation." Later on, the reporter asked a community member what he thought about the canal. "Fill it in," said Nick Monte—the owner of Monte's Italian Room, still clinging on for dear life after seventy-one years on the edge of the canal—told Rule. "Make it a park. Do something to clean this place up. The Federal Government is worried about protecting such things as penguins in North Alaska while New York City has to put up with this stinking, cancerous sore."

A few months later, the preliminary findings revealed that the canal was almost entirely devoid of free oxygen; there were "extremely high fecal coliform levels" (more simply, "full of raw sewage") as well as high concentrations of grease, oil, and sludge. When the full study was finally released in 1981, it revealed that only six industrial firms made use of canal in any observable fashion (as opposed to nearly fifty in the 1940s). In the last two decades, the amount of freight barged up the canal had dropped by more than 55 percent, and the number of times the drawbridges opened declined by nearly 70 percent. On average, more than thirteen million gallons of raw sewage emptied into the canal every day.

The study also recommended a number of physical solutions to improve the canal, such as reactivating the flushing tunnel, to increase the presence of oxygen in the water. It is almost ironic that more than a century after Major David Douglass submitted the preliminary designs for the canal to the leaders of the city of Brooklyn, the city still had not been able to address his primary concern: lacking the ability to clean itself, the canal would be rendered useless.[30]

KENTILE

10

Superfund Me! (1981–2010)

"By all reckonings it was the art party of the season," wrote Kay Larson in the art section of New York Magazine in June 1981. "The 'Monumental Show' is clearly this year's Event." This accolade was bequeathed to the Gowanus Memorial Artyard, a nonprofit artists group, and the Monumental Show was their "guerrilla" art exhibition in a warehouse at the corner of Third Avenue and Third Street—a seedy location often avoided by even the most streetwise Brooklynites at this time.

On the first day, May 16, more than "3,000 oglers jammed into the third floor of a nineteenth-century red munitions factory at 230 3rd Street" to witness at least six dozen huge sculptural objects, some more than fifteen feet high, on display (the "artyard" was supposed to be in a nearby vacant lot along the Gowanus Canal, but when the landlord balked the whole production was moved indoors, to the massive three-room studio of Frank Shifreen, one of the organizers).

In this "creative rehabilitation" of the former manufacturing space there were rock bands and performance art, curious, massive sculptures, paintings, and installations. A Russian émigré named Boris Zeldin deep-fried books and magazines in a small vat; there was a house-sized housefly by Duilio Pieri made from cardboard and plastic cups and a fifteen-foot-diameter silk balloon, surrounded by smaller balloons. An art organization called TODT "covered the walls of the rooms around the elevator shaft with ominous, gray-painted science-lab apparatus and vivisected bits of protoplasm; amid eerie rumblings, you walk on things that squelch." This last piece was jokingly dubbed *Arcane Art Scientism* by the "three artist-perpetrators," Michael Keane, George Moore, and Frank Shifreen.

All of these artists had strong connections to the thriving downtown arts scene of 1980s New York, and had yearned for the kind space needed to create large-scale art, as cheap loft space became increasingly difficult to secure in downtown Manhattan. The industrial lofts of Gowanus were much like those in SoHo, but farther out in a still-seedy domain. Keane—who conceived of the "Monumental" theme—was also in charge of des Refusés, a respected gallery in the legendary Westbeth complex, an artists' commune in the West Village. A great deal of successful contemporary artists spent that weekend in Gowanus. Keith Haring, who had associations with des Refusés but was relatively unknown at the time, displayed some of his "primitive" chalk drawings at the Monumental Show, an early display that precluded his intensely popular career throughout the 1980s. At the time, the most famous participants were "hallowed artists" Carl Andre and Nancy Holt, whose presence "was a magnanimous act of solidarity, especially since their piece—a thin line of rusty metal by Andre, a set of round mirrors on the floor of a smokestack by Holt—were indistinguishable from the mélange."[1]

The following year, Shifreen and his collaborators tried to outdo themselves with a second show. Although the idea might have seemed preposterous at the time, on the west bank of the Gowanus Canal, "at Smith and Fifth Streets, on a five-acre former dump rife with weeds, trash middens and expired auto bodies bloom[ed] the Gowanus Memorial Art Yard," wrote Grace Glueck of the *New York Times*. "A city-owned facility preempted for the moment by sculptors, it—along with two other indoor locations—serves as a setting for 'The Monument Redefined,' a vastly ambitious show with more than 150 participants, whose stated aim is to encourage new interpretations of the public monument." Among the wide array of experimental artwork, several sculptures were simply formed of garbage scattered through the yard: "Joseph Chirchirillo's 'Grizzly Bear Arch II,' a curving gateway structure assembled of indigenous debris," Glueck described, "or Roberta Williams's 'Monument to the American Dream: The Nuclear Family's Last Vacation,' which uses an old car body to depict a traveling family stopped dead in its tracks by an atomic event."[2]

This derelict lot was the original site of the Citizens' Gas-Light Plant—established more than a century earlier, whose name was long forgotten and replaced by Brooklyn Union Gas, a monopoly that coalesced in 1895 and operated until the early 1960s. Brooklyn Union Gas had owned two other plants along the Gowanus—now all were decommissioned, the plots sold to private owners. In 1974, the city had acquired the Fifth and Smith Street lots as a "public place," belonging to the community—supposedly ending a controversial disagreement within the neighborhood over the future of the derelict site. It was under the jurisdiction of the Parks Department, but was "in terrible shape . . . overgrown with weeds and littered with garbage and trash." Unbeknownst to the participants at the time, the ground was heavily polluted with coal tar—a carcinogenic by-product of manufactured gas production. A long public debate over what the land would be used for—proposals for a high school, a sports complex, a historic park, and subsidized housing had all been met with equal amounts of resistance—leaving the "Public Place" site, as it became known, in a perpetual state of limbo. Perhaps because of its derelict nature, the six-acre lot was a perfect setting for the New York showcase of unusual and experimental art.

Following the second Monumental Show, in 1982, Shifreen told local newspapers that he planned to seek the aid of the Gowanus Canal Community Development Cooperation—a nonprofit group dedicated to area development—to remove the heavier blocks of concrete and abandoned cars from the space, making it more welcome to the community. The GCCDC had also been a major source of funding for both shows, which had brought plenty of interest to the underused Gowanus waterfront spaces. The founder was none other than Salvatore "Buddy" Scotto. His advocacy—or advertising—of the Carroll Gardens and Gowanus area as ripe for development had stoked the interest of New York's real estate community. After the first monumental show, Shifreen's landlord, Milton Rinzler, had attempted to convert his factory loft complex into cooperative apartments with a developer named Philip Perlman. But the city Department of Health had concerns that one of the buildings had been used as a thermometer factory, and some potential mercury contamination had not been properly cleaned up. Instead of a sales meeting, Rinzler ended up in front of a tribunal.[3]

Leading up to the Monumental show, Scotto had been rubbing elbows with prominent New Yorkers, securing funding for his nonprofit development groups and networking with developers. His boat tours, and later neighborhood bus tours, stoked plenty of interest in the increasingly popular brownstone area. He had been invited to participate in the Partnership for New York City, a high-powered private development organization spearheaded by the philanthropist David Rockefeller. Back in 1977, the same year he was riding on canal boats with congressmen, Scotto invited Jerome Kretchmer, a former city administrator and developer, to consider developing the crumbling gray factory building on the lower end of Court Street, near the Brooklyn-Queens Expressway overpass.

Kretchmer was also a partner in a development company that had renovated industrial buildings in SoHo and TriBeCa and "made a handsome profit for it." The former Doehler Die-casting Factory Building, at 505 Court Street, was full of vacancies and unprofitable commercially, but Kretchmer could make use of a city tax abatement to redevelop commercial properties for into residential co-ops. Partnering with local bank branches and the Catholic diocese, Kretchmer and his business associate, an attorney named Ausin Laber, secured a city-backed loan from the Department of Housing Preservation and Development. The two bought the Doehler Die Building and four other underused buildings along Court Street in 1978 and began to renovate. The following year, Scotto formed the GCCDC and heavily promoted the loft-style apartment building as it was being refurbished into a 124-unit loft co-op with newspaper ad campaigns. His nonprofit development corporation then bought the four smaller Court Street buildings from Kretchmer, with the intention of developing them into a similar housing co-op. Father George Voiland, the pastor of the local St. Mary Star of the Sea diocese, called Scotto "the Garibaldi of Carroll Gardens."[4]

But as the years dragged on, community members began to voice their distrust of Scotto. In 1982, Fred Richmond, the congressman Scotto teamed up with five years before, resigned from office after pleading guilty to tax evasion, marijuana possession, and making an illegal payment to a government employee (Scotto later referred to him as a "kook" with a disastrous private life "but he sure as hell produced for us," referring to the earmarked money for the federal water study and to establishing the GCCDC). Scotto's family had "substantial real estate holdings," residents claimed, and his neighborhood tours had caused the gentrification that was pushing out lifelong residents—renters in particular, most of whom could not afford to compete with the increasing number of brownstoners. At the time of the second monumental show, Doehler Dye co-ops were intended to sell for sixty-five to seventy-five thousand dollars, solidly affordable for middle-class families who hoped to stay in the neighborhood. But skyrocketing interest rates, as high as 21 percent, left half of the apartments vacant.

At the time Scotto's most vocal critic was Celia Cacace, a no-nonsense fiftysomething woman who had grown up in Red Hook, and she staunchly referred to the area as "South Brooklyn–Red Hook"—relentlessly plugging what she considered the "real" identity of the neighborhood to be. Petite and striking with wide-set eyes, Cacace was a member of Community Board 6, the local citizens advisory group. Proudly working-class, Cacace never minced words, especially in a public forum, and insisted that Scotto's "marketing" of the neighborhood was forcing families out of their homes. "I don't call it gentrification, I call it genocide because they're killing off neighborhoods," she would often tell journalists, revealing her tendency toward hyperbole. The Doehler Die Lofts, she claimed, were never meant for local residents. They had been aimed at "outsiders," Cacace's term for wealthy Manhattanites—and when the cooperative failed to coalesce according to plan, the building was converted into a rental property, subject to the same conditions that were driving out the very residents it was meant to retain.

By the mid-1980s, the residents of Carroll Gardens were decidedly split, local papers reported. According to the Prospect Press, the area was "up and coming community, filled with brownstones far less expensive than those in Park Slope or Brooklyn Heights," themselves "pioneers bringing civilization to underdeveloped part of the borough." Community leaders like Scotto and Eileen Dugan (the former CGA member who became the neighborhood's state assemblywoman) said the new arrivals "saved the neighborhood from becoming a slum like nearby Red Hook," and that block associations like hers were formed to prevent housing deterioration—marketing the neighborhood was simply part of the process. But Cacace, and other older residents, remembered a time when she knew every person and family walking on her block. She had been living in the community for fifty years. "This wasn't a slum," she insisted. "There were no burned out buildings, no abandoned buildings." It was redlining that made obtaining mortgages impossible, whereas on Long Island it was easier, cheaper, she insisted. The renters had remained a stable community, but the new blood was beginning to price them out. Even the new neighborhood names offended her. At one point Cacace made T-shirts reading "I live in South Brooklyn–Red Hook."[5]

Cacace's favorite target was Buddy Scotto and his local entourage: "Even the Carroll Gardens Association was removed from the hands of local residents," she complained to local papers, and became an arm of Independent Neighborhood Democrats, or, as Cacace referred to it, the "political base for [Eileen] Dugan and 52nd district leader John Mazzitelli, also an employee of the CGA as well as Dugan's predecessor in that Assembly seat, Michael Pesce." In response Dugan charged that "Cacace would like to 'build a wall' around the community." Meanwhile plenty of owners who had purchased their townhouses for twenty-five thousand in past decades were benefitting from the neighborhood gentrification, reselling their homes for nearly ten times their investment. In response, Scotto insisted that his organizations were deeply concerned with tenants' rights, preventing evictions, and securing housing for seniors.

By the mid-1980s, they were already working on plans for a hundred-unit senior housing center to be run by Catholic Charities, one block from the Gowanus Canal. Both he and Dugan admitted that community displacement from gentrification was a delicate issue and tried to stoke interest in developing the Public Place site. Housing along the canal that was affordable to middle-income families, believed Scotto, "would be the best solution to Carroll Garden's problems with gentrification." Almost in spite of his convictions about Public Place, health studies suggested that the grounds might be heavily polluted with byproducts of gas manufacturing, including coal tar and ammonia. If they were found, declared Scotto, it would be the "government's responsibility to clean it up."[6]

Meanwhile, the Gowanus Canal remained a "Stygian mess, with a thick oily smear on the canal sides, and a thick coating of the same on exposed land surface," as claimed the 1984 archaeological survey of the area (as required for the digging of yet another sewer tunnel through this historical corner of Brooklyn). When the $458 million sewage treatment plant was finally finished in 1987, it became quickly apparent that a high-capacity sewage treatment plant "did nothing to restrict the continued inflow of water during heavy storms," as the nineteenth-century sewer design still lacked the capacity to contain surges.

The canal remained unable to support life beyond harmful bacteria, its floor covered in sludge, and—most of all—it stank terribly. Following the advice of the 1981 water quality report, the city made a new plan to restore the defunct 1911 flushing tunnel. It would add much-needed oxygen to the water and, officials hoped, filter out the flow of raw sewage—but again, the community would have to be patient while the city restored the defunct works. In lieu of much improvement, the seemingly unsolvable problems of pollution seemed to keep developers temporarily at bay well into the 1990s. Although nobody remembered, the community's complaints about the raw sewage and industrial dumping were almost identical to those made a century earlier—and the inability of the city to fix it was the same.[7]

The Carroll Gardens Renaissance

Smith Street, the closest commercial thoroughfare to the Gowanus, finally came back to life in the late 1990s. Named for Samuel Smith, a one-term mayor of Brooklyn, it had been the celebrated "furniture row" of early twentieth-century South Brooklyn—a bustling district with fancy awnings and showrooms, surrounded by an array of dry goods stores, clothing boutiques, and food markets.

But by the 1970s the furniture stores had all shuttered and pedestrians became increasingly scarce—only farther south in the Italian section were there some delicatessens, a few Laundromats, and shoe repair stores. By the early 1980s most of the storefronts were empty, and drug deals regularly took place on the shady corners. The sidewalks were literally cracked and caving in, which only made the area less inviting. It was poorly lit, and muggers regularly attacked people walking home from the subway at night.

The revival of Smith Street can be traced to 1987, when by a Park Slope woman named Bette Stoltz started the South Brooklyn Local

Development Corporation (SBLDC). A bespectacled blond mother with quietly cheerful demeanor, Stoltz had begun a career in civic improvement in her own neighborhood after organizing a grand street fair along Seventh Avenue in 1978, later regarded as a symbol of the neighborhood's revitalization.

"Park Slope is now ready for something like this," Stoltz told the *New York Times*, proudly recounting the restoration of the neighborhood's stately nineteenth-century brownstones and the positive effect on area street life. The fair boasted dozens of dance and musical performances ("from medieval to rock" and "belly to ballet") and three hundred fifty booths providing a diverse array of food, clothing, and crafts. "The revival can also be seen in the shops along Seventh Avenue," wrote Ari L. Goldman, the *Times* reporter, "many of which have switched from a service to a specialty nature and adopted catchy names such as Our Daily Bread, the F-stop, Heels n' Toes, Big Cheese," and so forth. Following the success of Seventh Heaven, as the fair was dubbed, city officials began to seek out Stoltz's advice.[8]

She became involved in a civic project to help revive Fulton Street in Downtown Brooklyn and spent the next decade learning about the world of community grants and jump-starting small businesses. Stoltz had no connection to Buddy Scotto's organizations or political allies, but her grassroots community work produced visible business results—she was well organized and cheerful, and knew how to talk to landlords and convince them to invest in their properties, and helped hopeful business owners to secure low-interest commercial loans. Her continued successes led to the establishment of the SBLDC—it helped that the Clinton administration had earmarked millions of dollars in local and federal funds to spur economic growth in dozens of urban areas across the country, and urban projects like Stoltz's had access to grant money that had not existed in previous decades. The region of Southwest Brooklyn, including Gowanus, Red Hook, and some corners of Sunset Park, was chosen in the mid-1990s as having a high likelihood of success.

One of Stoltz's biggest coups was procuring a twelve-million-dollar city grant for the SBLDC to restore the ailing Smith Street. An annual influx of money brought wrought iron, Victorian-style street lamps to brighten the corners, repaved sidewalks, and new awnings and restored facades for struggling, empty storefronts. Slowly, new businesses began to emerge out of the ashes of Smith Street. The SBLDC granted loans that helped thrift shops and 99-cent stores open at manageable rents. Then, independent of Stoltz's efforts, a new boutique selling kitschy knickknacks opened, followed by a French bakery. In late 1997, Patois, an upscale French restaurant, opened at Degraw Street, the first of its kind in the area. Within two years there were twenty new "small, trendy, upscale businesses": clothing boutiques, bars, restaurants, an upscale salon, a shop selling antiques and old records. Stoltz's years of hard work—convincing landlords to invest in renovations, encouraging businesses to settle in the area—showed tangible results.[9]

Carroll Gardens' bohemian-bourgeois identity attracted an increasing array of upper-middle-class families, but Smith Street also became the stomping ground of filmmakers, photographers, and artists. Like other particular corners of Brooklyn, the street became an enclave for tattooed young musicians in vintage clothing and writers wearing chunky-framed glasses—that burgeoning turn-of-the-century youth identity, the Brooklyn hipster. But Stoltz wanted the thoroughfare to retain a mix of hip entertainment and "normal services," to retain a "healthy mix." She had similar agendas for South Brooklyn–area businesses around Red Hook and the Gowanus Canal—the SBLDC sought to retain the hundreds of remaining industrial businesses and the jobs they provided.[10]

While Stoltz and the SBLDC were busy rebuilding Smith Street in the 1990s, the city of New York had been hard at work rebuilding the mechanisms of the Gowanus flushing tunnel. When finally switched back on, the refurbished pumping system would propel three hundred million gallons of oxygenated water from the East River into the Gowanus every day. After the failure of the Red Hook Sewage Treatment plant to clean the water, hope of canal-side development had stagnated—but a curiosity for the Gowanus had grown into a community of its own. Artists and musicians had taken advantage of cheap rents and warehouse building stock to set up studios and rehearsal spaces. Houseboats docked in odd corners of the canal, one of which was converted into a stained glass studio. Rowboats took "anxious visitors" on tours of the canal—fresh coats of paint appeared on structures otherwise covered in decades of graffiti; "for sale" signs appeared on buildings previously relegated to the "Gowanus wasteland."

In 1998, a documentary filmmaker named Allison Prete released *Lavender Lake*, aimed at educating Brooklynites on the outrageous amount of pollution in the canal. The film gained a sort of cult status as her contemporaries showed an explainable fascination for the canal, despite its toxicity. "Everybody thinks they're discovering something," Prete told the *New York Times*, trying to explain the phenomenon.[11]

Quite naturally, waiting in the sidelines for these environmental changes were New York's real estate developers. As an increasing number of people moved into city neighborhoods during the prosperous years of the Clinton administration, a housing crunch compelled more developers to meet increased demands for apartments by "seeking out locations once overlooked as blemishes—if not blights—on the urban landscape." Williamsburg, in the northern regions of Brooklyn, full of underused and neglected industrial buildings, had been "rediscovered" by downtown Manhattanites and was one site of great interest to developers; another was the up-and-coming Carroll Gardens.

In 1999 a developer called M. G. Huntington began to consider a three-story former accordion file factory building at 460 Smith Street on the southern outskirts of the gentrifying block for residential conversion. Huntington wanted to build a sixty-three-unit "affordable" co-op building, but it would require a zoning variance. One of the biggest proponents of this change was Buddy Scotto, who insisted that multistory industrial buildings were of no interest to developers—only residential buildings would increase the value of the neighborhood. "What it really comes down to is subsidizing market-rate housing at the expense of jobs for the working poor," Stoltz shot back.[12]

The Promise of a Cleaner Gowanus

After nearly forty years of inactivity, the Gowanus Canal flushing tunnel was activated on the first of May 1999. It was a historic day for the diverse community, which had endured an entire generation of stagnant, putrid water and failed attempts to curb sewage overflow. Within a few months, the difference was palpable. "Prior to the flushing tunnel, a dead dog would just float back and forth with the tides between Third Street and Carroll for maybe a week," David Lefkowitz, a real estate investor, told the *New York Times*. "Now, the thing could be gone in maybe 24 hours." He also noted that the surface water looked more like "old-fashioned slime" and less like chemical sheen antifreeze. By July, there were pink jellyfish visibly swimming in the canal, then schools of fish. Blue crabs scuttled along the bottom of the canal and over hubcaps. The quick rebound of marine life in the canal was a huge surprise, even to environmentalists; it had been forty years since crabs could be seen in the canal. The level of oxygen had greatly increased, and even the smell was greatly improved—on hot summer days, the canal had often smelled like rotten eggs and motor oil, and the smell of decay had greatly subdued. The canal was, quite literally, experiencing a renaissance.[13]

Few could have been happier about that development than Scotto, who was brimming with development visions after visiting San Antonio, Texas, that summer. Much like South Brooklyn, San Antonio had a polluted waterway running through a densely populated area, the San Antonio River. However during the 1980s, the environs of the waterway had been converted into the River Walk, "a tourist attraction lined with trees and shops that is, along with the Alamo, the centerpiece of San Antonio." It was an archetype for what Scotto—and many other hopeful developers—wanted to see in Brooklyn: a pedestrian waterway lined with housing, shops, and cafés. He called his trip to the River Walk "a shot in the arm" in envisioning a future for Brooklyn's waterway. But his dream, a sort of Venice on the Gowanus, ran "smack into the debate over waterfront use—manufacturing versus public access and commercial development—that is raging all over the city and in Brooklyn neighborhoods like Red Hook, DUMBO and Brooklyn Heights with varying degrees of success," wrote Matthew Sweeney of the *Brooklyn Paper* in 1999.

Although Scotto maintained that manufacturing no longer had a role to play in Brooklyn, Stoltz publically disagreed. New manufacturing companies were investing in the spaces along the Gowanus, she claimed, and one of these, an electronics manufacturer called Amtronics, recently had invested a million dollars into a twenty-thousand-square-foot warehouse space by the canal, and nearly doubled its staff thanks in part to help from the SBLDC. "Venice in Brooklyn sounds great," said Mario Cappucio, a vice president at Amtronics. "But I think you'll have a hard time getting rid of the industry that's here."[14]

The day after Christmas 2002, Linda Mariano approached a podium in a courtroom-like chamber on the sixth floor of 40 Rector Street, in Lower Manhattan. Staring at her from across a table were seven men, commissioners and directors of the New York City Board of Standards and Appeals, who watched as she placed a pile of paper on the podium. Linda's knees were knocking together and her arms were shaking. Her reading glasses kept falling off of her face. "It's like they're judging you whether you live or die!" she thought to herself, sweating. Still, she took a deep breath and reached in front of her, where a microphone was attached to the podium. She pulled it closer to her mouth, and leaned in, and then paused.

"I'm scared!" she finally croaked into the microphone. In unison, the men all burst out laughing. "Of *us*?" one of the commissioners asked, amused. "Yes!" Linda shouted, but the ice was finally broken. She looked down at her papers, adjusted her reading glasses. "Four Sixty Union Street is a small industrial building in the heart of Gowanus . . ." she began, as did her career as a neighborhood activist for industrial preservation.[15]

Nine months earlier, in February 2002, developers Jim Plotkin and Barry Leon had sent out a letter to all of the residents within 360 degrees and one mile of 460 Union Street, the empty industrial warehouse that extended to the edge of the Gowanus Canal. They were planning to demolish the building and replace it with a six-story, sixty-unit residential apartment building. But the Green Building, as it was known in Gowanus for its odd hue, was in an industrially zoned area. In order to build housing along the canal, the developers would have to apply for a zoning variance that proved to the Board of Standards and Appeals that the "unique conditions on a specific parcel of land would cause the property owner practical difficulty and undue hardship if it were developed" according to the original zoning. This process included a public hearing and commentary from affected community members.

Although the local community board had rejected Plotkin and Leon's proposal in 2001, such neighborhood groups had no real decision-making power, and so the developers appealed to the city directly. But to gauge the wider community's feelings about the possible development, the developers called for a community meeting at St. Mary Star of the Sea parish, on Court Street. Nothing was sacred in Gowanus: Plotkin had converted the Planet Mills Building, across the street from Linda's beloved brownstone, into a complex of "loft-style" condominiums. It all seemed so greedy to her, and upon reading the new letter, Linda was furious.

"Not in my backyard!" she later quipped. "This was a wonderful old industrial building and it belongs in this neighborhood—*my* neighborhood, Gowanus!" Although she had been living in the neighborhood for nearly thirty years, Linda hadn't really ever gotten involved in the various civic groups and community meetings that often determined its fate, except for volunteering to help restore Carroll Park in the early 1980s, when she was still a young mother. But she and Joseph, her husband, were both passionate about the unique industrial nature of their neighborhood, and attended the meeting in Manhattan a week or so later. The room was quite full, as the question of development always sparked debates in the dense and now-popular neighborhood. When the time was right, Linda stood up and asked simple, pointed questions—"Is it really wise to build housing for families and children right on the banks of a canal that we know is polluted?" and "Aren't there ways to reuse these buildings, instead of just knocking them down? Especially when we don't know what's in the ground under it?"

Linda's pragmatic, unabashed questioning of the whole development affair attracted the attention of other like-minded residents, which turned out to be exactly what she needed. Margaret Maugenest, an artist who moved from SoHo to a loft building on Nevins and Union Street in 1984, was one of these Gowanusians also at the meeting. She had seen a notice for it in a local newspaper and found the proposed development "totally inappropriate" when one considered the level of pollution in the canal. There Maugenest saw this outspoken neighbor she had never met before and felt a bit intimidated. But Linda was impressive, was well informed, and seemed to know what she was doing. "She's too smart for me," thought Maugenest, who was born in Indonesia, and lived in the Netherlands before moving to New York in 1978. "But I really want to know her—she's engaged and lots of strengths and I agree with her!" But too scared to approach Linda directly, Maugenest gave her number to Joseph, and told him that if they ever needed her help, she'd be glad to get involved with this issue. Maugenest wasn't the only person who noticed Linda at the meeting—and that was what the now-retired art teacher was hoping for. She and Joseph began to solicit other people, "more forces from the neighborhood," to help combat this development she disagreed with.

The fledgling group of like-minded, preservationist NIMBYites did research on zoning variances, and then prepared statements to read before the Board of Standards and Appeals. They went to at least a half dozen of these hearings over the next two years—aside from the Marianos, a number of other locals came to speak out against the zoning variance in front of the board, including Bette Stoltz, Celia Cacace, and Marlene Donnelly, an architect whose office was next to the canal. At first, the only people defending the developers at the hearings were Christopher Wright and Howard Goldman, the attorneys on the project. But as the hearings dragged on, a few community voices in favor of the variance emerged—most prominent among them Buddy Scotto. Even Bill de Blasio, the neighborhood city councilman who was not opposed to housing on the site, had spoken against the proposal due to its height and the style of the facade. He encouraged the developers to submit new designs, which they did in an effort to bargain with the community, bringing the building down to four stories. But Linda and her new neighborhood cohorts stuck together and presented to the Board of Appeals numerous pieces of evidence favoring their argument: the building had not been properly marketed for rent as an industrial building for a significant period of time leading up to the variance request; the surrounding lots were all industrially zoned. By the time of the final vote, impressed New Yorkers who were simply waiting for their own cases to be called up by the commissioners were asking Linda to speak on their behalf.[16]

On February 3, 2004, the Board of Appeals handed their decision to Plotkin and Leon: application denied. Among the numerous criteria reviewed over the past two years, the board found that allowing the variance would "change the essential character of the surrounding neighborhood."[17]

That evening, a squad of vindicated Gowanusians (and their allies) celebrated the end of their campaign with champagne and laughter at Margaret Maugenest's loft on Nevins Street, which boasts views on the canal. Having accomplished a near-impossible feat—defeating the best-laid plans of rich developers—the motley group decided they should form their own neighborhood organization. Through the buzz of success and drinks, the twenty-odd preservation activists attempted to come up with a name: something appropriately aquatic, reflecting their collective belief in environmental cleanup before development. It was Joseph Mariano who threw a twee acronym into the room, FROGG—Friends and Residents of Greater Gowanus.[18]

The FROGGs believed that any properties that slipped through their watch could open the real estate floodgates, creating precedent that would transform their neighborhood into something they didn't recognize. Living among light industry, studios, and commercial businesses suited their idea of community. When Margaret Maugenest moved to Gowanus to her loft on Nevins Street, it was because SoHo, where she had lived since 1978, had "lost its character" after the rag industry and trucking got priced out. The once-thriving artists were soon priced out too, and it became an anonymous place with no community. In Gowanus, she knew the faces of local workers and her neighbors. "The 'Mayor Bloomberg vision' of thousands of condos along the canal," she once said, "will mean you're going to deal with all of the tall buildings, and then of the community will be gone. The human scale, it's so important."[19]

The FROGGs did not rest on their laurels, but set right to work. They met once a month in Bette Stoltz's office on Smith Street and closely followed the news of every developer that submitted applications for variances and rezoning. They sat in on more hearings and performed hours of research on the intricate and hopelessly complicated web of zoning laws in New York City. By the end of 2005 they had stopped the conversion of a four-story warehouse at 255 Butler Street and a five-story warehouse at the corner of Third Avenue and Bond Street, all within a block of the canal. They couldn't win every battle: Jim Plotkin bought and subsequently razed a nineteenth-century stable house on Bond Street, one block from the Green Building. It was a crumbling structure that dated back to the Civil War, but was one of the last of its kind in the neighborhood. Bond Street had once been home to numerous stables and carriage houses—the Brooklyn headquarters of the ASPCA sat at the head of the canal at Butler Street, half a block from Bond Street. A former water trough made of concrete still sits in front of it.[20]

Although they didn't know it, FROGG's battles were still on the horizon. In 2004, Lev Leviev, a billionaire diamond mogul, teamed up with a developer named Shaya Boymelgreene on a venture called the Gowanus Village. They paid eight million dollars for several lots contaminated with pollution on the east bank of the canal. One of these lots including the long-abandoned Brooklyn Rapid Transit powerhouse building (known to many Brooklynites as the "bat cave"), a Romanesque revival building famous for its graffiti, youthful squatters, and bats. Their plan was to build a "hip village" of four hundred apartments in a complex of loft building and townhouses, although the land would also require zoning changes. The investors had also applied for the New York State Brownfield Remediation Program, which offered tax breaks in exchange for cleaning the lands that were developed.

In 2006, two more development announcements made the local headlines: Whole Foods, the high-end grocery store, was planning to open a massive retail location on the site of the former Coignet Stone Company factory, a mostly empty parcel at Third Street and Third Avenue. Even more surprising was that Toll Brothers, a developer of luxury suburban "McMansions," announced plans to invest five hundred million in new condominium developments across Manhattan, Brooklyn, and Queens. Thanks to their hired New York real estate guru, David von Spreckelsen, they were eyeing a parcel of two blocks along the Gowanus, across from the Leviev-Boymelgreene venture on the western bank of the canal.[21]

The frenzy of real estate in this period was hardly limited to Gowanus—developers were snatching up properties wherever possible in New York, particularly the "blighted" and industrial areas where young creatives had settled. Manhattan's Lower East Side, Long Island City in Queens, and the North Brooklyn neighborhoods of Greenpoint and Manhattan were all under intense scrutiny as the country experienced a swell of housing investment—in hindsight, partially the result of a growing real estate bubble. Although zoning around our storied waterway remained purely industrial through the 2000s, sensing the changing tides of real estate, the administration of Mayor Michael Bloomberg rushed to plan a comprehensive zoning change for the entire "Gowanus Canal Corridor." New York's real estate gurus were well aware of the plans, as nationwide housing prices peaked around 2006. Some twenty-five blocks of the Gowanus area were to be rezoned for nonindustrial use, and more than sixty sites with development potential were highlighted—projected tax revenues reached the hundreds of millions. For a company like Toll Brothers to elevate their business to national prominence, a strong position in an urban market like New York City was the next step. That the community was advocating for cleanup of the sewage-filled waterway made the nearby parcels only more attractive—regardless of the canal's putrid state at the time. Meanwhile members of FROGG and other like-minded community groups insisted they also wanted the existing industrial spaces used for their zoned purpose and encouraged manufacturers to make use of tax abatements. Since the restoration of Smith Street and the boom of Carroll Gardens, 125 new industrial businesses had reportedly opened in Gowanus.[22]

Specifics of the Toll Brothers development filtered down, with fantastic marketing language: Two full canal-side blocks, zoned for manufacturing, would be specially amended to a mixed-use district by the Department of City Planning to build 577 units of mixed-income housing, community and commercial space, and a swath of open space. Some 30 percent of the units would be earmarked as "affordable," below market rates, and a forty-foot-wide pedestrian greenway would run alongside the canal. Abutting this public walkway would be the two grandest towers of the development, rising twelve stories, about 125 feet, over the waters of the Gowanus. Supposedly, claimed the Toll Brothers, such a development and the wealthy condo purchasers it would bring to the community would "spur the cleanup" of the canal—and the Bloomberg administration appeared to concur. The concerned brownstoners couldn't believe that the city would consider the banks of the canal acceptable for residential building before the water and surrounding ground were remediated.

The Public Place site, once slated for community use, was also being considered for a large housing development: some four hundred units in a complex of buildings ranging from three to fourteen stories in height, also boasting affordable units. The Bloomberg administration had promised to choose a developer for the new project before leaving office in 2009. It was during this flurry of Gowanus development activity when in April 2007 Sludgie, the baby minke whale, swam to the mouth of the Gowanus Canal. She charmed thousands of New Yorkers and news readers across the country, before dying on a pile of oily rocks. For a short period, Gowanus pollution was nationwide story.

"The fear is not one site, it is the health of the whole area," Linda Mariano told the *Brooklyn Paper* in September 2007, regarding FROGG's opposition to the development. She spoke with great confidence during the rowdy, standing-room-only "town hall" meeting to discuss the proposed Toll Brothers development. "There is raw sewage in this canal and you should see the flooding. We are saying, 'Fix it now' before it gets worse." Meanwhile, environmental testing conducted by the city had found 150-foot-deep plumes of coal tar under the ground of the Public Place site. Community members were outraged that the city would consider building at all, even though there would be a significant cleanup and capping effort. Dr. Niloufar Haque, biology professor at City College, tested Gowanus water with her students and found strains of gonococci, the flu virus, and aggressive strains of disease-causing bacteria. She called the level of pathogens "scary," and said she wouldn't raise her child near that water.

Meanwhile, the city's Department of Environmental Protection and the Army Corps of Engineers presented some plans for cleaning up the canal. The DEP earmarked $125 million for the cleaning, which included modernizing the flushing tunnel and dredging some of the "black mayonnaise" coating the bottom of the canal.[23]

For the next two years, there were dozens of meetings and hearings as a battle of opinions raged in the community and among city officials about the onslaught of development. The Toll Brothers complex was too big to absorb, claimed the detractors, and would create too much density in an already overburdened community. All around the once-sleepy and derelict area, it seemed like every open corner or lot was being transformed into some high-rise tower, overlooking the low industrial district. "Ten years ago, I would have gone down on bended knee to get developers into that area," said Buddy Scotto in a public meeting in March 2008. Another community member at the meeting complained that the city was presenting residential condo development as the only path to getting the canal cleaned, which simply wasn't true. Bill de Blasio, the city councilman of the Gowanus and Carroll Gardens district (and future mayor of New York), supported the Toll Brothers plan as well.[24]

"A project with 130 units of affordable housing is a win for the community," de Blasio later told *Brooklyn Paper*. Tony Avella, a city councilman from Queens (and de Blasio opponent during the 2009 mayoral primaries), said, "The real-estate industry controls the agenda in this city." His comment secured "a guaranteed bloc of a dozen votes by playing to the anti-development crowd," the *Brooklyn Paper* quipped.[25]

FROGG and its other community allies wrote numerous letters to the City Council and attended more meetings with their comments, insisting that the development was much too high, completely out of scale and context for the reinvigorated neighborhood. Furthermore, by September 2008, the country was in the midst of a financial crisis. Major banking institutions were collapsing after facing defaults on highly traded securities backed by risky subprime mortgages. The inflated US housing market had betrayed itself. According to concerned residents, this should have shaken the foundations of real estate developers—especially those that build glass towers on former marshland, poisoned with more than a century industrial and human pollution.

In 2009, Shaya Boymelgreene abandoned his Gowanus Village plan, putting the site on the market for $27 million, more than three times what he paid for it. For the Toll Brothers, quite the opposite was true. They had spent more than $350,000 lobbying the city for a zoning change, and despite discovering deposits of arsenic, petroleum, mercury, and lead contamination in their site, they would continue to develop—and could still qualify for a brownfield cleanup tax abatement. The local community board voted in favor of the development, and then the City Council followed suit. Local newspapers followed the details in regular reports—the *Brooklyn Paper* dubbing it "the battle for the soul of the Gowanus Canal." Residents appeared at hearings to debate the height and context of the Toll Brothers site. De Blasio continued to voice his support for the development, stating the need for affordable housing and how the height would allow for the needed housing.[26]

The Arrival of the EPA

In December 2008, Alexander B. Grannis, commissioner of the New York State Department of Environmental Conservation, sent a letter to New York's regional administrator of the Environmental Protection Agency, formally requesting that the federal group nominate the Gowanus Canal for the Superfund National Priorities List.[27]

The Superfund, officially the Comprehensive Environmental Response, Compensation, and Liability Act, had been established in 1980 to clean up the most hazardous sites of environmental pollution across the nation. It was prompted by an infamous 1978 health crisis in Niagara Falls, New York, in which toxic chemicals were seeping into the homes and underground infrastructure of an area called Love Canal. The health effects were catastrophic in the neighborhood, including many unexplained illnesses and birth defects in children. After sampling sediment of the Gowanus, the EPA found the cancer-causing chemicals PAHs and PCBs—byproducts of coal tar—pesticides, heavy metals, and "volatile organic compounds." There was an average of ten feet of toxic sludge on the floor of the canal, found all along the 1.8-mile, 100-foot-wide canal and its branches. On April 23, 2009, the EPA nominated the Gowanus Canal as a potential candidate for Superfund site designation. On the rating system for the level of toxic pollution, the Gowanus scored a 50 out of 100, the same score given to the Love Canal in the early 1980s (in order to qualify for potential Superfund nomination, the minimum score is 28). Perhaps most interestingly, one of the primary reasons for the nomination was the presence of "subsistence fishing" near the mouth the canal—that is, the regular consumption of locally caught fish by some immigrant populations in the area.[28]

The announcement "surprised and enraged city officials, who warn that the 'stigma' of being included in the program could halt economic improvement indefinitely." One spokesman from the mayor's office claimed the program would take decades to complete, putting at risk "more than $400 million of private investment already committed to the area." Part of the city's fear was undoubtedly that a full Superfund designation would give the EPA legal power to compel any party responsible for causing pollution to pay for some of the cleanup.

The appearance of a federal deus ex machina was big news in all of New York City's media, including a faithful following of local blogs. Brooklyn remains the incubator for this ubiquitous form of Internet media, and the Gowanus, at the intersection of politics, the environment, real estate, and history, proved to be a compelling subject. Irony is the fuel that feeds the daily reportage of certain blogs, and it was ironic that Brooklyn's sewers polluted openly into a toxic waste site in the heart of a neighborhood mocked for its addiction to green living, kale, and progressive politics. The Toll Brothers, rightfully fearing the stigma, threatened to pull out of their investment if the nomination went through. The corporation had more than six hundred million in net losses for the year at the time of the announcement. "It'd be nice to point at the housing units the developers would build," Nydia M. Velázquez, the area's congresswoman told the *New York Times*. "But with the type of contamination that exists and the offer from the federal government, to say they oppose it and to go with a piecemeal approach is beyond me."

A filmmaker who lived a hundred yards from the canal agreed. "If there's any kind of flooding, these contaminants will be in people's backyards and homes. Simply saying there's millions of dollars of private money really is a separate issue than any cleanup of the canal. I'd love to see low-income housing and expensive housing for rich people, but I don't see how that works without a thorough cleanup." In response to these arguments, the city proposed an alternative plan several months in July, but Walter Mugdan, the EPA's regional Superfund director, questioned the viability of the plan, particularly its ability to collect the necessary funds.[29]

During the ninety-day comment period that follows the announcement of a Superfund site, the EPA usually receives approximately twenty comments from the local community (normally a Superfund comment period is sixty days, but an additional month was granted at the request of de Blasio, who was then assistant majority leader of the New York City Council). But after the announcement of the Gowanus Canal, more than thirteen hundred phone calls relaying all kinds of community opinions were made to the EPA's regional office. But with more than fourteen thousand people living in the immediate vicinity of the canal, and more than a hundred thousand in the area once known as South Brooklyn, the surroundings of this Superfund site make it unique—perhaps one of the most dense sites in the entire country.

More than one thousand of the comments supported the project, including phone calls from various senators, other politicians, and a bevy of nonprofit organizations dedicated to environmental and civic causes, such as Riverkeeper, FROGG, and the Center for Public Environmental Oversight. Around two hundred commentators were opposed to the listing, including the City of New York, the Toll Brothers, Buddy Scotto, and Bill de Blasio—the latter "questioned the Superfund's effectiveness." All of the opposed felt that it would be better to defer to the city's alternative cleanup plans, otherwise the EPA might overrule every plan already in effect and damage relationships with developers. They felt the Superfund designation should be used only as a "last resort." The City of New York also disputed the Gowanus Canal's Superfund site score, suggesting that it should be as low as 15.[30]

The Superfund assessment period lasted a year and included extensive environmental tests, private and public community meetings, and uncountable phone calls. EPA representatives met with dozens of potentially responsible parties, city officials, and business owners. They met with community groups, particularly FROGG and the GCCDC. Mayor Bloomberg personally called Lisa Jackson, the administrator of the EPA (a US cabinet-level officer), on two separate occasions to argue his case for the city's alternative approach. Meanwhile, throughout that time FROGG waged a battle of wills against the city. Certain that the Superfund designation would suit their own mission—to clean up the canal comprehensively and to preserve the industrial character of the neighborhood by scaring off developers—they set up a pro-Superfund campaign.

One artistic FROGG, Maryann Young, designed a cartoon logo of a blue whale spouting water underscored by the phrase "Gowanus Canal, Superfund Me!" and printed it on hundreds pins, buttons, signs, and postcards. Linda Mariano, Margaret Maugenest, local blogger Katia Kelly, Marlene Donnely, and a dozen other FROGGs distributed these items throughout the community. Spouting blue whales papered the windows of many Carroll Gardens brownstones in 2009, much to the chagrin of Buddy Scotto and members of the GCCDC.[31]

From their official perspective, more than anything the neighborhood would benefit from housing development, and a Superfund listing would stand in the way of that hope. By 2010, Buddy Scotto was eighty-one years old and concerned that his lifelong plan was in jeopardy. But his perspective stretches back to an age of Brooklyn long vanished, when industry betrayed the livelihood of an entire neighborhood, while any investment was good investment in a poor and dangerous place. When it came to trusting politicians and government, it was better to deal locally then with big government—better to let New York City and rich developers pave over the degradation of the past. Conversely, for Linda Mariano, who moved to Gowanus because of its decay, there is a certain romantic attachment to the odd and historic neighborhood. She calls it "emotional, visceral, I don't know!"

"I'm a preservation person at heart," she once said, "and I believe in this phrase people are starting to use, 'adaptive reuse,' and this is about just that." She paused, fingering the beads on one of the colorful Bakelite necklaces she uses to accessorize her handmade knitwear. "These buildings can be used rather than torn down." And while Linda knew from news stories and discussion with her neighbors that she and her family were living next to a toxic canal, she waved off any fears of long-term health effects with a sweeping hand motion—not out of dismissal, but a sort of "what am I gonna do?" attitude. She and her husband bought a house where they could afford it. "I smoked for 30 years!" she once said, as if to excuse her seeming indifference. "And it's not like I went swimming in it." Later on, she felt sheepish about that attitude. But she will never move, she has firmly maintained, and has always advocated for the cleanup of the stinking canal.[32]

On Wednesday, March 2, the EPA named the Gowanus Canal an official Superfund site. Marc LaVorgna, a representative for Mayor

Bloomberg, sent an email comment. “It’s disappointing,” he wrote. “We had an innovative and comprehensive approach that was a faster route to a Superfund-level cleanup and would have avoided the issues associated with a Superfund listing. The project will now move on a Superfund timeline, but we are going to work closely with the EPA because we share the same goal—a clean canal.”

“We did it!” whooped Linda over the phone that morning. “I always said it, and I never gave up hope! And now the Toll Brothers are out, ha!”

Epilogue

In July 2010, the Toll Brothers walked away from a $5.75-million down payment on their land abutting the Gowanus Canal. "It just didn't financially make sense to close on the properties and then have to wait 15 to 20 years until we could develop them," said David Von Spreckelsen, senior vice president.[1]

It was a surprise conclusion, for Gowanusians and developers alike—so rarely have grassroots activists bent on preservation been able to hold off the bottomless hunger of developers, movers, and shifters of New York City real estate. If you asked Natalie Loney of the EPA, it wasn't really activism that made the final decision for the federal government, but a purely scientific process. Of course, that's not how Linda Mariano and the other members of FROGG saw their campaigning. From their point of view, the battle for Gowanus took place on the streets and in the windows of the abutting neighborhoods. With politicians like Michael Bloomberg and Bill de Blasio pushing for a New York City–organized environmental cleanup, residents felt there was a real danger of never getting a fully cleaned Gowanus Canal. Not only did they get the support of federally regulated environmental cleanup, the designation scared off the up-zoned glass towers that these activists feared most.

In the years since the Superfund decision, much has been discovered. A team of environmental engineers, headed by EPA project leader Christos Tsiamis, has identified numerous pockets of coal tar and other contaminants deep under the soil of the Gowanus Canal and along its banks. Ultimately, the EPA will dredge approximately 9.5 million cubic feet of toxic material from the bottom of the canal, remove it to some form of waste remediation facility, and then cap the bottom of the canal to prevent any pockets of waste from repolluting the Gowanus. The various operations will cost approximately half a billion dollars. Yet the problem of combined sewage overflow, that is, the emptying of area sewers into the canal, does not fall into the purview of the Superfund program—ironically and much to the chagrin of Gowanus residents.

In fact, the complicated web of jurisdiction of the Gowanus neighborhood spans the city, state, and federal levels, requiring a seemingly endless amount of meetings, reports, debates, and concessions. Among the highest polluting "potentially responsible parties," as the EPA designates the various businesses and organizations that polluted the site (and hence, are financially responsible for the cleanup), are energy company National Grid and the City of New York. Unsurprisingly, the city has found itself at odds with many EPA decisions regarding the canal and has contested one particular conclusion, that runoff from the sewer system into the canal contains toxic elements. While the EPA stands behind its findings, the anxiety of city leaders is pretty obvious—if there is toxic material in the sewers, then the EPA has a legal power to compel the city to do what the EPA deems necessary in order to prevent any repollution of the canal. The EPA has designated the city as responsible for installing three massive retention tanks to catch sewage water in the case of large rain "events," as they are termed, to prevent the sewage from entering the canal. One site that the EPA suggested the city to consider was a public pool near several large public housing projects, as the ground underneath had been determined to be host to a large plume of toxic waste.[2]

This conclusion has led to all manner of protest from locals, community activists, and city officials. The confluence of politics, environmental science, and amenities for area residents has spawned much debate and conflict within the neighborhood—a "robust" response, to use a buzzword that often characterizes the sentiments of Gowanus residents when describing their love for this particular neighborhood and its unique, low-scale character. One of the defining characteristics of Gowanus is that it is a former wetland, the bottom of a watershed that is the collection point for the runoff waters from New York's torrential rains and sponge for the rising tides of New York Bay. For the past century and a half the floodgates, bulkheads, and drainage sewers have not contained the flooding near the Gowanus Canal banks. Since its construction in the 1850s, the local governments have attempted to fix this issue but always failed.

The problem is twofold: that engineering such a fix is impossibly complicated and therefore expensive, and the municipal powers can never be convinced to devote the money and resources necessary to finish this herculean task. Local residents have always found themselves knee deep in water at some point, and no amount of street regrading or half-conceived sewer patching has ever permanently fixed this urban problem. Yet people desire to live near the Gowanus, and during periods of real estate boom, as the Gowanus experienced in the 1870s, the late 2000s and beyond, the value of its land has climbed to grandiose heights. Developers see the potential of the water to provide value, despite the pollution inherent in its postindustrial existence. In the past, the Gowanus value came from its utility, but in the present day its uniqueness in the urban setting of Brooklyn has defined its potential.

This human devotion to Gowanus, as I hope to have shown, extends back to the earliest Dutch colonists in New York, and likely before them. The ultimate reason for this connection is its unique placement in the vicinity of an "arm of the sea," an estuary that travels inland, originally creating a wetland that functions as a transitional space between land and water. During colonization, this meant a healthy site for agriculture and an important means of transportation. It also lent itself to the proto-"industry" of tide mills—in the case of Gowanus, a remarkable Dutch invention that spawned a legacy of commerce and utility in the region. In the modern era, the canal has provided an unexpected sight in the middle of a growing industrial neighborhood, and with the help of human intervention, a solution to the wetland flooding—or so we would like to believe. When the first culvert at Bond Street was attached to the canal, it soon proved a nuisance. However stopping it up caused only greater problems for the settled neighborhood around the canal, and so residents have dealt with the problem in stride. Because of the resiliency required of those who live in urban environments, today residents continue to live with the aggravation, not to mention the medieval inconvenience, of a body of water that functions as an open sewer. In many ways, this dirty water led to the warehouses and factory buildings that have outlasted their original use, yet it also has provided a setting for new and wholly creative purposes. Compounded with human and industrial pollution, Gowanus presents a unique urban conundrum. How one can best make use of this body of water, despite the problems it presents?

Because of the dynamic nature of Gowanus, as the city of Brooklyn expanded, the presence of this water created unique opportunities, problems, and solutions through which we can observe the evolution of urban life. Historically, the Gowanus has spawned settlements, villages, shantytowns, docks, sewers, factories, chemical works, power plants, and numerous other innovations that have marked progress in our society. It acted as a buffer during the Revolutionary War, and later inspired poets, writers, and painters to record its existence into beautiful creations—even when the inspiration lacked conventional beauty. In the contemporary age, the spaces once devoted to industrial products have been rethought into creative outlets for art and music studios, entertainment, food, performance, museums, writings spaces, and collaboration for design and small-scale production of uniquely creative products suited to urban tastes. Such developments can be found in all cities, and in former industrial neighborhoods of New York, but this neighborhood defined by its waterway is unique in its long history and its deep-seated pollution.

As progress transformed the Gowanus Creek into a functioning tool for the growth of a city—providing the site and creation of building materials—it also rapidly transformed a thriving ecosystem into a cesspool, much to the dismay of the people who witnessed their rural lands become a frightening, indeed unrecognizable, version of themselves. While countless Brooklynites contributed to the development of the city of Brooklyn and to Gowanus, the efforts of people like Daniel Richards and Edwin C. Litchfield are significant to recall—not simply because they imagined a different landscape and had the initiative to execute it, but because they made mistakes.

These errors spawned a huge amount of community protest and push-back—the kind of civic involvement of local citizens that is uniquely American. Not only did Brooklynites feel a sense of ownership over the spaces they inhabited, they expressed these anxieties and desires in a manner that was unique in the world during the rapid changes of the nineteenth century. Certainly, the gap between rich and poor, powerful and impotent was enormous, but there are many similarities between the different eras of change described in the past chapters. In studying the actions of these developers, I hope to have shown how their arguably selfish visions for personal gain produced long-lasting results far beyond their own expectations. While Edwin C. Litchfield created his Fourth Street Basin against the wishes of the community, within fifty years it had been filled up and forgotten. Yet thanks to Litchfield, there is a neighborhood known as Park Slope and, for a time, a very functional Gowanus Canal. In the present day, the canal is the setting of one of the last "gritty" neighborhoods within a short distance to Manhattan, and therein lies its value.

The anxieties of nineteenth-century Gowanusians over the loss "pastoral" lands in the face of encroaching industry and urbanization parallel the anxieties of the twentieth-century brownstoners who settled in what they perceived to be unlikely and decrepit neighborhoods of the former South Brooklyn. The brownstoners' "authentic" Brooklyn neighborhoods, with uniquely low-scale architecture, village-like street life, and ethnic sociogeography, are now being challenged by the construction of high-rise residential buildings. These changes pose a threat to the brownstoners' unique way of life, not only by inflating the costs of living but also by changing the scale and the new stock of residents, creating a wholly different character. Such changes are to be expected in the dynamic cycle of urban life, but many Gowanus residents believed the pollution and unique building stock of their neighborhood would hold such development back.

The urban crises of the 1960s hit the Gowanus especially hard because the industrial utility it had provided became obsolete, and many of the jobs with it. This left the neighborhood with only its faults: pollution and a penchant for crime and violence. Yet the worst urban downgrade provided a perfect setting for renewal—a decay and recovery that happened simultaneously. The abandoned spaces were cheap and expansive—the freedom these spaces allow cannot be dismissed. The dynamic nature of Gowanus and its evolution is not cause and effect, but continuous. The seizing of opportunity where others saw abandoned space, like that of Dotty Bennett, who bought and repurposed an old barge amid the failing Depression-era old salts of Gowanus, represents a microcosmic version of the urban environment as a whole. As Gowanusians watched with a certain awe, Dottie and her coterie of professional "aristocrats" made a summer home out of their decaying livelihood, the simultaneous rebirth a sign of creativity where a majority saw depleted value.

Yet this same threat to a particular way of life can be ascribed to second- and third-generation Brooklynites of Gowanus of Buddy Scotto's generation. Holding out against the degradation of midcentury urban blight, they retained their identity as city dwellers and, in the case of much of the Carroll Gardens area, Italian Americans. When the brownstoners arrived and began moving into the run-down buildings, many in the population felt threatened by this first wave of gentrification. Celia Cacace expressed her feelings against gentrification with no shame or remorse, and yet befriended many of these gentrifiers, the very people whose additions to the neighborhood would drive up rents and ultimately render her unable to afford to live in the place where she spent her entire life. However neighborhood leaders like Scotto viewed the renewal of former industrial neighborhoods like SoHo as a model that would save Gowanus from its abandoned, dirty character—transforming it into a cleaner place that lacked the stigma of crime and pollution.

Sharon Zukin, the urban sociologist and author of the 1981 study *Loft Living*, in 2009 published *Naked City*, in which she expresses significant anxiety about the nature of "authenticity" and its meaning in contemporary New York. "Claiming authenticity," she writes, "becomes prevalent at a time when identities are unstable and people are judged by their performance rather than by their history or innate character." The "original" rural Gowanus is long gone, as is the Gilded Age entrepreneurial atmosphere that built the handsome red brick townhouses in the City of Churches, as Brooklyn was once known. Also gone is the thriving gashouse district of nineteenth-century Gowanus, with its colorful characters described in poetry by Michael J. Shay, the gas-drip bard who composed odes when he wasn't servicing gas pipes, or the "terrible gossips" among the working people of Planet Mills. The former danger associated with organized crime has also departed, leaving the stories and associations, but ultimately a new canvas for a redefined neighborhood. Zukin describes "two faces of authenticity," the tension between the historic preservationists of the 1960s and the desire to "develop centers of cultural innovation, which has become, since the 1980s, the goal of many who wish to find a magic motor of rapid commercial redevelopment."[3]

As Gowanus has become a center of Brooklyn's cultural innovation, the more affluent settlers of the once-degraded neighborhood have welcomed the influx of creative artists and "makers"—small-scale producers who have used the original industrial buildings as incubators for uniquely individual, noncorporate products (like clothing, furniture, and home goods, but also art, food, and performance). But at the same time they fear what Zukin describes as "the promotions of the media who translate neighborhood identity into a brand, and by the tastes of new urban middle classes who are initially attracted to this identity but ultimately destroy it." Hence, the neighborhood activists of FROGG fought against the destruction of old industrial buildings and the building of condos, as they believed the residents these landscape-changing constructions might attract would displace the same creative class that made the neighborhood so interesting to many in the twenty-first century.

Perhaps ironically, the pollution of Gowanus was both a reason to fight development and a way to keep the worst of it at bay. In their view, the "stigma" associated with the Superfund designation should preserve the industrial character of Gowanus, which set this neighborhood apart from its surrounding, increasingly gentrified brownstone quarters. Even before the Superfund designation, Linda Mariano had sought to nominate Gowanus as the first industrial district to be listed in the New York State Register of Historic Places. This designation would highlight the particular industrial character of Gowanus and introduce tax incentives to keep its shape and use intact.

In the opening passage of "The Need for Aged Buildings," the tenth chapter in *Death and Life of Great American Cities*, Jane Jacobs declares, "Cities need old buildings so badly it is probably impossible for vigorous streets and districts to grow without them. . . . As for really new ideas of any kind—no matter how ultimately profitable or otherwise successful some of them might prove to be—there is no leeway for such chancy trial, error and experimentation in the high-overhead economy of new construction. Old ideas can sometimes use new buildings. New ideas must use old buildings."[4] Echoing her predecessor, Zukin states that a "city loses its soul" when the continuity of a neighborhood is broken and the roots of past generations are paved over. Yet such is the case with Gowanus, whose landscape has already changed in the short time that I have been devoted to its history. Since 2013, surrounding the historic Coignet Building is a Whole Foods supermarket, the subject of great controversy and debate, but also much fanfare and use by the local community. The Kentile Floors sign, an unofficial landmark, was removed by its landlord in 2014. In that same year, across the canal from the new Whole Foods the Burns Brothers Coal pockets—towering concrete monuments that once housed coal for borough-wide delivery and, once abandoned by industry, an ecosystem of birds and bats—were knocked down despite their listing for consideration by the National Trust for Historic Preservation. For the real estate community, such nominations can be perceived as antithetical to progress and neighborhood development, hindering their ability to make use of this formerly decrepit space.

Following the 2008 recession, New York City real estate had a temporary slowdown, which made gleeful those preservation-minded citizens who didn't desire a rapid comeback. But in other parts of formerly industrial Brooklyn, particularly the northern neighborhood of Williamsburg, the up-zoning of waterfront spaces had already been executed and the effects had been felt. Previously affordable rents have skyrocketed, and high-rise luxury condo buildings have risen like mountains of glass where warehouses once sat. Farther north, the Polish enclave of Greenpoint is experiencing the same changes.[5]

Despite the Superfund designation of Gowanus and extensive flooding during Hurricane Sandy in 2012, in 2013 the former Toll Brothers project site was purchased by the Lightstone Group, a real estate company run by billionaire investor David Lichtenstein. Using the same zoning variance granted to the Toll Brothers, Lightstone planned to build a seven-hundred-unit rental complex, which would include twelve-story glass buildings on the banks of the Gowanus.

The purchase marked just one of many real estate transfers during this period that led one well-regarded real estate blog, *The Real Deal*, to declare that "Gowanus is the Williamsburg of 10 years ago."[6]

The essayist Philip Lopate writes about the urban landscape of New York and once captured his view of the Gowanus Canal from the Union Street Bridge during the height of housing mania: "Standing on the span, looking north, I see a good deal of sky and clouds and a vast sweeping view of Brooklyn that would have quickened the pulse of any Delft landscape painter. You can luxuriate in the profligate empty space ('waste,' to a developer's eye) framed by the canal. . . . I, a native Brooklynite, never romanticized the place as immune from modernity, nor do I see why it should be protected from high-rise construction when the rest of the planet is not. But if the sleeping giant Brooklyn were to awake and truly bestir itself, I would deeply regret the loss of sky."[7]

The sky in Gowanus certainly recalls a different era in New York, and Brooklyn before it. Every time the neighborhood has changed, the people have lamented, fought battles, and built bridges over it. Brooklynites barged in the bones of their city, block by block, along the canal, and then spit their waste into it. It remains their inland connection to the saltwater domain that covers most of our planet. One can only imagine what how many bones, oyster shells, old boats, and secrets are buried under the sludge, and the earth below it—how many shanty dwellers and sea captains touched its waters or were afraid to for fear of their health and hygiene.

Perhaps some idealistic city dwellers yearn for a seventeenth-century pastoral bliss long gone, when Gowanus was a wild and bountiful place, full of salt marshes and forests—yet still a quick boat ride from Manhattan. Such a thing is impossible, and it may be impossible to keep the postindustrial grit of Gowanus that has led to its renewal as a unique and hip place to live. In a relatively short period of time, Brooklyn has been reborn and rebranded in the imaginations of people across the world as the epicenter of hipness and culture in

New York. Some parts of Brooklyn are more expensive than Manhattan to live in, and as real estate in New York reaches enormous heights again, one must wonder what will happen next to the unique, formerly low-scale neighborhoods that once defined the post-2000s cultural shift to New York's once-forgotten borough.

To convince the officials in a place like New York City to play a long game—that is, to slow down development and invest in good infrastructure—is a difficult sell with no immediate returns. Like so many Gowanus settlers of the past, the newest developers here believe they can conquer the floodwaters of this estuary with high-rise towers. The rising sea levels will undoubtedly prove them wrong, but it's a chance they're willing to take.

In a way, Brooklyn is returning to former nineteenth-century, Gilded Age glory, when it was its own city that stood brightly in the shadow of New York, proudly singing of its own identity. This new urban setting seeks to define itself in twenty-first-century terms, and the battle for Gowanus is hardly ended. It remains the subject of great debate over ownership, authenticity, and the future of American cities and their postindustrial spaces. The Gowanus is just one small, 1.8-mile-long example of how this great debate has unfolded since the settlement of America. We should honor and protect its monuments and memories, and also clean up the pollution already—if not for history's sake, then for our own.

NOTES

Prologue

1 "Sludgie, We're Going to Miss You," *Gowanus Lounge*, April 19, 2007, gowanuslounge.blogspot.com/2007/04/sludgie-were-going-to-miss-you.html.
2 Ibid.

Chapter 1. Millponds, Oysters, and Early Origins (1636–1774)

1 Henry R. Stiles, *History of the City of Brooklyn* (Brooklyn, 1867), 1:24. Stiles does not include the southern Castateeuw purchase as integral in the establishment of Brooklyn, possibly because the lands were first used for agriculture and were not a proper settlement. Those purchases did develop into settlements, eventually the colonial villages of Nieuw Amersfoort (Flatlands), the 'T Vlacke Bos (Flatbush), and Midwout (Midwood), but not until the late 1640s. The great historian and polymath's neglect is just as likely to be a prejudice for recounting "proper" Brooklyn history, since the southern settlements were still separate towns, with unique identities from Brooklyn, when first his volumes were published in 1867.
2 Russell Shorto, *The Island at the Center of the World* (New York: Vintage, 2004), 40–45.
3 William G. Bishop, *Manual of the Common Council of the City of Brooklyn* (Brooklyn: The Council, 1868), 460.
4 Martha Bockée Flint, *Early Long Island: A Colonial Study* (New York: Putnam, 1896), 81.
5 Teunis G. Bergen, *The Bergen Family* (Albany: Joel Munsell, 1876), 22; Shorto, 41, 45.
6 Stiles, 1:22.
7 William Wallace Tooker, *Indian Names of Places in the Borough of Brooklyn* (New York: Francis P. Harper, 1901), 103, 291.

8 Bergen, *Bergen Family*, 33.
9 Teunis G. Bergen, *Register in Alphabetical Order of the Early Settlers of Kings County* (New York: S. W. Green's Son, 1881), 31.
10 Stiles, 1:25.
11 Ibid., 1:27.
12 Ibid., 1:44.
13 Hunter Research, *National Register of Historic Places Eligibility Evaluation and Cultural Resources Assessment for the Gowanus Canal . . . In Connection with the Proposed Ecosystem Restoration Study* (New York: Hunter Research, 2004), 2-1; and P. A. Keddy, *Wetland Ecology: Principles and Conservation*, 2nd ed. (Cambridge: Cambridge University Press, 2010), 497.
14 Hunter Research, 2-2.
15 Flint, 65.
16 Tooker, 31–32.
17 William M. Beauchamp, *Aboriginal Place Names of New York* (Albany: New York State Education Department, 1907), 207.
18 Lewis Henry Morgan, *League of the Ho-dé-no-sau-nee, or Iroquois* (New York: Dodd, Mead and Company, 1922), 139.
19 Email correspondence with Ives Goddard, March 21, 2013.
20 The full list: Cujanes, Cojanes, Coujanes, Cowanoes, Gawanes, Gauwanes, Gouanes, Goujanes, Gouvanes, Gouwanes, Gouwanos, Gouvanes, Gowannes, Gowanos, and Gowones.
21 Stiles, 1:59.
22 Peter Ross, *A History of Long Island from Its Earliest Settlement to the Present Time* (New York: Lewis, 1902), 58.
23 From the natives' point of view, the goods received from settlers were not payment for permanent ownership, but a sort of combined tribute, lease, and symbol of allegiance for the shared use of land and defenses. Shorto, 51.
24 Bailey O'Callaghan, *History of New Netherland*, vol. 1 (New York: Appleton, 1848), 308.
25 Flint, 82; Stiles, 1:45.
26 Edmund Bailey O'Callaghan, *History of New Netherland*, vol. 2 (New York: Bartlett and Welford, 1848), 186.
27 Ibid.
28 Ibid., 268; Bartlett Burleigh James and J. Franklin Jameson, eds., *Journal of Jasper Danckaerts* (New York: Scribner, 1913), 57.
29 Stiles, 1:114.
30 Bishop, 469–470; Stiles, 1:100.
31 Dan Wiley, *A Timeline of Gowanus* (Brooklyn: Hall of Gowanus, Proteus Gowanus, 2010).
32 Stiles, 1:69–69.
33 James and Jameson, xv–xxv.
34 "The passengers and crew were a wretched set. There was no rest, night or day, especially among the wives—a rabble I cannot describe." He did not give an exact number of passengers or crew, but there were around ten married women with accompanying husbands (many of whom were drunk most of the voyage),

and around a dozen crewmen. "I have never in my life heard of such a disorderly ship. It was confusion without end. I have never been in a ship where there was so much vermin." Ibid., 3.

35 Ibid., 40.
36 Ibid., 52.
37 Ibid., 53.
38 Ibid., 57.
39 Ibid., 57.
40 Ibid., 59.
41 Ibid., 91.
42 Ibid., 123.
43 Ibid., 175.
44 Ibid., 180–181.
45 Ibid., 229–230.
46 Bergen, *Bergen Family*, 119; Ross, 391.
47 Stiles, 1:39.
48 Georgia Fraser, *The Stone House at Gowanus* (New York: Witter and Kintner, 1909), 35–36; Stiles, 1:411.
49 Fraser, 37; City of New York Parks and Recreation, "J.J. Byrne Playground," www.nycgovparks.org/parks/B111/highlights/138.
50 Gabriel Furman, *Antiquities of Long Island* (New York: J. W. Bouton, 1875), 394.
51 Ibid., 323–325; Charlotte Rebecca Bangs, *Reminiscences of Old New Utrecht and Gowanus* (Brooklyn: Brooklyn Eagle Press, 1912), 96.
52 Denton's Mill or the Yellow Mill, in Gowanus, was also built upon Bout's patent, by Adam and Nicholas, the sons of Adam Brouwer, in 1709. The mill-pond was formed by the damming of a branch of the Gowanus Kil, and the mill was located on the northeast side of the present First Street, about midway between Second and Third Avenues. The dwelling house, which burned down about 1852, was in Carroll, midway between Nevins Street and Third Avenue (Stiles, 1:100).
53 Ibid., 1:96, 101.
54 The popular stories of this channel come from several sources, including one story told to the *Eagle* in 1861 by a Brooklyn woman named Diana, who claimed to be descended from one of Vecht's original slaves. Fraser, 47; *Brooklyn Daily Eagle*, November 30, 1861.
55 Bishop, 477.

Chapter 2. Bloody Waters (1776)

1 T. G. Bergen, "The Rising Sun Tavern and the Rockaway Pass," in *Manual of the Common Council of Brooklyn* (Brooklyn, 1868), 474.
2 Thomas Strong, *History of the Town of Flatbush* (New York: Thomas R. Mercein, Jr., 1842), 13.
3 Henry Onderdonk Jr., *Revolutionary Incidents of Suffolk and Kings Counties* (New York: Leavitt & Company, 1849), 139.
4 Bergen, "Rising Sun Tavern," 475.

5 John J. Gallagher, *The Battle of Brooklyn, 1776* (New York: Da Capo Press, 1995), 15.
6 Charles Francis Adams, *The Works of John Adams*. Vol. 9 (Boston: Little, Brown, 1854), 370.
7 Henry P. Johnston, *The Campaign of 1776 around New York and Brooklyn* (Brooklyn: Long Island Historical Society, 1878), 48–49.
8 Ibid., 54–56.
9 Ibid., 44–46.
10 Flint, 372.
11 Johnston, 65.
12 Ibid., 58–59.
13 Gallagher, 82–83.
14 Charles Francis Adams, Jr., "The Battle of Long Island," *American Historical Review* 1 (July 1896): 651.
15 Gallagher, 78–80.
16 William Henshaw, *The Orderly Books, October 1, 1775 through October 3, 1776* (Worcester, MA, 1948), 131; Johnston, 78–79.
17 Ibid.
18 Ibid., 57; Flint, 365–373.
19 Gallagher, 61.
20 Onderdonk, 81.
21 Pauline Maier, *American Scripture: Making the Declaration of Independence* (New York: Vintage, 1998), 242–243.
22 Flint, 389.
23 Gallagher, 66–68.
24 Francis B. Heitman, *Historical Register of Officers of the Continental Army* (Washington, DC: Rare Bookshop, 1914), 558.
25 Michael Pearson, *Those Damned Rebels: The American Revolution through British Eyes* (New York: Putnam, 1974), 161.
26 Letter of unidentified British soldier, September 23, 1776, War of Revolution Box 1, Manuscript Collection, New York Historical Society.
27 Pearson, 161–162.
28 Letter of unidentified British soldier.
29 Johnston, 139–141.
30 Stiles, 1:254–255.
31 Flint, 391–392.
32 Onderdonk, 133–134.
33 Stiles, 1:260; Flint, 391–392.
34 Edward J. Lowell, *The Hessians and Other German Auxiliaries of Great Britain* (New York: Harper), 61.
35 Johnston, 154–155.
36 Ibid., 160–161.
37 Ibid.
38 Johnston, 155–156.
39 Onderdonk, 148.
40 Bergen, "Rising Sun Tavern," 474.

41 Johnston, 271.
42 Stiles, 1:267.
43 Johnston, 168–174.
44 Adams, "Battle of Long Island," 668.
45 Stiles, 1:274–275.
46 Onderdonk, 152.
47 Ibid., 146.
48 Ibid., 142.
49 Johnston, 181.
50 Onderdonk, 146.
51 Joseph Plumb Martin, *A Narrative of a Revolutionary Soldier* (New York: Signet Classics, 2001), 24–26.
52 Johnston, 187.
53 Onderdonk, 155.
54 Linda Davis Reno, *The Maryland 400 in the Battle of Long Island, 1776* (Jefferson, NC: McFarland, 2008), 4, 170–171.
55 Johnston, 188–189.
56 Adams, "Battle of Long Island," 666.
57 Martin, 26–27.
58 Gallagher, 149.
59 Walt Whitman, *Leaves of Grass* (Philadelphia: David McKay, 1900).

Chapter 3. The Atlantic Docks and Basin (1812–1851)

1 "The Making of Brooklyn," *Brooklyn Daily Eagle* (*BDE*), February 27, 1900, 13.
2 David Ment, *The Shaping of a City: A Brief History of Brooklyn* (Brooklyn: Brooklyn Educational & Cultural Alliance, 1979), 25–31.
3 Ibid., 30–31, 36–37.
4 William Bright, *Native American Placenames of the United States* (Norman: University of Oklahoma Press, 2004), 84.
5 Abner Morse, *A Genealogical Register of the Descendants of Several Ancient Puritans, Vol. 3: The Richards Family* (Boston, 1861), 60.
6 Stiles, 3:73–74.
7 W. T. Bailey, *Richfield Springs and Vicinity* (New York: A.S. Barnes, 1874), 49–51.
8 William J. Brown, *The American Colossus: The Grain Elevator from 1843–1943* (Brooklyn: Colossal Books, 2013), 84–87.
9 "Deaths," *Western Recorder*, March 21, 1826.
10 Correspondence, Daniel Richards to Gen. George Morrell, April 17, 1827, Manuscripts and Special Collections, New York State Library.
11 John Noble Wilford, "How Epidemics Helped Shape the Modern Metropolis," *New York Times*, April 15, 2008.
12 Onderdonk, 117.
13 Stiles, 2:158–160.
14 *A Communication Addressed to a Committee of the Board of Directors of the Red Hook Building Company* (Brooklyn: Arnold & Van Arden, Printers, 1838), 4–8.

15 Ibid., 8.
16 Ibid., 12–13.
17 *General Index of the Laws of the State of New York* (Albany, 1859), 411.
18 Stiles, 3:578–579.
19 Daniel Richards, "An Act to Incorporate the Atlantic Dock Company, 1841," Atlantic Dock Company Collection, 1978.151, Brooklyn Historical Society, inside front cover.
20 Stiles, 3:579.
21 Ibid.
22 Daniel Richards, "The Origin of Atlantic Docks," draft, Atlantic Dock Company Collection, 1978.151, Brooklyn Historical Society, 8–12.
23 Ibid., 11–12.
24 "City Intelligence," *BDE*, August 22, 1846, 2.
25 Stiles, 3:579.
26 Ibid., 576.
27 "City News and Gossip: Atlantic Docks," *BDE*, March 2, 1848, 3.
28 "A Large Business. . ." *BDE*, November 25, 1848, 1.
29 "Sewerage in Brooklyn," *BDE*, September 21, 1847, 2.
30 Charles B. Stuart, "Major David Bates Douglass," in *Lives and Works of Civil and Military Engineers of America* (New York: D. Van Nostrand, 1871), 91–108.
31 David Bates Douglass, *Major Douglass' Report on the Drainage and Graduation of that Part of the City of Brooklyn . . .* (Brooklyn: Common Council, 1847), 10–13.
32 Hunter Research, 2-16–2-21.
33 Daniel Richards, *Plan for the Drainage of That Part of the City of Brooklyn Which Empties Its Water into Gowanus Creek & Bay* (Brooklyn: Common Council, 1848).
34 "Gowanus Meadows," *BDE*, February 16, 1849, 2.
35 Ibid.
36 "The City," *BDE*, March 4, 1850, 2.
37 "City News and Gossip: Sixth Ward," *BDE*, April 7, 1849.
38 "City News and Gossip: The Sixth," *BDE*, April 9, 1849 ; "City News and Gossip," *BDE*, April 12, 1849; "The Advertiser says," *BDE*, April 12, 1849, 1.
39 "More Strykerism," *BDE*, March 30, 1850, 2.
40 Stiles, 3:578.
41 Daniel Richards, "An Act Incorporating the Pacific Dock Company, April 14, 1857," Atlantic Dock Company Collection, 1978.151, Brooklyn Historical Society.
42 Stiles, 3:578.
43 "Great Atlantic Basin," *BDE*, April 19, 1885.
44 Ibid.
45 "Brooklyn," *BDE*, February 25, 1851.

Chapter 4. Sewers, Railroads, and the Castle on the Hill (1851–1857)

1 *Brooklyn Daily Eagle* (*BDE*), February 25, 1851, and February 11, 1852.
2 "Brooklyn City," *New York Times*, January 8, 1852; "Opening of the Gowanus Canal and Other Improvement," *BDE*, June 1, 1853.

3 *BDE*, March 17, 1853.
4 *BDE*, November 21, 1854.
5 Joseph K. Lane, "Edwin Clark Litchfield," *Park Slope Civil Council News* 29, no. 4 (April 1966): 13–15.
6 Robert Sobel, *Machines and Morality: The 1850s* (New York: Crowell, 1973), 64–67; Lynn Boyd Reener, "Litchfield Family of Three Brothers Provide the Name," *Litchfield News Herald*, August 1, 1953.
7 Sobel, 64.
8 "South Brooklyn Improvements," *BDE*, January 29, 1869.
9 Ibid.
10 Edwin C. Litchfield to Electus Litchfield, 1831, Litchfield Family Papers, New York Historical Society (TLFP: NYHS); Edwin C. Litchfield passport, 1868, TLFP: NYHS.
11 Edwin C. Litchfield to Electus Litchfield, 1831a, TLFP: NYHS.
12 South Carolina Historical Society, *Biographical Sketch of Colonel Richard Lathers* (Philadelphia: J. B. Lippincott, 1902), 50.
13 Edwin C. Litchfield to Alexander J. Davis, July 5, 1857, A. J. Davis Collection, Drawings and Archives, Avery Architectural and Fine Arts Library, Columbia University, New York.
14 Ibid.; Jane B. Davies, "The Litchfield Property and the Park," *Park Slope Civil Council News* 29, no. 4 (April 1966): 16–19.
15 Architect of the Capitol, "Minton Tiles," www.aoc.gov/capitol-hill/other/minton-tiles.
16 Davies, 18.
17 Sobel, 227–237.
18 "South Brooklyn Improvements," *BDE*, January 29, 1869.
19 "The Sanitary Condition of the City: How the Squatters Live in Brooklyn," *New York Times*, August 22, 1856.
20 "Down on Dowd's Island," *BDE*, October 7, 1888.
21 Ibid.
22 Sobel, 9.
23 "Brooklyn as a Place of Residence," *BDE*, March 17, 1853, 2; "Common Council," *BDE*, February 25, 1851. "By Ald. Lambert—That the Street Commissioner notify the contractor for grading and paving Bond street, that the work must be completed without delay, or it will be done at his expense: adopted."
24 "Who Are the Democracy?," *BDE*, September 11, 1852, 3.
25 Mark Silk and Andrew Walsh, "A Past without a Future?," *America Magazine*, November 3, 2008.
26 *BDE*, October 28, 1856.
27 American Society of Civil Engineers, "Adams, Julius Walker," www.asce.org/People-and-Projects/Bios/Julius-Walker-Adams/.
28 Julius W. Adams, *Sewers and Drains for Populous Districts* (New York: Van Nostrand, 1889), 175–177; Martin V. Melosi, *The Sanitary City: Environmental Services in Urban America from Colonial Times to the Present* (Pittsburgh: University of Pittsburgh Press, 2008), 58–59; "Sewerage," *BDE*, November 17, 1859.

29 Adams, *Sewers and Drains*, 177.
30 Cady Staley and George Spence Pierson, *The Separate System of Sewerage: Its Theory and Construction* (New York: D. Van Nostrand, 1886), 28–39.
31 Leonard Metcalf, *American Sewerage Practice* (New York: McGraw-Hill, 1914), 13.
32 *BDE*, August 12, 1857 and September 24, 1857.
33 *BDE*, March 19, 1861.

Chapter 5. The Brooklyn Improvement Company (1858–1869)

1 *Park Slope Civil News*, February 1965.
2 "Prospect Park Was Once Litchfield Land," *Brooklyn Daily Eagle* (*BDE*), April 11, 1930.
3 "South Brooklyn Improvements," *BDE*, January 29, 1869.
4 "Brooklyn Improvements," *BDE*, November 11, 1859; "Brooklyn Intelligence," *New York Times*, November 12, 1859.
5 Edwin C. Litchfield, correspondence from Albany with anonymous business partner, April 6, 1860, Litchfield Family Papers, New York Historical Society (TLFP: NYHS).
6 "Our Albany Correspondence," *BDE*, February 29, 1868.
7 "First Annual Report of the Commissioners of Prospect Park" (Brooklyn, January 28, 1861), 27–28.
8 Ibid., 23–25; Edwin C. Litchfield, correspondence, April 6, 1860, TLFP: NYHS; Clay Lancaster, Prospect Park Handbook (New York: Long Island University Press, 1972).
9 "Skating–Memories of a Revolution," *BDE*, November 30, 1861; *BDE*, December 26, 1861.
10 "The Newest Thing . . . on Ice," *BDE*, February 12, 1862.
11 "Base Ball on the Ice," *BDE*, February 5, 1861.
12 "Second Annual Report of the Commissioners of Prospect Park" (Brooklyn, 1862), 61–62.
13 "Skating," *BDE*, December 18, 1865; James L. Terry, *Long before the Dodgers: Baseball in Brooklyn, 1855–1884* (Jefferson, NC: McFarland, 2002), 91–95.
14 "Building Improvements," *BDE*, June 1, 1866.
15 "Our Albany Correspondence," *BDE*, February 16, 1866.
16 "Improvement of the Gowanus Canal," *BDE*, July 31, 1867.
17 "The Gowanus Canal," *BDE*, August 6, 1867.
18 "Management of the Hamilton Avenue Bridge," *BDE*, August 14, 1867.
19 Olmsted, Vaux & Co., *Preliminary Report to the Commissioners for Laying Out a Park in Brooklyn* (Brooklyn, 1866).
20 "The Bill Explained," *BDE*, March 14, 1866.
21 "View of Correspondents," *BDE*, January 16, 1867.
22 "Questions and Cross Questions," *BDE*, March 14, 1867; "South Brooklyn Improvements," *BDE*, January 29, 1869.
23 "University of the City of New York," *New York Times*, June 21, 1867.
24 "Gowanus Canal Improvement," *BDE*, February 17, 1868.
25 Ibid.; "Prospect Park Matter," *BDE*, March 7, 1868.

26 Edwin C. Litchfield, correspondence with N. J. Higbie from Paris, April 11, 1868, TLFP: NYHS.
27 Edwin C. Litchfield, "Memorandum for Mr. Higbie, July 24, 1868," TLFP: NYHS.
28 Ibid.
29 E. A. Livingston, *Brooklyn and the Civil War* (Charleston, SC: History Press, 2012), 49.
30 "Third Street Taxation Muddle," *BDE*, November 2, 1869.
31 "The Board of Aldermen," *BDE*, February 25, 1868.
32 Ibid.; "Third Street Commission," *BDE*, April 9, 1868.
33 "Winding up of a Special Commission," *BDE*, September 9, 1868.
34 Ibid.
35 Litchfield, "Memorandum for Mr. Higbie."
36 *Real Estate Record and Builders' Guide* (Brooklyn, 1868–1884); Joseph K. Lane, *The Brooklyn Improvement Company: A Brief History in Honor of Its One Hundredth Anniversary* (Brooklyn, 1966).
37 "Some Bills at Albany," *BDE*, February 4, 1869.
38 "The South Brooklyn Canals," *BDE*, February 17, 1869.
39 "South Brooklyn in Commotion," *BDE*, February 20, 1869.
40 "The Awards for the Litchfield Property," *BDE*, March 24, 1869; "Prospect Park Extension," *BDE*, March 20, 1869.
41 "Our Albany Correspondence," *BDE*, March 12, 1869.
42 "Third Street Commission," *BDE*, April 9, 1868.
43 "The Water Board," *BDE*, July 31, 1869.
44 "Gowanus Sewer and Third Avenue Bridge," *BDE*, July 14, 1869.
45 Nicholson pavement was cheap and popular and consisted of wooden blocks, sand, and coal tar to cover streets—it was hardly as durable as Belgian paving stones, which soon became the standard.
46 "South Brooklyn in Alarm," *New York Times*, July 29, 1869,
47 This is most likely "Boss" Hugh McLaughlin, leader of Brooklyn's Democratic Party machine, and, of no coincidence, master mechanic of the Navy Yard.
48 "The Third Avenue Bridge," "The Gowanus Canal," *BDE*, July 30, 1869.
49 "The City and Mr. Litchfield," *BDE*, July 31, 1869.
50 "The Third Avenue Canal; Gowanus Streets," *BDE*, August 5, 1869.
51 "How to Settle The Third Avenue Matter," *BDE*, August 6, 1869.
52 "Third Avenue Again," *BDE*, August 7, 1869.
53 "Third Avenue Canal," *BDE*, August 13, 1869.
54 "Third Avenue Canal—Letter from Mr. Litchfield," *BDE*, August 19, 1869.
55 "Our Correspondents Column," *BDE*, August 13, 1869.

Chapter 6. Foul Odors and Foiled Plots (1870–1885)

1 "Changes of a Decade" *BDE*, July 19, 1870.
2 "Brooklyn's Fast Growth," *New York Times*, October 2, 1888.
3 "South Brooklyn Terrors," *New York Times*, May 5, 1872.
4 "South Brooklyn Improvements," *BDE*, January 29, 1869.
5 "Local Gossip," *BDE*, September 19, 1871.

6 "B'hoy" is nineteenth-century American slang, inspired by the Irish pronunciation of "boy," and describes a working-class or ne'er-do-well young man.
7 "Treat" almost certainly meant buying a drink.
8 "Obstructing Travel," *BDE*, April 29, 1871.
9 "Artificial Building Stone," *BDE*, March 9, 1871.
10 "Local Improvements," *BDE*, June 22, 1872.
11 "New York and Long Island Coignet Stone Company Building" (New York: Landmarks Preservation Commission, 2006).
12 William Field and Son is remembered for raising the standard of tenement houses in Brooklyn (and several cast-iron facades in Manhattan, particularly the Hastings Building, a magnificent factory loft in SoHo).
13 "Business Structures," *BDE*, June 11, 1873.
14 "New York and Long Island Coignet Stone Company Building," 4.
15 "Artificial Stone," *BDE*, August 29, 1873.
16 Laura Raskin, "Birth of the Concrete Jungle," *Brooklyn Rail*, March 7, 2007.
17 "South Brooklyn Improvements," *BDE*, February 7, 1873.
18 "South Brooklyn," *BDE*, August 20, 1873.
19 "Brooklyn's Commerce," July 25, 1873.
20 James F. Rhodes, *History of the United States*, vol. 5 (New York: Macmillan, 1904), 40.
21 Ibid.
22 Jennifer Lee, "New York and the Panic of 1873," *New York Times* (*NYT*), October 14, 2008.
23 This is a popular quotation from *A Sentimental Journey through France and Italy* by Laurence Sterne.
24 Edwin C. Litchfield, correspondence with Edward H. Litchfield, September 27, 1873, Litchfield Family Papers, New York Historical Society (TLFP: NYHS).
25 Ibid.
26 Edwin C. Litchfield, correspondence with Edward H. Litchfield, September 29, 1873, TLFP: NYHS.
27 Edwin C. Litchfield, correspondence with Edward H. Litchfield, October 12–13, 1873, TLFP: NYHS.
28 Edwin C. Litchfield, correspondence with Edward H. Litchfield (from Frankfort), October 17, 1873, TLFP: NYHS.
29 Edwin C. Litchfield, correspondence with Edward H. Litchfield (from Berlin), November 10, 1873, TLFP: NYHS.
30 Edwin C. Litchfield, correspondence with Edward H. Litchfield (from Berlin), November 22, 1873, TLFP: NYHS.
31 Edwin C. Litchfield, correspondence with Edward H. Litchfield, December 12, 1873, TLFP: NYHS.
32 Ethan Allen, correspondence with Edwin C. Litchfield, undated, TLFP: NYHS.
33 Ethan Allen, correspondence with Edwin C. Litchfield, undated, TLFP: NYHS.
34 Ethan Allen, correspondence with Edwin C. Litchfield, January 12, 1874, TLFP: NYHS.
35 "The Tuxedo," www.henrypoole.com/history/the-tuxedo/.

36 Edwin C. Litchfield, correspondence with Edward H. Litchfield, March 4, 1874, TLFP: NYHS.
37 Ethan Allen, correspondence with Edwin C. Litchfield, undated, TLFP: NYHS.
38 Ethan Allen, correspondence with Edwin C. Litchfield, October 8, 1875, TLFP: NYHS.
39 Ethan Allen, correspondence with Edwin C. Litchfield, November 23, 1875, TLFP: NYHS.
40 "A Stench in the Nostrils of South Brooklyn," *BDE*, April 29, 1876.
41 "A Bad Smell," *BDE*, May 5, 1876.
42 "Proceedings of the Medical Society of the County of Kings" (Brooklyn, 1876), 148–149.
43 "Very Vile," *BDE*, September 3, 1877.
44 "The Gowanus Canal," *BDE*, February 26, 1878.
45 "The Respective Rights of the City and the Adjoining Property Owners," *BDE*, March 7, 1878.
46 "Brooklyn," *NYT*, October 9, 1878.
47 "At Albany," *BDE*, January 28, 1879.
48 "Gowanus Canal," *BDE*, June 18, 1880.
49 "Dewitt, William," in *The National Cyclopaedia of American Biography*, vol. 11 (New York: James T. White, 1901), 331.
50 "A Slight Difference in Valuation," *BDE*, April 25, 1882; "The Litchfield Case Is Heard," *BDE*, September 18, 1894.
51 This paraphrased quotation from Charles Reade's *The Cloister and the Hearth* was common nineteenth-century exchange during unfortunate moments. Here it translates, "We shall see. Strength, my friends, the devil is dead (as they say)!" Edward H. Litchfield to Edwin C. Litchfield, correspondence, April 6, 1883, TLFP: NYHS.
52 The ball ground reference refers to the Litchfields' Washington Park, which was leased to a man named Charles Byrne in 1883. The team he organized to play at this field would later become the Brooklyn Dodgers.
53 Edward H. Litchfield to Edwin C. Litchfield, multiple correspondences, April 6, May 18, May 25, 1883, TLFP: NYHS.
54 Edward H. Litchfield to Edwin C. Litchfield, correspondence, October 26, 1883, TLFP: NYHS.
55 "Darby's Patch," *BDE*, November 16, 1883; "Driving Them Out," *BDE*, September 27, 1883; "The Squatters," *BDE*, September 29, 1883.
56 Edward H. Litchfield to Edwin C. Litchfield, correspondence, December 14, 1883, TLFP: NYHS.
57 *BDE*, September 12, 1885.

Chapter 7. Industry, Identity, and Violence in Gowanus (1885–1898)

1 "In Peril from a Cyclone," *Brooklyn Daily Eagle* (*BDE*), January 10, 1889.
2 "The Machine Exploded," *BDE*, February 10, 1889.
3 "The Shore Line," *BDE*, June 24, 1888.
4 "Thrown Around a Shafting," *BDE*, January 7, 1889.

5 "Verdict in a Damage Suit Set Aside," *BDE*, December 9, 1882.
6 "Pinched Fingers," *BDE*, December 4, 1885.
7 "Lost Two Fingers," *BDE*, December 13, 1885; "Bobbin Girls," *BDE*, January 14, 1886.
8 "Lives in Peril," *BDE*, April 12, 1889; *BDE*, June 5, 1889.
9 "Violence," *BDE*, June 9, 1884.
10 "Not a Wake," *BDE*, June 23, 1884.
11 "Bond Street's Sewer," *BDE*, October 19, 1886; "Annual Corp Counsel Report," *BDE*, December 22, 1886.
12 "Brooklyn Outrivaling Cologne," *BDE*, August 3, 1887.
13 "Penny Wise and Pound Foolish," *BDE*, October 6, 1887.
14 "The City Sued," *BDE*, January 4, 1888; "Storm Sewers," *BDE*, March 15, 1887.
15 "The Aldermen," *BDE*, March 27, 1888; "The Board of Aldermen," *BDE*, October 11, 1887.
16 "The City Sued," *BDE*, January 4, 1889; "South Brooklyn Flooded District," *BDE*, January 5, 1888; "The Bond Street Sewer," *BDE*, January 19, 1889.
17 "To Close It Up," *BDE*, September 19, 1889; "A Disgrace to Brooklyn," *New York Times* (*NYT*), March 1, 1893.
18 "Brooklyn's Tardy Revolt," *NYT*, February 26, 1893.
19 James L. Holton, *The Reading Railroad: History of a Coal Age Empire*, vol. 1 (Laurys Station, PA: Garrigues House, 1990), 323–325.
20 "News of the Ball Field," *BDE*, April 27, 1891.
21 "The Gowanusians," *BDE*, August 14, 1892.
22 "A June Rose Festival," *BDE*, June 23, 1893; "Charity Drawing Room Entertainment," *BDE*, February 6, 1894; "The Queen of Gowanus," *BDE*, August 19, 1894.
23 "The Gowanus Canal in Song," *BDE*, January 10, 1898.
24 "Shay the Gas Man Poet," *BDE*, October 27, 1895.
25 "Down Where They Make the Gas," *BDE*, January 29, 1899.
26 "On East Baltic Street," *BDE*, March 27, 1887.
27 "Along Union Street," *BDE*, April 24, 1887.

Chapter 8. Strikes, Moonshine, and Mobs (1902–1949)

1 Jonathan Grossman, "The Coal Strike of 1902—Turning Point in U.S. Policy," in *Monthly Labor Review* (Washington, DC: U.S. Department of Labor, October 1975); Sydney Hale, *The Coal Trade* (New York, 1920), 71.
2 "Mining in Gowanus Canal," *Brooklyn Daily Eagle* (*BDE*), October 8, 1902.
3 "Encyclical of Pope Leo XIII on Capital and Labor" (May 15, 1891); *State of New York Department of Labor Bulletin* 5, nos. 16–19 (1903).
4 "Italians Cause Bloodshed in Blacksmith Shop Battle," *Brooklyn Standard Union*, May 11, 1903.
5 "How Hook-Gowanus Wars Ended," *BDE*,, May 20, 1945; "Faction Fighting Days," *BDE*, February 10, 1895; "An Old Feud Suspended," *Daily Standard Union*, July 12, 1903.
6 "Rain Floods City, Blocking Traffic," *New York Times*, June 30, 1903.

7 Charles F. Breitzke, "An Investigation of the Sanitary Conditions of the Gowanus Canal, Brooklyn, New York," *Technology Quarterly*, September 1908.
8 "Purifying the Gowanus Canal," *BDE*, August 30, 1906.
9 "Celebrate Cleanup of Gowanus Canal," *New York Times* (*NYT*), June 22, 1911.
10 Ibid.
11 Robert J. Schoenberg, *Mr. Capone: The Real—and Complete—Story of Al Capone* (New York: William Morrow, 1993), 23.
12 "Fifty-Four Killed or Injured by the Black Hand Since June 1," *New York Herald*, October 1, 1905.
13 "Tomboy Girl Chastised Man," *BDE*, August 22, 1905; "Beat Cop with His Own Club," *BDE*, May 1, 1907.
14 Peter Justice, "The Life and Times of Monte's Venetian Room," *Carroll Gardens Patch*, September 7, 2011.
15 "Moonshine in Gowanus," *BDE*, July 29, 1902.
16 "Rival Undertakers Led Battling Bands," *NYT*, August 8, 1915; "Wounded in Riot Caused by Rival Undertakers," *Evening Telegram*, August 9, 1915.
17 "Undertaker Sold Poisonous Liquor, Col. Porter Finds," *NYT*, December 30, 1919.
18 "Gowanus Tonnage $100,000,000 a Year," *NYT*, October 29, 1922.
19 Schoenberg, 32–33.
20 Ibid.
21 William Balsamo and John Balsamo, *Young Al Capone* (New York: Skyhorse, 2011), 126.
22 Schoenberg, 37.
23 "Fear Missing Policeman Is Victim of 'White Hand Gang,'" *Evening Telegram*, December 13, 1920.
24 "Murdered Man Found in Canal Tied in Sacks," *Evening Telegram*, August 3, 1923.
25 "Brooklyn Racketeer Found Slain in Canal," *NYT*, April 21, 1936; "Body of Slain Man Is Found in Old Trunk," *New York Sun*, August 5, 1936.
26 Schoenberg, 152–153; Balsamo and Balsamo, 126.
27 Balsamo and Balsamo, 126; "3 Gangsters Slain in Dance Hall Duel as Xmas Party Ends," *BDE*, December 26, 1925; "Three of Gang Slain at Brooklyn Dance," *NYT*, December 27, 1925.
28 "Seven Held in Murders," *NYT*, December 28, 1925; Brad Hamilton, "The Mob in Carroll Gardens Grew with Docks in 1920s," *Carroll Gardens–Cobble Hill Courier*, September 10–16, 1995.
29 "Two Ton Whale Seized in Gowanus Canal," *NYT*, March 14, 1928.
30 "Brooklyn's Own Whale Sold to Science for a Mere $50," *BDE*, March 14, 1928.
31 Hunter Research, 55 (2-40).
32 "Brewery Explosion and Fire Injure 3," *NYT*, July 4, 1933; "Agent Charges De Vito Made Death Threat," *Brooklyn Standard Union*, November 5, 1933.
33 "17th Century Fort Is Uncovered Here," *NYT*, May 5, 1933.

34 "$150,000 Still Seized in Brooklyn Raid," *NYT*, September 19, 1933.
35 Hunter Research, 55.
36 "Downtown Boon Seen in Proposed Bridge Plan," *NYT* January 29, 1939.
37 Robert Caro, *The Power Broker* (New York: Vintage, 1975), 520–525.
38 "Plans for Battery Tunnel Rushed," *NYT*, July 20, 1939; "President Breaks Ground for Tunnel," *NYT*, October 29, 1940.
39 Dorothy Agnes Bennett, *Sold to the Ladies!* (New York: G. W. Stewart, 1940), 1–37.
40 Suleiman Osman, *The Invention of Brownstone Brooklyn* (New York: Oxford University Press, 2012); Joseph Ingraham, "Brooklyn Tunnel Costing $80,000,000 Opened by Mayor," *NYT*, May 26, 1950.
41 Robert A. Beauregard, *When America Became Suburban* (Minneapolis: University of Minnesota Press, 2006), 10–12.
42 Joseph Mitchell, "The Mohawks in High Steel," *New Yorker*, September 17, 1949, 38–53.

Chapter 9. The Fall of South Brooklyn and the Brownstone Revolution (1950–1981)

1 Bert Hochman, "Time Becalms Gowanus," *Brooklyn Daily Eagle* (*BDE*), July 25, 1949; "Unknown Man Found Drowned," *BDE*, August 8, 1905.
2 Jack S. Nyman et al., *Reconsidering Gowanus* (New York: Baruch College/City University of New York, 2010)
3 Hunter Research, 55 (2-40).
4 Ralph Salerno and John S. Thompkins, *The Crime Confederation* (New York: Doubleday, 1969), 125.
5 Ibid., 132.
6 Tom Folsom, *The Mad Ones: Crazy Joe Gallo and the Revolution at the Edge of the Underworld* (New York: Weinstein Books, 2009), 26; Dan Hertzenberg, "Crazy Joe Kept a Lion in His Basement," *Newsday*, April 9, 1972.
7 Peter Justice, "The Life and Times of Monte's Venetian Room," *Carroll Gardens Patch*, September 7, 2011.
8 Salerno and Thompkins, 132–138; "Larry Gallo Dies in Sleep at 41," *New York Times* (*NYT*), May 19, 1968.
9 Salerno and Thompkins, 138; Jack Roth, "Gallo Sentenced to 7 to 14 Years," *NYT*, December 22, 1961; Fred J. Cook, "Robin Hoods, or Real Tough Boys?," *NYT*, October 23, 1966.
10 "5 Shots from Truck Hurt Two Ex-Cons," *NYT*, May 20, 1963.
11 Eric Pace, "Joe Gallo Is Shot to Death in Little Italy Restaurant," *NYT*, April 8, 1972; Nicholas Gage, "Story of Joe Gallo's Murder," *NYT*, May 3, 1973.
12 Mark Hay, "Buddy Scotto, on the Ramparts of Carroll Gardens," *Capital New York*, August 10, 2010; Max Lakin, "Only the Bred Know Brooklyn," *Gelf Magazine*, September 17, 2009.
13 Interview with Buddy Scotto, *Brooklyn Paper*, April 9–15, 1983.
14 Beauregard, 10–16; Osman, 45.
15 Hay; Osman, 201.
16 Osman, 82–86.

17 Ibid.
18 Osman, 196–197.
19 David Bird, "Tiny Brooklyn Road Job Grows into a 'Westway,'" *NYT*, April 3, 1979.
20 Osman, 202.
21 *Congressional Record* 145, no. 100 (July 15, 1999).
22 Stephanie de Pue, "Gowanus: By a New Name, Will It Smell as Sweet?," *Village Voice*, November 27, 1969.
23 Bendix was a radio personality who made light of a stereotypically "Brooklyn" working-class character.
24 "Neighborhoods: The Mood Is Changing along the Gowanus Canal," *NYT*, September 20, 1969.
25 de Pue.
26 Charles Grutzner, "Gowanus vs. Organized Crime," *NYT*, February 5, 1970.
27 Werner Bamberger, "Cleaner Gowanus Canal Looms," *NYT*, July 9, 1972; Max H. Seigel, "U.S. Agency Refusing to Dredge Gowanus," *NYT*, April 1, 1973.
28 Interview with Linda Mariano, January 24, 2010.
29 Monica Surfaro, "Dredgers Begin Cleanup of Gowanus Canal in Brooklyn," *NYT*, February 2, 1975.
30 Sheila Rule, "A Trip along Gowanus Canal Raises Hopes," *NYT*, September 24, 1977.

Chapter 10. Superfund Me! (1981–2010)

1 Kay Larson, "The Gowanus Gorillas," *New York Magazine*, June 8, 1981; Jonathan Schnell, "Big," *New Yorker*, July 27, 1981.
2 Grace Glueck, "Gallery View," *New York Times* (*NYT*), October 3, 1982.
3 Susan Paul, "Not Content with Success, Organizers of Gowanus Show Set Out to Top Original," *Phoenix*, July 8, 1982, 7.
4 "Doehler Die Comes to Life with New Co-ops," *Phoenix*, February 5, 1981; Fred Feretti, "Drab Factory in Brooklyn May Emerge as Cinderella," *NYT*, May 22, 1977.
5 Donald Allen Gross, "Gentrification in Carroll Gardens," *Prospect Press*, December 13, 1984.
6 "Carroll Gardens Still at Odds with Itself," *Phoenix*, January 2, 1986; "Richmond Sentenced to a Year and a Day, and Fined $20,000," *NYT*, November 11, 1982; Tracy Garrity, "Danger: Chemicals on Smith," *Brooklyn Paper*, January 26–February 1, 1985; Jim Miskiewicz, "Interest Rekindled for Canal Housing," *Brooklyn Paper*, September 10–16, 1983.
7 Ralph S. Solecki, "Stage I Archaeological Survey: Red Hook Water Pollution Control Project" (New York: Mason & Hanger-Silas Mason, May 20, 1984); Kevin Clarke, "New Study Eyes Toxic Lots on Smith Street," *Brooklyn Paper*, March 22–28, 1986; Hunter Research.
8 Ari L. Goldman, "Brooklyn's 7th Heaven," *NYT*, May 12, 1978.
9 Hope Reeves, "City Lore: Smith Street: A Hot Strip with a Storied Past," *NYT*, July 22, 2001.

10 Interview with Bette Stoltz, 2008.
11 Eleanor Randolph, "The City Life: Surviving the Gowanus Canal," *NYT*, May 23, 1999.
12 Paul H. B. Shin, "Factory Is Eyed for Apartments," *New York Daily News*, January 27, 1999.
13 Andy Newman, "Stench Is Out, Fish Are In," *NYT*, July 29, 1999; "City Activates Gowanus Canal Flushing Tunnel" (New York City Department of Environmental Protection, April 30, 1999).
14 Matthew Sweeney, "Buddy Envisions Texas on the Gowanus," *Brooklyn Paper*, November 19, 1999.
15 Interview with Mariano.
16 Ibid.
17 *Bulletin of the New York City Board of Standards and Appeals* 89, no. 7 (February 12, 2004).
18 Interview with Mariano.
19 Interview with Margaret Maugenest, January 25, 2010.
20 Jess Wisloski, "Gowanus Farewell to Bond Street Stable," *Brooklyn Paper*, May 14, 2005; Joseph Berger, "From Open Sewer to Open for Gentrification," *NYT*, November 28, 2005.
21 William Neuman, "A Developer Finds Many Opportunities," *NYT*, February 6, 2005; Jess Wisloski, "Gowanus Surprise," *Brooklyn Paper*, November 13, 2004; Mike McLaughlin, "Bell Tolls for the Gowanus," *Brooklyn Paper*, February 23, 2008.
22 Lisa Chamberlain, "A Suburban Builder Heads for the City," *NYT*, April 5, 2006; Andrew Rice, "On the Waterfront," *NYT*, October 25, 2009.
23 Ariella Cohen, "Booming Fall for Gardens, Hill," *Brooklyn Paper*, September 8, 2007; Robert Guskind, "Gowanus Canal Clean Up Coming . . . Eventually," *Gowanus Lounge*, October 23, 2007; Elizabeth Hays, "Gowanus Canal Sick with Germs, City Tech Professors Say," *New York Daily News*, October 5, 2007.
24 Ariella Cohen, "Booming Fall for Gardens, Hill," *Brooklyn Paper*, September 8, 2007; "Toll Brothers Gowanus Project Revealed," *Curbed*, February 14, 2008.
25 Mike McLaughlin, "Revolt Against This 'Toll,'" March 8, 2008.
26 "Toll Plan Has Merit," *Brooklyn Paper*, September 18, 2008; Katia Kelly, "Toll Brothers Spent $365,000 on Lobbying for Gowanus Rezoning," *Pardon Me for Asking* (*PMFA*), October 2, 2008; "Former Boymelgreen Gowanus Village Site Is on the Market," *Curbed*, February 26, 2008; Katia Kelly, "Not a Big Surprise: Full C.B.6 Votes Yes for Toll Gowanus Project," *PMFA*, November 13, 2008; "Toll Brother's Phase II Investigation Report for 363 Bond Street" (Environmental Liability Management of New York, May 31, 2005).
27 Eliot Brown, "Developers: Gowanus to Build or Not?," *New York Observer*, April 14, 2009.
28 Elizabeth D. Blum, *Love Canal Revisited: Race, Class, and Gender in Environmental Activism* (Lawrence: University Press of Kansas, 2008), 6; interview with Natalie Loney, March 14, 2014.

29 Mireya Navarro, "City Proposes New Plan for Gowanus Canal Cleanup," *NYT*, July 9, 2009.
30 "Support Document for the Revised National Priorities List Final Rule—Gowanus Canal" (Washington, DC: U.S. Environmental Protection Agency, March 2010).
31 Interview with Mariano.
32 Interview with Bill Appell, January 2010; Navarro; Joseph Alexiou, "'Hallelujah' for Gowanus Canal, Superfund Site," *New York Observer*, March 2, 2010.

Epilogue

1 Gary Buiso, "Toll Brothers Is Officially Stigmatized by the Superfund," *Brooklyn Paper*, July 9, 2010.
2 See epa.gov/region2/superfund/npl/gowanus/.
3 Sharon Zukin, *Naked City: The Death and Life of Authentic Urban Places* (New York: Oxford University Press, 2009).
4 Jane Jacobs, *The Death and Life of Great American Cities* (New York: Modern Library, 1993), 244–245.
5 Zukin, 58–59.
6 "Gowanus Gets Ready," *The Real Deal*, March 13, 2013, therealdeal.com/issues_articles/gowanus-gets-ready/; Terry Pristin, "Once Hobbled, New York Developer Aims for Comeback," *New York Times*, April 2, 2013.
7 Philip Lopate, "Brooklyn the Unknowable," in *Portrait Inside My Head* (New York: Simon & Schuster, 2014), 165–177.

INDEX

Note: Page numbers in italics indicate photographs and illustrations.

ABOUT THE AUTHOR

Joseph Alexiou is the author of the sixth edition of *Paris for Dummies*. His writing has appeared in the *New York Observer*, *Time Out New York*, Gothamist, and *New York* magazine's Daily Intel. He lives in Brooklyn, New York.